D1268015

THE EDGE OF THE PLAIN

Also by James Crawford

Above Scotland: The National Collection of Aerial Photography

Above Scotland: Cities

Victorian Scotland

Aerofilms: A History of Britain from Above

Scotland's Landscapes

Fallen Glory: The lives and deaths of the world's greatest lost buildings from the Tower of Babel to the Twin Towers

Who Built Scotland: Twenty-Five Journeys in Search of a Nation (contributor)

Scotland From the Sky

THE EDGE OF THE PLAIN

How Borders Make and Break Our World

JAMES CRAWFORD

W. W. NORTON & COMPANY
Celebrating a Century of Independent Publishing

First American Edition 2023

First published in Great Britain in 2022 by Canongate Books Ltd.

For permission credits, please see p. 383.

Printed in the United States

For information about special discounts for bulk purchases, please contact W. W. Norton Special Sales at specialsales@wwnorton.com or 800-233-4830

Manufacturing by Lake Book
Production manager: Louise Mattarelliano

ISBN 978-1-324-03704-0

W. W. Norton & Company, Inc.
500 Fifth Avenue, New York, N.Y. 10110
www.wwnorton.com

W. W. Norton & Company Ltd.
15 Carlisle Street, London W1D 3BS

1 2 3 4 5 6 7 8 9 0

To William, Maggie, Isabella and James

CONTENTS

INTRODUCTION

High up on the Alpine watershed between Austria and Italy a border melts and creeps downhill. In the centre of the United States, a ghost border is drawn back into existence by three men in a white Sprinter van. In the dusty margins where the African savannah meets the Sahara Desert, a green border of trees and crops struggles to take root and grow. On a shelf deep in the underground stores of the British Museum, a border sleeps. Lost for thousands of years, it has no idea how it came to shape the world.

A border sits on my desk. It's small enough to fit in the palm of my hand. I'm always surprised by how light it feels. It's roughly cuboid in shape. On five sides it's coarse, bumpy and grey. But on one side it's smooth, marked with splashes of yellow and orange. I bought this border ten years ago, on eBay. It's supposed to be a fragment of the Berlin Wall. It's very likely not. It's probably just a lump of concrete, scavenged from a building site and daubed with paint. I feel like I can live with this uncertainty.

When the wall fell, in November 1989, I was eleven years old. I remember watching on the news as Berliners danced along the top. The same footage was played over and over as one large rectangular slab crashed to the ground. In the days, weeks and months afterwards, people came from all over the world to try to grab their own pieces of the wall. *Mauerspechte*, they were called. Wall peckers. For a few Deutschmarks they'd hire a small hammer and hack away.

Of course, everyone wanted the western side. There was a wall-pecking pecking order. Pieces from the west were covered in iconic graffiti art, whereas pieces from the east were just flat, grey and featureless. Enterprising East Berliners, quick to embrace their new-found access to the capitalist economy, began spray-painting real fragments from their side to make them seem more authentic to buyers. I hope my piece is one of those pieces.

Today, the Berlin Wall is the world's most-travelled border. Bits of it can be found on six continents. They are exhibited in museums and galleries, erected on street corners. One slab is even used as a backdrop to a urinal in a Las Vegas casino. The shattering of the wall was, for some, supposed to be the beginning of the end of borders. The end of history, even. But history goes on. In fact, it has accelerated away from that moment. And borders have made a comeback. Or, rather, they never really went away at all.

One Monday morning in the middle of November 2018, a New York deli chain sent me an email with the subject 'Avocado Shortage'. Their message explained that 'no avocados have crossed the Mexico–US Border for the past three weeks' due to an import pricing dispute and, rather than 'serving a stockpile of frozen avocados and compromising on quality and taste', avocados were 'off the menu'. They promised to 'alert' me as soon as the situation changed. I have no idea how I was even on their mailing list. And I live in Edinburgh.

Two days later, the US President Donald Trump deployed 7,000 troops to America's southern border and authorised them to use 'lethal force' against what he described as 'an invasion' of migrants. The first 400 of those migrants – part of a walking caravan of more than 10,000 travelling from Honduras, Guatemala and El Salvador – had just arrived in the border city of Tijuana.

That same week, it was reported that North Korea and South Korea had blown up front-line guard posts all along the heavily fortified zone that has separated their two countries for seven decades, the first step in a tentative agreement to 'demilitarise' their border completely.

On the Thursday, the governments of India and Pakistan reached an agreement to establish a cross-border corridor to allow pilgrims to visit a sacred holy temple in Pakistan, the last resting place of Guru Nanak, the founder of the Sikh religion. On the same day, in the Middle East, fighting engulfed the Gaza Strip as thousands of Palestinian demonstrators clashed with Israeli soldiers, and tear gas, flying rocks, bullets and burning tyre smoke filled the skies above an eight-metre-high, concrete 'separation barrier'.

The week ended with the British Prime Minister, Theresa May, returning from Brussels to announce that she had brokered a Brexit deal with Europe that would 'end free movement once and for all'.

Avocados, 'invasions', spiritual corridors, human caravans, separation barriers, lethal force and a British prime minister celebrating the end of freedom . . . All in just seven days in November.

I don't think, in hindsight, that this was a particularly special week for borders. But it made me wonder, slightly more obsessively with each passing day, where borders *really* came from. When did they begin? How did they evolve and take root? How did they grow up into this vast network of lines – physical and virtual – running all over the earth? And why, today, are they seemingly the most volatile flashpoints for political and social conflagration across the globe? Is this just a symptom? Or could borders themselves be the cause?

A border is such a simple idea. Step across a line, whether you can see it or not, and you are somewhere else. The landscape may look exactly the same, one blade of grass to the next, but you are in another place, another country. Perhaps the people speak another language. Their cultures, practices, laws and ideas may be completely different. Perhaps you can be completely different too: who you are and how you live your life may or may not be permissible. On one side of the border may be the promise of wealth, on the other the certainty of poverty. What you read or who you love may be free for you to choose, or may be punishable by prison, even death.

It means that these lines, fences, walls or checkpoints – and the spaces they inhabit – possess immense power. Nothing is different and yet everything is different. This is, as the writer Amitav Ghosh put it in his description of the Indian Partition, 'the enchantment of lines'.[1] An enchantment that can be at once absurdist *and* fatal. I wanted to go in search of the source of this enchantment, to follow it all the way from then – whenever *then* was – up to now.

Everyone, I suspect, has their own, personal, border story. This is mine.

On 12 June 1908, three passengers – William, Maggie and Nellie – left the port of Liverpool on Cunard's steam turbine ocean liner *Carmania.* The ship was just three years old, built by John Brown & Company in Clydebank as the largest and the fastest in the fleet: 20,000 tonnes and 650 feet long; a top speed of eighteen knots; three giant decks offering 2,650 berths from first class down to steerage.

William was thirty-one, Maggie twenty-three and Nellie twenty-eight. They had left a farming community in Hawick in the Scottish Borders, where William had worked as a stable keeper. Now they were on their way across the Atlantic. On their way to America.

They arrived at Ellis Island on 18 June, into the stifling heat and humidity of a New York summer – the city's warmest on record. The ship's manifest gave only the scantiest record of who they were. Their ages. Their nationality ('Scotch'). William and Maggie's light-coloured hair, blue eyes and 'clear' complexions. Nellie's dark hair and brown eyes. William five foot nine, Maggie five foot six, Nellie five foot seven. That William and Maggie were husband and wife. That Nellie was William's sister.

The *Carmania*'s commanding officer signed an affidavit swearing that all passengers had undergone physical and oral examinations from the ship's surgeon. This confirmed that William, Maggie and Nellie were not 'feeble-minded', 'imbecilic' or 'insane'. That they were not infected with tuberculosis or a 'loathsome and dangerous infectious disease'. That they were not polygamists or prostitutes, nor had they been convicted previously of a crime of 'moral turpitude'. That they were not anarchists.

In the decade leading up to the First World War, Ellis Island was often processing more than a million immigrants a year. The previous twelve months had been the busiest in the island's history. After several hours waiting in line among a queue of thousands, William, Maggie and Nellie passed their medical and legal inspections. They could enter America. From New York they took the railroad west, travelled some 1,600 miles into the continental interior, to western Colorado. There they had secured work on a cattle ranch that occupied the high grasslands on the far side of the Rocky Mountains – William to look after the horses, Maggie and Nellie to look after the men.

Sixty years earlier, this land was Mexico. In the decades leading up to the twentieth century, the Native American Ute tribe had been pushed from the mountains and then out of the state entirely. And in their place came great herds of Texas Longhorn, driven north from the overgrazed grasslands to the south. This was open-range ranching, the cattle roaming over wide expanses to move back and forth between the snow-free valleys in the winter and the highlands in the summer. There was no town or settlement – not even another ranch – for a hundred miles in any direction. Just William, Maggie, Nellie and a troop of cowboys. Most were young men with no families. Maggie found them gruff and taciturn and soon began to resent her daily cooking rituals.

They stuck it out through two winters. But life on the ranch meant an abundance – perhaps even an over-abundance – of space, and the isolation grew too much for Maggie to bear. Soon they were making another journey, east this time, back across the Great Plains and the Mississippi, back over the Allegheny Mountains to the port of New York. Thousands of immigrants were still pouring into the country every single day. But for William, Maggie and Nellie, America's dream remained unfulfilled. They had not found what they were looking for in the New World. They moved against the flow: booked passage on an ocean liner and returned across the Atlantic. By 1911 they were working their own farm, on land that straddled the border between Scotland and England, near the village of

Roweltown. The following year Maggie gave birth to a son. John Dalgleish Short. My grandfather.

Just over a decade later, a seventeen-year-old boy called James crossed the border from Canada into Detroit. The US Immigration Service's Primary Inspection document from that day – 29 September 1923 – recorded that he was five foot three, with red hair and blue eyes. He had left the small harbour town of Fraserburgh in north-eastern Scotland the previous year, travelled alone to Glasgow and then by boat to Quebec City, where he lived for a time with distant relatives. His father John was a fisherman, as was his father before him. But James had other ambitions. As he arrived in America, he was asked his occupation. 'Mechanic,' he answered. He had come to the right place.

Detroit was all industry. Less a city and more a factory-metropolis with an insatiable demand for workers. At the beginning of the twentieth century, its population was just over 250,000 people. By the 1920s, it had surged to 1.25 million.

James was taken on by Henry Ford's Motor Company and began work in what was, for a time, the world's largest manufacturing facility – the Highland Park Plant. One hundred acres in size, it incorporated offices, multiple factories, a foundry and even its own power station. James took his place on what was the first-ever industrial assembly line. Car chassis were moved by conveyor belt along 150 feet of factory floor. Hundreds of workers manned each line, responsible for carrying out one of the eighty-four steps required to put together the 3,000 parts of the Model T motor car. In 1927, just four years after he had arrived in Detroit, the fifteen-millionth car rolled off the Highland Park assembly line.

In the summer of 1926, James met Isabella. Just a few months earlier, she had left her home and her family in Falkirk, travelled alone on the SS *Athenia* from Glasgow to Montreal, then continued her journey to reach Detroit at the beginning of May. Almost exactly a year later, on 9 May 1927, Isabella and James were married at the Northwestern Baptist Church. He was twenty and she was twenty-three. Their son John was born in December, just three days before Christmas.

They lived in a shared home on West Hancock Street in Midtown, rented for $33 a month. At the beginning of 1930, Isabella gave birth to a daughter, Margaret. By this time, however, Detroit's vast machine was beginning to falter. The Wall Street crash in October 1929 had triggered the Great Depression, and Ford's motor cars – designed and priced to be affordable to America's everymen – had been transformed almost overnight into luxury items. Production halved from 1929 to 1930. By the end of 1931 it had dropped threefold again. Tens of thousands of workers were being made redundant. Whole plants were shut down. At the peak of the Depression, unemployment levels across America were at nearly 25 per cent. In Detroit it was even higher – over a third of the population were out of work.

James had kept his job, but annual wages had shrunk by more than half to cope with the unprecedented scale of the downturn. Near the end of 1933, James and Isabella sat at their kitchen table in the house in West Hancock Street. James had a silver dime in his hand. They had been talking for months about the future, about what they should do. With discussion and reason exhausted, they resolved to trust to fate instead. The toss of a coin. Tails, they'd stay. Heads, they'd go. Stay in the city where they had made their home, where their children had been born. Stay in the city which was crumbling around them, where it was said hundreds were dying every day from hunger and homelessness. Or go. Pack their things, take John and Margaret, and return to Scotland. Go back to their families, and their history, and the lives they thought they had left behind.

James threw the coin in the air, watched it spin and land on the kitchen table, and brought his palm down on top of it. Then he lifted his hand. Liberty's head looked up at them. They had their answer. *Go.*

They left Detroit in early 1934. James, Isabella, Margaret and John Crawford. My great-grandparents, my grand-aunt and my grandfather.

I often think about that coin toss. There are, of course, innumerable moments when the course of a life can turn one way or another. Yet still. The flip of a coin offers something so pleasingly binary. It's not open to interpretation or nuance. Heads or tails. Go or stay. If it had landed tails, then I would never have existed. Two major branch lines of possibility flickered on and off as the coin spun around in the air of that Detroit kitchen.

There is another version of this story told among my family. That the decision to go had already been made. That the coin toss was about *where* to go. Back to Fraserburgh, where James was born. Or to Falkirk, where Isabella was born. But maybe there were two coin tosses? If you are going to let chance decide once, then why not twice? I was never able to ask my great-grandparents. Isabella died in 1990, and James two years later. Their story has already receded, acquired the polished veneer of family fable through second-hand retelling and misremembering.

Nevertheless, it still strikes me that my great-grandparents – on both sides of my family – were immigrants to America. And that, for whatever reasons, these ventures, these great leaps into the unknown, failed to deliver. James and Isabella Crawford. William and Maggie Short. They migrated over an ocean and a border – and, ultimately, they migrated right back again.

My great-grandparents did, at least, have a choice. For many now, there is no uncertainty about staying or going. There is only one option: movement. And so, a border becomes not just one line of possibility, but the *only* line – everything else is limbo. Beyond it lies a future, any future. To reach it, you just have to cross.

In today's world, that is far easier said than done. On the one hand, we are struggling to cope with the power of technology and globalisation to ignore and even annihilate borders. The world is shrinking – metaphorically and, as a result of climate change, also quite literally. Many borders, in response, are hardening, strengthening or even proliferating. Today, there are more borders in the world than ever before in human history. Nationalist rhetoric is only increasing in volume, and the lines are drawn harder, pulled tighter. Yet all the while, existential threats loom on the horizon that the 'enchantment' Ghosh described cannot prevent.

We are all of us now – in effect – standing on a border. Whether looking in or looking out, we are confronted, as never before, by the scale and extent of global inequality. The lines that separate us have become the ultimate conduits for both hatred and hope. The desire of some to turn away, 'build that wall' and 'end movement', will only increase the magnetic pull of borders. They have become a kind of litmus test for our world, evidence for the progress, or recession, of *all* human freedoms: social, political, cultural, economic and artistic. As Norman Mailer put it, 'One discovers how far one can go only by travelling in a straight line until one is stopped.' *The Edge of the Plain* is my journey to those stopping points.

In the course of writing this book I travelled in search of borders old and new. I went looking for ancient border markers and the mass grave of a border battlefield, in the Greek mountains. I walked the remote, abandoned outposts of the Roman Empire in the twilight of a Scottish summer. Two hundred miles north of the Arctic Circle, I met an artist who has dedicated his life's work to removing borders and reclaiming the language and divided landscape of his ancient culture. In Bethlehem, in the conflict-torn, border-obsessed West Bank, I stayed in the hotel with the 'worst view in the world'. High in the Ötztal Alps, I climbed into a world of vanishing border glaciers.

And then, as the months passed at the start of 2020, I couldn't go anywhere. On Thursday 12 March I flew from Tromsø via a deserted Oslo airport back to Edinburgh. That same day, Norway closed its borders to all non-nationals. The COVID-19 pandemic was rapidly shutting down the world. And borders – their permeability, their *hardness* or *softness*, became constant headline news. As the weeks and months of quarantines and lockdowns progressed, and with travel impossible, I sought out and spoke to people across the world whose lives, one way or another, have been consumed by borders. People who live and work on the margins, on the periphery, who, as the Spanish photojournalist Carlos Spottorno described it to me, 'put their feet on the line'.

My intention is to use these journeys, these conversations, these stories from the present and the past, to understand what borders are. How they are made, how they are constantly on the move, and how, increasingly, they are being bent and broken. No matter where you turn, it seems that the taut lines of borders are vibrating to – or even calling – the tune of global events. Their futures are connected intimately to our own. Controlling our landscapes, our memories, our identities. And our destinies.

How does one hate a country, or love one? . . . I lack the trick of it. I know people, I know towns, farms, hills and rivers and rocks, I know how the sun at sunset in autumn falls on the side of a certain ploughland in the hills; but what is the sense of giving a boundary to all that, of giving it a name and ceasing to love where the name ceases to apply? What is love of one's country; is it hate of one's uncountry?

– Ursula K. Le Guin, *The Left Hand of Darkness*

PROLOGUE

THE EDGE OF THE PLAIN

I was touching the oldest border in the world. Or, at least, the oldest border that still survives in a form that we can look at today and say, for sure, '*This* – this is a border.' My hands ran over its cool, limestone surface. It was a stout, creamy-white cylinder – streaked here and there with crystalline seams that glimmered like ice. At almost half a metre long, it was about the same size and shape as a concrete bollard.

How do we know that it is a border? Because it tells us. It is covered in inscriptions. They appeared to me, at first, like the impressions left behind by bird feet in wet sand. I let my fingertips run into their grooves, worn smooth by time.

Four and a half thousand years ago, someone bent over this stone cylinder, just like I was bending over it now, studying it beneath the beam of an Anglepoise lamp. With hammer and chisel (were they working by firelight or under the glare of the sun?) they began to chip and carve away. Long vertical lines were incised to make columns. And those columns were then filled with spidery, wedge-like characters. Our earliest known form of writing: Sumerian cuneiform.

I cannot read cuneiform. Those experts who can suggest that it takes a decade or so of study to learn the huge range of symbols: their potential multiple and contradictory meanings. But all the same, writing is writing. And that, at least, I do know. The script in front of me may have been alien, but the hand that produced it was not. I shifted the lamp so that oblique light was cast across the smooth surface, and, as I looked down and around the columns, I felt I could sense those moments where the impressions deepened, the shadows grew darker, and the narrative picked up pace: where the chisel had bitten hard into the meat, the gristle, of the stone.

On and on the author went, using almost every inch of space. What they were recording – carving, preserving – was the story of a border. It is the earliest one that we have. Perhaps, even, it is the first-ever attempt at writing history.[1]

This story starts at the beginning of time.

Enlil, the father of all the gods, granted to two of his immortal children, Ningirsu and Shara, a city each as their personal possessions. The city of Lagash was Ningirsu's, and the city of Umma was Shara's. Because the lands belonging to these two cities lay side by side, Enlil himself decided on a boundary line between them. A divine border.

But, the scribe tells us, the people of Umma would not observe it. They crossed Enlil's sacred line to try to take the lands of Lagash as their own. They seized Ningirsu's 'beloved fields', known as the *Gu'edina* – the 'Edge of the Plain' – a stretch of rich, fertile land lying along the northwestern frontier of Lagash. And so Enlil intervened, instructing his representative on earth, Mesalim, ruler of the neutral kingdom of Kish, to mark out the border once again: measuring it, digging a long boundary channel, and, to avoid future disagreements, inscribing the specific rights of territory and ownership onto a stone tablet, or stele, to be erected on the dividing line itself. This stele was 'the treaty of Mesalim': the oldest known peace treaty in history. One of the world's first-ever legal documents.

Peace did not last. A new ruler of Umma, Ush, refused to accept the border. He had the stele ripped out of the ground, he crossed the boundary channel and took the lands of the Edge of the Plain.

Years passed, a few decades perhaps. And so, deprived of his sacred fields and consumed with anger, Ningirsu created a new leader for Lagash: Eanatum, a super-heroic giant of a man, suckled at birth by the goddess Ninhursag and destined to overturn the sacrilegious land grab.

Eanatum rode out on his battle chariot, obliterated the forces of Umma, led at this time by Enakale, and re-established the border. More than that, he re-emphasised it, turning the boundary channel into a double embankment filled with the waters of a wide irrigation canal. He put the old, uprooted Mesalim stele back in place, erected new border markers of his own, built shrines to Enlil and Ningirsu, and instituted a kilometre-wide exclusion zone on the Umma side of the canal. As a concession, intended to avoid future conflict, he granted the Ummaites access to a small tract of the Edge of the Plain, on the condition that they paid Lagash a share of revenue from the barley they harvested there.

Yet the dispute would not go away. Resentment festered, passed down the generations. Soon Enakale's son Urluma, incensed at the 'shameful' terms agreed by his father, was preparing for war. After refusing to pay the duties owed to Lagash from the harvest, he marched on the border, tore out, burned and smashed Mesalim's stele and Eanatum's pillars, destroyed the sacred shrines, and proceeded to 'dry up' the canal by rediverting its water into the Ummaite lands.

It fell to Enmetena, nephew of the great Eanatum, to respond. He confronted Urluma, the 'field thief', on the very cusp of the border, at the 'hill of the black dog', where he drove back and slaughtered the Ummaite forces, sending Urluma running for his life across the boundary canal, 'leaving the bones of his personnel strewn across the plain'.[2] Urluma may have escaped, but his fate was sealed. He was murdered in a palace coup almost as soon as he returned to the city of Umma.

In the aftermath, Enmetena rebuilt the holy shrines, extended the boundary canal – so that it now ran for some sixty kilometres – and erected another series of border markers all along its length.[3]

The pillar that I was looking at now, that was telling this story, was one of those markers.

*

What a journey it has been on since then. It was early January at the beginning of the third decade of the twenty-first century. The pillar was lying on a soft rectangle of black foam, on a long wooden table, in the ornate study room of the Middle East Collection of the British Museum.

My table was at the centre of a line of tables, running through five vaulted archways. Above were three floors of wrought-iron balconies and shelving. Ten bays led off this central space, housing tray after tray of artefacts, protected behind tall cases of wood and glass. Alongside me, a woman was handling fragments of pottery from the ancient Assyrian city of Nimrud. Another table down, shattered cuneiform cylinders were arranged for study on mounds of white tissue paper. Even the chairs we were sitting on appeared to be artefacts – their leather upholstery so dry and cracked, and in places bleeding stuffing, that you could imagine they had been in use since this room was first opened in the middle of the nineteenth century.

I rolled the pillar over. It was spectacularly heavy. There was a compact, muscular density to the limestone. Cuneiform was most commonly written in wet clay, using a stylus made from river reeds. The task of carving it in stone, in such minute detail, must have been tough going: painstaking work.

As was the job of translation. It was only in 2018 that Irving Finkel, the Museum's Assistant Keeper of Ancient Mesopotamian script and one of the world's foremost authorities on cuneiform, came to decipher the pillar's long inscription. For at least a century and a half before that, it had lain in the vast basement beneath Bloomsbury. Just one piece of stone gathering dust on a shelf, one object among millions of others.

Exactly how and when it first got to those storage rooms remains unclear. The Museum's own acquisition notes say only that it was 'most probably acquired before 1884'. It must have travelled to London by ship, sometime in the latter half of the nineteenth century, sailed up the Thames to a waiting wharf, and been unloaded on the busy docks at Gravesend perhaps. Did it pass through the newly constructed Suez Canal en route, or did it take the long way round, navigating via the Horn of Africa? Before that, packed up in one of many wooden crates, it would have drifted by barge down the meandering course of the Tigris to the Shatt-al-Arab, the 'swift river' that empties into the Persian Gulf and the Arabian Sea.

The exact find spot remains unknown:[4] somewhere out in the dried-up deserts of the once lush plains of Mesopotamia – the place we now call Iraq. Many dig sites had appeared across the country in the nineteenth century, excavation trenches spreading their fingers out over the sands. Was there an excited shout of discovery? Or a weary shrug as yet another object was added to that day's haul? Either way, the moment came when this cylinder was drawn from the dust, to meet the light of day for the first time in thousands of years.

It is only now, however, that we realise its true significance. As Finkel worked through the inscription, he became aware of anomalies within the text. Like any form of language, cuneiform changed and evolved over time. Yet the account on the pillar continually used some of the oldest, most archaic forms of the Sumerian script – symbols first written over 800 years earlier. Some markings were shallow or half finished, made to look, even at the moment of writing, as if they had been eroded away by time. The very deepest cuts in the stone were reserved for Ningirsu, whose name was supplemented with three different versions of the cuneiform for 'god'. By contrast, where the text mentioned Umma's god, Shara, the chiselling work was so faint and erratic as to be almost illegible. This, it seems, was deliberate. The scribe was both taunting the Ummaites *and* fabricating evidence – it was fake news and trolling, in cuneiform: an attempt to manufacture proof that Lagash's right to the Edge of the Plain went back to the very beginning of language, even to the very beginning of the world.[5]

There was something else, however, one particular phrase that appears in the inscription. On this pillar, for the first time that we know of in human history, you can read the words 'no man's land'.

The author used them to describe the exclusion zone first established by Enmetena's uncle along the Umma side of the boundary channel. It was just a throwaway line, a literal term for a stretch of territory to be left empty and untouched, that 'no man' should enter. Four and a half thousand years ago, it was a phrase that was virtually weightless. But it has travelled on through history. And, far from being lost and buried, it has experienced a constant process of accretion: growing exponentially over the millennia – and during the last century in particular – to reach a supermassive, tragic density.

No man's land.

Today, the words evoke history gone wrong. They cut to the heart of humanity's troubled nature: our endless capacity for fighting over space. And here the phrase was, carved into our oldest surviving border marker, in our earliest form of writing, in one of our formative attempts at recording history.

Here lies our first story. Once upon a time, across no man's land, there was a border . . .

I had Finkel's translation on the table alongside me, with the Sumerian characters for 'no man's land' picked out. I tried writing them myself in my notebook: a process of copying without comprehension. The original script was made up of a series of lines ending in triangles – like tiny flags – arranged to form discrete shapes. My attempt was messy, the lines wobbly and ink-blotted, the shapes haphazard. I tried again, better this time: the lines formed with more confident strokes, helped by treating each 'flag' like a letter.

I was determined to find where the phrase was carved into the pillar itself. I bent over it, peering through a large magnifying glass, moving back and forward over the markings, heaving the pillar round to switch from one column to the next. It was easy to get lost in the mass of scratched and chiselled inscriptions.

At last I found it: that same arrangement of characters. Though faint in places, the carving was intricate, elegant. I touched it – the pillar still cool despite the heat of the lamp.

No man's land.

To have this phrase at my fingertips, preserved at the very instant that it was brand new, the sensation was electric, charged. I couldn't stop looking. Under magnification, the crystalline limestone glistened like spun sugar. This was a beautiful object. Beautiful, and terrible.

The pillar's story ends with victory for Lagash. After describing generations of violent border confrontations, the author draws the dispute to a close. And, if the reader were in any doubt, the inscription's last lines offer a dire warning to anyone who would seek to reopen the wound:

> If the Umma leader crosses over the boundary channel of Ningirsu . . . to take away the fields by force, whether he be the Umma leader or any other leader, may Enlil destroy him! May Ningirsu, after casting his great battle-net upon him, bring down upon him his giant hands and feet! May the people of his city, having risen up against him, kill him there within his own city![6]

When it was first erected, around 2,400 BC, it was set upright, cemented into a wide pedestal, and then positioned on the summit of the border embankment – a deliberate eye-catcher, glimmering in the sunlight, flashing its message out over the plain. This was history as artefact and document in one: the long tale of the border told by the border itself. *History*, but not, perhaps, as we know it.

The pillar tells of a world where the actions of gods and men intertwine. Where deities mark out boundary lines in the earth, breastfeed future kings, and take to the field of battle alongside their mortal subjects. At the same time, there is remarkable bureaucratic specificity – that the border runs for some sixty kilometres 'from the Tigris to the Nun canal'; that Umma owes Lagash interest on 44 million hectolitres of barley, but only repaid it on 18 million.[7]

It is a fragmentary story, told in fragments – because this pillar is not the only source. The tale of the Lagash–Umma border conflict recurs across a small collection of similar objects that have emerged from the Mesopotamian sands over the last two centuries. There are cuneiform inscriptions on broken clay tablets and jars; two densely marked stone slabs; a pair of large, ovoid, river-worn boulders carved with identical accounts of the dispute.[8] Most impressive of all is one large stone sculpture, rediscovered by French archaeologists in the 1880s. Now held at the Musée du Louvre in Paris, it is known as the 'Stele of the Vultures', and it offers a graphic depiction of one of the pivotal battles for the border.

Carved in relief into its broken limestone surface are the figures of the god Ningirsu and his superpowered champion Eanatum. On one side of the stele, Ningirsu appears as a giant, holding captive beneath his great 'battle-net' a tortured jumble of nude Ummaite soldiers and bringing his mace down on the head of one unfortunate figure who is trying to wriggle free. On the reverse, there is Eanatum in his chariot, at the head of a mass of shielded warriors, spear held out ready to strike. Beneath his army's feet are the trampled bodies of fallen enemies. In the top corner, vultures carry the severed heads of Ummaite soldiers in their beaks – the gory detail that gives the carving its modern name.[9]

Further down the stele, a panel shows the aftermath. Bodies are piled in a heap so high that workers with baskets on their heads have to climb ladders to throw soil down upon them. Eanatum sits on his throne, watching as the burial mounds rise, animals are prepared for sacrifice, and sacred plants are placed in the ground and watered.[10] Those tall embankments, created all along the length of the border, were not just heaped mounds of earth. They also contained within them mass graves, the stacked-up bodies of the fallen. A border inscribed in blood and bone.

In these alternative accounts, the frontier shifts and changes. Sometimes more detail is added; at other times events conflate or diverge, chronology becomes confused. The boundary pillar was trying to summarise all that had gone before, to be the definitive text, placed in situ on the Edge of the Plain. But it was only telling the story *so far.*

What followed is shown, rather bluntly, by the fabric of the pillar itself. I could see quite clearly where a huge blow had cleaved away a section from the top. An attempt had also been made to hack away at the inscription – three thumb-sized depressions had defaced one section of the text. Given the hardness of the stone, the effort just to erase this tiny area must have been considerable.

I peered at the bumps, pressed my fingers into them. In breaking the rock's surface, the dense crystal interior was exposed. Over time, impurities had oxidised, leaving faint circles of dark orange. They looked like burn marks left by stubbed-out cigarettes. Finally, there was the base. At some point, brute force had been used to detach it from its pedestal and overturn it. This action had left an ugly, frayed – and partly blackened – stump. Just like the markers that came before it, this one did not last. How could it have been any other way?

As for what happened to it: the tale was picked up on a shard of cuneiform-inscribed clay, also now held in the Louvre. Written some fifty years after the border pillar was put in place, this fragment offered no preamble; it just launched into a long and exhaustive list of devastation, like a rolling news report. The Ummaites, it said, had set fire to temples, buildings and statues all across Lagash. Each site was named in turn, along with details of how their treasures had been plundered. It recorded how the barley of Ningirsu's 'beloved field' had been spoiled. It described how *all the border posts* (including the one lying in front of me) had been broken and uprooted. And then, finally, it told of the sacking of the city of Lagash.

The culprit was named as the Ummaite ruler Lugalzagesi. With a final note of defiance, the scribe called a curse down upon him: 'because the Ummaite destroyed the bricks of Lagash, he committed a sin against Ningirsu; Ningirsu will cut off the hands which had been lifted against him'.[11] Lugalzagesi was already concerning himself with wider horizons. In a triumphant pronouncement, preserved on the broken remains of a four-millennia-old vase, he talked of how he would bring prosperity to all the people of his lands. Lands which, he claimed, had been granted to him by Enlil, and which stretched 'from the rising of the sun to the setting of the sun', and 'from the lower sea, along the Tigris and Euphrates, to the upper sea'.[12]

And so the Edge of the Plain was no longer the edge. After some 150 years, the border dispute really had ended: with the destruction and subjugation of Lagash. The boundary canal became just another irrigation channel. The frontier shifted, was pushed outwards, beyond sight and mind. With the border gone, Lugalzagesi's inscription declared that a new age of peace could begin:

> may all mankind thrive like plants and herbs . . . may the people of the land look upon a 'fair earth'; the good fortune which the gods have deemed for me may they never alter, and unto eternity may I be the foremost shepherd.[13]

Lugalzagesi's 'eternity' did not last long. Within a few years, he was brought, bound in neck chains, to the gates of the city of Nippur. The 'king of all lands' was reduced to an abject figure – prisoner of Sargon the Great, ruler of Akkad, history's first empire.[14] Umma, too, had been sacked and destroyed, barely outliving its great rival. The curse had come true. One land, swallowed by another, then swallowed by another.

Once upon a time there was a border . . .

And what is a border, if not a story? It is never simply a line, a marker, a wall, an edge. First, it is an idea. An idea that is then presented as a reality. It doesn't just exist in the world. It can only ever be *made*. It can only ever be *told*.

There were borders before this pillar, before the war over the Edge of the Plain. There must have been – although their true stories, and in particular their physical remains, are almost entirely lost to us. Certainly, humans have been marking territory for millennia. In the prehistoric world, hunter-gatherers would cut notches or symbols into trees, hang the bones or viscera of animals from branches. Prominent burial sites were positioned on the periphery of hunting grounds, so the souls of the dead could stand sentry and ward off intruders.

In the Aboriginal communities of northern Australia, bodies were sometimes carried for days, to be buried at the tribal edgelands – where graves were strung out at intervals, creating a sort of spiritual boundary line.[15] There is some speculation that even our earliest works of rock art, from tens of thousands of years ago – finger markings on soft surfaces, cave paintings, engravings in boulders – were, in part, attempts to demonstrate a connection to space, to imbed something human and personal in the landscape, to say, 'This place is mine.'[16] *Mine, and not yours?*

So territory was being defined even then. But it was also, always, being redefined. Communities lived on the move, shifting from site to site, following the wild herds or shoals of fish as the seasons changed. In southern Scandinavia, elevated wooden burial platforms were built on high ground or strung between tree trunks. Known as 'air graves', the deterioration of these structures, along with the decay of the bodies they held, were intended as visible signs that territory was equally impermanent.[17]

The Lagash pillar was something different: the next evolutionary step, if you like, in the process of *owning* the earth. In its inscription, territory is eternal – apportioned by god and marked out at the very beginning of time. The pillar describes a line that runs for sixty kilometres, that has been cut into the very ground itself, and which says that it must not be crossed. It warns that those who *have* crossed it, who ignored its power, have been punished by the gods. Our earliest written account of a border – and it is the story of an argument.

So this is where I begin. A line is drawn. And then another and another and another. We haven't stopped drawing them ever since.

I reached out to the pillar one last time. Some objects just have an aura, a presence, call it what you will. The pillar was so solid, so dense, that it felt as if it had its own gravity well – it kept pulling me back in. I was thinking of that scribe, chipping away at the limestone; of the hands that set the pillar in place on the embankment; and the hands that later tore it out again. All the people that once touched it, just like I was touching it now.

What emotions something as simple as a line can stir, what actions it can provoke. Borders don't just divide the landscape. They multiply it, creating new worlds, new realities. They've been doing this now for thousands of years. Unrolling across the earth. Casting their strange magic out over the plains. Inscribing their stories in the dust and the dirt.

PART 1
MAKING

1
LINE OF BONES

'They said that there was no population here. That was their thinking. This was no man's land. Wilderness.'

I was crouched beneath the eaves of the artist-mapmaker Hans Ragnar Mathisen's attic studio in his home in Tromsdalen, 214 miles north of the Arctic Circle. Hans was sitting beside a large plan chest, pulling out sheet after sheet of semi-transparent plastic foil, each one covered with lines and names marked in pencil or black ink. Through a window, across the waters of the fjord, I could see the lights of the island city of Tromsø. Tiny snowflakes pressed themselves up against the black of the glass and then vanished.

Hans opened more drawers.

'When I came to secondary school, you know you got different subjects – history, geography, languages and so on? And I was very fond of this workbook we had in geography. There were maps that had not been coloured in, and you had to colour them. The mountains, the middle lands, the forested areas – you made them all different colours. So that's how it began.'

He handed me several sheets to hold as he dug deeper into the piles inside one drawer.

'Ah, yes! This is the original of my first proper map. Well, not quite the original. It is a replica because the *original* original was lost.'

He pulled a sheet out and held it up.

The map was startlingly colourful. It showed the great hooked arm of Scandinavia extending west to the bent elbow of Russia's Kola peninsula. In the top left was a fiery sun, like a compass flower.

In the top right, surrounded by a dark blue sea, was the moon. The mountains were marked in reds, oranges and browns, the lowlands in rich greens and yellows. The map was framed by drawings of ribbons, which met and wrapped around an ornamental walking stick on one side. There were more drawings: an ancient rock carving, a shamanic drum, a wooden drinking cup, a crib, a decorated spoon.

In the bottom right corner was a map within the map. It was centred on the North Pole, which was shown as a bright yellow star. The northern hemisphere revolved around it: Russia, Siberia, Alaska, Nunavut and Greenland. Scandinavia was at the top of this map and was positioned, in conventional terms, upside down. Next to this insert – and drawn as a piece of elaborate embroidery – was the map's title: *Sápmi*.

Sápmi is both a territory and a concept. It describes the living space of the Sámi people, made up of tundra and taiga, mountains and forests, rivers and seas. But it also describes the Sámi culture and way of life, which has existed on the Fennoscandian Peninsula for thousands of years, going as far back as the end of the last Ice Age.

'I wanted it to be very beautiful,' Hans said. 'Because we Sámi have experienced such bad things. I wanted it to be beautiful for us.'

In the map, Sápmi stretches all the way across Norway, Sweden, Finland and into Russia. But there are no borders. The names and boundaries of the four nations that now occupy this terrain are not included. Instead, Sápmi reaches out over the earth – free, unfettered and unconstrained by lines.

'That was an easy thing. Because I saw no reason to include the borders. Because Sápmi is our homeland and that's that.'

He looked away from me, down at the map. He sighed.

'I was the first Sámi mapmaker. No one before me did this. Yes, there were other maps. But not made by Sámi. The Sámi did have maps of course. But the maps were in their heads.'

A day earlier. A strong wind was blowing in from the north. It tugged incessantly at the thin layer of fresh snow on the frozen surface of

Lake Kilpisjärvi, sending streams of powder gliding and skittering out over the pan-flat expanse. The snowmobile bucked and twisted underneath me. My guide, Thomas, had led me, slowly at first, through a birch forest, picking a route between the trees. But now, out on the lake, we could open up our throttles. I watched my speedometer climb past thirty, forty, fifty, sixty, seventy kilometres per hour. In the distance a gap appeared in the grey clouds. A shaft of sunlight drew a perfectly straight, golden line across the landscape.

The lake was surrounded on all sides by hills – low, interlocking rises covered in a thick black fur of birch. But beyond the hills were huge, bare mountain ridges, snow-smoothed and bone-white. The temperature was six degrees below zero, not including the wind chill: mild for early March. Just the week before it had been minus twenty-five.

'The ice on the lake is about two metres thick right now,' Thomas had told me. 'You only need about ten centimetres for it to be safe for snowmobiles. At twenty centimetres, you could land a jumbo jet out here.'

Our route ran northeastwards for the whole, eleven-kilometre length of the lake. It also took us – exactly – on top of an international border. The line dividing Finland and Sweden cuts right through the middle of Kilpisjärvi. For around four months of the year, it lies on the shifting, shimmering water. But from October through to June, this border is encased in ice.

Snow continued to fall. It whipped up under my helmet's visor to sting the exposed skin above my facemask. Another snowmobile passed in the opposite direction, pulling a heavily laden sled with a black dog sitting on top. The dog jumped up to bark at us, spun around on its sled to watch us go. We reached the end of the lake, then rode another hundred metres or so up a gentle hill. Thomas glided to a stop and I pulled up behind him.

'Did you see the dog?' he asked me. 'That's a Sámi dog. A reindeer herder's dog. The herd must be somewhere out in the mountains right now.'

He gestured back down over the frozen lake.

'Last year I saw – I don't know – it must have been a thousand reindeer out there? I'd never seen so many together in one place.' He laughed. 'You know, it was like something out of a wildlife film, a David Attenborough film. It was winter, midday, the sun really low – just after the end of the polar night. And the reindeer started running down the lake, and they kicked up all this snow around them, a huge cloud. It looked amazing in that sunlight. And the herders were after them on their snowmobiles and their dogs were after them too. And the dogs were just barking like crazy.'

I looked at the lake below us. It was a pristine expanse. A beautiful, flat, empty blankness. The one disturbance was the passage of our snowmobiles: a long, solitary line receding into the distance. Like we had drawn the border ourselves, carved it into the snow.

The way ahead took us back into the forest. We climbed for a few minutes, weaving a trail through the mass of birch branches, then we descended again, riding out into what appeared to be a wide clearing, open at its far end. It was, I realised, another frozen lake.

Some ten or so metres out across the lake was a giant, circular concrete block, topped by a small grey stone. If we *had* been drawing a border, then this would have been our end point. I climbed off my snowmobile, brushed at the ice encrusted on the surface of the block. The windward side was completely white, but on the lee there were patches of yellow paint shining through. I walked round it clockwise. And every few paces I found myself in a different country. Sweden to Finland. Finland to Norway. Norway to Sweden. Sweden to Finland to Norway again.

It is not just one line that meets here, but three. In fact, rather than an end, it is a nexus – what's known as a 'tripoint'. The northernmost extremity of Sweden joins up here with the westernmost point of Finland. And beyond them both, to the north and west, lie Norway and the Arctic Ocean. In 1897, this marker was erected as a simple pile of stones. Thirty years later – after the stones kept collapsing due to the extremes of winter weather – it was reconstructed as it remains today, a three-metre-tall, four-metre-wide conical frustum, an artificial island lying just off the shore of Lake Golddajávri, and which, for three quarters of the year, is buried in snow.

Up close, I could make out that the little slab on top of the cairn was three-sided. Each side was carved with a representation of the country it faced. Three crowns for Sweden. A coat of arms topped by an axe-wielding lion for Norway. And finally, and very simply, on the third side, the word *Suomi* – the Finnish for Finland. Of Sápmi, however, there was no mention.

This tripoint – this 'three-country cairn' as it is called – sits right at the heart of the Sámi lands. Seen one way, it is a cartographical curiosity, a place where you can jokingly cross three national borders in a few seconds (and indulge in some time travel: Finland is one hour ahead of Sweden and Norway). Seen another way, however, it is a symbol of how a territory that has been known and occupied for countless generations can be claimed and marked out by incomers. Seen *that way*, the great concrete cone becomes a stake hammered into the ground, fracturing a landscape into three. It sends borderlines rippling out over the earth like geological fissures. You may not see these lines, not in the land at least. But they see you. They mean something. And they come with consequences.

In the summer of 1904, two Danish sisters, Emilie and Marie Demant, holidayed in a log cabin by Lake Vassijaure in northwestern Sweden, right alongside the Norwegian border. They had travelled there on a brand-new railroad, built to transport iron ore from the vast mines of the prospector town of Kiruna, over the mountains to the ice-free Norwegian port of Narvik. After a few days hiking across the open landscapes of the high plateau, they reboarded the train at Vassijaure – its stop so new that it had neither station nor platform – and continued on to Narvik. On their return to Kiruna, they shared a carriage with a Finnish traveller and another man with 'lively eyes', who was dressed in fur tunic and hide trousers, and carried a large knife in a sheath fashioned from animal bone. With the Finnish passenger acting as translator, they began to talk.

The man's name was Johan Turi, and he was a former Sámi reindeer herder turned wolf hunter, on his way to visit his family at their summer camp on the northern bank of Lake Torneträsk. Turi had just turned fifty years old. He had been born in 1854 in Kautokeino, 140 miles to the northeast, in the heart of the vast expanses of the Finnmark region of northern Norway. But at the age of three, his family had relocated south to Sweden, to the Sámi town of Karesuando.

The ceding of the Grand Duchy of Finland from Sweden to Imperial Russia in 1809 had fractured the Scandinavian landscape in three. Tensions had escalated between Russia and Norway, and then, in 1853, Russia completely closed the Finnish–Norwegian border. In an instant, Sámi herders were denied access to the pasturelands that their reindeer had grazed on for centuries. Many, like Turi's family, had no option but to move. They remained at Karesuando for thirty years until, in 1889, Russia also closed Finland's border with Sweden.[1] Once again, the crucial wintering grounds of the herds were cut off. This time, Turi's father decided to head westwards, taking his reindeer to the forests of Lake Torneträsk, near the Sámi market village of Jukkasjärvi – just a few miles away from a small, ramshackle settlement of turf-roofed, wooden huts. Ten years later, those huts would explode into the mining town of Kiruna.

Turi explained how he had grown tired of his family's pursuit of reindeer herding. While his two brothers had established their own herds, he had opted instead for the solitary life of a trapper, hunter and fisherman. Long periods alone, out by himself in the landscape, had given him much time to think – and to dream. It had reminded him of his desire, since he was a boy, to not just tell, but *write down*, the story of his people and their way of life.

Emilie, thirty years old and the younger of the two sisters, offered up her own long-held dream in return: that she had always hoped one day to travel with the Sámi herders across the landscapes of the north. 'I had had since childhood,' she said, 'a nearly mystical desire to live among the mountain people.' In those moments, as their train rattled through the Swedish highlands, a deal was struck. Emilie would help Turi to write and publish his story. And Turi would arrange for Emilie to live and work with his brother's family, following the reindeer on their annual migration.[2]

The reindeer have known this landscape for longer than anyone. Some 10,000 years ago they moved northwards in the wake of the retreating inland ice. People – hunters, the original ancestors of the Sámi – followed.

For the reindeer, the winter cold is no threat. Their fur is of thick, high-density, hollow hair fibres, offering incredibly effective insulation. They can maintain core body temperature up to fifty degrees below zero. Their challenge, however, has always been finding sustenance when the land is frozen and snowbound.

Over the millennia they have evolved very specific migration patterns. In winter they move through the lowland forests, digging down into the snow to reach their main food source, ground lichens. In spring, when calves are born, they seek out pastures where snow melts early, feeding on grass and plants to regain weight lost in the coldest months. In summer they retreat to the mountains, to escape the heat and the mosquitos. By August, they have moved to lower pastures, for the rut to begin. Autumn is a brief interlude, holding on to the last warmth of summer before a rapid climatic shift back towards the impending polar darkness.[3] For nearly 9,000 years, little changed in the rhythms of life for the Sámi hunters and the reindeer. But by the ninth century, outsiders had moved into the lands of Sápmi.

Visiting the court of the Anglo-Saxon King Alfred the Great around AD 890, the Norse chieftain Óttar recounted how he regularly received tribute from the Sámi in the form of reindeer, marten, bear and otter skins, bushels of down feathers and ship cables made of whale hide and seal skin. This was, Óttar boasted, his main source of income.[4] Even so, it was not until the thirteenth century that the first Norse village was established in Finnmark in northern Sápmi – along with the first church – and, over the next few hundred years, most new settlements clung to the coastal fringes.

Inevitably, however, the pressures on the land only increased. In 1542, the Swedish king Gustav Vasa announced that 'all permanently uninhabited land belongs to God, us, and the Swedish Crown, and nobody else'. Vasa had led the breakaway of the Swedish nation from the Kingdom of Denmark, which still controlled Norway. This began the process of drawing fault lines through Scandinavia. The implications for the Sámi people were stark. A 1591 Swedish census listed one community of nearly 300 Sámi living on the northeastern coast, and recorded how they were paying taxes, *at the same time*, to the crowns of Sweden, Denmark and Russia.[5]

As a result, demands for fur and meat rose sharply. Hunting intensified to serve the needs of the traders and the taxmen, and it soon became clear that the impact on reindeer numbers would be unsustainable. Instead, by the seventeenth century, a new bond had developed between the Sámi and the reindeer: a semi-domestication that saw the mountain and forest tribes live and move with the herds all year round as they migrated across the northern expanses – managing their numbers in an attempt to ensure that they would not be hunted to extinction.

There was also a new use emerging for the landscape. In 1634, a Sámi man, Peder Olofsson, discovered traces of silver ore in the northwestern highlands at a place called Nasafjäll in the mountains that formed the – still undefined – border between Sweden and Norway. A year later, a mine was in full operation, with a silver works for smelting the ore established some forty kilometres away, on the shores of Lake Sädvajaure, at a site the Sámi named as Silbojokk: the 'silver stream'.[6]

The constant need for charcoal to fuel the smelter's furnace saw the near-total felling of the pine forests surrounding the lake: tree cover which has still never returned. Industrial by-products

– great heaps of slag and waste material – poisoned the water-courses and transformed the shape of the surrounding environment. The local Sámi were persuaded, initially by tax exemptions, to use their now semi-tamed reindeer to transport ore from the minehead down through the mountains to the silver works. Increasingly, however, they refused, concerned as they were about the physical impact on the reindeer and the consequences of interrupting the migration of the herds. Some accounts tell of how the Swedish mineworkers forced the Sámi to comply, tying herders to timbers, and pushing them down into river rapids until they changed their minds. Others talk of how the ore road was littered with 'bleached reindeer skeletons' – a line of bones, left running all the way from the mountains to the lakeside.[7]

Soon, almost all the local Sámi had abandoned this landscape, many going north or west into Norway. The mines and silver works only lasted for a couple of decades before they were destroyed by Norwegian troops during a 1659 conflict with Sweden. Working conditions had been extremely hard, and the amounts of silver produced failed to generate the hoped-for riches. Yet, all the same, the eyes of both the state and private prospectors had been turned northwards. For the first time, people were looking deep into the Sápmi interior, wondering not just about what was on the land, but also, what was *in it*. And, of course, who owned it.

The issue of territory only grew more contentious. Disputes over land pitched Sweden and Norway into constant conflict. Finally, in 1734, the two crowns agreed to the formation of a border commission which would, as Christian VI of Denmark put it, 'compose a complete map and drawing of the boundary line and area between Norway and Sweden on both sides'. A border that should be 'approached geometrically, with all lines, angles and curvatures stated in their net length and breadth'.[8]

This required a ground survey of the whole extent of the mountainous spine of Scandinavia, from the Baltic Sea to the Arctic Ocean. Much of this initial work was carried out by one man – a Danish-

Norwegian military officer and jurist, Peter Schnitler. In 1742, Schnitler embarked on a four-year field study, travelling across the northern landscapes and interviewing local communities – almost all Sámi – about the border. Once his study was complete, he sent his personal maps and journals to a team of military surveyors, who followed in his tracks to create an accurately measured and fully drawn borderline. The result, as agreed by the Treaty of Strömstad in 1751, remains the longest border between two countries in Europe – a single, unbroken line, running for 2,200 kilometres.[9]

This treaty came with a codicil attached, informed by Schnitler's field interviews. Thirty clauses offered special provisions for the Sámi people (then known as 'Lapps' or 'Lapplanders') to regulate and acknowledge their unique place in this divided landscape. 'Since the Lapps need the land of both countries,' it said, 'they are to have the right, in keeping with the old custom, in the autumn and the spring to move with their reindeer to the neighbouring country, and henceforth as before in common with the subjects of each country to use land and shore for the maintenance of themselves and their animals; and they are to be amicably received, sheltered and assisted.'[10]

It was the first written, legal acknowledgment of Sápmi, and the first recognition of the rights of the Sámi people to move freely across the land, wherever the borderlines were drawn. At the same time, the Sámi had to assume either Swedish *or* Norwegian citizenship. This was often determined by where a community's winter lands were located. In many cases, however, even these were divided by the border, and so they were simply given the choice. As a direct benefit, after centuries of exploitation, the Sámi only had to pay tax once, in one country.

The codicil was a curiously ambivalent document. It has been described as the Sámi 'Magna Carta' – enshrining the existence of a discrete people and culture, and their ancient landscape.[11] Yet, ironically, it did this as part of the very process of carving up that landscape. Rights, once given, can still be taken away. And borders – once drawn, once opened – can still be closed. It was telling that, from the very moment that Sápmi was written into existence, it was split down the middle, cut in two.

Emilie Demant returned to Denmark with her sister, but she did not forget her arrangement with Johan Turi. She kept up an irregular but enthusiastic correspondence with him, while at the same time meeting with a professor of comparative philology at the University of Copenhagen, Vilhelm Thomsen, who taught her the rudiments of the Sámi language. In June 1907, three years after her first visit, she was back on a train bound for northern Sweden. She passed through Kiruna, and then, a little further to the northwest, disembarked at a small station overlooking the still partly ice-bound waters of Lake Torneträsk. A few days later, Turi arrived to meet her. At midnight, with the sun still sitting above the horizon, they rowed across the lake to its northern bank and then walked to the encampment where Turi's brother, Aslak, was waiting.[12]

Aslak lived with his wife Siri and their five children as part of a community called a *siida* – a Sámi word which encompasses a group of families, all the land that they use and the specific place they are inhabiting at any one time. A *siida* is, in a sense, both a governance structure *and* a territory, but a territory that is always shifting and mutable, its borders drawn and redrawn by the movement of the reindeer and their herders as they migrate across the country.

Emilie arrived at the *siida* just as the thaw had taken hold and they were preparing to move to their summer camp. After saying goodbye to Turi, one of her first tasks was to help her host family pull down their tent and pack it into boats alongside sacks of flour, dried meat, cooking pots, skins and bedclothes. Travelling northwest up the lake, through the permanent sunset of the earliest hours of the morning, they made for the far shore, climbed up into the forest and raised the tent again – covering the earth inside with a mat of fresh birch twigs and arranging a circle of stones for a hearth. 'From outside,' Emilie wrote, 'the tent glowed like a coloured lamp against the violet mountain where the snow lay in long strips. Inside burned the fire I'd longed for, for so many years. The reality far exceeded my dreams.'[13]

For the next eight months, from high summer through to March of the following year, Emilie's life alternated between the grand expanses of the landscape and the tiny world of the Aslak's family's tent. 'The exterior setting is magnificent enough,' she wrote, 'mountains, sun, dark, storms, the huge sky, stars, northern lights and a vast countryside. Who in our society has such a backdrop for his work?'[14] Yet, as the light faded and the cold advanced, the one constant, the place of return, was always the tent. 'The tent is moved from place to place, but the tent is always the same inside and out.' As the polar night enveloped the north – 'the dark time' the Sámi called it – Emilie's existence shrank down to the smallest footprint, a circle just a few metres wide. 'The fire drew people and dogs together, as the fog walled us in,' she wrote. 'We had a home as far as the fire reached. Sparks from the fire flew into the air like little red stars and were put out by the mist . . . Then the fire was extinguished and we were one with the dark.'[15]

Emilie participated in all aspects of Sámi life. She gathered and chopped wood; cooked, stretched hides and made clothing from reindeer skin; packed up the reindeer's burdens and walked alongside them. Some of her most vivid accounts captured her thrill at living and moving with the herd. There were nearly 3,000 reindeer in the *siida*, and when they came together it was in 'grey waves' that 'rumbled, like thunder coming from the underworld', a living mass that 'rushed over the mountainside like a hailstorm'. Emilie wrote of how she couldn't help but 'feel shivers' at the spectacle. But it was not just her; she observed that even the Sámi, despite their intense familiarity with the animals, still 'experienced a sort of intoxication at the sight of the herd'.[16]

At the end of March 1908, she took the opportunity to leave Aslak's *siida* and join up with another Sámi family at Karesuando. Rather than cross back over 'the same tracts of land . . . which would be a little humdrum', she wanted to experience 'new people, new conditions and new territories'. The Karesuando *siida* was about to embark on a long and arduous spring migration: a journey of over 200 kilometres, travelling northwest to cross over the mountains from Sweden to Norway, bound for the pastures of Tromsdalen, overlooking the city of Tromsø. Emilie trekked with a husband and wife, Heikka and Gate, for another four months, through the high, windswept passes where the rapid thaw made conditions ever-changing and treacherous. 'There, between the peaks, is our passageway,' Gate told her, 'a place where we can see the dark forest under us as a hell and the steep mountain above us as a heaven.'[17]

She reached Tromsø at the very end of June and, after a few weeks spent at the summer camp, made the journey south. Just over a year on, she came back to the railway station at Lake Torneträsk. From there, it was a short hike up the mountain to a small prospector's wooden shack. Inside, Johan Turi was waiting for her. Over the next four months, through the summer and into the autumn, Emilie would uphold her part of the bargain – she would help Turi write his book on the Sámi people.

Muitalus sámiid birra – 'An Account of the Sámi' – was published two years later. Emilie convinced Turi to write it in the Sámi language, which she then had to translate into Danish, with the two versions sitting alongside each other. Many who met Turi liked to portray him as a kind of noble savage, or primitive *savant* – but he was far from ignorant of the modern world. Turi had lived and participated in this world, adapted to it, and attempted to integrate it with his own Sámi way of life. His very reason for writing the book was to give voice to his concerns over the changes he had experienced all around him: to assert the rights of his people and show how they were equal to those of any other nation. While *Muitalus* was both an ethnography and a history – with stories drawn from folktales which bled into detailed, practical descriptions of reindeer husbandry or traditional medicine – it was, at heart, a polemic.[18]

'I am a Sámi' was Turi's very first, declamatory line. 'I have been thinking that it would be best if there were a book in which everything was written about Sámi life and conditions,' he continued, 'so that people wouldn't have to ask how Sámi conditions are, and so that people wouldn't misconstrue things, particularly those who want to lie about the Sámi and claim that only the Sámi are at fault when disputes arise between settlers and Sámi in Norway and Sweden.'[19]

In 1901, the pre-eminent Danish explorer Knud Rasmussen had spent time with the Sámi in northern Sweden, which he detailed in his book *Lapland*. Recalling a conversation with a Sámi man, he offered a fatalistic view of their future. 'The reindeer herds will disappear, and your friends will die along with their wilderness,' he had said. War had come to Sápmi, he continued, 'and those fighting are two cultures. And the new one must be victorious, because it bears the future within itself.' As a result, the Sámi would be 'oppressed in their own land and give way with the quiet resignation of those sentenced to death to the new people, those who charge ahead with their trains and dynamite. And they will die as quietly and unnoticed as they have always lived up here.'[20]

Turi's work represented a refusal to submit to this 'quiet resignation': it offered instead a deliberate act of resistance, a voice to break the silence of Sápmi's so-called 'wilderness'. Emilie, who had read Rasmussen's *Lapland* and remarked 'how thin it is in its pages, and superficial',[21] was soon to produce a book of her own. In 1913, she turned the letters and journals from her year of nomadic life into one volume, titled *With the Lapps in the High Mountains*. Taken alongside *Muitalus*, it offered a remarkable account of an ancient culture moving through a time of rapid political, economic and social change. And it captured how Sápmi was shrinking – metaphorically and literally – right before her eyes. Encroachments and threats came from almost every direction, closing in like the polar darkness around the hearth fire. Mass industrialisation, agriculture, expanding settlements, intensive forestry – and borders. Always borders.

Some of the most poignant passages in Emilie's book came during her migration with Heikka and Gate from Karesuando to Tromsø.

Her route had followed the line of the Sweden–Finland border, which itself followed the Könkämä river all the way to Lake Kilpisjärvi, Lake Golddajávri and the three-country cairn. She wrote of how they made camp along the way, their tents 'high up on a hill, from which there was a broad view into "the forbidden land"' – Finland. 'The only border was the river that lay thick with ice, underneath the ridge, and the reindeer can't respect a frozen river as a state boundary'.[22] The animals continually strayed over the line, with anxious herders and their dogs chasing them back to the Swedish side.

Days later, as they were on the move again, she observed that 'one of the men herding the stray reindeers had lain down on a hill while the reindeer rested. He looked over Finland close by; it was easy to guess his thoughts . . . Over there to the east on the other side of the river, the lichen was grey and heavy; there he and the animals could find strength and courage . . . But all the goodness was blocked by state boundaries, behind which lurked legal statutes.'[23]

To cross the border into Norway, they turned westwards, away from Lake Kilpisjärvi and 'the forbidden land' of Finland, climbing higher up into the mountain plateau, to a place called Kåbmejaure: the 'ghost lake'. It was midsummer, but the conditions were atrocious: high winds, snow, hail, rain. They had to weigh their tents down with granite boulders to prevent them being torn apart in the maelstrom. The Sámi called it 'death weather'.[24] They were on the very cusp of the Norwegian border.

Gate told Emilie that she could hear the 'Haldas' – the spirits of the underworld – 'cry at night'; and Emilie agreed that 'there was something so eerie in the wind along the mountainsides'. Sámi folklore from the region spoke of a very specific type of Halda – known, in Finnish, as a *rajanhaltija*. It was a creature that haunted a border, screaming when it was moved or when it was crossed. Whether the cries on the wind were anguished laments for the lines that had been drawn through Sápmi, or warnings to the herders of the dangers they faced when passing from one land to another, Gate did not say.

(A decade later, however, the final prohibition came: a 1919 Swedish-Norwegian border convention that banned the movement of the herds between the two countries. More pastures, more calving grounds gone. Millennia-old migration routes cut off, in an instant.)

Those days of following, traversing and crossing the lines of the fractured terrain of Sápmi had made a powerful impression on Emilie. A Sámi, she wrote, 'is a migratory bird who moves his living places. He follows the reindeer; he settles down where they find fodder and puts up his grey tent where it's beautiful and where he can see far and wide.'

In one of the final lines of her book, she turned to the reader to ask a question which was at once plaintive and accusatory: 'You, who close the borders and take the earth from him, do you know what you do?'[25]

I had followed Emilie's route, partly by snowmobile, but mostly by bus, all the way to Tromsø. Long streets of compact, wooden-slatted houses sprawled lightly across the humped back of an island about half the size of Manhattan. Fjords and mountains surrounded it in every direction. Despite the sharp-edged uprights of chain hotels clustered around the waterfront, it still retained the earthy, just-built feel of a frontier town.

Hans Ragnar Mathisen had asked me to meet him at a Chinese restaurant just a short walk uphill from the main harbour. He was in his mid-seventies, and he cut a slight, almost frail figure. His silvery-white hair fell in long, thin strands down either side of his balding head, framing the blackest eyes I'd ever seen. Eyes that seemed all pupil, nothing else. They reminded me of a passage I'd read in Emilie's book: how she said that you could 'see the whole landscape in the reindeer's eyes, as in a black concave mirror . . . and see omens inside'.[26]

Hans was born on 1 July 1945 among the bombed-out wartime ruins of the port town of Narvik, one of a pair of twins. His brother did not survive infancy, his parents died soon after, and his own childhood was blighted by ill-health. When he was around two years old he contracted tuberculosis and was hospitalised for almost nine years, seven of them spent in a sanatorium in Tromsø. On his release in 1956 he was taken in by a foster family who were also Sámi – something he didn't discover until much later in life. He told me how one day, when he was in his teens, he was looking through books and papers in his foster parents' home, when he came across an old map of Tromsø county.[27]

'I saw on this map that there were some place names in parenthesis next to the Norwegian names and I wondered what is this? It was another language. It was Sámi. And at that time Sámi was kind of taboo. I knew that *I* was a Sámi, but I couldn't speak it or read it then.'

A new Norway was emerging in the aftermath of the Second World War. A Norway built on the concept of the welfare state and driven by the idea of 'equality' – but an equality so purist that it did not want to acknowledge difference. Like, for instance, the difference between a Norwegian and a Sámi. In this new Norway, there were set standards of behaviour, diet, living and education. One nation needed only one language, one history. All teaching in schools had to be conducted in Norwegian. Sámi was a language of the past, a relic of an older world; and the time had come to phase it out. It was a policy known as Norwegianisation.[28]

'Even when I was still in the hospital I knew I was being Norwegianised,' Hans said. 'I remember there was one patient who came to the hospital. And she didn't talk. And everyone said, "Oh, she can't talk." That was their conclusion. But she could talk, but not the Norwegian language; she could talk only Sámi.' He shook his head, then fixed me with those black eyes. 'This is outrageous. It's a crime in my opinion. To deny children – people – the use of their mother tongue. It is a spiritual torture. And Norwegians have too easily been acquitted of such things.'

Finding that map of Tromsø, at that time, had offered an illicit thrill, a glimpse of a world denied: a world that Norway said was no longer there, had never really been there in the first place. Hans got a thin scrap of paper, the thinnest he could find, placed it over the map and traced the coastlines. Then he added just the Sámi names, deliberately leaving out the Norwegian ones. It felt, at the time, like some kind of transgression – a small, but important, victory.

'I saw this map and I thought, *perhaps it is not so bad to be Sámi after all*.'

When he was twenty, Hans began to relearn the Sámi language he had lost as a child. His foster parents couldn't afford to send him to university, so he worked as a teacher and then a technical draftsman in an architectural practice. By 1973 he had earned enough to pay his way through university and had been accepted as a student at the Oslo National Academy of the Arts.

'I asked my tutor if it would be all right to use one year to make a map,' Hans told me. 'And he said yes. So I thought, okay, but I can't make just *any map*. It has to say something, because it is an artwork, you know? So it started off as political.'

Straight away, however, he had a problem. The Sámi homeland stretched so far that he couldn't find any one map that showed the whole area at the same scale. He went to the Norwegian Mapping Authority, who told him that no such map existed. Then they explained that, actually, there *were* maps, but they had been produced by NATO and were not available to the public. Hans convinced the authority to release the maps: they turned out to be flight navigation charts used by military pilots.

'I got them and I still have them!' Hans told me gleefully. 'And so I put them together and I traced them – and that was my outline for Sápmi.'

Next came the names. He pored over old maps and books, contacted Sámi communities in Norway, Sweden, Finland and Russia. He assembled a list that ran just short of a thousand valleys, mountains, rivers, pastures, fjords and settlements. Many of these had also been subject to Norwegianisation, translated or transliterated into bizarre distortions of their originals: the Sámi for 'dark-time valley' became 'valley of shame' in Norwegian; 'lonely bay' became the nonsensical 'home air'. Or they had just been replaced entirely.

Everything on his map was drawn by hand, the names handwritten. All of a sudden a landscape that had been seen by outsiders as wild, untouched – and nameless – was shown filled to the brim.

'The Sámi place names are so descriptive and exact,' he said, 'that a Sámi hearing them, he can already see the landscape.'

Because in Sámi culture, nature is not empty – and never was. To name is to know. What Hans was producing was a map of 'lived land', where geography was not arranged politically or nationally, but culturally. History was turned upside down – just as Scandinavia was turned upside down on his map. The borders melted away, because they had no meaning. And why draw something that didn't really exist?

'I showed it to some of the Sámi I knew in Oslo who were a bit older, and they saw it and said, "You know, this will make you famous." And I never thought of that,' he laughed and shook his head, 'I never thought of that.'

Completed in 1975, the map became a potent symbol of burgeoning Sámi political consciousness. It combined the beauty of a unique cultural artwork with the defiant spirit of provocative, anti-colonial activism. Hans sought funding from the Oslo Sámi Association and the Norwegian Cultural Council to mass-produce copies of the map.

'Of course I knew it was a risky thing to make a map of the Sámi homeland,' Hans told me. 'I remember that when I showed the proof to the Cultural Council, they were a bit worried. I could sense that. They were worried that this is a slap in the face of Norwegian feelings of supremacy. And it was meant to be! And they recognised that. Yet all the same, they said I could have the money.'

In 1978, Hans moved to the tiny Sámi village of Màze in Finnmark, where he co-founded an artist collective – called the Màze Group – who lived together in the same small house. They were all graduates of Norwegian art schools, and they all wanted to use their work to highlight the struggles – and more simply the existence – of the Sámi people to the wider world.

Four years earlier, the Sámi had become founder members of the World Council of Indigenous Peoples. Hans had even attended the Council's first meeting, at Port Alberni in British Columbia, taking copies of his Sápmi map with him and encouraging others to redraw and reclaim their territories in the same way. Land rights were seen as the most pressing and precarious issue: how to prevent governments and transnational corporations from developing or extracting resources from traditional cultural landscapes. This was of immediate relevance to Hans and the Màze Group.

The village of Màze was set on the floor of the steep-sided valley of the Alta-Kautokeino river, the largest salmon river in the world, which flowed directly northwards to empty out into the Arctic Ocean. And it was, according to Norwegian government plans, scheduled to be drowned by the creation of a vast hydroelectric power scheme.

'The original plan was that the dam should be so high that the tip of the church spire would be fifty metres underwater,' Hans told me. 'And the church is on a hill above the village!'

Mass protests against the scheme began in 1978. It was a unifying moment for Sámi cultural expression, with artist-activists like Hans creating a visual and political language for the demonstrations. Slogans like 'We will not move again!' and 'We came here first!' merged into the rallying call of '*Čájet Sámi Vuoiŋŋa!*' – 'Show Sámi Spirit'. A member of the Màze Group, Synnøve Persen, had designed a flag for the Sámi people in colours of red, gold and blue, which was brandished at every demonstration.[29]

'We discussed how to protest against Alta,' Hans told me. 'Because there had already been violence. A bridge was blown up. And a Sámi had lost their hand in the process. There were some who thought we should do more of the same. But I said – like the Sámi boy who outsmarted the giant Samo – we need to be smarter than them. So I suggested a hunger strike. They were not enthusiastic. But I said, no, it is the best solution. It will be such a sensation.'

The hunger strike started outside the Norwegian Parliament in Oslo in October 1979, demanding an immediate stop to the Alta project and the legal recognition of Sámi land rights. It attracted attention from media around the world, and by 1980 it had forced the government to halt work on the dam and appoint a commission to explore the issue of Sámi rights. However, work started again on Alta in 1981, and despite constant interruptions from demonstrators invading the construction site, the dam was eventually completed six years later.

Yet the protests had not been entirely in vain. The project's plans were changed to avoid flooding the village of Màze, and in 1988, the Norwegian constitution was altered, acknowledging state responsibility for 'enabling the Sámi people to preserve and develop their language, culture and way of life'. The creation of a Sámi parliament followed in October 1989. Alta had been the catalyst for a remarkable cultural and political renaissance.

'Our thoughts flew out of closed cages,' Synnøve Persen wrote of that time. 'A movement was born . . . We wanted back our land, our language, our self-esteem, our culture, our property. We wanted back everything that had been taken from us through the centuries.'[30]

After dinner, Hans drove me across the fjord to his house in Tromsdalen. Snow flitted through the beams of our headlights. Directly ahead, at the far end of the bridge, the interlocking, concrete fins of the Arctic Cathedral were lit up by spotlights. Beyond loomed the huge bulk of the 4,000-foot-tall Sálašoaivi mountain. (In Norwegian it's called Tromsdalstinden. But the Sámi named it first . . .) Just a few miles down the coast was the summer camp that Emilie Demant had travelled to with the Karesuando herd.

Hans lived in the same, simple, boxy wooden house that had belonged to his foster parents – one of a long line of houses that climbed street by street up the lower slopes of Sálašoaivi. We passed through the porch and into his living room. It was a space that had long ago lost any connection to the concept of order. Every flat surface was piled high with books and papers. Some larger piles had become ad hoc surfaces for smaller piles, creating paper ziggurats that listed at precarious angles from chairs or tables. One whole side of the room was given over to a cage for two budgerigars, who sang enthusiastically on our arrival. Hans switched on the radio and smiled towards the birds.

'They love classical music,' he said.

The sound of a violin concerto filled the room. In an alcove off to one side was a sofa – covered in papers, of course – that faced an open-ended cardboard box lined with glue pots, balanced on a coffee table.

'That is my book-binding station,' Hans explained. 'For years I have been collecting old books about the Sámi people. And I take off their covers and rebind them. It is my new hobby! Look, this one I bound in reindeer hide.'

He pulled a volume off a shelf and handed it to me. It was a very soft, light-brown leather, and had been embossed with an elaborate pattern. I asked Hans what it was.

'It is the impression of an artwork from an old Sámi shaman's drum,' he said. He pulled at one of the piles on a side table and revealed a beautiful woodblock print showing dancing figures, stars, mountains and galloping reindeer. The radio started playing 'Climb Every Mountain' from *The Sound of Music*. A border-crossing anthem. It was hard not to laugh at the timing. The song echoed around the house as Hans led me upstairs to his studio.

I wanted to know how many maps he had made over the years.

'It is about fifty,' he said. 'Most of them of Sápmi – in whole or in part. But also maps of the lands of other indigenous peoples around the world.'

Yet, as he pulled sheet after sheet out of his plan chest, I could see that it was far more than fifty. When you counted up all the versions that went into one completed map, the total must have run into hundreds, even thousands. Time after time, Hans had drawn the almost impossibly detailed Scandinavian coastline, traced its intricate crenulations, followed its fjords as they narrowed into rivers, its rivers as they led inland to mountains. I could imagine that it all now remained in his hand as muscle memory, something that could be switched on and off like an automaton. As if, in drawing Sápmi into existence, he now couldn't stop.

I asked if he kept up with any of the new generation of Sámi artists. Had he seen the work of Katarina Pirak Sikku, for instance, who had drawn her own map of the Sámi nation? Where Hans had erased the borders, she had, instead, imagined Sápmi as a defined political-geographical state – with a population of 4.5 million people, an official language of Sámi and a capital city in Tromsø. Her new nation bordered Sweden and Finland but appeared to have absorbed, or colonised, Norway. Her map was drawn in simple black ink on a scrap of A4 paper, with the borders marked in green biro.[31] And, just as Hans had done, she had inverted the traditional perspective, swapped north with south.

Hans shook his head. He had not heard of her, he said. But he appreciated her spirit. 'Artists always have to surprise. Get the attention of people,' he said. 'I am an old-fashioned artist now. I had my time as a revolutionary.'

And what about the future of Sápmi, its place in the modern world?

'Like all other cultures,' he said, 'the Sámi way of life is always changing, adapting. Because there is no choice. There are still some places where the Norwegian way of thinking has not gone so deep, where they keep the *siida* system in practice. My older cousin, he is one of the last people who lives the old way. Inland hunting in the winter, then when the summer comes he goes to the coast. But you must remember not all Sámi are reindeer herders. It is the minority. Most Sámi now are settled more or less. They live in towns. They live in cities.'

It was almost half a century since Hans had laid out the full extent of Sápmi in his map. In erasing the frontiers of four nations in the process, he had also staked a claim for the land. Or rather a counter claim. 'We were here first!' – as the slogan went. The borderless set against the borderers. But the debate, the fight even, over what that land is for, what to do with it, who it belongs to, still goes on. Hans told me about a vast copper mine at a place called Biedjovággi, near Kautokeino, that first started operating in the 1970s, before it closed due to a global collapse in prices.

'After they finished, they just left this giant hole in the ground. That was what they did. Because they said there were no people, nothing there, so what did it matter? Still there is this kind of thinking.'

Today, the demand for copper is rising exponentially – for use in mobile phones and laptops, to power electric cars – and private extraction companies are bidding to open Biedjovággi once again. Indeed, the race is on to dig and drill at sites all across the landscapes of the boreal north.

'The prospectors are in a hurry. There is work going on now to try to make sure that the Sámi areas are protected from unwanted exploitation. But if the government, the companies get a grip before that happens, then . . .' Hans tailed off for a moment. He looked pained, wearied. 'Well, then many things will be lost.'

The next morning I was sitting in an achingly hipsterish coffee shop just off Tromsø's main square, scrolling on my phone through the website of the Sámi artist, Máret Ánne Sara.[32]

Four years earlier, on 1 February 2016, Máret Ánne had arrived in a truck outside the Finnmark district court in the town of Tana and deposited a pile of 200 reindeer heads on the ground. There was a photo on her website of the grisly pyramid she arranged on the snow, with a Norwegian flag planted right at the top. The severed heads still had their fur and eyes, and, although frozen, were spattered in blood.

Máret Ánne's younger brother, Jovsset Ánte Sara – then just twenty-four years old – was to appear in court later that day, bringing a case that challenged an order for the forced slaughter of 35 per cent of his reindeer herd. The percentage reduction was a blanket requirement across all herders – essential, the government said, for preventing overgrazing and ensuring the environmental protection of the tundra. For Jovsset, however, it threatened to reduce his reindeer numbers below the threshold required for a licence, which would put him out of business – violating, he argued, the state's legal requirement to protect his right to practise his culture and way of life as a Sámi.

Máret Ánne had sourced the 200 reindeer heads from a slaughterhouse which was already working on the government cull. She told the media that it was a work of protest art, created in support of her brother's case. It was called, she said, *Pile o' Sápmi* – the title a direct reference to the colossal piles of bones left behind by the extinction of the Native American buffalo herds in North America in the nineteenth century. A slaughter which had, of course, been sanctioned by the governments of the United States and Canada as a means of stamping out indigenous culture. Máret Ánne was not trying to be subtle.

Jovsset won his case, but the Norwegian government appealed. In January 2017, the trial moved to the Regional Court in Tromsø. And *Pile o' Sápmi* moved with it. Over the course of the previous year, Máret Ánne had taken the reindeer heads, skinned them, removed their muscles, lips, eyes and jawbones, then boiled and dried them, leaving just their skulls. Laid bare like this, they also revealed their – non-traditional – method of slaughter: a single bullet to the head that left a gaping hole in the bone of every temple. Outside the courthouse in Tromsø, just a few hundred metres from where I was sitting, she encased thirty-five of these reindeer skulls in a plexiglass cube, suspended in rows from one wooden spar.

Jovsset won his case again, but the government appealed, again. The trial moved to the Supreme Court in Oslo. Máret Ánne continued to evolve her artwork in response. Right in front of the Norwegian Parliament, in the same space that had been occupied by the Sámi hunger strikers four decades earlier, she erected a giant curtain of 400 reindeer skulls strung on wires from a four-and-a-half-metre-long metal pole. She had carefully arranged the skulls according to their shade of bone, to create a deliberate echo of Synnøve Persen's design for the Sámi flag created during the Alta demonstrations in the 1970s. And she had given her work a new name – now it was *Pile o' Sápmi Supreme*.

On this occasion, however, Jovsset lost. The account on Máret Ánne's website ended with a link to a – now disabled – 'go fund me' page, to support an appeal to the United Nations Committee on Human Rights. Jovsset had succeeded in raising enough to take the case forward, but the final decision is still pending (as of December 2021). In a strange twist, the National Gallery of Norway bought *Pile o' Sápmi Supreme* from Máret Ánne for its permanent collection. An artwork protesting against the oppressive control and bureaucracy of the state has become state-owned. Whether its display will help, or merely fetishise, the Sámi struggle, is a matter for interpretation. But was that, I wondered, exactly Máret Ánne's point?[33]

I finished my coffee and set off to walk to the Arctic University of Norway, at the very southern tip of Tromsø. It was a bright, windless, bitterly cold day. Roads and pavements were layered in ice worn clear as glass. My route climbed gently to follow the ridgeline of the island, and I could see south and east to the long row of white mountains encircling the fjord.

Máret Ánne and Jovsset's story was so bizarre that it stayed in my thoughts throughout the walk. The way it acted like an echo of – and testimony to – Sámi history. The way it merged art and activism, just like Alta, and Hans and the Màze Group before it. The raw brutality of Máret Ánne's work and the way she evolved and adapted it. It was like Hans had said to me the night before: *the Sámi way of life is always changing, adapting. Because there is no choice.* But if you adapt so far that the herds are gone and all the land is taken, then what do you have? The starkest reading of *Pile o' Sápmi*'s curtain of skulls is that too much adaptation leads, eventually, to death.

I was going to the university to meet Ivar Bjørklund, a cultural anthropologist specialising in the study of indigenous peoples. Passing through the building's lobby, I was confronted by the giant skeleton of a *nebbkval* – a northern bottlenose whale – arranged artfully on a bed of rocks. More bones. A giant ribcage. Vertebrae like a row of axe handles. Tromsø, of course, was once one of the largest, busiest whaling stations in the North Atlantic. A lot of bones ended up here.

A receptionist took me through a security door and led me to Ivar's office. It was a quiet, spacious room, looking out onto a cluster of birch trees. Ivar was in his early sixties, with a mop of thick grey hair. Tall, loose-limbed, avuncular. Quick to smile and always, it seemed, on the verge of laughter. I told him about meeting Hans the previous night.

'You know, I was in the university in Oslo at the same time as him in the 1970s,' he said. 'And when I first saw his map I thought, *what a revelation!* It was a map with impact. You could find it on the walls of every student dorm. It was a new context. A new way of looking upon the world. It's like if you had taken the map of Great Britain and turned it upside down! It told a new story.'

Ivar was now playing his own part in this story. In 2018, he was appointed to a Truth and Reconciliation Commission set up by the government to investigate the Norwegianisation policy and the injustices it perpetrated against the Sámi people.

'The mandate is threefold,' he explained. 'What happened? What is the situation today? And what could be done in the future?'

The commission is to report its findings by the autumn of 2022.[34] I asked him how things were going, now that he was two years into the process.

'Hard to say,' he said. 'We're still digging into the past. And trying to agree on it. Because when it comes to Norwegianisation you have two kinds of politics – everybody thought, okay, we'll look for the laws. The ones that had a specific aim to assimilate. Well, those are easy to find. But what about all those laws and regulations that had other aims, but whose consequences were assimilation? Acts aimed at bringing welfare and making things more profitable, but you had to do it *our way*. Which is the Norwegian way. The reindeer herding of today is a prime example of this.' He gave a wry laugh. 'How you say, "The road to hell is paved with good intentions"? A lot of good intentions. But the consequences were complete assimilation.'

I told him that I'd just been reading about Máret Ánne and Jovsset, and their legal battle against the government cull of the reindeer herds.

Ivar nodded vigorously. 'There is so much at stake, and it is resulting in big confrontations. Because the young generations of Sámi are very politically involved – which you see in their art. One generation ago, it was land grabbing because of welfare politics. Everybody in Norway should have a good life and we should develop a welfare policy. Today, it is because of global interests. We have climate change, so we should develop green technology; that's why we need more land grabbing – windfarms and mining and so on. So the Sámi and their resource base are always the target for whatever political agenda the Norwegian authorities are up to.'

I thought again of how Hans had drawn a map of a land with no borders. But it seemed that his vision for Sápmi was slipping away. Everywhere, nooses were tightening. The reindeer and their herders were being corralled by the landscape itself, as it was taken over by massive infrastructure projects. Mines for iron and copper. Plans for high-speed trainlines to cut right through the heart of Finnmark. Huge areas of tundra – the same tundra the government wanted to protect from overgrazing – earmarked for vast windfarms. The rise of what has been called 'green colonialism': large-scale 'rewilding', reforesting or green energy projects carried out for the sake of the planet, but which displace those who live off the land – the Sámi – in the process.

'Come look at this,' Ivar said. He brought up a map on his computer of a fjord a hundred kilometres or so to the northwest of Tromsø, along the Arctic coast.

'The people living here are defined as coastal Sámi. They have a right to fish here. In Norway, in principle, all the fish in the sea are owned by the people. In principle all the fish is *owned by me*. But the ones with the political strength are the salmon producers.'

He brought up a second, more detailed map, with the areas of the fjord marked out in a series of irregular, different-coloured blobs.

'What you see here is fishing activities and different fishing grounds. And different kinds of technology used in fishing. So basically what it tells you is that the whole fjord is intensely used by fishing. This black line shows you the area the Sámi have lost to fish farming. These are fish farms, fish farms, fish farms, and it goes all the way round here.'

Ivar explained that it wasn't only the fishing areas that the coastal Sámi lost, it was also the fish themselves. The farms caused pollution so the cod no longer came into the fjord. Wild salmon used to return every spring to spawn, but they contracted sea lice from the farmed salmon, decimating their populations.

'It's a mess,' he said. 'But the mess makes money. This is the second biggest money-maker in Norway after oil.' He pointed again at the map of the fjord. 'And now they are wanting to put new fish farms here and one out here. So a new battle is coming.'

It was increasingly clear to me that Sápmi wasn't just a land cut in four – it was cut into thousands of pieces. Not just cracked along major international fault lines, but entirely shattered. Borders were everywhere, large and small. Lines drawn in the tundra, circles inked not just on the land, but also out over the waters of the fjords.

'Then there is this,' Ivar continued, turning to a map on his wall and pointing to a stretch of coastline near Norway's most northerly point. 'This is the new Alta. The Alta for the twenty-first century. Kvalsund. A huge copper mine – they've been planning it for ten, fifteen years.'

Containing an estimated 72 million tons of copper ore, the mine has been described by the Norwegian Minister for Trade and Industry, Tørbjorn Røe Isaksen, as crucial for effecting the 'green shift' in the country's economy, moving it away from its dependence on oil.[35] Even if it does this by destroying the surrounding natural habitat in the process.

'So the front lines are very clear now,' Ivar said. 'Everyone has dedicated themselves to this – as it was in Alta. It's all the Sámi and the Norwegian environmental organisations that are dead against it. But for the government it's very good business. It's a crazy project because it's going to disturb or destroy reindeer herding pastures for many herders and their families. But it is also going to destroy life in the fjord for the Sámi coastal fishermen because all these deposits are going to cause pollution and kill the fish. There's nobody who can say it's not dangerous, that it's okay for everybody. The main argument for the government is money.'

I asked Ivar what he thought about the Sámi ability to adapt, about what Hans had said to me, and the message in Máret Ánne Sara's *Pile o' Sápmi*.

'Well, look at the reindeer herding,' he said. 'People think that reindeer herding is just what it was one hundred, two hundred years ago. But it's not. The only two things which have been continually the same are the person and the animal. The way they do things has been changing. It is extremely technologically driven now – snowmobiles, ATVs, even helicopters, you name it. They are extremely smart around how to make herding fit with the contemporary situation: politics, legislation, whatever. They always find a solution.'

Surely, though, I wondered, this isn't sustainable. Eventually, a point will be reached beyond which there can be no return. What, for instance, about the impact of climate change on the herders themselves? The polar regions had been experiencing record high temperatures. Wildfires had been ripping through the forests *north* of the Arctic Circle.

Ivar nodded. 'Yes, I just returned the other day from the winter herding pasture areas in Kautokeino and they have problems now. You get sudden freeze, sudden thaw; snow gets harder. The reindeer can't dig down to the lichen. It's getting problematic. The winters are not as stable as they used to be. So, yes, up till now they have found *temporary* solutions. But there is always a limit. If there is no pasture left then it is gone.'

I thought of the shift from Hans's free, open, unconstrained map to Katarina Pirak Sikku's defined Sámi state. Was this the last adaptation, the one that would save them? Did Sápmi need borders?

'Well, this is part of the suspicions from certain Norwegians. *You are just looking for autonomy, you want to put up your own state.* This has never been said by any Sámi politician. In rhetorical terms it is fun, of course. It's provocative.'

Ivar thought for a moment, then continued. 'But it depends what you mean by territorial autonomy. Many Sámi would argue that they need control over their resources. The reindeer herders don't want *ownership* of territory. They want very strong user rights. Which is a kind of a border, you could say. With the coastal fishermen it is the same thing. They don't want ownership but strong, strong user rights. Much stronger than today. So, in a way you could say yes, they want some kind of a border. They want protection.'

I left the university and walked back towards the centre of Tromsø. The sun was dropping fast, and it painted the surrounding mountains first yellow, then orange, then an iridescent pink.

Here was a border story that was far older, in many ways, than that of Lagash and Umma. A story that went back to the end of the last Ice Age. Actually, you could say it went even further than that. Twenty thousand years ago, reindeer had been the staple diet of the hunter-gatherers of central and southern Europe. Their bones had been found scattered all over the Palaeolithic artist's studio of the Lascaux caves – used to make tools, weapons, even musical instruments.

For a time this story had moved at a geological pace. The ice retreated and slowly, slowly, slowly the borders advanced. So slowly, there was no real moment of collision, just a steady, incessant – but now rapidly accelerating – creep. Sápmi is a fascinating, remarkable thing. A land with no borders, an ancient land, still living, still subsisting, but within the confines of four modern nation states. But is this a story of survival or of decline?

There has been constant, incremental loss: acre by acre, pasture by pasture, animal by animal. Degree by degree. Because even climate change now threatens this habitat, shrinks the reindeer migration routes, pushes the herds to the very brink of the continent, threatens to tip them off into the Arctic Ocean. While, at the same time, the governments pledging to fight this climate change take more land away to feed the demand for more 'wilderness', more forests, more mobile phones, more electric cars; kill the reindeer for eating too much grass. It seemed absurd almost to the point of surreal.

'It's a big irony. A huge irony,' Ivar had said. 'Compare reindeer herding to fish farming, say. Seventy-five per cent of the fodder the farmed salmon eats contains soya from Brazil – where they burn the tropical rainforests to be able to grow soya beans. And then they send the soya beans all the way across the world to the fish farms in Norway, to produce vegetarian salmon food. Which pollutes the local environment in the fjords, kills or chases away the wild fish. Set against that, reindeer herding seems a very sensible way of using the land.'

At the same time, Sámi culture seemed to be thriving. Not much more than half a century ago, being Sámi was a stigma, a source of shame. 'Now it's a chic thing,' Ivar had told me. 'It's popular to become a Sámi, even if you have no connection to the Sámi way of life, the history, the language or anything. This development might have consequences for Sámi politics in general. Because what kind of constituency is it? They all are under thirty years old and live in the cities. So maybe you need some kind of a territory to define the resource base?'

Can you survive as a people without land, without territory? Can you last? Or is that just our westernised way of thinking? Our obsession with ownership: the way we have constructed our world. To border or not to border? I thought of another Sámi artwork I had seen, by Anders Sunna, a young Swedish reindeer herder turned artist.[36]

Produced in 2016, it is a five-metre-long, two-and-a-half-metre-high tableau painted in dark, sombre colours – blacks, browns, blues and crimsons. On one side are four sinister, almost faceless figures. They wear brown shirts with red armbands, and one of them is drawing the outline of a border in red, to run through the white landscape of Scandinavia. On one side of this line is a huge, black abyss. Another one of the figures holds a tiny reindeer and two herders in his hand, poised over the hole, about to drop them down into it. This map is surrounded by fences and the stencilled impressions of reindeer skeletons. Watching this scene play out, on the right-hand side of the picture, is the much larger figure of a Sámi herder with his reindeer, set against the backdrop of a white mountain and a blood-red sun. The herder is pointing an accusing finger at the four figures. The sun is casting the shadows of herder and reindeer, which are shown as half-vanishing skeletons. The work is called *Colonialism Inc.* The business of bordering.

It is a haunting image. Once seen, it is hard to forget. Like *Pile o' Sápmi*, its message is stark, unflinching and unsubtle. And, like Hans Ragnar Mathisen's map, it identifies borders at the root of the problem. Would the Sámi even want them if they were offered? Would they go and draw a line around the pastures, the tundra, the fjords, the migration routes and say, *these are ours now*? And if they did, would that, in fact, be the final act of colonialism, the endgame of assimilation? Turning *them*, at last, into *us*.

2
THE ENDLESS MARGIN

Somewhere among the Parnon mountains – the great, grey, limestone massif that runs in a diagonal line through the southeastern corner of the Peloponnese – there lies a mass war grave. It is said that exactly 598 soldiers are buried there: the casualties of a battle that left only two men alive.[1] Today, all trace of it has gone, the gravestones collapsed or disappeared, the bodies concealed within any one of the many humps and wrinkles of a landscape that rolls in waves down to the Gulf of Argolis and the Aegean Sea.

When the Greek geographer Pausanias visited the site in the second century AD, the grave markers were still there. In his *Description of Greece* he wrote of following a steep, narrow path, which rose up and away from the coast, meandering through olive groves to reach an open plateau. It was on this flat tract, he said, that the battle took place, where the soldiers fought and fell, and where their tomb was carved out of the earth and memorialised in simple stone.

Pausanias continued on from this lonely site, up to the heights of Mount Parnon, to a place he called *Hermai*. The name came from the three 'herms' he found standing there: rectangular stone columns sculpted with male heads and genitals (most commonly depicting the god Hermes, hence the name). These herms were ancient border markers.[2] And they were the reason for the battle that had taken place on the slopes below.

In this corner of the Peloponnese three territories met. The frontiers of the Spartans, the Argives and the Tegeans rubbed up against each other, creating a fragile and continually contested landscape. To the east of the mountains, where the terrain flattens down to the sea, was a fertile stretch of farmland known as the Thyreatic plain. In the sixth century BC, the Spartans occupied this plain, annexing it from the Argives. And so, the story goes, the Argives assembled their armies and set off to fight for their stolen land. War was declared, but an agreement was reached to fight it on very specific terms. Three hundred men from each side would meet in pitched combat, with the rest of the forces withdrawing behind their respective borders. Whoever won could rightfully claim the Thyreatic plain as their prize.

So evenly matched were the sides that the battle up on the plateau became an exercise in mutual annihilation. As dusk fell, just two men were left standing, the Argive warriors Alcenor and Chromius. They looked out over the field of broken bodies and, judging themselves the only survivors, set off for Argos to bring home the news of their victory. Yet there was one other still alive among the carnage – the Spartan general Othyrades. Unconscious and wounded, he awoke later in the night surrounded by the dead. Propping himself up on the makeshift crutch of a broken spear shaft, he began moving silently among the corpses, stripping them of their weapons, shields and armour. By dawn he had assembled a heaped sculpture of spoils, which he dedicated in writing – using his own blood – 'To Zeus, Guardian of Trophies'.[3]

When the two main armies met again the next day, both claimed victory. The argument escalated and soon erupted into fighting. The war, which this 'Battle of the Champions' was supposed to have avoided, broke out anyway. The deaths of the 597 men were just an overture. In the ensuing conflict, there were heavy casualties on both sides. Eventually, the Spartans prevailed. The Thyreatic plain was theirs.

One among them, however, could not be consoled by the triumph. Othyrades, either traumatised by what he had witnessed, or shamed that he had survived when all of his comrades had fallen, refused to leave the battlefield on the mountain and return to Sparta. Instead, he killed himself there – adding one more body to the slaughter.[4]

*

A lone figure bends to the ground, places two objects on the earth: a simple carved statue; a flat stone to use as an altar. This figure is standing on the *eschatia* – the furthest limit, the end. Behind them is the country that they know. Ahead of them is *eremos chora*: no man's land.[5] What the Homeric Hymns describe as a wild, desolate place, 'undivided and uninhabited, where beasts/which eat raw flesh roam through the shady glens'.[6] And not just beasts. Gods roam there too. Dangerous, capricious gods. Artemis the huntress. Dionysus, god of crazed drunken excess, the divine embodiment of uncontrolled passion and violence. Pan, half man, half goat, who haunts the woods and high hills. Patron of shepherds and their herds, he is capable of inspiring blind terror with his sudden appearances and stentorian voice. It is Pan who gives us the word *panikon* – panic.[7]

The figure lingers on the edge, looks out to a land where order, rationality, control – even life – fray and disintegrate. Because death lies out there. To enter the wild places is to walk along the razor's edge. Violent confrontation awaits in the dark forests or exposed mountain-sides. That is what the old stories say anyway, the ones that tell of heroes who go there to prove their worth – or die trying. The *eschatia* is the route out of the land of the living; it is the liminal space that leads on to the domain of the dead – the underworld, Hades. Beyond the *eschatia*, civilisation breaks down. So too does time itself. In the unstructured, untamed wilderness, there is nothing to anchor the past and the present.[8]

The figure offers a prayer, leaves a bowl of food or drink on the altar. They make a libation, pour wine into the soil. Then they turn away, walk back on familiar, comforting paths to their home, their village. But they have unravelled an invisible thread. Their passage has tethered the centre to the periphery.

They make this journey again. Others go with them. More objects are left, more offerings made. The simple altar grows, is surrounded by walls and pillars. It becomes a sanctuary, a site that is bound to the divine. The rituals enacted there ask the gods to look over and protect this edgeland from trespassers, outsiders, the chaos of the wilderness. Other sanctuaries emerge across the countryside. The village grows into a town, the town into a city. A space is being defined – a *polis*. At its heart is the *asty*, the urban centre, and surrounding it is the *chora*, the agricultural hinterlands – fields, olive groves and cultivated earth which stretch right up to the *eschatia*. The sanctuaries are nodes, fixed points in the landscape that combine with the natural geography – the mountains, hills and rivers – to mark the edge line. They represent the outer limit of the *polis*: the border.[9]

Everything inside the border belonged to the citizens. Or more precisely, to the men. Women and children could play their parts in the rituals and ceremonies that celebrated the history of the *polis*, but they couldn't lay claim to land or buildings, they couldn't participate in politics. Citizenship of the *polis* was a men's club. It saw the civilising instinct as a male preserve – and space itself as gendered. Men represented the city's order and rationality. Women, on the other hand, were considered febrile, unpredictable and volatile, just like the *eschatia* and the wilderness beyond. *Eremos chora*, no man's land, became a literal truth. Pass over the border and you were in a dangerous, threatening – and overwhelmingly *female* – terrain.[10]

It was women, not men, who enacted rituals beyond the boundary lines. Maenads, the female followers of Dionysus, left the city for the mountains in long procession. Once in the wilderness they removed their shoes, dressed in animal skins, drank to excess, and, to the sound of fast, urgent, percussive music, danced themselves into a state of euphoric frenzy.[11] The accounts of the maenads both captivated and terrified. They became the potent subject of myth and drama. The playwright Euripides put them at the heart of his tragedy, *The Bacchae*. Audiences watched as Dionysus, disguised as a priest of his own cult, wreaked havoc on the stability and order of a city. The god had taken all the women, 'stung them with frenzy, hounded them from home up to the mountains, where they wander, crazed of mind', to live 'beneath the silver firs on the roofless rocks'.[12] He then tricked the king of the city to go with him to the mountains to spy on the maenads – wearing a wig and dress as disguise. But the king was discovered, and in their frenzy the women tore him limb from limb. At the bloody centre of this violent murder was the king's own mother, who returned to the city carrying her son's head in her hands, believing, in her ecstatic reverie, that it was the head of a lion.

In the popular imagination, the border was seen and understood as far more than just a territorial marker. It was the margin between many things: sanity and madness, society and anarchy, man and woman, mortal and god, peace and violence. A place at once to be feared and honoured. Without it, the *polis* could not exist. It needed the edge to understand what it was, what it stood for and what it believed in.[13] It is a story of identity that began with that lone figure on the *eschatia* making an offering to the gods. This was the moment that created the border, that planted the seed. And from it emerged the very soul and psyche of the city.

Athens, around 2,500 years ago. A group of young adolescent boys, known as *ephebes*, are about to begin a two-year stint of military training. At the end of this period they will become full *hoplites*, citizen-soldiers, able to own land and property. But first they must leave the city, leave the countryside, and travel to the *eschatia*. There they will be known as *peripoloi*, those 'who patrol around'. Their basic task is to occupy the border forts among the mountainous terrain that separates Athens from the lands of the rival state of Boeotia to the north. From these marginal outposts the boys will set out to walk the land, spending their days learning the true, physical nature of the edge, implanting it in their bodies by their very movement through the landscape.[14]

There is, of course, a clear rationale for this: when they become full citizens, this land will be *theirs*. They are the future soldiers, merchants, politicians and leaders of Athens. They need to know and understand the extent of their *polis*. But it is more than just that. There are symbolic reasons for sending them to the borderlands. The history and myths behind the formation of the city and its territory are to be found there too.

There is a story of a fight that once took place on the *eschatia*, a bout of single combat between the king of the Athenians, Thymoetes – the last descendant of the Minotaur-slaying Theseus – and the king of the Boeotians, Xanthos, 'the fair one'. This duel was agreed as a means of settling a dispute over contested land, to mark the position of the borderline. But when it came to the bout, Thymoetes, who was an old man, stood down, and another Athenian warrior, Melanthos – 'the black one' – took his place.

During the contest, Melanthos shouted out to Xanthos that he was breaking the rules. 'Look,' he cried, 'there is someone fighting by your side!' As the Boeotian king turned in surprise, Melanthos slipped in and killed him. In some versions, there was a figure – Dionysus, clad in a black goatskin – who appeared as a distraction alongside Xanthos. But most of the stories simply celebrate Melanthos's cunning, the *apate* – the trick, the deception – that won him the duel: and the right of Athens to claim the borderland.[15]

Whether this is a real event or not is in some sense irrelevant. Either way, the tale is woven into the imagination and ritual culture of the Athenians. So too is the idea of the border as a metaphor for the journey from boy to man. This region out on the margins, defined by the prospect of transition from one space to another, is seen as the perfect backdrop for adolescent transformation. The *eschatia* is where the oppositions and contradictions of the Greek world are at their rawest and most exposed: reality and myth, citizen and outsider, wilderness and civilisation.

At the ceremony that makes them *ephebes* – aged sixteen – the boys sacrifice their long hair. They are given a black cloak to wear, in honour of Melanthos, 'the black one'. In other rituals they are encouraged to cross-dress, to disguise themselves as girls and take part in processions leading from the city to the border sanctuaries. And then, when their two years are complete and they are ready to become citizens, they swear an oath to 'the boundary-stones of the fatherland, the wheat, the barley, the vines, the olive trees and the fig trees'.[16]

In this moment, they signal that their youthful dalliance with the ambivalent frontier is over. They have passed through, and now they are men, bound to the world contained *within* the border, the world of rules, of certainty, of wheat, barley and vines – cultivated, tamed land: the world of order.

Such rites of passage are not just confined to Athens. In Sparta there is an equivalent institution known as the *krypteia* – the 'secret', the 'hidden'. These are also boys on the cusp of manhood, and they too are sent to the borderlands. But rather than forming part of a cohort, they roam either in small groups or entirely alone. Their task is to survive in the wilderness by any means, travelling light, armed only with a dagger – if they have any weapon at all. By day they must stay hidden, but at night they roam the fringes of the frontier, allowed to capture and kill with impunity any Spartan slaves – known as *helots* – that they find.

Everything they do is in direct opposition to what they will become: the Spartan *hoplite*, the ideal of the disciplined, principled soldier, the pillar of the community. In the *krypteia*, boys must trust no one, must live by their wits, steal, deceive, trick and even murder.[17]

The whole process amounts to a grand symbolic performance. It is nothing less than adolescence itself that is being sacrificed, out there on the border.

This fixation on the edgelands in the Greek world only increased. As the *poleis* and their populations grew, there was pressure to claim and use the marginal lands that lay between them. Border disputes became near constant. Settlers moved into the *eschatia*, cut down the forests or occupied what had been common pasturelands. Once the city states were islands of civilisation amid a sea of wilderness. Now the opposite was true. It was the *eremos chora*, the tracts of no man's land, that were surrounded.[18]

Some *poleis* submitted their border claims to arbitration, to be assessed by neutral parties. Officials were sent out to walk the land, to interview herders and shepherds – those who knew the frontier territory best – to interrogate claims of historical use or authority. Stone markers were placed in the ground, known as *horoi*, which combined with the natural features and the fixed points of the sanctuaries to further delineate borders in the landscape. A new role was created: that of the *horistes*, an official entrusted with drawing, recording and marking borders. A 'technology' emerged – the development of knowledge and expertise to survey and apportion the landscape.[19]

Political and philosophical thought turned to the dynamics of borders, how they organised the *polis* and how they were used to regulate and manage contact with the world beyond. Aristotle argued that the edgeland must always be seen as a bridge, a place to negotiate essential contact with others. 'In laying down the laws,' he wrote, 'the legislator must have his attention fixed on two things, the territory and the population. But also it would be well to add that he must take into account the neighbouring regions also, if the city is to live a life of intercourse with other states and not one of isolation.'[20]

At the same time, he warned that those who lived by the periphery may be changed or altered through their regular interactions with it. He was wary of the fluid nature of the border, the way it could inculcate different, even competing or opposing views from those held at the urban centre. There was the danger, he suggested, that political affiliations could fray at the edgelands and threaten the unity of the *polis*. To counter this, he recommended enacting a law that allocated two plots of land to each citizen, one at the core and one on the border. 'Where this system is not followed,' he wrote, 'one set of people are reckless about quarrelling with neighbouring states, and the other set are too cautious and neglect considerations of honour.'[21]

Boundary marking and border making were professionalised, established as central to the definition and operation of the *polis*. But if you trace the origins of these lines, it still brings you back to the interwoven fragments of stories. Stories of territory won by duels and battle, and land ordained and claimed by divine gift. Stories of great, heroic moments that tell the people who they are and how their city was formed. Stories that were re-enacted year on year in grand civic ceremonies and festivals.

In Aristotle's Athens they still celebrated Melanthos's cunning victory over Xanthos out on the *eschatia.* In Sparta they commemorated the 'Battle of the Champions' fought for the Thyreatic plain: the fate of their 300 fallen warriors was held up as the ideal of 'beautiful' death. They held a festival known as the Gymnopaedia, where they honoured them with 'Thyreatic wreaths' and sang hymns to their sacrifice. In time, this battle evolved into a *shared* ritual between Sparta and Argos. Each year, as a coming-of-age initiation, 300 *ephebes* from each city met to re-enact the fight as a kind of non-lethal sparring contest.[22]

Borders, then, were the wellsprings of memory, of collective origin. And their influence appeared everywhere. There was the board game called *polis*, or *petteia* (meaning 'pebbles'), where the aim was to advance your pieces, your *petteia*, over a central borderline on a board divided into squares, hemming your opponent in and capturing their territory.

Or there was the ball game known variously as *episkuros*, *epikoinos* and *ephebike.* It was played on a field divided into two halves, with two marked baselines at either end and a central line formed out of small, white, limestone chippings, called *skuros. Episkuros* was played as an explicit dramatisation of a border contest.[23] The word '*skuros*' has its root in '*skiron*', a name often given to peripheral regions, to borderlands. A ball was placed on this central line, and two teams would first contest possession and then force their rivals backwards by throwing the ball towards the opposition side. And so the ball, and the contest, moved back and forth until, eventually, one team pushed the other back behind their baseline, their border, to claim possession of the entire field – and victory.[24]

One of the alternative names for the game, *ephebike*, referred to the adolescent *ephebes.* Players were most often young military trainees enacting yet another symbolic moment of transition. Teenagers, on the edge of manhood, contesting the border ball game.[25]

Yet amid all these bloodless rituals, there was still real war, real conflict. The *ephebes* and the citizen-soldiers were increasingly called on to fight. Processions of men, young and old, would make their way to the borderlines. In the fifth and fourth centuries BC, Greece was consumed by the Peloponnesian and Corinthian Wars. City state against city state, neighbour against neighbour. The Athenian politician and orator Demosthenes deplored this new world, saying that 'nothing has undergone greater change and improvement than the art of war'. Where once conflict was 'conventional and forthright', governed by rules and principles, even arranged by the seasons, now, he said, it was permanent, indiscriminate and brutal. No one played by the rules any more. There were no rules.[26]

Centuries later, another famous Greek orator, Dio Chrysostom, was asked to intercede in one of the constant border disputes between his home city Prusa and its neighbour Apamea.

'The wrangling and hatred of men who are such near neighbours, who share common borders,' he said in a speech to the people of Prusa, 'is like nothing else than insurrection in a single city.'

Borders, he said, should be tools of unity, not division – they were like ties of blood, of marriage, the physical manifestations of kinship drawn across the landscape.

'The very land and sea and mountains in every way bring you people together and, even if you did not wish it, compel you to deal with one another.' And yet, still, it was the 'folly and corruption of mankind' to seek out conflict. Look, he said, at 'the ceaseless circling dance of the planets, which never get in each other's way'; consider how the earth, the sea, the atmosphere 'strong and great as they are, submit to their partnership with one another and continue free from hostility'. So why then, 'cannot such puny, petty towns of ordinary mortals, such feeble tribes dwelling in a mere fraction of the earth, maintain peace and quiet and be neighbours to one another without uproar and disturbance?'[27]

But then that was never the message that was spliced with the making, sacralising and mythologising of borders. The prevailing story was always opposition, contradiction, the edge line as a place of contest: claimed either by taming the wilderness or by taking it from others in tests of strength, in battle. The border was unique: it was yours, it was *hard won*. It was where you grew up, where you came of age. Perhaps even – and this, for some, was the greatest honour – it was where you died. A poem by Dioscorides celebrated this very idea, as the body of a Spartan warrior, Thrasybulus, is returned home after a border conflict with the Argives.

> Dead on his shield came Thrasybulus,
> having received seven wounds from the Argives,
> exposing his whole front to them,
> and old Tynnichus,
> as he laid his son's blood-stained body on the pyre, said:
> 'Let the cowards weep. But I will bury you, my son, without
> a tear,
> you, who are both mine and Sparta's.'[28]

Generations of young men – still just boys really – prepared for war. Many threw themselves around the *episkuros* field in that graceful mockery of combat. Homer even described an early version of the game in the *Odyssey*. Two Phaeacian princes put on a demonstration of their skills for Odysseus, one taking a ball and:

> hurling it towards the shadowy clouds
> as the other leaping high into the air would catch it
> quickly, nimbly, before his feet hit the ground again.
> Once they'd vied at throwing the ball straight up,
> They tossed it back and forth in a blur of hands
> As they danced across the earth that feeds us all
> While boys around the ring stamped out the beat.[29]

Think of those fields marked out in the *polis*. The ball games played back and forth across them. The mood joyous, elated, as one team would send the other running behind the *skuros* – the border – towards the baseline, so that they teetered on the very edge. With the next throw the ball would arc high through the sky. Would it carry the baseline, force their opponents off the field completely? The players, the crowd – all watched and held their breath.

*

It was early evening on the island of Skyros in the Northern Aegean Sea. Twelve men carried a body ashore from a ship moored off the southwest coast. They followed the path of a dried-up riverbed into a narrow valley. There, in the shade of an olive grove, a hole had been dug in the dusty ground. The body belonged to a young man – just twenty-seven years old – who was sailing to war. Another young man, Achilles, had come to this island too. His mother had hidden him here, disguised as a girl to try to stop him from being taken by the war fleet bound for the plains of Troy – the place where, she knew, he was destined to die.

This young man had been headed for the same coast as Achilles. He had been happy, excited, reciting Homer throughout his journey, convinced that he was being borne onwards by the 'winds of history'. He was a poet, a soldier-poet, and as the day of battle came nearer, he could sense the building tension, wrote of how he could even feel the spirit of Achilles, stirring alongside him 'in the darkness'. But then he fell ill on the voyage. A simple insect bite wracked his body with fever, and within a day he was dead.

Evening was turning to night. The twelve men gathered by the grave. One of them will later tell the young man's mother that her son is buried in 'one of the loveliest places on this earth, with grey green olives round him . . . the ground covered with flowering sage'.

'Think of it,' he will say to her, 'under a clouded moon, with the three mountains around and behind us and those divine scents everywhere. We lined his grave with all the flowers we could find.'[30]

It was past midnight now. Some of the men had returned to their boat. Five remained, erecting a stone cairn on top of the grave. Of those five, only two will survive the war to come. Some years later, the young man's mother will ask a sculptor to create a new grave marker, replacing the cairn with a small tomb carved out of creamy-white marble. One of her son's poems will be inscribed on the stone. 'If I should die, think only this of me,' it begins. 'That there's some corner of a foreign field/That is forever England.'

The young man was Rupert Brooke, and he died on 23 April 1915. This was two days before the Gallipoli landings. He did not live to see what would follow.

A ball flew into a powder-blue sky. The players went after it, setting off across the field. It was not a Mediterranean sky. It was another sky, another field. All the same, the weather, after the morning mist lifted, was 'heavenly'.[31] It was a hot summer's day. The ball was not thrown but kicked. One spectator talked of how 'the ball rose and travelled well',[32] soaring up, resting for a moment in stillness at its apex, and then curving back to the earth, towards the opposition line.

Another man described following its path, down on the ground. 'I see men arising and walking forward; and I go with them.' They all chased the ball. But then, 'some seem to pause with bowed heads, and sink carefully to their knees, and roll slowly over, and lie still'. Something was wrong with the game. Something was happening to the players. 'Others roll and roll, and scream and grip my legs in uttermost fear, and I have to struggle to break away, while the dust and earth on my tunic changes from grey to red.' Yet he continued. Because what else was there to do but chase the ball? Try to force the other side back behind their line, off the field of play. 'And I go on with aching feet, up and down across ground like a huge honeycomb, and my wave melts away, and the second wave comes up and also melts away, and then the third wave merges into the ruins of the first and second, and after a while the fourth blunders into the remnants of the others, and we begin to run forward.'[33]

It was 1 July 1916. The first day of the Somme.

The man who kicked the ball was the twenty-one-year-old Captain Wilfred Nevill of the East Surrey Regiment. There was a second ball too. On one was written 'The Great European Cup-Tie Final. East Surreys v Bavarians. Kick off at zero.' On the other the words, in block capitals, 'NO REFEREE'. Seconds after he put boot to ball, Nevill was dead.[34]

Nearly two weeks later, the story appeared in the British newspapers. The *Daily Telegraph* wrote that 'the gallant captain himself fell early in the charge, and men began to drop rapidly under the hail of machine-gun bullets. But still the footballs were booted onwards, with hoarse cries of encouragement or defiance.' The *Daily Mail* paid tribute with a poem:

On through the hail of slaughter,
Where gallant comrades fall,
Where blood is poured like water,
They drive the trickling ball.

Siegfried Sassoon watched the advance as it happened. At 7.45 a.m., fifteen minutes after it began, he sees the reserves still cheering on the men in front like spectators at a football match. By 10.05 a.m., when more than 30,000 are already dead, he described 'looking at a sunlit picture of Hell. And still the breeze shakes the yellow charlock, and the poppies glow below Crawley Ridge where a few shells have fallen lately.'[35] By the end of the first day, the dead or wounded numbered 60,000.

Nearly 600 soldiers dead on a mountainside in Greece. Over 60,000 in a field in France. The Somme was supposed to be the climactic moment of the war: the great fight – the largest single battle that the planet had ever seen. It pitted the two opposing lines, the two concentrated forces, against each other on one small stretch of ground to decide a winner. Who would come out on top? As Sassoon's friend and fellow poet Edmund Blunden wrote: 'By the end of the day, both sides had seen, in a sad scrawl of broken earth and murdered men, the answer to the question. No road. No thoroughfare. Neither race had won, nor could win, the War. The War had won, and would go on winning.'[36]

Two lines running through 400 miles of landscape. Two *front lines*, that is. Behind them were support lines and reserve lines, communication lines and firing lines, and 'saps' – lines which reached out beyond the front line like thin, gnarled fingers. These lines were holes in the ground: trenches.

They started on the North Sea coast of Belgium, ran south through Flanders and over the border into France, then down through Artois and Picardy to cross the River Somme, before turning at Compiègne, just forty miles north of Paris. From there they went east, through Champagne and past Reims, hooked around Verdun and Saint-Mihiel, then turned south again to end, finally, at the Swiss border at Beurnévisn.

They were not straight lines. The trenches were all curves and sharp angles, endless zigzags, to contain the blasts of shellfire. If you could somehow have grabbed them all, pulled them out straight and joined them together, end to end, they would have run for far more than 400 miles. Closer, in fact, to 24,000 miles – making one super-trench long enough to encircle the entire earth.

These lines were not borders. But they were both a product and a grotesque simulacrum of borders. For four years, from the winter of 1914 to the autumn of 1918, they offered the most extreme, physical, man-made division of a landscape ever seen in human history. They were fixed, rigid, barely moving a hundred metres in any direction. They were the *èschatia*, the edge – and beyond them, and between them, was *eremos chora*. No man's land.

Just like the *eschatia* of ancient Greece, the trench line was the margin between order and chaos. It was the gateway to the land of the dead. Except, the underworld had risen up to the surface, shown itself to the overworld. It was right there, yards, even inches away. It told the history of the war in real time. The trophy piles it amassed just grew larger and larger. 'It was a morbid but intensely interesting occupation tracing the various battles amongst the hundreds of skulls, bones and remains scattered thickly about,' wrote P. H. Pilditch, a British major. 'The progress of our successive attacks could clearly be seen from the types of equipment on the skeletons.'[37]

Everything was reduced, simplified. Saturated in oppositions. There was the good side of the line and the bad side. 'This side of our wire everything is familiar and every man a friend,' wrote Charles Carrington, while 'over there, beyond the wire, is the unknown, the uncanny.'[38] The soldiers were surrounded by individuals, men with names and faces and families, each with their own stories to tell. But just a few hundred metres away was the enemy, almost never seen, but always present – a featureless mass, hovering below the parapet. To the Allied troops, the Germans were phantoms, wraiths, occupying what the infantrymen thought of as 'other' – a place beyond imagination, a 'mysterious, vacant yet impenetrable land'.[39]

'The mere fact that in a certain direction there are German lines seems to alter the feeling of a landscape,' reflected T. E. Hulme, another soldier-poet. The result, he said, is that 'you unconsciously orientate things in reference to it. In peacetime, each direction on the road is, as it were, indifferent, it all goes on *ad infinitum*. But now you know that certain roads lead, as it were, up to an abyss.'[40]

There were rituals to be performed out there in no man's land, on the edge of the abyss. Twice a day, first at dawn and again at dusk, was the hour of 'stand-to'. All along the trenches men took up their weapons, fixed their bayonets, and climbed up onto their firing steps. And then they waited in silence. On the other side of no man's land, it was the same. Both sides poised, but unmoving, just staring into the near distance. Stand-to was 'strict and binding anywhere in the forward zone, under any circumstances whatever,' wrote the soldier and painter David Jones. It was, he said, an hour of 'peculiar significance' and 'solemnity' as 'from the sea dunes to the mountains, everywhere, on the whole front the two opposing lines stood alertly, waiting any eventuality'.[41]

It was, in essence, a ritual of stalemate, of entrenched warfare – those soldiers prepared for 'any eventuality', yet knowing that nothing would really change. The lines they occupied didn't move, but from time to time battles were played out in front of them on the stage of no man's land, and all the participants were killed or wounded. It took the ancient idea of the border conflict, the 'Battle of the Champions', and just played it on repeat. *Best two out of three. No, best three out five. No, best five out of seven . . .* The battles themselves were also rituals, a 'fatal ceremonial parade across No Man's Land'.[42] The minutes of stand-to ticked by in soundless meditation. The sun rose. The sun set. The sun rose again. 'The poignant misery of dawn begins to grow,' wrote Wilfred Owen of yet another morning stand-to.

We only know that war lasts, rain soaks, and clouds sag stormy,
Dawn massing in the east her melancholy army,
Attacks once more in ranks on shivering ranks of grey,
But nothing happens.[43]

The common thought was that this was the new state of being. That all of this would go on for ever. That the trenches may as well have been endless. Stanley Casson, a classical scholar, archaeologist and eager philhellene was overawed by their sheer extent. 'Away to right and left stretched the great lines of defence as far as eye and imagination could stretch them,' he wrote. 'I used to wonder how long it would take to walk from the beaches of the North Sea to that curious end of all fighting against the Swiss boundary; to try to guess what each end looked like; to imagine what would happen if I passed a verbal message, in the manner of a parlour game, along to the next man on my right to be delivered to the end man of all up against the Alps. Would anything intelligible at all emerge?'[44]

Within days of arriving at the Western Front, Edmund Blunden was overcome by the 'prevailing sense of the endlessness of the war. No one here appeared to conceive any end of it.'[45] Robert Graves summed it up with the bleakly wry comment that everyone held two irreconcilable beliefs: 'that the war would never end and that we would win it'.[46] Captured during the Battle of the Somme, a German prisoner admitted that he saw 'no end to it'. It was, he said, the 'suicide of nations'.[47] Isaac Rosenberg, in his poem 'The Immortals', depicted killing without end: 'I killed them/but they would not die . . . for faster than I slew/they rose more cruel than before.'[48]

No man's land, the *eschatia*, was transformed into the ultimate site of dread and death. The landscape of no return. 'The parapet, the wire and the mud,' wrote Henry Tomlinson, the official correspondent for the British Army, had become 'permanent features of human existence.'[49] This was bordering, and border technology, taken to gruesome extremes. Barbed wire was an invention of the frontier, first used in America at the end of the nineteenth century as a means of containing cattle. Now it was strung out, maybe a million miles or more, throughout the desolation of no man's land. It was the perfect, mass-produced, modern-industrial symbol of division.

Perhaps it had always been leading up to this. Writing home from the front in May 1915, Alexander Douglas Gillespie, a twenty-six-year-old second lieutenant with the Argyll Highlanders, contemplated this strange rupture in nature. He talked of walking 'among the ghostly cherry trees', while 'star-shells' rose and fell to the north and south. The moon came up and a nightingale began to sing.

'It was strange to stand there and listen,' he said, 'for the song seemed to come all the more sweetly and quietly in the quiet intervals between the bursts of firing.' It was, he thought, as if 'the countryside were singing gently to itself, in the midst of all of our noise and confusion and muddy work'. He had already lost his brother, Thomas, to the war. As he stood there he thought 'of all the men and women who had listened to that song, just as for the first few weeks after Tom was killed, I found myself thinking perpetually of all the men who had been killed in battle – Hector and Achilles and all the heroes of long ago, who were once so strong and active and now are so quiet.'[50]

It was early in the war, a year before the Somme, and Alexander believed that he could still see an endpoint. In another letter, this time to his old headmaster, he wished that the whole line of the Western Front, once peace returned, would be transformed into a *Via Sacra*: 'one long avenue between the lines from the Vosges to the sea'. In his vision, he said he would 'make a fine broad road in the "No Man's Land" between the lines, with paths for pilgrims on foot, and plant trees for shade, and fruit trees . . . Some of the shattered farms and houses might be left as evidence, and the regiments might put up their records beside the trenches which they held all through the winter. Then I would like to send every man, woman and child in Western Europe on pilgrimage along that *Via Sacra*, so that they might think and learn what war means from the silent witnesses on either side. A sentimental idea, perhaps, but we might make it the most beautiful road in all the world.'[51]

Four months later, Alexander Gillespie was killed at the Battle of Loos.

I once went into the Parnon mountains, looking for the grave site of the 'Battle of the Champions'. Driving from the coastal town of

Astros, I followed a narrow road that climbed into the Peloponnesian highlands via a series of dizzying switchbacks. My guide was a crumpled printout of a map, produced originally by a professor of art history at the University of Toronto called Frederick Winter.[52]

Along with his wife Joan, a constant companion on his fieldwork expeditions, Frederick had come here nearly forty years ago, when he was in his mid-sixties, with the aim of connecting the ancient sites recorded by Pausanias to actual points in the modern landscape. The couple summarised their travels in a long academic paper, which offered a critique (at times bewildering) of some fifty years of competing theories on the location of the battlefield and its graves. Their map of Pausanias's route – a best guess given the limited and fragmentary evidence available – identified a site amid the rolling uplands north of Mount Parnon, just a couple of kilometres west of the hilltop village of Agios Ioannis.

The village seemed almost empty when I passed through. No people, no cars. Just a few stray cats slinking along the roadside or staring at me defiantly from the lids of large wheelie bins. White-walled houses with red-tiled roofs were arranged in terraces down the hill, facing north. I passed the village square, fringed by pine trees, a couple of tavernas, and then I was out the other side. A couple of minutes later and I was pulling off the road onto a faint, stony path, overgrown with grass and scrub bushes.

The day was grey and overcast, punctuated by distant rumblings of thunder somewhere out over the Aegean. I followed the path on foot for a few hundred metres, walking around the crown of a hillside and out of sight of my car. The way ahead then straightened to follow a shallow ridgeline up to a wide, rounded summit. Near the top were the broken walls of a roofless building – an abandoned shelter or shepherd's hut. Apart from that there was nothing. I was standing amid a desolate vista of yellow-brown hills and mountains, their slopes studded with green clumps of trees.

Maybe there *were* 598 bodies buried beneath my feet. Or maybe there was only a thin covering of soil, and then layer after layer of empty, honeycombed limestone. The map was not exact, and I could easily have been in the wrong place. There was also, of course, the possibility that the battle had never happened at all. That it was just another story of the Greek borderlands: invented, passed down, embellished and polished by repeated telling. Translated from folklore into history. Had Pausanias, just like Frederick and Joan Winter eighteen centuries later, been hunting a phantom? Unpicking fact from myth and memory can be a hard – even impossible – task.

A decade later, and I was driving to another grave site: this one much simpler to find. It was signposted for a start, and set within a flat landscape of wide, open fields. I could see it from miles away. A copse of bottle-green trees and, rising above it, a blocky head of red brick. From a distance it looked like the top of an old factory clock tower.

I parked, walked through an avenue of trees, along a wide pebble pathway. And then there it was, at the top of a very gentle slope: a monument of staggering immensity. It stands in Lego-brick simplicity. Front on, it appears as two oversized feet, supporting legs that meet in the middle to form a high archway. It is palpably, almost ostentatiously, *rooted.* Bottom-heavy, clamped to the ground, hunkered down. Those two feet actually divide into sixteen, eight on each side, threaded by smaller archways, all faced in white stone. This does nothing to diminish the scale. The grave here is unmissable. It is the bodies that it commemorates which are lost.

This is the Thiepval Memorial in Picardy, northern France. The Memorial to the 'Missing' of the Somme. Carved into its white stone are the names of 72,315 unrecovered men, those who lost their lives somewhere out among the surrounding fields. When the monument was first completed in 1932, that number was 73,357. Since then, more human remains have emerged from the earth. A fraction of the missing are now found. The rest are still gone, perhaps for ever. Thiepval is their collective headstone.

I looked around at the grass, the trees, the flowers, the pathways – everything was immaculate. Cut and clipped and pruned and ordered. There was no unruliness, no wild, untamed growth. The land here was pristine. Pristine and silent. In August 1916, one soldier looked out at this same expanse – dug out, turned over, ripped up and blown apart – and wrote home to his sister that, surely, it was now changed for good. 'How ever they will get it smoothed out again,' he wrote, 'is more than I can imagine.'[53] And yet here it was. Flattened, empty. Fields all around as far as you could see, lit golden in the late afternoon sun, monotonous in their uniformity.

I'd brought with me a battered old copy of one of the most remarkable books ever written about the First World War. Published in the 1970s, *The Great War and Modern Memory* was the work of Paul Fussell, an American professor of literature who had served in the infantry in the Second World War. It is not a history of events, a litany of dates and battles, but rather a study of the impact of the conflict and its aftermath on all of western culture. In one memorable passage, Fussell writes of coming here, to this very landscape.

> Today the Somme is a peaceful but sullen place, unforgetting and unforgiving. To wander now over the fields is to appreciate in the most intimate way the permanent reverberations of July, 1916. When the air is damp you can smell rusted iron everywhere, even though you see only wheat and barley. The farmers work the fields without joy. They collect the duds, shell-casings, fuses and shards of old barbed wire as the plough unearths them and stack them in the corners of their fields . . . Lurking in every spot of undergrowth just off the beaten track are eloquent little things: rusted buckles, rounds of corroded small-arms ammunition, metal tabs from ammunition boxes, bits of Bully tin, buttons.[54]

All those trophy piles, stacked up, honouring – unknowingly – the old gods. It's said that the trees here can't be planted in straight rows, because their roots will inevitably reach down and find something that should be left alone – canisters of unexploded mustard gas, toxic shell casings. The unlucky trees will wither and die, and the rows will lose one or more from their ranks. It is, perhaps, too acute a metaphor. So, yes, this land *is* smoothed out again, after all. But under its surface it still roils with bones and debris, fragments that are spat periodically back up into the world. Ghosts of the vanished lines.

How did we get here? You can't follow the trenches and look for an answer. They are all but gone. Perhaps the reasons are just too numerous: as many as there are names etched in the white stone of Thiepval. But here is one reason. One that can be found, ironically, in a *peace* settlement which ended decades of European conflict.

Three and a half centuries ago, some 250 miles east of Thiepval, a congress was convened in the Westphalian cities of Münster and Osnabrück. It involved thousands of diplomats and their staff, representing nearly 200 different provinces, states and empires. The first six months alone were taken up with arguments over protocol as to who should sit where and in which order the various dignitaries should enter any given room. Negotiations continued for another four years. War had torn continental Europe apart, and, in particular, had devastated the land that would later become Germany. The parties involved in the conflict were legion, but the causes were simple: religion, power and money. Thirty years of unceasing war needed an end.

In 1648, amid an incessant to and fro of envoys and countless exchanges of letters, a framework for peace was agreed. What was proposed was, in effect, an entirely new political order, led by the principle of *cuius regio, eius religio*: 'whose realm, his religion'. This recognised, on the most basic level, the right of a prince or monarch to impose their own religion on their subjects. But, rather more than that, it also established their supreme and exclusive authority – including over government, taxation, law and the military – *within a specific geographical area*. This was the notion of sovereignty.[55]

In feudal, medieval Europe, territorial claims had been fluid and overlapping. Political dominion was almost impossible to map in any spatial sense. In its most basic terms, it stretched to wherever any one ruler could collect taxes. But it was also determined by complex hierarchies of vassals and lords, bonds of allegiance and fealty, all of which led upwards to God himself, represented on earth by the Pope and the Roman Catholic Church. Except, of course, even God was now divided, split apart by the emergence of the Protestant faith.[56]

Those hundreds of exhausted men in the meeting rooms of Münster and Osnabrück, stricken by interminable war and dogmatic schisms, resolved to do away with all this. To make it simpler, *clearer*. Lines were the answer. Autonomy of governance by defined area. The subjects of each prince or monarch to be corralled by cartography. This was the beginning – albeit tentative and incomplete – of the modern nation-state. The formation of clearly defined and measured territories, with discrete populations and resources. The race was on to draw borders.[57]

Over time, this process of 'definition' also came to include not just a preference for religion, but also unified language, culture and ethnicity. There was a need for stories that told of shared histories and identities. 'Nation' comes from the Latin word '*nacio*': birth. Countries were being 'born' anew. The nineteenth-century German geographer and theorist Friedrich Ratzel – inventor of the term 'geopolitics' – even went so far as to claim that a nation-state was a kind of biological entity, that it was alive. As such, it needed space to live. And to grow. He called this '*Lebensraum*'. Borders, in Ratzel's view, were an epidermis. They were organic and they could move and expand and absorb other lands. Indeed, he said, they had to, in order for the entity inside them to survive.[58]

In 1914, this 'skin' pushed halfway across France and Belgium. The flesh of nations collided on the Western Front, and for four years – wounded by a thousand, sixty thousand, a million cuts – bled unstoppably into the earth.

Nowhere more so than where I was right now. Here, on the Somme, it was as if a border artery had been severed. Except the damage wasn't fatal. Great reservoirs of fresh blood were merely transfused into the trenches, and so the flow continued, unabated, unstemmed.

F. Scott Fitzgerald captured this very image in *Tender Is the Night*, his novel suffused with the pain and guilt of post-war ennui. In 1925, Dick Diver and his friends travel to visit the restored Newfoundland trenches, looking out over the parapet to Beaumont-

Hamel and Thiepval. The sky is 'dingy' and rain is on the way. Here, Fitzgerald observes, 'the very weather seems to have a quality of the past, faded weather, like that of old photographs'.

Dick points into the distance, turns to his companions. 'See that little stream,' he says. 'We could walk to it in two minutes. It took the British a month to walk to it – a whole empire walking very slowly, dying in front and pushing forward behind. And another empire walked very slowly backward a few inches a day, leaving the dead like a million bloody rugs.'[59]

Dick notes the peculiar intimacy of this war, suggests that centuries of changes in culture and art and society had all been leading – fatalistically – to the abrasive, skin-on-skin embrace of the trenches.

'This took religion and years of plenty and tremendous sureties and the exact relation that existed between the classes,' he says. 'This kind of battle was invented by Lewis Carroll and Jules Verne and whoever wrote *Undine*, and country deacons bowling and *marraines* in Marseilles and girls seduced in the back lanes of Württemberg and Westphalia. Why, this was a love battle . . . All my beautiful, lovely, safe world blew itself up here with a great gust of high explosive love.'[60]

I walked towards the memorial, its facade brightened by the lowering sun, my long shadow in step ahead of me. Up the wide steps and beneath its high central arch, and I was surrounded by a profusion of hard angles: everywhere the walls, floor and passages bisected by lines, geometric patterns of light and dark. Directly in front of me was the Stone of Remembrance. It is just one of hundreds that were erected on any site commemorating a thousand or more war dead. All follow the same, unified design envisaged by the architect Sir Edwin Lutyens.

Writing in 1917 to Fabian Ware, the founder of the Imperial War Graves Commission, Lutyens explained his initial idea for the monument. 'On platforms made of not less than three steps, place one great stone of fine proportion 12 feet long and finely *wrot* – without undue ornament and tricky elaborate carvings – and inscribe thereon one thought in clear letters so that all men for all times may read and know the reason why these stones are placed throughout France

– facing the West and facing the men who lie looking ever eastwards towards the enemy.'[61]

The 'one thought' came from Rudyard Kipling. Caught at a slight angle by the sun behind me, its carved letters appeared in striking black shadow against the grey-white Portland stone: *Their name liveth forevermore.*

Lutyens took direct inspiration from the architecture of classical Greece. The remembrance stones were carved according to the same principle of *entasis* from the Parthenon of Athens – eschewing straight lines to create an optical illusion of depth and scale. The style was deliberately clean, simple, unadorned. And secular. When Lutyens was commissioned to design the Cenotaph in Whitehall – the name itself coming from the Greek '*kenos taphos*', meaning 'empty tomb' – he took its shape from the grave markers of the ancient Anatolian city of Xanthos. When the monument was first unveiled in 1920, the *Catholic Herald* called it 'nothing more or less than a pagan monument, insulting to Christianity'.[62]

The rest of the hulking structure at Thiepval is down to Lutyens too. Here, however, the classical gives way to a kind of imperial-industrial heft, as if a giant factory has swallowed up, and absorbed into its bright-red brickwork, a series of triumphal arches. I passed out the other side of the memorial, walking directly west, where the land slopes down a little and a neat formation of graves is laid out on the grass: flat, rounded headstones for the British on one side, crosses for the French on the other.

I had had a sentimental urge to come here at dusk, at 'stand-to', to observe the ritual of the lines, that silent hour of border meditation. In the preface to his book, Fussell writes about how 'the dynamics and iconography of the Great War have proved crucial political, rhetorical, and artistic determinants on subsequent life'. The war, he says, 'was relying on inherited myth', at the same time as 'generating new myth, and that myth is part of the fibre of our own lives'.[63]

At one point he considers a novel by Anthony Burgess, *The Wanting Seed*, written in the 1960s, but set in a dystopian Britain of the twenty-first century beset by overpopulation and food scarcity. The novel's protagonist, Tristram Foxe, finds himself unwillingly conscripted into a British Army about to fight a large, yet undefined war. The sense of the surreal increases as Tristram and his battalion 'ship out' overseas, and everything around him seems lifted from the aesthetic of the First World War: uniforms, weapons, gramophones, songs, Kitchener posters, bully beef . . . and trenches. Tristram marches through ruined villages to the front line. Leading the platoon into battle is Mr Dollimore, an ideologue who glories in the coming conflict and talks in clichés that meld, unironically, the words of Rupert Brooke and Shakespeare's *Henry IV*. Dollimore, Burgess writes, 'was ready to lead his thirty over (some corner of a foreign field) in brave assault, owing God a death (that is for ever England)'.[64]

As the whistles sound, and the soldiers go over the top and charge forward, Tristram watches on in mute panic. 'It was slaughter, it was mutual massacre.' Playing dead in the trenches, he later manages to escape from the battlefield, and discovers to his horror that he was on a large 'set' constructed in southwestern Ireland. Later, picked up again by the army, he is told that he was the only survivor of an 'E.S.' – an Extermination Session – as a major informs him 'that's what the new battles are called'. The war is no real war. It is a solution to the overpopulation problem: staging fake, but still lethal, re-enactments of the Great War trench battles over and over again, as a means of demographic culling. In a final act of grotesquery, the bodies of the fallen are turned into bully beef, to help alleviate the food shortages.[65]

The Wanting Seed, Fussell writes, is 'animated by a profound appreciation of the way the Great War established the prototype for modern insensate organised violence'. In it, he says, Burgess has 'sensed both the alliance between war and theatre and the necessity of our approach to the Great War through the channels of myth and cliché. Which is to say he located War as a major source of modern myth. The book is permeated by an understanding of the modern world as the inevitable construct of a whole series of wars.'[66]

I moved between the gravestones, then passed the Cross of Sacrifice at the memorial's far western edge, where it gives out to open fields, running off to the horizon. There was no one else here now. I was alone, and I was thinking of Fussell's book, and Burgess's nightmare future of performative war on repeat. As if the Great War had stamped the ultimate, perfected template for conflict and suffering. Yet to perfect something means to have practised and refined it, honed it to its sharpest edge. If you go looking for origins, then older myths of war keep rising up to the surface.

What was the Somme – and *The Wanting Seed*'s 'Extermination Session' – if not a futuristic incarnation of the 'Battle of the Champions'? It was here that the border ball games of the *poleis* found their mirror image in Wilfred Nevill's footballs, kicked just yards away from where I was standing. Had I been on this exact spot just over a century ago I could have seen them soaring through the sky. Think of all those adolescent *ephebes* being sent in their millions to these artificial borderlands – now just fields once again – to be preserved for ever in *kenos taphos*, 'empty tombs', where they 'shall not grow old', memorialised by Lutyens' white, minimalist, classical austerity. And perhaps, as time passes – and as the reality dims and the myths intensify – this is all coming closer to the romantic, Spartan ideal of 'beautiful death' than we might like to admit. Blood-red poppies, in place of 'Thyreatic wreaths', laid around countless Stones of Remembrance.

The modern world, Fussell wrote, formed as the inevitable construct of a whole series of wars . . . Or, you could say, *the inevitable construct of a whole series of borders*. This performance of war – and, ultimately, of bordering – has been going on for a very long time. Here, perhaps, was the greatest, purest, most devastating performance of all. But not the last. Never the last. There is always an encore. And as more time passes – not just a century, but a millennium, say – will we still believe what really happened here? Will the Somme – our twentieth-century Battle of the Champions, that exercise in postmodern mutual annihilation – seem scarcely credible to some *future* generation?

The sun set on the Western Front once again. Yellow into orange into purple: a Technicolor curtain fall. The hour of 'stand-to' was over. I walked away, back through Thiepval's great stone archway, across the darkening and ageless lawn.

3
LIMITLESS

One evening, just a few days after midsummer, I walked the line that, for a brief time, marked the northernmost edge of the Roman Empire: a border between the known, conquered world and the end of the world. Beyond this line were marshes and forests, wild reaches where, it was said, the sea was 'not restricted to the coast, but passes deep inland and winds about, pushing in even among highlands and mountains as if in its own domain'.[1] And beyond *this*, the land just stopped. Apart from another brief stretch of sea, containing the tiny islands of the *Orcades* and *Thule*, there was nothing. Just what the Greeks called *Okeanos* – the World Ocean – the endless waters that encircled and bounded the earth.

In the summer of AD 82, the Roman governor Gnaeus Julius Agricola mustered his legions and led them into these edgelands. Agricola's son-in-law, the renowned orator, historian and biographer Tacitus, wrote of the campaign in gripping, near-cinematic detail. All of Britannia had been secured up to the 'narrow neck of land' between the Clota and Bodotria rivers. 'The enemy,' said Tacitus, 'were pushed into what was virtually another island.'[2] Caledonia.

After a year spent penetrating deep into the highland landscape, Agricola brought the Caledonians out into the open for a climactic battle beneath a mountain that Tacitus called Mons Graupius. As their forces assembled, the leaders of the two armies delivered passionate speeches.

A man called Calgacus, the heroic champion of the Caledonians, addressed his troops as the 'last men of earth and the last of the free'. After them, he said, lay no other nation, nothing but waves and rocks. They were about to fight their final stand against the brigands of the world, an empire driven by a rapacious desire to consume and control everything. 'Robbery, butchery, rapine, these the liars call *empire*,' Calgacus exclaimed, 'they create desolation and call it peace.'[3]

Agricola's address to his legions was to put 'the final edge on their courage'. He told them that they had braved both enemies and nature, surpassing anything achieved by any Romans before them. 'We grasp the furthest reaches of Britannia,' he said, 'not by report or rumour, but by encamping here in force.' Now all it would take was one last effort to give meaning to all the miles of hard marching, all the woods threaded, all the estuaries crossed. He said that he had made up his mind long ago that no army and no general should ever turn back. 'A death of honour is better than a life of shame . . . And, if we must perish, it would be no mean glory to fall where land and nature end.'[4]

As Tacitus reported it, this battle on the edge of the world soon became a rout. When the fighting moved from the slopes of Mons Graupius to the open ground, the spectacle was 'awe-inspiring and grim'. The Caledonian resolve was broken, and those who still could fled for the forests and the mountains. 'Everywhere were weapons, bodies, mangled limbs and soil soaked with blood.' The next morning, there was nothing. Just an awful silence, deserted hills, houses smouldering in the distance. The Roman scouts could find no signs of life. Was this peace? Or desolation?

Victory came just as summer ended. The emperor Domitian ordered the recall of Agricola and his legions, saying there was greater need for the troops elsewhere. For Tacitus, however, the real reason was jealousy – that Agricola's momentous achievement would see the governor's name raised above that of the emperor. 'Britannia was thoroughly conquered and immediately abandoned,'[5] he lamented. The end of the world had been reached, grasped and let go.

Forty years later, this end point had retreated far to the south of

Mons Graupius. Work was underway on a structure conceived as a monumental physical symbol of the extremity of empire. A barrier of earth and stone, running for some seventy-four miles across a largely empty landscape. A wall built on the orders of the emperor who gave it its name: Hadrian. Another twenty years on, Hadrian's immediate successor, Antoninus Pius, ordered this imperial frontier pushed further northwards. Three legions – the Second, Sixth and Twentieth – marched to Tacitus's 'narrow neck of land', where the two great Caledonian estuaries carved inwards from east and west, and they began to dig.

I was walking through the results of all of that digging. At about the halfway point between the Bodotria and the Clota – better known today as the Forth and Clyde rivers – the frontier line reaches its highest point, at a place called Bar Hill. Beyond a quiet, stony farm track, just west of the small village of Croy, a deep, wide and unmistakable 'V' cuts through the landscape. The bright, lowering sun picked it out in shadow, and I climbed down into its darkness, wading through tall, pink-tipped, wild grass, to follow its hard, black line. From a flat stretch, the ditch briefly dipped down and then reared upwards, rising to a summit of just over 500 feet.

This earthwork once belonged to what the Romans called a *murus caespiticus*, a turf wall. A frontier in four parts, it began as a mass of turf and clay slabs layered over a stone base, making a rampart over ten feet tall. Immediately in front was a stretch of levelled ground, the 'berm', that sank down into a ditch – twelve feet deep and anything from twenty to forty feet wide. Finally, there was a second hump on the north side of the ditch, an 'upcast mound' formed by the heaped mass of spoil thrown up by all the digging. The rampart was topped by a wooden palisade and walkway. And behind it, to the south, was a road, the 'military way', that connected some twenty, roughly equidistant Roman forts, almost all built right up against the line of the rampart.[6] Now imagine all this running, uninterrupted, for over thirty miles, from sea to sea. Cutting the land, literally, in two.

From the top of Bar Hill, the view stretched out in all directions. I could follow the line the wall had once taken over the undulating terrain to the east and west. It was nearing ten o'clock but the sun still hung lazy above the horizon. Looking north, the ground dropped, flattened, and then rose again into the low spine of the Kilsyth Hills and the Campsie Fells. In silhouette the hills had turned a rich purple. It was that time of year when darkness would never quite come.

'Their day is longer than in our part of the world,' Tacitus had written of Caledonia. 'The night is bright . . . so bright that you can barely distinguish the evening from the morning twilight.' This, he concluded, was the product of living on the edge. 'The flat ends of the earth cannot, with their low shadow, raise the darkness to any height; night therefore fails to reach the sky and its stars.'[7]

You wonder if the soldiers who built this wall and manned its forts thought the same. Or their families, for they lived here too – the stylish leather sandals of women and children were pulled out of an infilled well discovered just a short distance from where I was standing. Some soldiers would have been Britanni, conscripted into the army. But others were veterans from Hispania, Thrace, Gaul and Gallia Belgica (modern-day Spain, Bulgaria, France and Belgium). The cohort stationed here, at Bar Hill, were archers from Hama in northern Syria. What did they think of the permanent gloaming of a Scottish summer? How did they feel about making a home and a life on a frontier that fringed the very 'flat ends of the earth'. Proud? Fearful? Utterly bored? And what about the Caledonians? What was their reaction to this vast construction project, this great unfurling of imperial might?

The official story was that Antoninus Pius, like Hadrian before him, had built the wall as a bulwark against the 'barbarians', the uncivilised hordes of the north. Yet the suspicion, the likelihood even, was that there was no conquest, no great military campaign. Instead, the advance from Hadrian's Wall proceeded largely unopposed. And then to the awe, and perhaps the bemusement, of the locals – who had been trading and interacting with the Romans for decades – the legions set to work. This territorial leap northwards was an easy win for an emperor with no military pedigree. The wall offered a great symbol of power in a far-flung province. And its construction kept the soldiers busy.

You can imagine the planning, the surveying, the design. The evictions of communities who found themselves right in the wall's path, the setbacks, the days lost to torrential rain, those brutal sections, one just to the east of Croy, where they had to cut through tough, igneous, dolerite rock. This was no simple, earth-moving task, but a complex engineering project that refined the work of Hadrian's earlier frontier and included, among other things – because this was Scotland, after all – a sophisticated drainage system.[8]

The completion of every section was marked by a series of carved sandstone 'distance slabs', placed in pairs with one on the north face of the wall and one on the south. Every slab included a dedication to Antoninus, 'the father of the country', along with the name and number of the legion that built it, and the exact length of the work in either feet or paces (the recorded distances ranged from the wonderfully specific '3,666½ paces' to the vaguer 'over 3,000 feet'). Many of the stones featured detailed carvings – the goddess Victory, an imperial eagle feasting on captive enemies, the legionary mascots of a running boar, a Pegasus and a Capricorn.

Most elaborate of all was the slab that marked the eastern terminus of the wall, where the frontier met the waters of the Forth estuary. On either side of the dedication to the emperor were two graphic scenes. In one, a Roman cavalryman waded into a scene of battle, sword held high, scattering his barbarian enemies, one of whom he had already beheaded. In the other, an animal sacrifice was performed, perhaps a closing rite to dedicate the construction of the wall to the gods. Both scenes were framed by columns of classical architecture, pointed references to the superiority and sophistication of the Roman civilisation. It was a lot to pack into one squat block of sandstone – power, conquest, dominion, supremacy, piety. And distance. Because even in the midst of all this potent iconography, recording the length of this last, eastern section – 4,652 paces – was still given prominence.[9]

Nothing quite like these slabs was created anywhere else in the empire. Inscribed building markers *were* common, but they were basic, unadorned blocks that simply gave the name of the legion involved in construction. Yet on the Antonine Wall, every step, pace and foot across its whole length was measured and memorialised, the true extent of the physical exertion required to build the frontier carved repeatedly into the frontier itself. This was bordering as a grand performance, an almost ceremonial, self-conscious transformation of the native land – its soil, its clay, its rock, its wood – into one vast sculpture, a thirty-seven-mile-long symbol of the Roman ability to tame wilderness and nature.

There was something overblown and bombastic about it all. As if a kind of deep-rooted, unspoken insecurity was being woven into the very fabric of the frontier. Why had an empire as mighty as Rome built an endpoint at all? First came one wall and then, twenty years later and a hundred miles north, came another. When is a wall not a wall? When it's a sign of a profound, existential crisis.

In the early years of the Roman Empire, after Julius Caesar's son, Octavian, had ended decades of civil war by replacing the Republic with rule by *princeps* ('first citizen', an emperor by any other name), one work of literature came to be raised above all others. It was produced by the son of a farmer, born in 70 BC in a small village in northern Italy. His name was Publius Vergilius Maro: or, more simply, Virgil.

His early poetry had caught the attention of Octavian – who now called himself 'Augustus', a quasi-spiritual title meaning 'illustrious one' – and Rome's new leader soon became Virgil's all-powerful patron. (Robert Graves, the author of *I, Claudius*, couldn't forgive what he saw as this political corruption of art by autocratic fandom. 'Few poets,' he wrote, 'have brought such discredit as Virgil on their sacred calling.')[10] Around 29 BC, perhaps under commission from Augustus, Virgil embarked on an epic poem, which took inspiration – and characters – from Homer's *Illiad* and *Odyssey* and bent them into a grand creation myth for Rome.

Called the *Aeneid*, it tells of Aeneas, the son of Venus and a prince of Troy, who flees his city's destruction by the Greeks and, with a rag-tag crew of fellow refugees, sets off across the tempestuous seas, pursued by the rage of the goddess Juno. The story's narrative arc is established very early on, when Venus, distraught at her son's plight, comes to her father Jupiter and asks why Aeneas is being singled out for such punishment.

The king of the gods soothes his daughter's anguish. Yes, he says, years of hardship lie ahead for her son. When he comes at last to land on the shores of Italy, he will have to 'wage a long, costly war'. But at its end awaits a great destiny. He will build a new homeland, and its people, the 'Romans', will emerge as the 'lords of the earth'. 'On them I set no limits, space or time,' Jupiter says. 'I have granted them power, *imperium sine fine*.' Empire without limit. Rule without end.[11]

It offered the ultimate tale of triumph over adversity: the greatness of Rome sprung from the desolation of Troy. Throughout the poem Aeneas is given tantalising glimpses into Rome's future (which, for contemporary readers, was actually its historical *past*), along with its heroes and villains, its triumphs and tragedies, leading all the way up to Virgil's own time and Augustus himself, who is presented as a direct descendant of the Trojan prince. At one point, Aeneas travels to the underworld and meets his dead father, who foretells that Augustus will 'expand his empire . . . to a land beyond the stars, beyond the wheel of the year, the course of the sun itself'.[12]

It is hard to overstate the impact of the *Aeneid* on Roman society. Here was a manifesto for global supremacy – boundless empire, boundless power – wrapped up in a glorious, violent and achingly dramatic Homeric epic. Myth, history and real life were melded together into the ultimate Roman blockbuster, a magnum opus at once breathtakingly ambitious and cynically populist. Even before its completion, the hype had begun, with a younger poet, Propertius, urging all other writers, past and present, to 'give way' because 'something greater than the *Iliad* is being born'.[13] The *Aeneid* was an instant classic. Copies spread and multiplied, moving from the high-born, chattering classes to becoming the pre-eminent set text of the schoolroom and quotes being scrawled liberally on city walls throughout the empire.

As time passed, its reputation only grew. The book took on a quasi-religious potency. Those seeking prestige and influence treated it as a kind of oracle, believed that it had the power to predict the future. This practice became known as the *Sortes Virgilianae* – the Virgilian Lottery. You opened the book at random, blindly chose a passage, and whatever you found beneath your finger foretold your destiny. One of the first people known to have played this lottery was the ambitious son of a senator, a cousin of Emperor Trajan. The line he landed on was 'I recognise that he is that king of Rome'. This was the Virgilian equivalent of picking the winning ticket. And the reader's name? Hadrian.[14]

Hadrian became emperor in AD 117, nearly a century and a half after the *Aeneid* was first published. He inherited the empire at its greatest ever extent. Trajan had pursued the grand Roman project of conquest and dominion, claiming huge swathes of new territory in every direction. Yet it was Hadrian who would call a halt to the relentless outward surge that Jupiter (or rather Virgil) had prophesied. He began imposing *limes* – limits, actual physical frontiers – on the limitless empire, from his wall in Britannia and the barriers running along the Rhine and the Danube, to border roads and fortifications in the remote deserts of the Sahara and Persia. He gave Rome hard, defined perimeters. Symbolic endpoints. Or, at least, *edgepoints*. Was Hadrian, that diligent student of Virgil, really turning away from the *Aeneid*'s central, expansionist message? Had the new emperor lost his nerve?

The thing is, there was more than one way of reading Virgil: what have become known as the 'optimistic' and 'pessimistic' interpretations. For the optimists, the poet was mounting a heartfelt justification for empire, portraying the personal struggles and sacrifices required to bring peace to the world: where *pietas* – duty – was the greatest virtue, and the ultimate aim of conquest and expansion was to see 'the Terrible Gates of War . . . bolted shut'.[15] Here Virgil nodded, unabashedly, to his patron Augustus, who had ended the internecine bloodshed of the Republic and replaced it with paternalistic stability. He was the emperor who was destined – to paraphrase an infamous modern slogan – to Make Rome Great Again.

To others, however, Virgil – far from the poet who 'bartered his talent for social security' (Robert Graves once more)[16] – was in fact lacing the *Aeneid* with a subtle yet sustained critique of the whole imperial project. Perhaps, the pessimists suggested, he was showing through Aeneas's travails that the cost of empire was too great: as was the risk. Because *imperium sine fine* wasn't just about unchecked territorial ambition, but also unchecked *personal* ambition. In an emperor, the power wielded by one individual was equally unconstrained by time or by boundary. What was to stop any one man's sense of duty from being corrupted by limitless authority? In the end, the message was that empire will always be built on, governed through – and brought down by – violence.

Was Hadrian a pessimist? It seems an unlikely quality in an emperor. Yet there is no doubt that he worried Rome was stretched beyond its means. He spent nearly two decades travelling to its extremities, wanting to see and walk the borderlands himself. Perhaps he was the first emperor to really, *physically*, confront the imperial edges, to question if anything, truly, can be without limit.[17]

Virgil both inspired and haunted the Romans who came after him. The *Aeneid* had blurred the lines between reality and myth, and at the same time highlighted the inherent contradictions between the glittering greatness of empire and its moral offences and innate fragility. When Tacitus wrote his account of Agricola's Caledonian campaign, he echoed these same concerns. In the speeches that he recounted before the battle of Mons Graupius, he followed a standard trope of Roman literature: the key players delivering their lines to heighten the emotional drama in advance of a pivotal event. And so he invented Calgacus's speech – in fact he may even have invented

Calgacus himself. Agricola, at least, was real. But the words he spoke were, almost certainly, made up.

Instead, this was a dialogue between Rome's split personalities, a meditation on tyranny and its discontents. On one side, Tacitus had Agricola appealing to his soldiers' ingrained sense of duty, urging them to get things done, just like Aeneas would have: because no good Roman ever turned back. Yet, into Calgacus's mouth, Tacitus put an excoriating condemnation of empire. He cast the Romans as arrogant, greedy and lustful, the scourge of the earth, bringing not peace to all lands, but bondage, slavery and death.

It was an astonishing attack, which channelled the *Aeneid*'s deepest misgivings. The Romans were a 'motley agglomeration of nations', held together only by weak bonds of 'apprehension and terror'. Break those bonds, Calgacus (or, rather, Tacitus) said, and 'where fear has ended, hatred will begin'.[18]

It was a speech filled with high Roman anxiety. Even as the empire grew bigger than ever before, it was stalked by the spectre of the fall, by the prospect of a collapse that seemed at once unimaginable – and inevitable.

On another summer evening, a few years ago, I flew over the Antonine Wall in a Second World War biplane: a vintage Tiger Moth owned and piloted by William Mackaness, a professor of geography at the University of Edinburgh. Leaning out of the open cockpit, I could see how, in the low sun, the wall's earthworks still left hard lines in the modern landscape: its ditch etched in black, its rampart bulging in shadow beneath the taut skin of fields and moorlands, like the wriggling body of a giant worm. It would vanish for some sections then reappear again, running behind a line of terraced houses or through the middle of an estate of high-rise flats. At times it was as clear and true as the motorway or railway that ran alongside it.

When we came to land at Cumbernauld's small airfield, the wall was exactly parallel to the runway. I could still see its deep depression just beyond the boundary fence, overrun by wild grass, flickering black and gold in the sunset, less than a hundred yards away. A frontier, a *border* – dug out by spade nearly two millennia ago – and it was still there.

This is, perhaps, even more remarkable when you consider just how briefly it was actually in use. The wall took twelve years to build – and was occupied for another eight – before, all at once, it was abandoned. Forts were carefully demolished: timbers taken down and sometimes burned, stone structures pulled to the ground. Valuables were packed up and taken away. All that was left behind, often dumped into wells or ditches, were fragments of metal or pottery, nails and broken arrowheads and all those piles of worn-out sandals.[19]

As the years passed, people came to forget who had built it. As early as the sixth century, the historian Gildas said it was created by the Britons, not the Romans, because it was made of turf rather than stone. By the later medieval period, it was no longer known as a wall at all. It was referred to locally as 'Grymisdyke' or 'Grim's Dyke', and was said to be the supernatural work of the Devil, or even a plough line left behind by ancient giants.[20]

It was only much later that its Roman origins re-emerged. The first discovery of one of the distance slabs came at the end of the seventeenth century: a huge block, pulled from the muddy banks of the River Clyde, revealed a sculpture of the goddess Victory, with a Latin inscription which dedicated the wall to Antoninus Pius (and – of course – recorded a construction length of 4,411 feet). Soon, other slabs began to appear, their hard corners poking up out of farmers' fields or discovered built into the stone walls of cowsheds.

By the later eighteenth century, a new line, the Forth and Clyde Canal, was slicing Scotland from east to west, running alongside – and often right on top of – the wall. This was one of the great arteries of Scotland's industrial revolution, and its building works pulled yet more fragments of the Roman frontier out of the soil. John Anderson, a professor of natural philosophy at the Glasgow College, was given the task of travelling the length of the canal and securing whatever artefacts he could. His expenses claim to the

College included accommodation at various inns, 'horse hire for my servant', payments to those who 'assisted in lifting the stones', and 'drink-money to the workmen'.[21]

One of his most significant recoveries came after canal diggers broke into a Roman rubbish pit at a farm in Auchendavy, just north of the town of Kirkintilloch. Five stone altars were pulled out of the heavy clay soil, all dedicated by one man – the flamboyantly named centurion, Marcus Coccieus Firmus – to no less than twelve different gods. These ranged from Jupiter, Victory, Mars, Minerva, Diana and Hercules to the Celtic horse goddess Epona and even the *genius* – the 'soul' – of the 'land of Britain'.[22] It was a remarkable example of spiritual spread betting. A symptom, perhaps, of the inherent uncertainty of life on the frontier, where mundane, everyday rituals were suffused with a constant apprehension over an unknown threat lurking somewhere over the northern horizon. But did Coccieus Firmus ask the gods for peace or for some action to break the monotony?

I grew up on that horizon: some twenty-five miles north of Bar Hill and the Antonine Wall, just outside the little town of Auchterarder. As a teenager, I used to ride my bike on summer evenings down a single-track road to the remains of another great Roman earthwork, a place called Ardoch fort, built by Agricola in the late first century to support his Caledonian advance.

It was one of a network of military outposts he established, known today as the Gask Ridge. Its watchtowers, camps and forts ran, almost exactly, along a geological schism: the Highland Boundary Fault, a solid, unwavering line passing diagonally through the centre of Scotland, from southwest to northeast. A line where soft lowland rocks meet an impassable igneous barrier, where the land suddenly rears up in a concertina of hills and mountains (mountains now known as the Grampians – a corruption of Tacitus's Graupius due to, of all things, a typesetting error in the earliest available print edition of his works). It is, in many respects, as 'true' a border as you will find anywhere in the world. And Agricola used it as a sort of proto-frontier, a forerunner of Hadrian and Antonine's walls.

I would cycle to Ardoch fort and sit high up on one of its defensive ditches, resting my back against the heaped earth, my face turned northwest towards the mountains and the setting sun. I'd read a book or listen to music on the chunky, cassette Walkman I clipped to the waistband of my shorts. I rarely saw another soul and was largely indifferent to the site's long history. It was just a nice place to stop.

You wonder how the Romans spent their time on the frontier. We know much about what they ate: wild fruits like blackberries, raspberries and strawberries; game, fish and shellfish; lentils and porridge. They imported olive oil, macaroni wheat, figs, coriander, dill and opium poppies from the continent. Wine was brought from southern France.[23]

Amid the ruins of the fort of Vindolanda, on Hadrian's Wall, wooden writing tablets were discovered which offered a rare and intimate insight into border life in the early second century. There was much recording of humdrum tasks and duties: inventories of food, a request from a soldier to take leave, a note asking to borrow a hunting net. But there was also a touching letter from a woman called Claudia, the wife of a soldier, to her friend Sulipicia, the wife of the camp commander, inviting her to a birthday party and signing off with '*anima mea . . . karissima*', 'to my dearest soul'.[24]

On several tablets there were lines from Virgil's *Aeneid*. Many of these seemed to be writing tests, either for children or soldiers (one was even marked with the terse comment 'slack'). Still, it is tempting to think of some centurion, or maybe the commander's wife, climbing one evening to the summit of Bar Hill, with a cup of wine and their copy of the *Aeneid*. Glancing up, occasionally, at the dipping sun and the land beyond the wall, looking out over the limit of their empire. Watching the hills, and wondering, and waiting – always waiting.

There is a poem by another great chronicler of empire, an Alexandrian Greek called Constantine P. Cavafy. Although he wrote some nineteen centuries after Virgil, he was similarly concerned with Mediterranean antiquity and its fraying extremities, with fate and loss and the personal costs of history. His poem 'Waiting for the Barbarians' opens with all the people of some great, unnamed city – ordinary citizens, senators, consuls, praetors, orators and even the emperor – frozen in horrified anticipation of the arrival of the 'barbarians'. The city has ground to a halt, the hours pass slow and agonising, and everyone looks to the city gates – thrown wide open – and into the distance; 'because', as the poem tells us repeatedly 'the barbarians will arrive today'.[25] Yet, by the time night falls, they still haven't come.

> And some people have arrived from the borderlands,
> and said there are no more barbarians anymore.
>
> And now what's to become of us without barbarians.
> Those people were a solution of a sort.

Was *this* life on the Antonine Wall? Manning a barrier built as an expression of imperial power in a land where the true threat was intermittent or even imaginary? The legions carved their line. Built it up and bolstered it. And then they waited. Hoping, perversely, for the attack to jolt them into war, the crisis that would once again propel the flagging momentum of their empire. And it never came. Two decades passed, and then the Romans packed up their wall, and looked for their solution elsewhere.

The Romans had a story about another endpoint – and another wall – to be found at the very opposite extreme of their Empire from Caledonia. This time, however, they were not its creators. Writing in the first century, the historian Josephus described how, some 400 years earlier, Alexander the Great had closed a mountain pass with a massive iron barrier gate, built to keep out the 'barbarian' threat of the Scythians – a nomadic, horse-riding people who had spread all the way from Siberia to the northern coast of the Black Sea. This barrier could be found, Josephus said, in the Caucasus Mountains, somewhere among its ridge of high peaks, which stretched in a perfect line from the Black Sea to the Caspian Sea. To the Romans this was the very edge of the known *northeastern* earth, with the Caspian Sea thought to be a giant bay leading out to the world-encircling ocean.[26]

In the early Christian era, the (wildly popular) accounts of the exploits of Alexander became mixed up with the sacred texts of the scriptures. The Talmud and the Old and New Testaments had talked of two dark, subhuman figures called Gog and Magog, who were described as an 'evil' in the north,[27] living in a 'barren and desolate'[28] land surrounded by impassable mountains. They were said to command a huge army, 'all of them riding upon horses',[29] which would, at the moment of the apocalypse, be 'loosed out' of their prison to 'go forth and seduce the nations'.[30]

These threads and fragments of stories became intertwined and, as time passed, the tale of Alexander's gate evolved to imply that it wasn't just some ordinary foe that was barricaded up in the mountains, but Gog and Magog themselves, the two biblical bogeymen. After all, Josephus had written in his original account that the Scythians were descended from Magog.[31] Could it be that, behind that great iron wall, waited the ultimate barbarian horde, the agents of global destruction?[32]

It was this fantastical interpretation which made its way into what was known as the *Alexander Romance*, a work of semi-mythical biography that circulated for centuries around all of Europe and the Near East. A sort of early medieval bestseller, it was translated into numerous languages, including Arabic, and eventually the account of the barrier was included in the Qur'an, which described how the 'two-horned one' (the Islamic name for Alexander, after the helmet of ram horns which he was shown wearing on coins minted during his rule) 'dammed up the valley between the Two Mountains' with iron blocks and molten brass, so 'Gog and Magog could not scale it, nor could they dig through it'.[33] At the same time, the Qur'an also included a version of the old prophecy: that Gog and Magog would eventually break free of this prison and come racing through the breach with their invincible armies. Their ensuing campaign of pillage and destruction would, it was said, bring about the end of the world.

Some eight centuries after Josephus had first set this story running, al-Wāthiq bi'llāh, the ninth caliph of the Abbasid empire, woke in his palace in Samarra, troubled by the lingering memory of a dream. In his sleep, he had seen a vision of Alexander's barrier. And its gates were cracked wide open.

Al-Wāthiq was so disturbed by this ominous portent that he called in his advisors and ordered that the barrier be found and its condition inspected. An expedition party was assembled, led by a multi-lingual polymath and traveller known as Sallam the Interpreter. In the summer of AD 842, Sallam left Samarra, and headed north. After travelling for some sixteen months, he finally began to pick up the barrier's trail. He recorded reaching the ruins of towns and cities, so many that it took twenty days to pass through them all. When he asked the locals what had happened to them, he was told that, long ago, they had been invaded and destroyed by Gog and Magog.

Then he came to a fortress, set above a gorge in the mountains. The people there spoke Arabic and Persian, and they were Muslims (they said they had been converted many years previously when a man came to them riding a camel and told them of the Qur'an and its teachings). They explained that their fortress was one of a line of defences leading up to the base of the barrier itself. They told Sallam that he was very close now, just three days away. The route ascended steadily, through small villages overlooked by watchtowers, towards a circular mountain range. At the very end of the third day he saw two more fortresses, each clinging to outcrops of rock on either side of a narrow pass. Between them was Alexander's barrier.

Sallam described an immense structure. He judged it over thirty metres high, fifty metres long. It appeared to have been fashioned from a colossal single slab of iron. 'Air cannot penetrate by the gate nor by the mountainside,' he said. 'It is as if it is created in one piece.'[34] Running across the gate was a huge bolt, prevented from opening by an equally huge padlock. A key was suspended from a chain that was riveted against the surface of the gate.

In one of the fortresses, Sallam found the remains of the tools used to construct the barrier: forges and giant brass cauldrons and iron ladles, all now piled up and stuck together with rust. In the other, he met a commander and his men, whose job it was to guard the gate. He heard how, every Monday and Thursday, the commander would ride out at dawn to the gate, climb up a ladder and strike the bolt with an iron rod. A moment later, 'he hears them' – Gog and Magog – 'making a noise like a hornets' nest, after which they are quiet'.[35] The commander would do this twice more, at midday and again in the afternoon, each time bending his ear to the gate to listen, and then he would sit until sunset, leaving only as darkness fell.

Sallam wanted to know if the gate had ever been damaged and was told that it had not – the only breach in its smooth surface was one tiny crack 'as wide as a thin thread'. The commander was not worried about the fabric of the gate, he said, because its iron was over two metres thick.

Returning to the gate, Sallam knelt by the hairline crack, pulled a knife from his boot and scraped away at the iron there, breaking off some small fragments and tying them up in a piece of cloth to take back to the caliph. He noticed then, high up on the barrier and written in iron, the prophecy that told how, when the end times came, God would destroy the gate and unleash Gog and Magog on the world.

Sallam took another year to return to Samarra. He reported everything that he had seen to al-Wāthiq, and also to a young official in the caliph's court, Ibn Khurdādhbih, who included the account, seemingly verbatim, in a work called the *Kitāb al-masālik wa-l-mamālik* (*The Book of Routes and Realms*). There was one – rather significant – problem, however. Despite Sallam's precise, and sometimes fantastical, detail, it still wasn't clear exactly where Alexander's barrier was.[36]

When Sallam embarked on his journey to the gate, the Caucasus were not the remote lands that they had been in Josephus's time. And the threat beyond the frontier was no longer the marauding Scythians. History and myth had both mixed up and moved on.

Sallam had, in effect, been sent out by the caliph to find a legend. Is it any surprise then that he returned with a tale of fantastical discovery about a colossal gate in a strange and distant land? A barrier manned by faithful Muslims, and which was surrounded by the very instruments of its construction – the forges and heaped cauldrons – that the Qur'an had described?

Ibn Khurdādhbih faithfully recorded Sallam's travelogue in his *Book of Routes and Realms*. Even at the time, other geographers were sceptical – or outright dismissive – questioning what Sallam had seen, and even whether he had made the journey at all. Yet this did not stop Khurdādhbih's book becoming a key reference work for generations to come. It served, in particular, as a crucial source for early cartographers, the creators of the *mappaemundi* that began to emerge in the eleventh century.[37]

The Arabic geographer Muhammed al-Idrisi relied on it for his famous and hugely influential 1154 world map, produced for Roger of Sicily, which showed Alexander's barrier as a long and imposing black wall with one gate, which cut off a thin stretch of eastern land pressed right up against a circular ocean. The great Ebstorf and Hereford maps, made in Germany and England in the late thirteenth century, both featured it too. On the Ebstorf map, there was a peninsula, surrounded by mountains on two sides and a wall on the other two, containing the figures of Gog and Magog, who were shown eating body parts and drinking blood. The Hereford map dispensed with this explicit graphic detail, but included, inside a peninsula walled off by Alexander's barrier, an inscription explaining that 'the horrors in this place are worse than can be imagined . . .

The inhabitants are without culture, feed on human flesh and blood, descend from Cain and were enclosed by God through Alexander the Great.' It finished by warning that it was inevitable that they would one day break free and 'devastate the world'.[38]

Indeed, for some, it was self-evident that the more time that passed, the more imminent the arrival of the apocalypse must surely be. The immensely popular fourteenth-century book *The Travels of Sir John Mandeville*, prophesied that the cataclysm was going to be brought about any day by a simple fox foraging for food, who would dig a hole beneath Alexander's gate and create the passage that would allow Gog and Magog to escape. Others, however, were growing weary of all of this doom-mongering. Henry of Harcaly, a fourteenth-century chancellor of the University of Oxford, wondered why, going back for many hundreds of years, you could 'so often find the claim that the chasm of Alexander has been broken', and yet the world was 'not showing any more sign of ending than before'.[39]

As world maps grew larger and more extensive, Gog and Magog still remained – but always on the periphery. Which meant that Alexander's gates were moving continually, a mirage on the far horizon, never coming closer. They leapt from the Caucasus to the lands beyond the Caspian Sea, shifting steadily further north and east into Mongolia, China and Siberia.

The location kept changing, and so too did the faces. Over the course of more than a millennium, Gog and Magog were identified with peoples ranging from the Scythians, the Huns, the Turks and the Magyars, to the Mongols, the Goths, the Jews and the Celts (there was even an account among the Samoyed tribes of the Arctic Circle of a people trapped behind mountains in the polar north, who spoke an unintelligible language and were constantly trying to cut their way out of their icy prison).[40]

At the very beginning of the sixteenth century, the Spanish cartographer Juan de la Cosa, who had sailed with Christopher Columbus in 1493, produced a map that included both the 'new' and the 'old' worlds, yet still featured, in its far northeastern corner, the land of

Gog and Magog. Rumold Mercator's 1595 map of Asia put their territory at the very edge of Siberia but split it in two, into 'Ung, called Gog by us', and 'Mongul alias Magog'. Even at the beginning of the eighteenth century, the Venetian geographer Vincenzo Coronelli featured Gog and Magog on his *Libro dei Globi*, as a shadowy presence, right on the eastern cusp of the map.[41]

In the latter half of the nineteenth century, a Dutch orientalist, Michael Jan de Goeje, came into possession of a newly discovered version of Ibn Khurdādhbih's *Book of Routes and Realms*. This edition, which had been found in the Egyptian city of Alexandria, included significantly more detail about Sallam's journey to Alexander's barrier. As de Goeje worked through his translation, he began to piece together an itinerary that connected the descriptions of *terra incognita* to real, identifiable geographic locations. A route began to emerge, which saw Sallam travelling over the Caucasus mountains and then turning east around the northern coast of the Caspian Sea to meet up with a branch of the ancient Silk Road. From there, de Goeje speculated, he must have pushed on further east, beyond the massive salt lake of Lop Nor on the fringe of the Taklamakan Desert, all the way to Yumenguan, the frontier post of the 'Jade Gate', found at the very western end of the Great Wall of China.[42]

This theory, first published in 1888, received much the same reception as Khurdādhbih's original account of Sallam's tale: a mixture of excited congratulation, scepticism and even ridicule.[43] Fractious disagreements over de Goeje's interpretation still continue to this day – perhaps because the prospect it offers is just too tantalising, too perfect. Sallam sets out to find the barbarian extremity of the earth. He makes his way across mountains and deserts and wide empty steppes until, at last, he meets a road traversed by merchants and travellers, who tell of a huge wall and gate further to the east. He presses on and then, at Yumenguan, he finds a version of what he seeks: fortresses and watchtowers and a giant structure – a 'Jade Gate' – controlling entry and exit between China and the 'Western regions'. It may not be Alexander's gate, but it is an ideal surrogate. And so he returns to his caliph with a story, greatly embellished and altered to fit the mythology and the words of the Qur'an, but still rooted in some kind of tangible reality.

The irony, of course, is that the Great Wall of China was also built – at least symbolically – as a defence against barbarian invaders: its 4,500 miles of stone a bulwark against the pernicious threat of the outside world. Sallam, in reaching Yumenguan (if, of course, he ever made it there at all) had brought 'the other' right up against the *other* 'other', collapsing two perspectives into one. The gate built to keep the barbarians *in* was also the gate built to keep the barbarians *out*. It was two sides of the same wall, the place where the western horizon collided with the eastern horizon.

What he had discovered was nothing less than a geographical singularity. Either everyone was a barbarian, or there were no barbarians any more. This was, perhaps, the real prophecy hidden within Sallam's great journey – and excavated a thousand years later by de Goeje's translation: that the barbarians weren't biding their time. They were simply disappearing, fading from existence.

One day, a small crowd crossed China's border. Then more came. Some were stopped and turned back, but the numbers kept increasing. Thousands were pouring in. Those thousands became millions. The Chinese authorities scrambled frantically for ways to stop the incomers. They began searching for accomplices *inside* the country, dissidents who were working to help these incursions over the borderline. They found a man called Lin Hai, a small-time merchant. He was arrested, put on trial, and imprisoned for attempting to overthrow the state. But the incomers were everywhere by this point, arriving from all sides.

So China began to build a *new* wall – a huge new wall, with hundreds of thousands of guards, and patrols manning its perimeter day and night. The crowds kept coming, but now they broke against the wall, found the way ahead blocked. Yes, there were still breaches. Holes appeared and had to be sealed up. But the great threat had been repelled. The wall stood firm.

The wall's chief architect was a man called Fang Binxing. He came from Harbin, the 'Ice City' of the Heilongjiang province in far northeastern China. But he didn't build his wall from turf, or wood, or iron, or even stone. Rather, he fashioned it from blocks of code, domain-name system filters, fibre-optic gateways.

Construction began in 1998 and has been going on ever since. This wall's fabric is continually shifting, changing, evolving – growing more complex and multi-layered. It is known as the Great *Firewall* of China, and it was conceived as a barrier against the limitless expanses of the internet.

What Fang Binxing had created was a monumental national border – in cyberspace.

The incomers crowding China's gates weren't people. Not exactly, anyway. They were data packages, information flows. Before Fang built his wall, they travelled into China from foreign servers, via millions of links and clicks and emails.

One of their entry points was Lin Hai – the 'merchant', the early internet entrepreneur. A software engineer in Shanghai, he had built up a substantial list of Chinese email addresses as a client database. In 1997, he passed 30,000 of these addresses to Li Hongkuan, a Chinese émigré in Washington, D.C., who ran an email newsletter called *VIP Reference*. The name was taken from the classified reports produced during China's Cultural Revolution – *da cankao*, meaning 'big reference'. They collated censored foreign news reports and were only available to high-ranking members of the Communist Party.

The deal was reciprocal: Lin gave over his email addresses and Li gave him back another 30,000 in return. For Lin, it grew his marketing network. For Li, it boosted his newsletter's circulation. *VIP Reference* was put together by Chinese activists living in exile – with the help of anonymous journalists still working inside the country – and it featured allegations of corruption, detailed critiques of party leaders, editorials on democracy and free speech, and translations of articles from across the global media. (Li himself had been one of the student protestors at Tiananmen Square in 1989, and had left just hours before the tanks rolled in and the shooting started.) By the end of 1999, he claimed to be sending nearly a million emails of *VIP Reference* a day, straight from his computer in Washington to homes and offices all across China.[44]

The authorities sought out the email 'traffickers', the 'smugglers' of border-crossing data. Lin Hai was seized by the Shanghai police in March 1998, and all his computer equipment, modems and floppy disks were confiscated. He was accused by the prosecutors of 'inciting subversion of state power and overthrow of the socialist system', a charge which came with a maximum penalty of life imprisonment. The trial took place behind closed doors, and in just four hours the court ruled on a two-year jail sentence. Lin Hai became China's first-ever internet prisoner.[45]

Others would soon follow. These were high-profile cases, offering a very public demonstration of the potential personal costs of 'misusing' the web in the eyes of the state. The number of people going online in China was rising rapidly. From just around 80,000 in 1996, it had climbed to 7 million by 1999. Prosecution of individuals might act as a deterrent, but the government wanted something more substantial. By this time, Fang Binxing had been appointed Deputy Chief Engineer of the National Internet Emergency Response Centre. He had created his blueprint for a digital wall and, under his direction, its immense fabric was taking shape.[46]

Although this was a barrier in cyberspace, it still had real, physical foundations. There were only three main points that connected the internet in China to the rest of the world, via fibre-optic cables. Two undersea lines led into the country from Japan – one into Beijing to service the north, the other into Shanghai to access the central coastal region – while a third ran from Hong Kong to the south. All internet traffic had to pass through these national gateways, and so Fang and his team installed autonomous network 'sniffers' to patrol the lines: border guards that inspected the content of all data on arrival to decide whether or not it should be stopped or let through.[47]

In essence, the wall was a kind of 'megafilter', and over time its methods of surveillance and censorship grew ever more sophisticated. It began by blocking Domain Name Systems and Internet Protocol Addresses, the unique identifiers of specific websites and webpages: digital passports, if you like. Many sites were blacklisted, turned away at the very point of trying to cross the border. They ranged from the religious movement Falun Gong – banned by the Chinese government, membership is treated as a criminal act – to the web presences of organisations including Amnesty International, Reporters Without Borders and Human Rights Watch. In particular, any site connected to the so-called 'Three Ts' – Tiananmen Square, Tibetan independence or Taiwanese separatism – were instantly denied entry.[48]

Western news outlets like the BBC, CNN, Reuters, Bloomberg and *The New York Times* were switched on and off at will, their access to China revoked during periods of political sensitivity or whenever they ran a story that the government deemed objectionable. (Again, this bled into the real world. 'Offending' media groups might find requests for new journalist visas denied, or barriers put in place to obstruct the renewal of existing visas; some 'news assistants' – who were Chinese nationals – would be subject to telephone harassment or even detention).[49] By 2005, Li Hongkuan's *VIP Reference* was no longer slipping through gaps or climbing over the wall. The mass spamming of emails that had once been so effective was now reduced to a trickle. Almost none were crossing the border, and so, on 30 May of that year, Li pressed send on his last-ever issue.[50]

Today, the wall's filtration system has reached the point where, rather than block whole sites, it can target and block individual pages or even single images that contain 'forbidden' material. 'Good' news stories can pass through the gates. It is only the 'bad' ones that are turned away. Creating the impression, for the ordinary reader in China, that they were never there at all.

When it comes to social media, however, the wall was designed as an impassable barrier. Facebook, YouTube, Twitter, Flickr, Instagram and WhatsApp were – and are – all blocked. Instead, the state has encouraged, indeed nurtured, the development of specific Chinese-built alternatives, from the social media site Renren and the video-hosting platform Youku Tudou, to the blogging app Weibo and the mobile messengers WeChat and Weixin. Developed and run by private enterprise, these services still rely on government licensing, and so are subject to Chinese laws and media controls. Companies sign 'voluntary' public pledges to manage the internet 'in an ethical way' and avoid hosting any content that might 'jeopardise state security and disrupt social stability, contravene laws and regulations and spread superstition and obscenity'.[51]

So broad and vague are these guidelines that it forces profit-driven companies to build caution and conservatism into the systems themselves. Weibo users, for instance, are told explicitly the limits of acceptable discourse, and made aware from the outset that their posts are under constant scrutiny. State controls are first outsourced to private enterprise and then passed down, through the act of using social media itself, to the individual. Censoring, over time, becomes self-censoring.

Working alongside all this is an evolving 'social credit' system, a kind of accounting mechanism for online ethics, which assigns values to what the Chinese government deems positive or negative web behaviours. Operating both at a personal and corporate level, low credit scores can see you expelled from cyberspace, and, in the real world, can close off the Chinese market to your business, or even, for individuals, result in losing your job – or ending up in jail.

Then there are those given the task of manning the wall. This has become one of the fastest-growing professions in China, with cyber guards now numbering over 2 million. But rather than looking outwards beyond the frontier, their eyes are trained *inwards*. Known as network managers, they eavesdrop on digital discussions, always on the hunt among user-generated content for banned words or phrases, rooting out dangerous ideas.[52]

In an essay published in 2018, Zhuang Rongwen, the newly appointed chief of the Cyberspace Administration of China, explained the need to monitor the 'spiritual garden' of the web in order to 'control public sentiment concerning hot social issues, sensitive events, and sudden incidents. Promptly refute mistaken online thinking trends; resolutely control harmful political information that distorts Party history, the nation's history, and military history, or rejects the Party's leadership and the Socialist system'.[53] Helping in this task are an incentivised network of informants: members of the general public who pass on details about 'harmful' material to the state-run China Internet Illegal Reporting Centre and receive cash rewards for any valid tip-offs.[54]

China's president Xi Jinping says this is about 'cleaning up' the internet, filling it with 'positive energy'. For Xi, 'no internet safety means no national security'.[55] And so Fang Binxing's wall has mutated into something much bigger than a barrier for repelling 'barbarian' data and information. Its colossal superstructure has woven itself inwards from its external borderline, infiltrating almost every aspect of daily life in China. (At the time of writing, the country has over 800 million 'netizens'. By the time you read this, it will likely be over a billion. That would be nearly twice the entire physical population of the European Union.)

This walled-in internet, with its custom-built rules of conduct and interaction – learned through trial and error as part of the very process of using social media – has become a vast training ground. It teaches the parameters of personal and political discussion. Provides instruction on how to behave and not to behave, what to believe and what not to believe – backed up by punishments increasing in severity from social credit-score deductions to the death penalty. Netizens learn, in essence, what it is to be Chinese. The wall isn't just a tool to protect national identity from corrupting external influences. It's also a mechanism for shaping national identity itself. The wall, in a sense, *is* national identity.[56]

The ultimate aim of all this is what China calls 'national internet sovereignty'. 'Information dissemination knows no national boundaries,' says Zhuang Rongwen, 'but sovereignty exists in cyberspace.' So, while 'China's great gates of openness to the outside world will not close', they are still gates, and they will only allow 'information flows that are lawful, free and orderly . . . and realistically protect national security and the people's interest'. Just like nations can control the flow of goods and people across its borders, Zhuang says, so they should be able to control the flow of data and communication. At the same time, travelling out beyond the wall will be 'the story of Chinese people striving for a dream, and the story of China persisting in peaceful development, cooperation and win-win, to let the world understand China even better'. To do this, the country – and, indeed, Zhuang argues, all countries – must have a defined, sovereign presence on the internet: what he calls 'a real, three-dimensional and complete China'.[57] A web nation to mirror the physical nation.

Borders have made the leap to cyberspace. More giant walls are rising up to divide the – once seemingly limitless – expanses of the internet. In December 2019, Russia ran its first live test to disconnect from the World Wide Web. For years, Vladimir Putin's government has been planning and passing legislation with this goal in mind – including insisting that all international corporations that host data on Russian citizens have to physically keep that data inside the country itself, bringing their servers within its geographical borders. Russia has taken the blueprint of the Great Firewall and attempted to retrofit it into their own system, creating a hybrid web enclave known as RuNet. In crude terms, it's a vast copy of the internet, designed to operate independently of the rest of the world. And, just as with China, it's subject to intensive surveillance and censorship, and is governed and controlled by Russian law.[58]

This form of digital nationalism is spreading rapidly across the world. China has been exporting a model of its own internet infrastructure, part of what it calls the Belt and Road Initiative – connecting Asia to Africa and Europe through a network of overland corridors, shipping routes and telecommunications channels. Internet packages are offered up that include not just the technology to build a digital border wall, but also the information systems, censorship training and model legislation required to man and operate it. Some sixty countries, including Iran, Egypt, Morocco, Uganda, Zimbabwe, Ecuador and Venezuela, have already invested in China's plug-and-play solution, many of them sold on the idea of avoiding colonisation by a 'Western' internet, dominated by corporations from Silicon Valley.[59]

A great rift is emerging in the fabric of the web. As the former Google CEO Eric Schmidt put it in a speech in San Francisco in 2018, 'the most likely scenario now is not a splintering, but rather a bifurcation':[60] an eastern internet led by China and a western internet led by America. Two huge, cyberspace blocs. With one colossal border running between them. And then will more walls rise up inside these blocs? Walls within walls within walls? Britain already has one. It began constructing its own version of a Great Firewall in 2016; initially designed to repel cyberattacks, it is now evolving to filter out its own version of 'harmful' content.[61]

It seems like the barbarians have made a comeback. Or that, at least, is what we are being told. We thought they were gone for good. But now they are everywhere. They are in our pockets. We can hold them in our hands. We can hear that incessant angry buzz, that digital thrum, like the agitated sound of Gog and Magog behind their iron gate, restless to break free.

National firewalls are built to keep them out, to keep us safe. Cyberborders are reinforced to help us remember who we are and what values we uphold in *our* country, on *our* side of the line. We thought the internet was limitless, but maybe that was pride, maybe that was naivety. We thought it was free and open. But the fear spreads that unstable, antagonistic, even dangerous information flows are roaming its digital plains.

The spectre of Gog and Magog, of the *other*, has re-emerged on the fringes: in the dark spaces of the web, in the angry cacophony of social media, in the faceless, remorseless armies of bots who muster among the cracks of cyberspace. Look to the horizon, over the parapet of your digital frontier. And once again – or so the story goes – the barbarians, 'those people', *are* a solution. Of a sort.

PART 2
MOVING

4

WALLED OFF

The taxi pulled off the road onto a fringe of scrub ground directly beneath the wall. Huge, slate-grey concrete slabs were topped by iron Ys holding curlicues of razor wire. We climbed out and Baha led me down a street between a group of houses. The taxi driver had agreed to wait for us – but I noticed that he kept the engine running. We continued for a hundred metres, until the street opened out and the slope steepened then dropped away to offer a view across the lands to the north and west. A series of rounded hilltops framed the Wadi al-Sarar and the Rephaim Valley, an ancient route leading from the Judean desert to the Mediterranean Sea. The clouds had thickened throughout the day and now the sky was hard and heavy. Mist had already begun to obscure some of those distant hills.

We walked off the road onto a patch of gleaming marble floor fringed by a scattering of small rocks. Then larger ones. We kept going. In a few steps we were clambering up onto huge chunks of rubble that sprouted bent and twisted tendrils of rebar. A soft, persistent rain started to fall. Baha said that we were standing on the ruins of a demolished house. He pointed to an apartment block, further down the hillside, where the family who had built this house now lived. Their home – the one that we were standing on – had been deemed illegal and so was bulldozed to the ground. Because it had found itself on the wrong side of a line. Just like the rest of this village.

Baha pointed out to me the route that the wall took through the landscape. How it undulated down and around the hillside off to the east. How, near the bottom of the valley, it changed from concrete slabs to an eight-metre-high stretch of razor wire enclosing the village's entire northern edge. How one house had found itself on the other side of this barrier, and so the family living there were only able to access their home through an underground tunnel with an electronic gate, operated remotely by military guards. He continued to trace the wall's line, to where its construction continued – from west to south and all the way round to where our taxi was waiting, back up the slope behind us. According to its plans, the wall, once completed, will be a closed loop. It will encircle this whole village.

The rain was heavier now, falling in fat drops among the rubble. I had come to the most bordered place on earth.

Opened in 2018, a high-speed, double-decker train runs from Tel Aviv through Ben Gurion airport and on to Jerusalem. A journey that can take an hour and a half by bus or car has been reduced to a little over twenty minutes. For more than a century the only rail link between Jerusalem and the coast had been an Ottoman-built line that ran south from Jaffa then wound its way slowly through the hills and valleys to the west of the city. The new route does rather less in the way of winding. As it turns southeast and away from the coastal plain it meets the rising hills head on, dives through tunnels cut deep into the bedrock. Most of the journey is spent underground, interrupted by brief interludes of landscape as the train rushes over one tall viaduct or another, spanning the gaps between the mountains and the darkness.

This played havoc with the mobile signal – and the animated, vociferous phone conversation – of the woman sitting opposite me. At the back of the carriage, taking up four seats each, were a young man and young woman, both wearing dark blue T-shirts tucked into green trousers that cinched at the ankle into heavy, matt-black boots. They exuded the kind of languorous self-confidence that, I assumed, came from cradling the assault rifles laid across their laps.

The train pulled into a station platform hollowed out of the rock eighty metres below Jerusalem. This burrowing beneath the city is set to continue. Just the day before I arrived, Israel's Transportation

Minister Bezalel Smotrich had announced official approval for plans to extend the trainline further east, all the way to the Old City and the Western Wall. (Smotrich's predecessor, Israel Katz, had first proposed the development in 2017, suggesting that an Old City station be named after President Donald Trump.) Within hours of this latest announcement, the Jordanian foreign ministry was condemning the decision as a 'flagrant violation of international law'.[1]

Up on the surface, the warm sunshine of Tel Aviv had been replaced by a low ceiling of dark grey cloud and an insistent wind, carrying with it the strong scent of approaching rain. It was dusk, the daylight fading fast. I caught a taxi and we nudged through heavy traffic towards my hotel. Unwittingly, I had booked into a property that had been the subject of a fifteen-year legal battle.

The New Imperial Hotel stands just inside the Jaffa Gate in Jerusalem's Old City. In 2004, its owners, the Greek Orthodox Church, sold a ninety-nine-year lease to a shell company for Ateret Cohanim, a Jewish settler organisation whose stated aim is to 'redeem the land in and around the walled Old City . . . rekindling the flame of Jewish life in the heart and soul of Jerusalem'.[2] The Church has been contesting this sale ever since, alleging that it was conducted illegally by a corrupt former employee who had taken bribes and forged documents.[3] All the while, Ateret Cohanim have been demanding fifteen years of unpaid rent – adding up to over £2 million – from its Palestinian proprietor Abu Walid Dajani, whose family have run the hotel since 1949.

The hotel itself is older still. First built in 1884, the groundwork for its foundations revealed the remains of a cistern which, locals said, was the very pool that Bathsheba bathed in when she caught the wandering eye of David, the first king of the Israelites. It was their son, Solomon, who built the original temple of Jerusalem on a nearby hill that his father bought from a local farmer for fifty silver shekels. The destruction of that temple, its reconstruction and subsequent destruction *again*, haunts this city.

Property, ownership, presence, absence, *belonging*. In the cramped, claustrophobic streets of the Old City, Judaism, Christianity and Islam press up against each other in an incessant, unruly scramble for space. It is what prompts organisations like Ateret Cohanim to amass funds from diaspora donations – most particularly from America – for land and lease purchases, to establish what they call 'footholds' to help them in their mission of 'securing and rebuilding a Jewish Jerusalem'. 'Making,' as they put it, 'the Old City young again.' Taking it back to those heady days of King David.

In the summer of 2019, the Supreme Court of Israel upheld the sale of the hotel and an eviction notice was served on Dajani. 'The Christian properties have been a target for seventy years, but this is the most dangerous so far,' said a spokesman for the Orthodox Church in response to the verdict. 'It is aimed at marginalising Palestinian influence and weakening the Christian presence in the Old City . . . Jerusalem is sacred to the three monotheistic religions, the purpose of the move is to transform the city into a place of hatred and struggle.'[4]

I had put very little thought into booking the New Imperial Hotel. It had simply popped up near the top of my internet search and appeared to offer convenience, affordability and the chance to breathe a little of the recycled air of history. Kaiser Wilhelm II stayed here in 1898, and then two decades later the hotel hosted the British general Edmund Allenby, who addressed the people of Jerusalem from its balcony after he officially accepted the surrender of the city – bringing the curtain down on four centuries of Ottoman rule. Today, its guests are backpackers and tour groups. The clientele may have changed, but the play remains the same. Who owns and controls this land? Who has the right? How far back can you trace your claim? Back to the time of David, when the king was buying up Jerusalem real estate with silver shekels? Back even further than that?

Dajani's family have lived and owned land in this city for at least a millennium. They trace their heritage to the grandson of the Prophet Muhammad, and for 800 years they have been the keepers of the keys to King David's tomb on Mount Zion. Now Dajani frets over suspicious web reservations, believes that guests linked to Ateret Cohanim are taking rooms through Booking.com as a way to force their occupancy of the building.[5] To gain a foothold *in* the foothold. Since the Supreme Court ruling, the settler organisation has called Dajani a 'squatter'. News of his case has even reached the unlikely figure of Vladimir Putin, who, under pressure from the Russian Orthodox Church, has called for the annulment of the sale.

It's not every bed for the night that can offer up such a volatile – and ancient *and* incessant – backstory. As the fate of this hotel hangs in the balance, a new borderline blinks in and out of existence. Lines upon lines upon lines. Running through the lobby, along the corridor, maybe even across the floor of my room. You can't move here for tripping over them.

I was woken early the next morning, just after six o'clock, by the sound of praying. Down in the courtyard, directly below my window, a tour group had gathered. A loud, clear American Midwest accent was praising God for the beautiful day and thanking him, in advance, for the sights that awaited in his holy city.

'We are about to follow in the footsteps of our Lord, Jesus Christ,' the voice said. 'We are walking into history.'

Murmurs of excitement. An 'amen' chorus echoed off the flagstones.

A couple of hours later, I checked out of the New Imperial Hotel, walked around the perimeter of the Old City to the Damascus Gate, and then along Nablus Road to the 'Arab' bus station. I found the 234 bus and climbed on.

The driver pointed past me to another bus. 'That one is for Bethlehem,' he said.

'But this one goes to Checkpoint 300?'

'Yes.'

'That's okay. That's where I want to go.'

The driver shrugged and looked away. 'Five shekels.'

I paid, took the ticket and found a seat. The bus was half full. All the other passengers were young Palestinian students, residents of

East Jerusalem on their way to attend classes at Bethlehem University. On the other side of the wall.

The bus route followed the line of a border. Or a sort of border. Well, not really a border at all. It has been called a 'Ceasefire Line', an 'Armistice Demarcation Line' and, most simply – because of the colour of wax pencil that was first used to mark it on a map – the 'Green Line'.

The Green Line was drawn on 30 November 1948, by Lieutenant Colonel Moshe Dayan and Lieutenant Colonel Abdullah al-Tal. Dayan was a commander in the armed forces of the new state of Israel – a state that had only declared its existence six months earlier – whereas al-Tal was an officer of the Jordanian military and the leader of the combined Arab Legion in Jerusalem. Two men – representing two opposing sides – meant *two* lines. Dayan drew his in green, al-Tal used red, and both marked the areas controlled by their respective armies.[6] Their lines came inland from the middle of the Dead Sea, curved around the lower slopes of the Hebron mountains and bent northeastwards to cut right through the heart of Jerusalem. From the city, they turned west to leave the high ground, twisted north to run along the fringe of the coastal plain – parallel to the foothills of the Wadi Ara – and then eastwards again to meet the northern stretch of the Jordan Valley.[7]

Mostly, the two lines sat directly on top of each other, but in some places they diverged, creating swathes of empty, demilitarised 'no man's lands'. These two lines contained with them two wildly different stories. Two competing and instantly diverging realities. Drawing them marked the ultimate schism in this land – the moment that two parallel worlds were created. And, really, how do you go about mapping those?

Thirty years earlier, when General Allenby entered Jerusalem and Britain assumed administrative control over Palestine, the country had no clear, defined shape at all. Its borderlines proved elusive. They were already an argument. With insouciant imprecision, a 1919 British

Foreign Office memorandum stated that the territory 'may be best described as the Palestine of the Old Testament, extending from Dan to Beersheeba. There is a question as to the exact boundaries, and these will have to be settled by commissioners.'[8] This settling would take years. And all the while, a scramble was going on – had been going on for decades – to occupy and, more importantly, *own* this Old Testament landscape.

In the latter half of the nineteenth century, and in particular after the Russian pogroms of the 1880s, a small yet steady stream of Jewish immigrants started arriving through the port cities of Haifa and Jaffa. Communities bought up plots of – often bare and stony – earth from local Arabs and the Ottoman administration. Discrete pockets of agricultural settlements formed and grew all along the coastal plains of Palestine: *moshavot*, Jewish colonies.[9]

The influx of people brought new opportunities for trade and income, but also, inevitably, led to disputes over territory and boundaries. Absentee owners sold farms that had been worked by tenant families for centuries. Settlers would come to claim their land and evict anyone living there. As one Bedouin group protested to the Ottoman authorities, 'the farm, which was ours since the times of our fathers and grandfathers, was forcefully taken from us by the strangers who do not wish to treat us according to the accepted norms among tillers of the soil, and according to basic human norms or compassion'.[10]

Tensions were rising. The first significant violent clash came in 1886, at one of the original *moshavot*, Petah Tikva (Hebrew for 'door of hope'). It began with a haphazard land sale and a disagreement over grazing rights. Tenant farmers from the Arab village of Yahudiya were asked to vacate fields which they still believed they owned. They proceeded to plough one of these contested fields and confiscated a horse belonging to a Jewish colonist. In response, the Petah Tikva settlers seized nine donkeys. The two communities met to try to resolve the issue, but negotiations broke down. Frustrated, a large group of villagers came to Petah Tikva to take back their donkeys. Accounts vary as to what exactly happened next, but it seems that the Yahudiya men, when they discovered that their animals were not there, began breaking into houses and smashing windows, injuring five settlers in the process. One of them, Rachel Halevy, died several days later – possibly from shock exacerbating an already serious health condition.[11]

Accounts of that day were told and retold, circulating in particular among the Jewish communities in Palestine and abroad. Some dismissed it as a simple conflict over property and money. Others saw in it the sinister echo of the pogroms. In this land of stories and storytelling, where myth and reality everywhere intertwined, it became a kind of settlers' parable, a tale that was as much about the shifting identity of its tellers as it was about the actual events themselves. It offered a simple template – a mob of angry, aggressive Arab males facing off against outnumbered young Jewish male colonists. This template could be changed, embellished and ultimately transformed. What started as a story of victimhood, a cautionary, horribly familiar tale of oppression, was turned into a founding frontier myth, a tale of strength and resilience straight out of a pulp western.[12]

Over time, a new character, Sender Hadad – the son of the unfortunate Rachel Halevy – was introduced into the story as a grand, heroic matinee idol, described as 'a giant of a man . . . with muscles like whip cords, huge fists . . . A heavyweight mounted on a splendid Arab horse, he rode into the thick of every fight, scattering by sheer fury of onslaught, superior numbers.'[13] In original accounts, Hadad had not even been there when the villagers came to Petah Tikva, and returned later to the settlement, taking his ailing mother to Jerusalem for treatment, only for her to die on the journey. Yet increasingly he appeared as the tale's avenging angel, a paragon of physical strength who had, it was said, fought off the horde of murderous villagers almost single-handedly. He was a new kind of Jew – 'a strong man who brought down his heavy hand on all. The Arabs were afraid of him'[14] – the sort of man who could make, and then defend, a country of his own.

It was this very thought that inspired the creation of the Zionist Organisation in Basel, Switzerland, in 1897. 'Zionism,' its founders said, 'aims at establishing for the Jewish people a legally assured home in Palestine.' This was the grand narrative that these individual stories – frontier *moshavot* like Petah Tikva, heroes like Sender Hadad – fed into. Once the land was settled and secured, it could be unified, the colonies brought together to create something more, something greater. A defined space. Perhaps, even, a brand-new state.

Twenty years later, this Zionist cause received a remarkable public and political endorsement. On 2 November 1917, British Foreign Secretary Lord Arthur Balfour wrote to the Zionist Organisation to say that 'His Majesty's government view with favour the establishment in Palestine of a national home for the Jewish people'. What was perhaps most startling about Balfour's declaration was that, just two years earlier, Sir Henry McMahon, the British high commissioner in Egypt, had made a similar commitment to supporting *Arab* independence in Palestine. As the quip went, this ancient country, this Promised Land, had suddenly become the *twice-promised* land.

For the next three decades these two competing – and seemingly irreconcilable – futures first pulled and then finally ripped Palestine apart. New arrivals had continued to shift the country's demographic. Jews had made up less than 10 per cent of the population at the turn of the century. By the start of the 1930s it was nearly 20 per cent and it was rising all the time.[15]

In 1936, Arab discontent over immigration spilled over into militancy, rioting and a co-ordinated general strike. Lord Peel, a former secretary of state for India, was commissioned to investigate the unrest. His assessment was grim. 'An irrepressible conflict has arisen between two national communities within the narrow bounds of one small country,' he wrote. 'There is no common ground between them. Their national aspirations are incompatible. The Arabs desire to revive the traditions of the Arab golden age. The Jews desire to show what they can achieve when restored to the land in which the Jewish nation was born . . . the conflict is aggravated by the uncertainty of the future. Who in the end will govern Palestine?'[16]

A decade later, the United Nations Special Committee Report

painted an even bleaker picture of social and political disintegration. Published in 1947, it cited acts of Arab and Zionist 'terrorism', and outlined an organised Jewish campaign of 'lawlessness, murder and sabotage' designed to ensure that 'nothing should be allowed to stand in the way of a Jewish state'.[17] The previous ten years had seen the rise and fall of Nazi Germany and the terrors of the Holocaust. Palestine had experienced a massive new wave of immigration, and now over 600,000 Jews were resident in the country, while the Arab population had grown to 1.2 million. 'Two sizeable groups,' as the UN report put it, 'with intense nationalist aspirations are diffused throughout a country that is arid, limited in area, and poor in all essential resources.'[18] Division, they said, was the only option.

On 29 November 1947, the UN General Assembly voted to partition Palestine into an Arab and a Jewish state – with the city of Jerusalem to remain under international control. As one world was born, another collapsed. For the Jewish people, the cherished homeland was finally within reach. For the Arabs, however, the inconceivable was happening. They saw no compromise, only injustice and betrayal. The UN's proposed borders were, they said, 'a line of blood and fire',[19] fracturing the land of Palestine, *their* land. They would oppose them at all costs.

As the British withdrew, the country erupted into civil war. What unfolded over the next year was vicious and chaotic. There were massacres and atrocities, villages were destroyed, and people were forced from their lands and their property. Long lines of refugees criss-crossed the country. Some 700,000 Arabs fled or were expelled – amounting to around half of Palestine's Arab population. The Jewish militias and military, emboldened by the heroic frontier myths of Sender Hadad and the first colonists, and haunted by the recent memory of an attempted genocide, were uncompromising and brutal. Communities and families were riven and scattered.

And at the end of it all, two men bent over a map and – with red and green pencils – sketched out an alternative reality. Palestine had gone. Nearly 80 per cent of it now had a new name: Israel. The rest, situated in the West Bank, in East Jerusalem and in Gaza, was to be administered by Jordan and Egypt. Many Palestinians were now refugees in their own land, a land without a name, but with lines running through it that they could not cross. They could not go back to their homes and villages now that the shooting had stopped, could not even collect their belongings, and those who tried were called 'infiltrators' and were arrested or shot. The Arabs called it the *Nakba*. The catastrophe.

A line of freedom and independence. A line of exile and humiliation. That's quite a bus route. Highway 60 – known as Road One – now lies on top of the Green Line. My bus joined this highway and moved slowly through the morning traffic, dropping down into the valley alongside the Old City and Mount Zion, joining up with the Hebron Road that leads south to Bethlehem. In the aftermath of 1948, this had been no man's land. A long, winding strip of concrete walls, barbed wire, minefields and fortified observation posts that ran through the whole of Jerusalem: the Green Line as a jagged, bristling reality.

The Palestinian writer and philosopher Sari Nusseibeh was just a boy when the city was cut in two. His bedroom window overlooked the 'shoot-to-kill zone' that separated his family home in East Jerusalem from the Mea Shearim, the Jewish neighbourhood of the strictly religious Haredim – the 'Awestruck Ones'. 'Between the back of our garden wall and the State of Israel,' he wrote, 'were: one lonesome, semi-destroyed and bullet-ridden cement structure; a UN observation and border crossing station; and scattered rocks and thistles growing among the odd landmine. There was also a grapevine that had managed to survive all the fighting. In springtime I used to stare for hours at the vine's new leaves, and in the fall I watched the juicy grapes grow big.'[20]

On the other side of no man's land, less than a mile to the west of Nusseibeh's home, was another writer in the making – the ten-year-old Amos Oz. Born in Jerusalem to Lithuanian and Ukrainian immigrant parents, Oz described himself as a 'little Zionist-nationalist fanatic' who, 'in the days of the original intifada – the one instigated by us Jews against the British occupation', joined in with all the other children in his neighbourhood to throw stones at the British vehicles that patrolled the streets. One of his favourite childhood preoccupations was playing war games: 'moving troops, besieging a castle or a city, routing, taking by storm, starting a resistance movement in the mountains'; overseeing a constant territorial to and fro across his living-room floor, 'extending or contracting frontiers marked out by matchsticks'. Now, a real frontier had come to him. 'Sometimes we were woken up in the early hours by machine-gun salvoes from the direction of the armistice line . . . or the wailing of muezzin on the other side of the new border: like a hair-raising lament the howl of this prayer penetrated our sleep.'[21]

Both boys found themselves drawn inexorably towards the line. Here was a psychic rift in the fabric of Jerusalem, the only city they had ever known. For Nusseibeh, the 'forbidden territory' began at the end of his own garden, and so hardly a day would go by that he didn't spy on the streets on the other side of no man's land, observing the 'strange' buses, cars and people as they moved around. 'Sometimes the bearded creatures looked back at me,' he said. 'It was almost like being in a dream.'[22] Oz too would 'stare wide-eyed at the other Jerusalem – frightening yet alluring, with all its concealed enchantments, its warrens of narrow streets that were forbidden to us and threatened us out of the darkness, a secretive, malign city, pregnant with disaster'.[23]

It was never supposed to be a border. The UN Armistice Agreement maps – which were simply copies of Dayan and al-Tal's map – stated explicitly that 'this map must *not* be considered an authority on the delimitation of international boundaries'. The Armistice Agreement itself, signed in 1949, stressed that the 'Demarcation Lines' were established 'without prejudice to future territorial settlements or boundary lines'.[24] The Green Line was always intended as a quick pencil stroke, contingent and temporary: a way to mark the ceasefire, the pause in hostilities, in geographical space. Yet the pause stretched out longer and longer. Months passed. Then years. Then a decade.

As the two boys grew older, they came more and more to probe this dividing line, exploring the strange constrictions and contusions that had been formed by hacking the urban landscape apart and then hastily sealing up the wounds. 'I walked to the shrapnel-lashed Damascus Gate,' wrote Nusseibeh, 'and into the labyrinth of streets and alleys, and then all the way to the Jaffa Gate, which had been sealed shut after the war. Did the gate lead nowhere or everywhere? Maybe both.'[25]

Oz, by then a lovesick teenager, would exorcise his nihilistic urges by sneaking out of his house every night, and mooching along the perimeter. 'I felt attracted to the barbed-wire fence and the minefields that divided the city,' he said, 'and once, in the dark, straying perhaps into one of the areas of no man's land, I accidently trod on an empty can which made a noise that sounded as loud as a landslide, and immediately two shots rang out from quite nearby in the dark and I ran away. Still, I went back the next evening and the following ones to the edge of no man's land.'[26]

Gradually, this division, this length of concrete and corrugated iron, felt almost normal. 'No man's land seemed as immutable as the desert at our back,' said Nusseibeh. 'It had become a benign presence.'[27] Benign, and seemingly permanent. Beyond the city and into the countryside, however, the Green Line had almost no physical presence. In the 1950s, the Israelis made basic attempts to mark it in the landscape – fixing iron posts into blocks of concrete, setting up lines of barrels and oil drums – but even this process was fraught with difficulty. Dayan and al-Tal's lines had been drawn on two separate 1:250,000 British survey maps (which then had to be taped together). The scale meant that the width of the pencil marks themselves equated to nearly one hundred metres. Given that the Green Line ran for a total of 310 kilometres, this created one long, snaking corridor of imprecise, debatable land. It was a shadow border, defined by its own innate imprecision, a blur in the rift between the two parallel worlds of Israel and not-Israel.

Then, in 1967, nineteen years after it was first drawn, an attempt was made to erase the Green Line completely. The Six-Day War, which stemmed, initially, from clashes between Israel and Syria over water resources, escalated to follow the same pattern as 1948. The combined Arab forces of Egypt, Syria and Jordan were arranged against the Jewish homeland. It was a story that went all the way back to Petah Tikva – with Moshe Dayan, now installed as Israeli Minister of Defence, taking the Sender Hadad role. The war was a disaster for the Arabs and a stunning victory for the Israeli Defence Force. They pushed Egypt out of Gaza and all the way back to the Suez Canal; took the Golan Heights from Syria; and removed Jordan from Jerusalem and the West Bank entirely. Everything that was once British Mandatory Palestine was now under Israeli control.

In December of that year, the Israeli government took the decision to have the Green Line removed from all published maps, atlases and textbooks.[28] Yet, apart from the area around Jerusalem, they did not officially annex the land gained during the war. Under international law, Gaza and the West Bank were deemed 'occupied territories': a space where the Israeli military, as opposed to the Israeli government, would hold legislative, executive and judicial control. With the Green Line now effectively gone – and only ever marked in the most cursory and haphazard fashion anyway – it meant that even Israel's shadow border had dissolved. The blurring of territory now extended for hundreds of miles, all the way to the Dead Sea and the River Jordan. There was no border and there still isn't. How can there be? The land today remains 'occupied' because the war has not officially ended. To put it bluntly, no one really knows where *exactly* Israel ends and the Occupied Territories begin.

In Jerusalem, no man's land was dismantled. The presence of a long strip of waste ground in the heart of the city offered a perfect, empty, unowned space for new road construction. It meant that routes like Highway 60 – the road I was travelling on now – could follow the old line perfectly through the city, running from north to south. For those Palestinian families still living in Jerusalem, the removal of the barrier induced a kind of dazed shock. Nusseibeh, by then a student at Oxford University, travelled home and was stunned.

'It was miraculous to see how the barbed wire and shoot-to-kill zones, things I had lived with since childhood, were gone,' he wrote. 'It was only then that it dawned on me how the war had ended the division of my country. *Defeat had given me back my homeland.*'

It did not take long, however, for his optimism to sour. The morning after he returned, he jumped over the garden wall behind his house and onto the once forbidden stretch of land. The grapevine was still there and he picked a grape eagerly and popped it in his mouth. 'The taste wasn't the sumptuous burst of flavour I had long imagined. It was bitter, and I spat it out.'[29]

A new period of limbo began. The occupation continued for months, then years. There appeared to be neither the prospect nor intention of withdrawal. The new masterplan for the Jerusalem municipality, drawn up in 1968, had as its 'cardinal principle' the intention to 'build the city in a manner that would prevent the possibility of its being repartitioned'.[30] The city boundaries were redrawn to loop in as many Jewish communities around the periphery as possible – including villages and farms. Meanwhile, Arab and Palestinian leaders were suddenly arguing for the reinstatement of the 1949 agreement – the return of the Green Line.

'They wanted the wall back,' wrote Nusseibeh. 'No man's land had allowed them to hide the reality of the Jewish state behind a veil of concrete, as one might hide an object of shame.'[31] Over time, he watched as Jerusalem was transformed by massive Israeli construction and infrastructure projects, yet it was 'nearly impossible' for Arabs to get building permits. Everywhere he saw attempts to marginalise and segregate Palestinians and maintain what was called the 'demographic balance', ensuring there were significantly more Jewish than Arab residents in the city.

'An invisible no man's land was being created,' Nusseibeh said, 'this one by ideology and psychology rather than by concrete and barbed wire.' Increasingly, he felt like he was witnessing not so much a division of his home, as a vivisection: 'a slow act of homicide, the killing of a city that constituted the soul of my family and of my people'.[32]

My bus left Jerusalem behind. Traffic eased as the highway emerged from the city into a stretch of open countryside. Green, stony hillsides, still wet from the previous night's rain, glittered in the morning sun. On one side of the bus I could see, in the distance, the sandy-brown mountains that led off towards the Judean Desert. On the other, houses and roads under construction, the footprints of Jerusalem still extending steadily southwards.

We passed a terraced hill on our right, and then, beyond it, the land unfurled gently into an open plain covered with a huge, sprawling olive grove. My gaze followed the olive trees downslope – until they all stopped abruptly. A huge concrete wall snaked across the hillside. It was studded at intervals with circular watchtowers, and it curved and bent, a sinuous, unbroken grey line that stretched far off over the hills and out of sight. In this land, the borders come in waves: rising, falling, subsiding, then – when the storms arrive, as they inevitably do – soaring up above the earth.

The road continued on, up to the very base of the wall. We all filtered off the bus to walk through a metal gateway: Checkpoint 300. A large blue sign above our heads read '*Bon Voyage*' – there were similar good-byes in Arabic. I followed the small procession of students through a tight turnstile, then down a long, narrow, high-ceilinged concrete tunnel, painted with grey and red stripes – the pattern directing you downhill, out of Israel and into the Occupied Territories of the West Bank.

'You push people out physically, but that's not the first step. The first step is you push people out mentally, right? You take away the humanity of a person, and then you treat them like shit. And then at the end of the day you say, *well, they're not a person to begin with*.'

I was sitting with Baha Hilo in the Singer Café in the small town of Beit Sahour, just a mile or so southwest of Checkpoint 300. Baha, a sociologist and activist, is a co-founder of To Be There, a grassroots collective of local Palestinians, whose work ranges across human rights and refugee support to youth mentoring and political tourism. He was thickset with long, curly black hair tucked into a huge, crocheted hat, and he liked to roll his own cigarettes as he spoke lugubriously.

'They accuse us of leaving, you know? The State of Israel says Palestinians were not expelled. We just left because we felt like going out for a walk. We all collectively decided to walk away. Of course we did! Many nations have the urge of just going out for a hike, right?'

Baha had spread a map out across our table. It was covered in lines and blotches of colour, showing areas and zones: Israeli roads and Palestinian roads and military roads; Israeli settlements and Palestinian towns and military bases and checkpoints. It was like looking at a microscopic cross-section of bone tissue, at once familiar and utterly alien.

The café was busy – with free Wi-Fi, it's a popular spot for UN and NGO workers – and it had filled up throughout the morning. It was called Singer after the famous American sewing-machine manufacturer, and a number of beautiful old machines were positioned in alcoves or hung over the bar or even set into the tables. (I had asked Baha about the significance. 'There isn't any really,' he said. 'The artist-owner is a wealthy guy. He just liked how the sewing machines looked so he bought some.') The Singer Café was one of the first of a wave of arts-led redevelopments of Beit Sahour. Over the past few years, a number of the Old Town's derelict buildings, with their thick stone walls and ornate, vaulted ceilings, had been transformed into galleries and artisan work spaces. And, of course, coffee shops. The massive, chrome Italian coffee machine behind Singer's bar was a statement of intent. The coffee was very good.

I was talking to Baha about land, about the events after 1967, when the occupation began. What has happened, he told me, is the same thing that has been happening since the nineteenth century – a continual process of removal and replacement.

'Everything about the State of Israel, from day one, is about robbing Palestinian families of their land,' he said bluntly. 'The government is about passing laws to legalise land theft. The army does the same thing. Private sector does the same thing too. Even God, in the state of Israel, is a god who works as a real-estate agent. He has signed this piece of land – this particular piece of land – he has signed that to the Jewish people. Not an inch bigger, not an inch smaller, not an iota to the right. The exact same land.'

So was it God, I asked, who drew those borders?

'God, to a person with racist mentalities, is a God that *makes mistakes*,' Baha replied. 'So it is down to them to correct God's mistakes. So God gave this land to the Jewish people, but he made the mistake of creating Palestinians on it. So then the State of Israel has to come along to correct God's mistakes.'

Baha paused, rolled a cigarette paper back and forth in his fingers.

'Jewish nationalists have always viewed Palestine as a land without people. "A land without people for a people without land." But to say Palestine is a land without people you have to erase 10,000 years of human history.'

For Baha, Europe, and the European mindset, was to blame.

'What is happening here comes from Europe. It is settler colonialism. The ideology that rules over Palestine is a European ideology. This is why when you landed in Tel Aviv it felt like you were in Europe. You didn't feel like you are in the Middle East, right? It is Europe in the Middle East. They called it "Switzerland in the Middle East". What do we have in common with Switzerland?' He paused and fixed me with a look. 'Pine trees.'

Here, even the trees have been politicised, given a role to play in defining and claiming the land. According to the Applied Research Institute of Jerusalem, more than 800,000 indigenous olive trees have been uprooted by Israeli authorities and settlers since 1967.[33] At the same time, organisations like the Jewish National Fund (JNF), which was established in 1901 to buy and develop land exclusively for the benefit of the Jewish people, has planted in excess of 250 million pine trees.[34]

'Pine trees are not native,' Baha said. 'Their needles are acidic. They destroy the soil. I have no idea if Israeli environmentalists or Israelis in general care about the destructive impact of pine trees. They just wanted something that grows fast and changes the landscape.'

I thought of the Palestinian writer and lawyer Raja Shehadeh, who has chronicled, with mournful eloquence, the physical transformation of this land: a land that he has known his whole life. In his book

Palestinian Walks, he describes seven journeys made on foot across the hills and *wadis*, taken over the years between 1978 and 2007. 'In two and a half decades,' he writes, 'one of the world's treasures, this biblical landscape that would have seemed familiar to a contemporary of Christ, was being changed, in some parts beyond recognition.' On the subject of pine trees, one particular passage by Shehadeh had stuck with me.

'All it took was for one tree to establish roots. Then when it seeded, its cones would open, spreading seeds from terrace to terrace, multiplying the pines at the expense of those trees that had been there long before them . . . they grew tall and large, forcefully claiming the land where they struck root. Like the olive trees their roots remained close to the surface, knotted and smooth like knuckles, scrambling for the same piece of ground, making it hard for them to coexist.'[35]

Scrambling for the same ground. Hard to coexist.

'Are the trees a metaphor?' I asked Baha.

He was silent for a moment, giving me another one of his looks. 'No,' he said. 'They are actual trees. I think there's no metaphors here.'

Since 2001, Baha has been a co-ordinator of the Olive Tree Campaign, which invites visitors to work with Palestinian farmers on their olive harvests, and which has, over the past two decades, overseen the planting of some 90,000 new olive trees, sponsored by donations from individuals and organisations across the world. Yet it is an effort that is dwarfed by the activities of the JNF over the same period.

In 2010, the multi-million pound 'greening' of the Negev desert began, including the planting of a million pine trees to create the 'GOD TV forest' – named after its sponsor, an evangelical Christian television channel, whose owners Rory and Wendy Alec have said that God himself told them to plant the trees to prepare the land for the return of Jesus. In the process, the Bedouin desert village of al-Araqib was completely levelled – its houses demolished, its population expelled.[36] The JNF, however, claimed that they were redeeming a 'dead' landscape, pioneering afforestation technologies in a harsh environment which they can then export 'to countries where farming has the potential to prevent starvation'.

I could see why Baha was resistant to metaphors.

Trees have become physical actors, surrogates for real people, and have been given a significant role in the perpetual battle for territory. Recent research has found that some eighty-six villages evacuated in 1948 now lie beneath JNF forests.[37] It is a process that the Israeli historian Ilan Pappé calls 'memoricide'[38] – turning lived landscapes into pristine 'nature' and 'wilderness', erasing or hiding the physical traces of Palestinian history beneath a kind of artificial, prelapsarian forest canopy.

Baha told me that Israel still enforces an Ottoman land law from 1858, which says that any land left uncultivated for three years reverts to 'state' ownership. As a result, one of the main aims of the Olive Tree Campaign is to help Palestinian farmers maintain possession of their property. Because once olive trees are planted, it is evidence that land is being cultivated.

And so the pine forests and the olive groves jostle for position all across the countryside, creating physical and symbolic frontiers between Israeli and Palestinian space. These two tree species have been co-opted to create a multiplicity of borderlines, their planting and management creating an ecological power struggle, a living form of border control. For a time, the pine forests were confined to the 1948 boundaries of Israel. But, after 1967, they began to spread into the hills and mountains of the West Bank. And people came with them.

The erasure of the Green Line had created a new frontier. The Occupied Territories offered a 'wild' space where young, idealistic Jewish nationalists could live out the rugged, mythologised lives of their pioneering forebears. It began in the most basic fashion: small groupings of caravans or mobile homes driven up to hilltops, then arranged in a circle like wagons in a John Ford western. For the settlers, this was 'God-given' territory – not the West Bank, but the biblical land of 'Judea and Samaria', part of 'Eretz Israel': Greater Israel. For the state, because these rocky, windswept summits were uncultivated, ownership could be claimed under the old Ottoman law, despite this being deemed illegal under the terms of the Geneva

Convention. As the settlements grew, they pushed further into Palestinian land, often leading to clashes with local farmers or villagers. It was Petah Tikva all over again. Except this time, Sender Hadad came in the form of the Israeli Defence Force.

Protracted legal disputes would play out in the Israeli courts, but more settlements kept appearing, the so-called 'youth of the hill' using the bureaucratic confusion and the tacit – or increasingly explicit – support of the government or private enterprise to stake their claims. Over time, these ad hoc communities were transformed. Gone were the mobile homes, and in their place came sturdy, red-roofed limestone villas, arranged into huge, master-planned, multi-million-dollar suburban estates crowning hilltop after West Bank hilltop.

Throughout his many years as a lawyer and human rights activist, Raja Shehadeh fought these developments. Yet any victories were hard won and fleeting. 'As a child I used to cast my eyes across the elusive divide between the West Bank and Israel,' he wrote. 'The town was here and over there was usurped Jaffa on the horizon. And nothing was in between . . . When Israel began establishing settlements, opening roads though the hills, flattening hilltops and connecting far-flung places with water and electricity I was filled with awe. And fear.'[39]

Today, more than 500,000 Jewish people are settled in the Occupied Territories, in nearly 200 settlements. Networks of roads – most of which Palestinians are prohibited from using – soar over valleys or cut through mountains to connect the settlements to the coastal plain and the cities. Where once the division between Israel and Palestine was a simple pencil line, now the border has become entirely elastic. It is stretched at will by the growth of more and more settlements, the construction of roads and infrastructure, and the continued appropriation of 'uncultivated' land for purposes ranging from 'security' to 'conservation' (almost a quarter of the Occupied Territories are now designated 'state land').[40] In fact, it is not useful to think of one continuous line. Rather, the 5,655 square kilometres of the West Bank have become a sort of border archipelago, a series of shrinking and expanding islands: ebbing, flowing, never fixed. And then into this dynamic and fragmented landscape has come the ultimate symbol of rigidity and permanence: the Wall.

The wall emerged out of the relentless violence of the early 2000s. The second *intifada* – an 'uprising' to the Palestinians, a 'terror campaign' to the Israelis – led to years of protests, riots, murders, rocket attacks, suicide bombings, sieges and unrestricted urban warfare. Thousands were killed. The fluidity and multiplicity of borders meant that the battle lines were everywhere.

The Israeli government response was to make absolutely clear the lines of *separation* throughout the entire landscape. They would build a vast, fortified barrier, the most expensive single project in the history of the state. The first section opened in June 2002, running through an olive orchard in the town of Selim in Jenin. Almost two decades, 700 kilometres and $3 billion later, construction continues. Perhaps it will never stop.

'But you know Israel has different walls, right?' Baha said. 'You can see visible *and* invisible walls. Invisible walls meaning that there is a reason that Palestinian communities do not grow naturally in an urban way. There are Palestinian communities in Israel who have not been allowed to grow by *an inch* since 1949. Because they are not given permits to build on their property. The State of Israel sometimes recognises that your family property *is* your family property. Which means, "We've still not found a way to rob your family of your property, so it's yours. But, until we find a way to rob your family of your property, you are not allowed to build on it."'

Baha got out his phone, tapped in a number, and began to talk in Arabic. 'A taxi is coming,' he said.

We went outside to wait, and Baha smoked his roll-up. The sun had gone, replaced by a flat grey sky. A cold wind was blowing through the narrow streets of Beit Sahour.

'Not far from here there is a village,' he told me. 'Al-Walaja. It is a place that has *everything*, all at once.'

We climbed over the rubble of a bulldozed house in al-Walaja and looked out across the valley towards al-Walaja. Down in the valley was the Green Line. The al-Walaja on the opposite hillside was the old al-Walaja. We were in the new al-Walaja. All that was left of the old town were a few ruined stone buildings. In this al-Walaja, however, the ruins were brand new.

In the summer of 1948, Israeli forces attacked the old village and the people fled southeast, across the *wadi*. When the war ended and the Armistice Line was drawn, almost all of al-Walaja's lands were included within Israel. Yet a small portion of cultivation terraces, with groves of olive, fig and apricot trees, remained on the other side, in the hills of the West Bank. Around a hundred villagers chose to settle here, rebuilding their lives and their community within sight of their old homes.[41]

But borders just would not leave al-Walaja alone. After the occupation in 1967, Israel redrew the municipal boundary of Jerusalem to run right through the centre of the village. Suddenly, half of al-Walaja was in the city, while the other half was still in the West Bank. Yet those now deemed to be living within the Jerusalem boundary were not given residency rights. They existed in a kind of nowhere zone, a geographical limbo. Over the years, many of these residents were detained or arrested for entering Jerusalem illegally – without ever leaving their homes.

Then came the land seizures and the house demolitions. Large stretches of the hillsides were appropriated from al-Walaja for the construction of the Jewish settlements of Gilo and Har Gilo. Homes were bulldozed to the ground because they had been constructed without building permits – permits which villagers were either denied or, in the case of those living within the Jerusalem municipality, not even allowed to apply for.[42] Because, well, you can't build in a vacuum, can you?

The ruins we were standing on belonged to a house that had been demolished just a couple of years earlier: one of more than eighty knocked down in al-Walaja over the past three decades. Baha pointed out house after house that had a demolition order hanging over it. Buildings living on borrowed time.

But still there was more. When the plans for the construction of the wall were first revealed, the intention was to run it along the Jerusalem boundary line: cutting al-Walaja in two. The community successfully appealed to the Israeli High Court, and the wall was re-routed – to encircle the whole village instead. And so now the wall clings tightly to its built-up areas, leaving most of the agricultural lands on the other side in what is known as a 'Seam Zone' – those parts of the West Bank that find themselves between the wall and the 1948 Green Line. Farmers have to pass through gates in the barrier to work their fields or gather their harvests. Then, in 2013, the Jerusalem Municipality approved the establishment of a national park which extended into this seam zone, right on top of al-Walaja's farmlands.[43]

This was less separation than *suffocation*. The village was hemmed in, constricted, surrounded by walls and fencing, its lands left on the outside steadily picked off and given over to development, construction or recreation.

'This wall,' Baha said, 'is about leaving as many Palestinians as possible on one side and as much land as possible on the other. What Israel wants is the land; what Israel doesn't want is the people.'

Yet still al-Walaja persists. Further down the village, just a few metres from the stretch of razor wire that marks out its northern edge, grows what is thought to be the oldest olive tree in all of Palestine. It is a massive presence – rising twelve metres high, its trunk twenty-five metres in diameter, a tangle of huge, gnarled knots – and it still produces olives every season, up to 600 kilogrammes of them in a good year. Baha said it was four, maybe five thousand years old. A wonder, 'a blessed tree'. A tree that has witnessed so much of the human history of this landscape, it has lived through the Old and the New Testaments, seen empires come and go. The wall is so close to the tree now that it rests beneath the shade of its branches. And underground, its roots stretch out, down into the earth, spreading far and wide – perhaps, even, working their way beneath the fencing and the razor wire, and into the land on the other side.

The rain suddenly came on heavy. Huge, cold splashes detonated among the rubble. We jogged back up the hill towards the taxi. Ahead of us was the wall. Beyond it, on the hilltop right behind al-Walaja – built on the stony, 'uncultivated' summit – was the settlement of Har Gilo. Over the top of the barbed wire I could see a balcony window on the upper story of one of its houses. A figure, indistinct behind the glass, seemed to watch us all the way, until we were obscured from view behind the wall's grey concrete.

'This wall doesn't really separate Palestinians from Israelis, you know,' Baha said. 'Because there are Palestinians and Israelis on one side and Palestinians and Israelis on the other side. But the wall is an *obstacle*. Is it an obstacle for a Jewish Israeli person? No. A Jewish Israeli doesn't experience a checkpoint. They greet you, give you a nice wave. That is a checkpoint *for them*. As a Palestinian it is something else. The wall is an obstacle between Palestinians and Palestinians. The checkpoint is an obstacle between Palestinians and Palestinians. And the wall is an obstacle between Palestinians and their property.'

It was late afternoon. The roads were busy as we tried to make our way back east towards Bethlehem. Down in the next valley was a pristine stretch of fast-moving, dual-laned highway, fringed on both sides by massive, overhanging concrete barriers. It disappeared at each end into tunnels cut through the hillsides. For Palestinians living in the West Bank, it was a prohibited road. For Jewish settlers living in the West Bank, it was an expressway home. Right in the centre of this road's concrete barrier I could see a massive graffiti mural that read 'Stand Taller than Walls'.

Baha turned around and said to me, all of a sudden, 'I'm forty years old and I've never known freedom. In twenty years I'll be sixty and I still won't have known freedom. I'll never know freedom.'

It felt like he had said these words before. Perhaps many times. To journalists, visitors, political tour groups. There was something rehearsed, almost performative in the phrasing. That did not make it any less sincere. But it did hint at a weariness I sensed in him. There is a phrase in Arabic – *sumud*, 'steadfastness' – that has become the ideology of Palestinian resistance to the occupation. It is about a sense of rootedness in the land, of always holding on, no matter what. Of enduring. *Resistance through existence.* But it must exert a heavy mental toll. I recalled something Baha had said to me earlier that day.

'Seventy years of oppression does make people accumulate a form of numbness. It is not normal. But it becomes common. It becomes something we are used to.' Another thing to struggle with – finding the space, the seam zone, between anger and numbness. It *is not* normal.

Traffic clogged the roads of Bethlehem. We were near a checkpoint. Queues of vehicles were backed up, and the air was filled with exhaust fumes and the sound of car horns. We squeezed through gaps and made our way slowly across town. Throughout the journey, stretches of the wall came in and out of sight. Now we were right alongside it again, following its path through the urban landscape until it turned at right angles to run down a narrow lane.

We had reached my stop. The hotel with the worst view in the world.

In 2017, a century after Alfred Balfour signed his declaration promising British support for a Jewish homeland in Palestine, a hotel opened in a derelict pottery works in Bethlehem, set just four metres away from the West Bank Wall. The construction and installation had taken fourteen months and was carried out in absolute secrecy. Even its staff of forty-five local Palestinians did not know the identity of their new boss. All that changed when its owner released a statement to the world's media.

'It is exactly one hundred years since Britain took control of Palestine and started rearranging the furniture – with chaotic results,' it read. 'I don't know why, but it felt like a good time to reflect on what happens when the United Kingdom makes a huge political decision without fully comprehending the consequences.'

The statement was signed off by the elusive and enigmatic British graffiti artist Banksy. This was, arguably, his most ambitious work. A hotel in the West Bank, conceived as a living, fully functioning and permanent art installation, made up of nine bookable rooms, a piano bar, a museum, a gallery and a bookshop. Its name was set – literally – in lights above the front door: The Walled Off Hotel.

The result was one giant, Banksy *matroyshka* doll – an artwork containing artworks inside artworks inside artworks. I sat in the piano bar at a candlelit table, eating a plate of salty za'atar and drinking a local Palestinian beer. Opposite me, a baby grand – its make concealed beneath a white smear of spray paint – played by itself. Although programmed with bespoke arrangements, it can also be operated remotely, and it has welcomed 'live' performances from musicians such as Hans Zimmer, Trent Reznor, Massive Attack and Elton John. The whole aesthetic of the lounge was a kind of shabby, British-colonial chic: part gentlemen's club, part tea room. There were leather chesterfield sofas, cut-crystal glasses, and palm trees with small, tattered and dusty Union Jack flags sticking out of their pots.

Banksy's artwork covered every wall surface. Behind the piano was a blocked-up, graffitied window, outlined in shifting neon light. Dangling in front of it were three cherubs, two wearing makeshift gas masks, the third reaching out for a mask but missing, caught in a pose of forever falling towards the ground. On another wall, crucifixes had been refashioned as giant grappling hooks, while security cameras were mounted on wooden shields like hunting trophies. In a fireplace near the lobby door, artificial flames glowed beneath a 'flammable' sign and a pile of rubble and rebar. Even my room key was an artwork, designed as a six-inch-high replica of a T-shaped segment of the wall. The hole for the key chain was the hole found at the top of every real concrete slab, used by cranes to lift and lower sections of the wall into place.

From my seat I could also see, down a short corridor and past a white marble bust wreathed in a circle of tear-gas smoke, a life-sized dummy of Alfred Balfour. He was sitting at a desk with a pen in his hand, a map of the Sykes–Picot Agreement on the wall behind him. A sign invited you to 'Press button for historic re-enactment'. I walked over to press it and watched as Balfour's hand circled chaotically over a replica of his declaration, madly signing his name again and again until, after a while, his automatic arm juddered to a halt.

Before I left him, I had asked Baha what he thought of Banksy's hotel.

'I don't think,' he said. 'I'm not a person who thinks a lot.'

Unsatisfied with this answer – Baha was clearly a person who thought a great deal – I had probed him a little more.

'You know, King David was born in the city of Bethlehem. Jesus Christ was born in the city of Bethlehem. Now Banksy has a business in the city of Bethlehem,' he said, giving a wry laugh. 'You have to talk about the important things that happened in Bethlehem, you know? King David, Jesus and Banksy . . .'

Since the hotel opened, it has proved enormously popular, both for guests and for daytrippers. Some reports suggested that it is even rivalling the Church of the Nativity – the birthplace of Jesus – as Bethlehem's most popular attraction. It was clearly intended as a work of protest art, channelling Banksy's particular brand of humour and subversion. But did Baha, as someone who had been born and brought up in Bethlehem, feel like he shared in this protest?

'That's irrelevant,' he said. 'With the Banksy hotel, the debate is very simple. People say it's good. People say it's bad. That's all. What I think is irrelevant.'

He was quiet for a while longer and then he continued. 'Look, what the debate on the Banksy hotel does is that it intentionally shifts the conversation about four metres. *Away from where the Israeli wall is.* Because the wall did not only destroy the building the hotel is in now. It destroyed the entire northern part of Bethlehem. It destroyed businesses on the highway that once connected Bethlehem, Jerusalem and Hebron together – one of the oldest routes in Palestine. Joseph and Mary walked on these routes. Abraham walked on these routes. So when you are talking about something that has been functioning for thousands of years, and then the State of Israel comes in and destroys it, it becomes a little bit more interesting, you know, than whatever an artist from Bristol has come here to do. So I'm not going to say it's a positive thing or a negative thing. It's just a thing, you know?'

I drank my beer and looked out the window. I was sitting just metres away from the de facto border between Israel and the West Bank. It certainly had my attention. I could sense its restlessness. It had pushed deep into Bethlehem, a long finger of concrete. But it wasn't a symbol of permanence. Rather, it was one of movement. I could tell that it was anxious to push further, to self-replicate, to keep going. To smash through the glass of the lobby, through the hotel and then the streets beyond, to reach even deeper into the city. Look away from it for a second, and you could imagine it creeping forward, stealing another metre or two, coming close enough to press up against the glass and peer in at you. It was dark outside now. The graffiti was faded and indistinct in the gloom. Inside the bar, the piano played on.

My bedroom was like a set from a Wes Anderson film. Bright blue walls and massive red Persian carpets. A desk and side tables with everything arranged just so: piles of books, ceramic dishes, candlesticks, a cocktail shaker, two ice buckets, an antique radio, a black and gold teapot, a glass bottle stuffed with five red feathers. On first entering the room, I'd been given a spiral-bound booklet that itemised everything I'd find there – even down to the number of fake flowers in one small porcelain jug (thirteen, in case you're interested). Photographs showed exactly how it should all be arranged. I had to check off each item and notify reception if anything was missing or out of place. As the hotel explained, this was a property that was full of 'valuable works of art, some of which you are permitted to lock yourself alone with overnight'. Above my bed was a very large Banksy original, depicting the crucifixion in the style of the graffiti-art pioneer Jean-Michel Basquiat. I decided not to go anywhere near it with a glass of water.

Later that night, I watched a video on my phone of a man walking through Jerusalem carrying a can of green paint. There was a hole in the bottom of the can, and so, as the man walked, a thin, constant stream of paint ran out to leave a line on the ground. The video was only seventeen minutes long and was made up of a montage of moments from a twenty-four-kilometre journey on foot through the city – along roads, past the Jaffa Gate and the Old City, through Palestinian neighbourhoods and Jewish neighbourhoods and derelict ground and even military checkpoints.

The man was the Belgian conceptual artist Francis Alÿs, and the route he was taking followed, as closely as possible, the path of the Green Line – redrawing the phantom border in green paint (fifty-eight litres, as it turned out).[44] Alÿs then showed his video to a number of people and recorded their reactions over the top of the footage. One of those people was Yael Dayan, the daughter of Moshe, the man who first drew the Green Line. It was this version of the video that I was watching.[45]

Yael's voice was rich and gravelly, a smoker's voice. 'I wish it was that simple, to just walk with this can,' she said, watching Alÿs move through Jerusalem. 'The Green Line is not even a reality. It is a symbol. It means different things to different people. For the majority it means the end of conflict – *if we can return to it*. It means a smaller Israel, and safer. Although the line is a false thing, it will bring about *normalisation*. But some say the Green Line is a disaster. A suicidal line.'

Very faintly, in the background, Alÿs asked Yael if her father ever talked about drawing the line.

'It was not a bedtime story and he did not give it importance,' she replied brusquely. 'It doesn't matter. It wasn't meant to be the final line . . . Because it was very clear to my father, as it was to others, that borders cannot be decided by war.'

Yet now the Green Line, once the defining mark of conflict, could become, she said, 'a peace line'. Just like Alÿs's fine trickle of paint, it offered the prospect of 'an open border. Workers coming to and fro. There will be students, there will be population movement. You can't think of a hermetically closed border.'

In the seventy years since her father drew the line, it has surged out across the landscape. Now it was here in Bethlehem, several miles away from where it first began, standing right outside my hotel-room window. It didn't look like it wanted to go backwards anytime soon.

The next day, I walked the wall. It had rained throughout the night, but the morning was bright and clear. The sun saturated the still-wet streets, bounced off the asphalt and the limestone and the concrete and bathed everything in a pale, yellow light. The wall's path through Bethlehem was shifting and erratic. Rarely did it ever travel in a straight line. Rather, it knifed through the city in a series of sharp turns, before opening out into long parabolic curves. Graffiti covered it, on a spectrum ranging from banal to beautiful. There were countless messages of love and peace, invocations to tear down the wall, to 'Fuck Walls', or to 'Make Hummus, Not Walls'.

Right below one watchtower was a huge, strikingly lifelike portrait of the teenage activist Ahed Tamimi – the sixteen-year-old girl who became an iconic figure after she was videoed slapping the face of an Israeli soldier in retaliation for her fifteen-year-old cousin being shot in the head with a rubber bullet. The mural was the work of the Neapolitan street artist Jorit, and was created to coincide with Tamimi's release from an eight-month prison sentence. Jorit himself was arrested and detained – for three days – by the Israeli military for painting the wall, before he was deported back to Italy.

In many sections of the wall, layers of graffiti had stacked up, new murals and messages written on top of the old, over and over again – a decades-long stratigraphy of protest. Banksy's work, of course, remained untouched: two cherubs attempting to crowbar two sections of the wall apart; a young girl lifted off the ground by a bunch of balloons and rising to the top of the wall; a white dove of peace wearing a flak jacket and caught in the sights of an infrared crosshair.

What soon became clear to me was that almost all the messages, whether sprayed, scrawled or stencilled, were in English. They were speaking to the western world. Many were also the work of visitors *from* the west. A shop attached to Banksy's hotel – Wall Mart – offered spray cans for hire to paint the wall. Many Palestinians rejected the idea of painting the barrier at all, arguing that it should not be beautified, it should simply be torn down. Banksy himself recalled a story of being approached by an old Palestinian man while he worked.

'You paint the wall, you make it look beautiful,' the man said to him. Banksy thanked him. But the old man replied, 'We don't want it to be beautiful. We hate this wall. Go home.'[46]

I followed the wall westwards to where it formed the hard edge of the Aida refugee camp. Once a scattering of tents and temporary shelters for those who had been forced from their homes in 1948, today it is a chaotic assemblage of concrete and brick, confined to an area of less than a square kilometre. Its buildings, some reaching four or five storeys high, house nearly 5,000 registered refugees. This was a seventy-year-old, temporary home for generations of families who are still waiting for the day that they can return to their old villages, on the other side of the border – a border once miles distant, which had now come to them, with its concrete and its soldiers and its watchtowers. A sign on the wall as I entered the camp welcomed me to 'the most tear-gassed place in the world'.

I met Saeed there, a boy in his early twenties, who had lived in Aida his whole life. 'I was six years old when the Wall went up,' he said. 'It is all I've ever known.'

We were standing opposite a blackened and broken-looking watchtower. He told me the story of how this tower was the final piece of the wall to be put in place next to the camp in 2005, and how it was targeted that same day by local boys, who set tyres alight at its base, blackening the concrete and the one-way windows that looked out from the tower into the camp. Then Saeed told me about Ali Jidar (Wall Ali) – the sixteen-year-old boy who built himself a wooden ladder, placed it up against the wall, and then climbed to the top to wave a Palestinian flag. He was arrested days later in a night-time military raid and sentenced to eight years in prison. The response from the youth of Aida was to create a makeshift monument to Ali. They jammed slats of broken wood into a crack between two sections of the wall to form the sculptural impression of a ladder – a symbol that this wall was not insurmountable, that all you needed to cross it was willpower and some planks.

Saeed told me that people from the camp didn't tend to graffiti the wall. I'd barely seen one message in Arabic. For a time, on the corner just along from the burnt-out watchtower, someone had sprayed a famous line in Arabic from Tunisian poet Abu al-Qassim al-Shabbi's

'Will to Live': 'Inevitably the night will come to an end and the chains will be broken.' Now it was lost beneath an elaborate mural of the Dome of the Rock and a painting of the Basque flag. Yet, even though it could no longer be seen, Saeed said, that did not matter. Often, when the wall was being built, messages were spray-painted onto the bottom of the concrete sections as they lay on their sides awaiting assembly. Seeding the very idea of resistance into the hidden spaces, where they would stay, awaiting the day when the barriers would come down and the words would be revealed again, like prophecies.

Standing there, beneath the watchtower, I thought that the wall looked anything but permanent. Instead it seemed fragile, tawdry – already semi-ruined. Yet perhaps that is the point. Its identical segments are like clones, endlessly replaceable. The Israeli architect Eyal Weizman describes the wall as 'like a worm sliced into segments, each assuming a renewed life':[47] everywhere growing and stretching, surging into the West Bank to loop around the Jewish settlements on their hilltops and the networks of private roads that connect them. Or, in places like al-Walaja, Bir Nabala, Qalqilya, Hableh or – largest of all – Gaza, surrounding Palestinian communities on every side. Walling them off from the rest of the world.

In his book *The Least of All Possible Evils*, Weizman tells the surreal, Kafkaesque story of how the route of the wall was shaped and reshaped in the Israeli High Court of Justice. How it was intended to follow the path of the Green Line, yet it continually drifted away from it, further and further into the West Bank. Its original draughtsmen, the Israeli Ministry of Defence, argued for these deviations on the principles of security and structural expediency given the undulating nature of the terrain. Yet the proposed route almost never strayed onto the Israeli side of the Green Line. It always pushed the other way.

In a test case for the construction of the wall, concerning a stretch running through the land of the Palestinian village of Beit Sourik, the High Court was confronted with a complex series of arguments and counter-arguments concerning spatial realities, ranging from the layout of the villages, the gradient of the slopes earmarked for construction, the positioning of the fields and orchards, lines of sight and even the relative ranges of different forms of offensive weapon. Unable to make a decision based on the presented maps, plans and aerial photographs, the judges demanded that the petitioners return with a physical scale model.

'It was made in a computer-controlled milling process in high density foam,' Weizman explained, and it was painted to show the locations of the relevant fields and orchards. 'And so the first model of the wall to have ever been produced was not made by the party erecting the wall, but rather by those opposing it.' When the model was displayed in court, judges and lawyers had to leave their benches and seats to cluster round it. 'Models are like toys,' Weizman said, 'reduced worlds under control . . . The legal process came to resemble a design session, with the parties making their points on the model, sometimes balancing their pens on its miniature topography to try out alternatives.'[48]

And there was the rub – not one of those alternatives was *no wall at all*, which was the ultimate basis behind the legal challenge. And so, just over a week before the International Court of Justice ruled that the whole concept of the wall was illegal, the High Court of Israel also ruled *against* the 'Separation Barrier' in Beit Sourik. The judges decided that the original Ministry of Defence route would impact too severely on the life of the village, and so they recommended the construction of one of the compromise routes that had been marked on the scale model. For them the wall, it seemed, was a given. The only question was exactly which way it went.

This was a question that was asked again and again in the Israeli courts. Segment by segment, the wall was challenged, pushed, pulled, shaped and altered. The human rights lawyer Michael Sfard, who took on many of these cases, spoke of how he realised, with no little horror, that he was 'in fact and in practice one force that designs together with other forces the final route of the wall . . . We find ourselves helping the authorities design a better wall, a wall that goes through a route that is more sustainable . . . It is very difficult for me to say it but there are several places where I designed the actual route of the wall. It has become clear to me that in fact I am one of its architects'.[49]

Another of its architects – its chief architect, if you like, the Ministry of Defence planner Danny Tirza – described the endlessly shifting path of the wall as 'a political seismograph gone mad'.[50] All the tensions in Israel and Palestine were sculpted into and reflected by a 700-kilometre-long – and growing – barrier. An elastic borderline of concrete, razor wire, electric fencing, surveillance equipment, roads, ditches and watchtowers which, just like the conflict that gave birth to it, seemingly has no end.

Back in the lounge bar of Banksy's hotel that evening, eating a plate of hummus that came with flatbreads arranged like a section of the Wall (complete with holes in the top of each slice), I was reading a book of short stories called *Palestine +100*. This collection asked twelve Palestinian writers to imagine what their country would look like in the year 2048, a century on from the *Nakba*, the 'catastrophe' of the 1948 expulsion of 700,000 Palestinian Arabs from their homes.

One story, Saleem Haddad's 'Song of the Birds', was set in a future Palestine that seemed idyllic and peaceful, except for a wave of suicides afflicting teenagers – including the narrator Aya's older brother Ziad. Soon Ziad was coming to visit Aya in her dreams. Over the course of several nights he explained to her that his suicide was not about death but about life. 'What you're living in,' he said, 'it's all just a simulation. They've harnessed our collective memory, creating a digital image of Palestine. And that's where you live.' Killing yourself was the only way to reach the real world. 'We are the first generation to have lived our entire lives in the simulation. We are at the frontier of a new form of colonisation. So it's up to us to develop new forms of resistance.' He told her to listen to the song of the birds – a pre-set loop that repeats over and over. And so Aya crept closer and closer to taking her own life, to enacting her right to 'digital return'. It is a chilling story, inspired, in part, by the author's own experience as a Palestinian in exile – do you make a home elsewhere in the world, where there is no conflict? Or do you return, to struggle and to suffer, and in the process face the harsh reality of resistance?[51]

Another story, 'N', by Majd Kayyal, strayed even further into the realms of science fiction. In his Palestine of 2048, the conflict with Israel was over. But only because technological development had opened a quantum portal, allowing the existence of two parallel worlds – one for Israelis and one for Palestinians. This dimensional border was set up by the 'Agreement', which included, as its most crucial caveat, Article 7: that those born before the Agreement cannot travel between worlds. They were still 'living a trauma they can't overcome' and had to choose one world and stay put, while the younger generation, unencumbered by memories of conflict, were allowed to travel back and forth. But even then, some people refused to go to their partitioned world. The narrator's father told of an old family friend, a Palestinian activist, who decided to stay in the Israeli dimension: 'He refused . . . This victory, he thought, was essentially a hi-tech, scientific apartheid.'[52] Division is division, dimensional or not.

Visions of the past and the future have always bled together in this land, saturating the soil with both traumatic memory and cataclysmic prophecy. Go back a century, and Ze'ev Jabotinsky, the founder of the Revisionist Zionist party, was doing his own future gazing. Writing in 1923, in an article titled 'The Iron Wall', he predicted that the Jews 'must either suspend our settlement efforts or continue them without paying attention to the mood of the natives. Settlement can thus develop under the protection of a force which is not dependent on the local population, behind an iron wall which they will be powerless to break through.'[53] Jabotinsky's 'iron wall' was meant as a metaphor for unassailable military supremacy. Today it has become a near-literal reality. I thought of what Baha would say. *There are no metaphors here. It's an actual wall.*

Or what about the renowned Israeli scholar Yeshayahu Liebowitz? In his 1968 essay 'The Territories', he warned of the dark future that lay in store for his country if the occupation continued. 'The Arabs would be the working people and the Jews the administrators, inspectors, officials and police – mainly secret police. A state ruling a hostile population of 1.5 to 2 million foreigners would necessarily become a secret-police state, with all that this implies for education, free speech and democratic institutions. The corruption characteristic of every colonial regime would also prevail in the State of Israel.' The policy – and logic – of occupation, he continued, could lead only one way: 'concentration camps would be erected by Israeli rulers'.[54]

Maybe VR simulations and parallel worlds aren't so far-fetched after all. Whichever way you look at Israel and Palestine, it is hard not to see the spectre of dystopia. I kept thinking of Weizman's description of the wall as a worm cut in slices, whose segments regrow relentlessly. It conjured, of all things, the image of that old Nokia phone game, *Snake*. In the game you start as a dot that grows into a longer and longer line with every passing second – the snake – and you have to guide that growing line through the fixed space of your phone screen until it fills it all up and you inevitably crash. The West Bank was the phone screen, and the wall was the snake: the ever-increasing borderline. You try to divide a space so much, that all you have left is the division, the apparatus of separation. As Raja Shehadeh wrote near the end of *Palestinian Walks*, 'whether we call it Israel or Palestine, this land will become one big concrete maze'.[55]

Later that night, in my bedroom, I could hear shouting or chanting from outside, somewhere nearby. I got up and went onto my balcony. Perhaps I had been reading too much science fiction, but the view seemed to me then almost apocalyptic. A wild, bitter wind was blowing, howling through the artificial, concrete canyon between the wall and the hotel. My room was on the second floor, and so I could see over the top of the wall. To what? A car park, a huge empty car park waiting to be filled the next day by the cars and buses of visitors travelling there from Jerusalem to see the tomb of Rachel, favourite wife of Jacob and mother of Joseph and Benjamin.

Some 3,000 years ago, a heavily pregnant Rachel set off on a journey south from the city, went into labour on the way, and died giving birth. Her body is said to have been buried somewhere in the earth just a few metres away from this car park. This was why the wall had pushed so far into Bethlehem. To cradle Rachel's last resting place with concrete and security cameras. The wall narrowed from the expansive car park to a thin passage, overlooked by watchtowers, which pressed right up against the sides of her tomb.

In the distance, up on the hillside to the west, I could see the bright lights of Gilo, the huge Israeli settlement that was built on al-Walaja's West Bank land. Reflecting off the low, stacked clouds, Gilo's bright lights turned the sky into a sodium-orange firescape. The noise continued, mingling with the raucous wind to fill the night. But I couldn't work out what it was or where it was coming from. It was impossible to tell if it was a joyous celebration, an argument, a party, a demonstration – or all of them at once.

I was about to graffiti the wall. I hadn't really meant to, although I *had* thought about it. But the previous night I had decided that I definitely wasn't going to. I was there to observe, to talk to people. I was worried about this idea of 'conflict tourism', that the wall was becoming a kind of virtue canvas for western visitors, that it was less about showing solidarity and more about voyeurism and 'insta' adventures. I could paint it and then leave it behind, cross back to the other side of the wall and get on a plane and fly home (which was, in fact, exactly what I was going to do, later that day). But if you were a Palestinian, you had no option but to look at it, every day of your life. It bordered your very existence. From that perspective, covering it in a mix of cartoons and scribbles and well-meant but ultimately empty homilies seemed a little childish.

I'd explained all this to the owner of Wall Mart, the shop next to the Walled Off Hotel, when I'd come in for a look and he'd asked me if I wanted to hire a spray can.

'That's fucking bullshit,' he had said to me. 'Just paint the wall.'

'Look,' he continued. 'Most people, they come in here, and they are desperate to paint something, but they don't know what. They just want to paint.'

I had told him that, actually, I did know what I wanted to paint, even if I wasn't sure that I actually wanted to do it. I got out my notebook and showed him the copy I'd made of the ancient Sumerian script for 'no man's land', first written on the Lagash border pillar 4,500 years earlier.* Then I showed him the pictures of the pillar itself, taken on my phone when I was in the study room of the British Museum. Another man, who had been working on a drawing in the corner of the shop, came over for a look. He introduced himself as Mario – as it turned out, he was a Polish graffiti artist, going by the handle *Cake$*. I told them that I had thought of taking this phrase, conceived during the world's earliest-known border dispute, and writing it on the wall. They both nodded.

'It's good,' Mario said. 'You must do this.'

There was something pleasingly complex about the process of translating the script from my notebook onto the concrete. The first step was to photograph it. Then I had to email it to the shop's computer. Once the file was on the computer it could be projected – and enlarged – onto a blank piece of cardboard stuck to the far wall. I drew in pencil around the outside of the Sumerian lettering and, once that was done, moved the card to a cutting board, and used a scalpel to cut along the lines to make a stencil. Mario had gone back to his drawing, and as I worked we talked about borders. He told me that his grandmother was from Silesia, that her family had actually voted to become part of Germany in the 1921 plebiscite, but instead, the border was redrawn to include them in Poland. Just under twenty years later, it was one of the first places to be invaded by the Nazis at the outset of the Second World War.

* See Prologue

Once the stencil was done, I was handed a can of black paint and told to go and find somewhere on the wall. I stuck the card over an empty space on the concrete and with furtive glances either side – and in particular in the direction of the watchtower a hundred metres away – I pressed down on the nozzle. The text was just a foot or so long, and it only took a few seconds. I let it dry, peeled the stencil away, and there it was. *No man's land.* A phrase first chiselled into limestone around 2,400 BC, now brought up through the layers of history: copied, photographed, emailed, outlined, cut and spray-painted.

I realised that almost no one would be able to read it. That it would likely be covered up by other graffiti in the weeks or months to come. And I was fine with that. In fact, I *wanted* it to become buried somewhere beneath the layers of paint, to join the other hidden messages of the wall. It was a kind of border barcode, like I was marking the wall with its stamp of origin, its place of manufacture. Another line made real. Another descendant of the Lagash–Umma conflict, running out across the plain, cleaving the earth into pieces.

All of this took rather longer than I anticipated, and so I had to dash north through Bethlehem, to Checkpoint 300. Crossing back was a very different experience from leaving. I joined a small crowd of about twenty Palestinians: men, women and children. We had to walk through a series of long tunnels that ended in cramped metal turnstiles, pass our belongings through an – unmanned – X-ray machine, and then queue to show ID cards or passports to a Palestinian Authority attendant in a plexiglass booth. An Israeli soldier with a machine gun waited on the other side. On several occasions, when the attendant allowed someone to pass through, the soldier asked to see their papers and sent them straight back again. When he did this to one old woman, she started to remonstrate with him in Arabic. He shook his head, took one hand off his gun, and made a sweeping gesture towards her. '*Yalla, yalla,*' he shouted at her. *Hurry up. Over to your side of the line.* She came back through the turnstile and just stood there, not knowing what to do.

When it was my turn, the attendant stared briefly at my passport, the soldier ignored me. I passed through to the other side of the wall, climbed onto one of the waiting buses, and soon was travelling back over the hills to Jerusalem. The day was warm and sunny, almost cloudless, and the bus was hot. It was a Friday – *Shabbat* would begin at sundown and the early afternoon traffic was heavy as people made their way home. Back at the Arab bus station, the city streets were quiet. I'd missed my airport bus and trains did not run on Fridays, so I had no option but to find a taxi.

The ranks were full, but all the taxis were empty – their drivers, I assumed, gone to lunch. Eventually, a car pulled up and we agreed a fare for the airport. The taxi driver was a Palestinian man, in his early sixties. We made rapid progress out onto the highway and we drove with the windows down, the cool breeze defusing the heat of the day. At one point he gestured to some tumbledown ruins on a valley side – an abandoned village – but I didn't catch the name. We settled into a comfortable silence and after a while he lit a cigarette and began to sing softly to himself in Arabic.

I was thinking about the old woman back at the checkpoint. How easy it was for me to pass through a land I hardly knew, yet how she was barred entry to the only place she had ever known. *Not today. Try again another time.* Sometimes it can be hard *not* to indulge in metaphors. But I could see why Baha was so sceptical of them. I had, for instance, been envisioning the wall as some kind of entity, an out-of-control organism, voracious and persistent and driven by its own desire to grow as long and as large as it could. A temporary border that never stopped moving, because it was, in some sense, *alive*. But of course it isn't. It always has to come back to people. It is people who invent the line, who draw it, who design it, who shape it, who argue over its route and what it is for. People who fight for it. People who die because of it. An *iron wall*. A *concrete labyrinth*.

In his book *Language of War, Language of Peace*, Raja Shehadeh tells of a shoemaker in Hebron who adds a small amount of Palestinian soil into the soles of the shoes he fashions, so that refugees, the deported and the departed, those who are denied return, can always stand on a tiny piece of their land. Some physical part of Palestine can travel with them wherever in the world they go. Maybe we all carry the lines with us. Maybe we are the lines.

In Israel, in Palestine, those lines, and the stories they contain, are like one vast convolution, a knot so dense and so complicated, and going so far back in time, that it cannot be unpicked. What does it mean to belong to a place and how *long* can you hold on to that *longing*? Is there a statute of limitations on leaving, or expulsion, or return? Should that feeling ever expire? Isn't that the reason why we tell stories about our people and our pasts – as the only way to truly preserve our culture when most of the stones have turned to ruin? But what story will the wall tell about Israel, and what story will Israel tell about *itself*, one thousand, two thousand years from now?

For Shehadeh, everything that has happened in this land is proof that 'the only borders are in people's minds, artificial creations that come to be acknowledged and recognised by us, the people living here, because we have no choice. By creating this surfeit of borders, Israel has made a mockery of them and finally brought home the point that the only real borders are those which we come to accept.'[56]

Not long before his death in 2018, Amos Oz, albeit in a different way, reached the same conclusion as Shehadeh. 'The State of Israel can be a monster or a cartoon caricature with expansive borders, just as it can be a fair, moral, creative society that fulfils its heritage and lives in peace with itself, inside narrow borders', he wrote in an essay entitled *Dear Zealots*. 'It is madness to allow the question of borders to enslave and distort all other issues. This issue has never, in all of Jewish history, been the only one or even the first one on the agenda.' Surely it was time, he said, for Israel to 'finally awaken from the hypnosis of the map'.[57]

01

5
THE LOST BORDER

The first day of July on a beach overlooking the Pacific Ocean. Two men are working in the dune grass above a long strip of clay-coloured sand. It is morning and mist hangs heavy over the scene. The coastline blurs and then disappears into the near distance. Waves roll in suddenly, emerging out of a blank, offshore wall. Driftwood lies everywhere along the high tideline. Trees snapped, bent and broken, bleached the pale, brittle-grey of bone.

The men manoeuvre an object into position in front of the dunes. The object is six feet six inches tall, an obelisk fashioned from galvanised steel and set on a square wooden base. Just below its pyramidion is a number, in heavy black: 01. They check their position, precisely 42° north. Just a few metres over the California state line, into Oregon. They have hit their mark. This is the beginning. From here, they have 2,400 miles to go.

The two men are Marcos Ramírez and David Taylor. A third man, José Inerzia, is filming this moment. His camera pans across the empty beach, follows the waves breaking on the shore, then it comes to rest on Marcos and David, now standing back to back on the sand. They are positioned on either side of the line of latitude: Marcos facing south, David facing north. David is standing in the United States. Marcos is standing in what was once Mexico.

'The first obelisk,' Marcos writes in his journal, 'will breathe in the breeze from the Pacific, hear it roar, and there it will stay until it rots or is stolen. After planting it, we will head east to discover the history, and find the lost landscapes, of a Mexico that was – and that suddenly slipped away.'[1]

Marcos, David and José leave the beach behind, and climb into a Sprinter van filled with the flat-packed parts required to fabricate more obelisks. Later the same day, twenty-five miles to the east along the line of 42° north latitude, they build and erect Monument 02 in a mossy glade, between the trees of a redwood forest. In the afternoon, another fifty-five miles further east, they put Monument 03 in a grassy meadow, set between a quiet backroad and a railway track.

On the side of their van is written, in bold black lettering, *Binational Commission of Historical and Geographic Borders*. Alongside is a circular logo in black and gold which shows North America with a line cutting it in two. The line works its way diagonally downwards in a series of steps, from the northwest to the southeast. It is drawn to show the route of the border between Mexico and the United States. Not the current border, however, but the one that was created two centuries ago: the one that lasted for just thirty years, from 1821 to 1848. It was a border that existed on paper, defined by the words and clauses of a treaty. But, unlike the borders that came after, it was never marked in the land.

'We are sewing the old dividing line,' Marcos writes. 'We go through it between federal, state and neighbourhood roads, until invariably we find the ideal spaces to plant these markers, full of history and nostalgia.'[2]

It is a journey that will take them from Oregon's Pacific coast through Montana, Nevada, Idaho, Utah, Wyoming, Colorado, Kansas and Oklahoma, all the way to Texas and Louisiana – ending on the circular concrete platform of an old gun emplacement, at the very southern tip of the land, where the Sabine River empties out into the great expanse of the Gulf of Mexico.

'Let's not forget,' Marcos continues, 'that fortunately or unfortunately (however you want to see it) borders, like life itself, have an expiration date.'[3]

*

'I had been spending time in Van Horn, down on the Rio Grande, and I decided I needed to go check out the borderline west of El Paso,' David Taylor told me.

'And I drove to the border, on this access road, and looked to my right, and there is this obelisk standing there, six and a half feet tall, and it was just this sort of stately presence. And I thought, *what is that?* And it doesn't take long to figure out what it is. It says *Boundary of the United States* on one side and *Limite de le Republica Mexicana* on the other. And it had the number seven on it. So that means there are more, right? So how many of these things are there? That's what started it.'

David was talking to me from his house in Tucson: white walls behind him lit a warm yellow by the morning sun. He had a quiff of wavy grey hair, black-framed glasses and a square jaw. David is an artist and a professor of art at the University of Arizona. He was born in South Carolina, but moved as a child to Massachusetts, to live on the northeastern coastline of the United States, between Boston and Cape Cod. In 1999, he took a job at New Mexico State University.

'I was living in a place that was just forty miles from the southern border,' he said, 'but I didn't really have any depth of understanding or experience of it.'

And so, in 2006, he responded to a call for public artwork from a new Border Patrol station that was under construction in the Texan town of Van Horn. David's idea was to ride along with the agents, to photograph both their daily lives and the marginal landscapes they inhabited. He would go on to spend over 700 hours on patrol with them.

'I ended up being fascinated by the agents,' he said. 'They are complicated characters ultimately. Maybe as complicated as the border itself. There's an enormous number of Latino and Mexicano agents, for instance. And so much was changing. The border was changing. The border has changed more in the last twenty years than in the previous hundred.'

He called this project 'Working the Line'.[4] It was the beginning of a fifteen-year obsession with the border which he has not yet been able to shake. 'At one point I was thinking a few years ago that I need to move on to something else. And then I just find myself coming back. It became so clear to me that it is this enormously complicated and nuanced space. And so, it felt urgent to stick with it.'

It was during his time with the border agents that David first encountered obelisk number 7. Right away, he knew he wanted to find the other markers – *'there has to be at least a six and an eight, right?'* He began to seek them out, amid a rapidly emerging new border landscape: patrol roads, vehicle barriers, pedestrian fencing.

The oldest markers dated back to the 1850s, erected in cast iron under the terms of the 1848 Treaty of Guadalupe Hidalgo. This agreement, which marked the end of the brutal, two-year Mexican–American War, stipulated that a joint 'Boundary Commission' would oversee the drawing of a 'boundary line with due precision, upon authoritative maps, and to establish on the ground landmarks which shall show the limits of both republics'. The line was to travel from the mouth of the 'deepest channel' of the Rio Grande, following its course upriver to the 'town called Paso' – the present-day, bifurcated city of El Paso and Ciudad Juárez – and then travel directly overland to the Pacific Ocean where it would cut California in two, with Alta in the north going to the United States, and Baja in the south remaining with Mexico.[5]

On this western stretch, which covered some 690 of the border's near-2,000 miles, there was no consistent natural geographic feature – like the Rio Grande in the east – to act as a surrogate boundary. So the obelisks became the physical incarnation of the line. To begin with, there were only seven – because, as the Boundary Commission put it, 'the land was barren and can never be cultivated by either party'. The seven grew to fifty-two by the end of the 1850s, designed to be 'visible by line-of-sight by a person on horseback': a vista of one monument to another across hundreds of miles of desert and mountains.[6]

This border was, however, beset by disputes. Many of the markers were dismantled and repurposed as building materials. Ranchers and prospectors removed them in order to claim more acreage for cattle or mining. Native Americans destroyed them in protest at the continued carve-up of their indigenous lands. One marker – number 26 – was even incorporated *inside* a saloon, the building constructed around it to turn it into an ornamental feature, set up against a back wall.[7]

This blurred and uncertain line was resurveyed in the 1890s. The fifty-two monuments were to become 258, the broken and missing ones replaced, and the rest added to make the division much more pronounced in the landscape. The obelisks were now to be spaced just two to three miles apart, sometimes even closer. A photographer from Albuquerque, Daniel Robert Payne, was contracted by the US section of the Boundary Commission to record every single one, capturing them as they were being put in place. This expedition travelled the whole route on horseback, with baggage wagons pulled by pack mules. Payne was photographing the obelisks using heavy, eight-by-ten-inch glass-plate negatives, developing the images in a darkroom tent carried on the back of one of the wagons.[8] It was the discovery of this photographic survey that was the catalyst for David.

'What I recognised after exploring a few of the monuments was that this is a great organising principle for a piece of work,' he said. 'I felt like there is all this new border infrastructure going in, so this is the time to make these photographs again. So it was sort of an urgent, reflexive act. I *had* to do it.'

From the first photograph to the last took him ten years. He had to find and record 276 monuments in total – the 258 having been supplemented by another eighteen in the early years of the twentieth century.

'I would go out for a week, maybe two weeks at a time. Manage to photograph say forty of them, and then have to go back to teaching or whatever.'

David followed the line in a rough sequence, starting at number 1, on the west bank of the Rio Grande where the states of Chihuahua, New Mexico and Texas meet, and moving westwards to the final terminus alongside the Pacific sands of Playas de Tijuana. Often he would camp out in the borderlands, hike from one obelisk to the next. As he moved along the line he intersected with smugglers, migrants, Border Patrol agents, the Mexican army, cartel-controlled lands, prehistoric archaeological sites and makeshift shrines stuffed with prayer notes asking *Dios* for safe passage across the border.

'I was happy to throw a cot down within sight of the boundary. I've even had people coming through camp in the middle of the night, when I was in the mountains, followed by a Border Patrol helicopter.'

These encounters were 'usually furtive', he told me. 'You see someone, say hey, then they just dissolve into the vegetation, disappear over the hill.'

In the more remote locations the obelisks remained almost unchanged: sentinels in a lonely landscape. David's photographs show them as curious objects, at once antique and somehow entirely out of time. Or, as the author Cormac McCarthy put it, having the 'look of some monument to a lost expedition'. In other places, however, they had been framed – dwarfed and dominated – by fencing, walls, razor wire and CCTV cameras, or swallowed up by growing urban landscapes.

'And so it ends up being a geographic cross-section but also a temporal cross-section,' he said, 'because of the bordering structures that were getting built increasingly as I moved west. So you see fences and barriers more and more prevalent as you move west through the series of images.'

When David reached Tijuana he was introduced to Marcos Ramírez for the first time. Marcos offered him a place to stay, helped him locate the last few obelisks, hidden amid the confusing layout of the modern city, where the border runs past everything from industrial estates filled with *maquiladoras* (manufacturing plants), customs facilities and an international airport, to slum housing, a bullfighting ring and a wildlife refuge.

It was during this time, Marcos told me – as I spoke to him from his workshop in Tijuana – that they first began to sketch out a new idea. Marcos was a stocky, compact figure, with a full beard, now mostly grey, but still flecked here and there with patches of dark brown. He had lively eyes, creased heavily with laughter lines.

'We talked over a few beers, then some tequila, about how there was an older border. The one before the one that is here now. And so maybe it would be nice to somehow marry David's project photographing the obelisks with the idea of recuperating to Mexico the land that was lost in the war with the United States.'

Marcos was referring to the territorial division agreed by the Treaty of Adams–Onís – first signed in 1819 between America and the Kingdom of Spain, and then re-ratified in 1821, after Mexico gained its independence. In the words of the treaty, the boundary line was to begin 'on the Gulf of Mexico, at the mouth of the River Sabine in the Sea, continuing North, along the Western Bank of that River, to the 32nd degree of Latitude'. From there it was to turn to follow the course of the Red River until it reached 100° west, then run north to meet the Arkansas River at what is now Dodge City, 'thence, following the Course of the Southern bank of the Arkansas to its source in Latitude 42 North and thence by that parallel of Latitude to the South-Sea'.[9]

Drawn as a line, it looked like two steps climbing upwards through the heart of the continent, rising to meet a flat platform that stretched across to the Pacific Ocean. Seen in modern terms, it meant that all of what is now Texas, New Mexico, Arizona, Utah, Nevada and California – along with half of Colorado and small portions of Kansas, Oklahoma and Wyoming – *was Mexico*. Half a million square miles. Fifty-five per cent of Mexico's total landmass at that time. The treaty also included a promise from the United States to 'renounce forever, all their rights, claims and pretensions to the territories west and south' of the new territorial line.[10]

Forever lasted just twenty-seven years.

'So we asked ourselves, *how can we mark it?*' Marcos told me.

How could they find a way to represent this lost border, this northern *frontera* of a now half-vanished Mexico? A line that was described on paper, but never *inscribed* in the earth.

'And that's when it came to us – let's make replicas of the border markers. But make them weaker and lighter versions. And then we place them in the actual landscape and photograph them. We mark something that was never marked. It was also like an experiment, to do something that history forgot to do. And then just forget about it too. Get rid of the feeling.'

For David, it was a perfect way to capture the ephemerality of borders.

'The idea was that our obelisks could be stolen, tripped over, blown over. The whole notion was that this work would be transitory. It would recede over time. And so it really ends up being emblematic of the fact that this border didn't really exist for any great period. We wanted to create a gesture in the land that really acknowledged its existence, made its claim to history. But then allowed it to take its course from there on out.'

Marcos was born in Tijuana in 1961 and has lived there for much of his life. His home, he told me, is on sixteenth street.

'The numbering starts at zero at the border,' he said, 'then counts up from there. I live in the oldest neighbourhood in the city, and it is right next to the fence that divides Mexico and the United States.'

His father came from central Mexico, and worked as a projectionist from the age of fourteen until he was twenty, when he crossed the border to America to try to find a job in Hollywood. His dream of a career in the movie industry faltered, however, and he was later deported, sent back across the line. He then set up home in Tijuana, where he raised a family.

'Growing up in my house, there were two things that were never missing,' Marcos said. 'We always had something to eat, and we always had books.'

He remembered clearly the day his father brought home two huge encyclopaedias: one was a history of the world, the other a history of art.

'So I always saw there were two histories: one written by the people who won the war, who had the power; and then we had another history that was the history of the artists. I was always attracted to the idea that in art history, nobody was a winner or a loser.'

Marcos was a 'kind of revolutionary kid' he said, a 'left-wing kid' who was against capitalism and big business. He studied for a law degree at the Universidad Autónoma de Baja California, then moved into practice after he graduated.

'But there was all this corruption in the system, and in order to function I needed to become part of this system. And I was against that.'

He quit his job as lawyer, crossed over to San Diego, and found work through his cousin, who was a foreman for a crew of carpenters.

'I ended up working for seventeen years as a carpenter. But about eight years into that, I started doing art on the side. And then I decided I wanted to become an artist full-time. I did that more than twenty years ago. I quit my last job with a boss, and I've never been back. I've been able to survive.' He a gave deep, throaty laugh. 'A struggling artist! But not *too* struggling.'

The themes explored by his work have never strayed far from a preoccupation with the border. In 1997, he built and installed a huge sculpture at the main San Ysidro Port of Entry to the United States, overlooking the lanes of asphalt and traffic concertinaing into one of the busiest land border crossings in the world. Called 'Toy-an Horse', it was a ten-metre-tall wooden horse – a representation of the mythological Trojan Horse, with two heads which shared the same body, but faced in different directions. One looked north to the United States, the other south, back into Mexico.

The structure of the horse itself was deliberately incomplete, so that you could see into its hollow body – it would have been impossible to hide inside it, as the Greek soldiers once did. It appeared as a giant, oversized toy. Yet it also held within it the echoes of war. It was symbolic of an interminable siege, of one nation camped right up against the wall of another, trying every means possible to get inside.

'All of this came together with my personal history, the history of my father, my time as a lawyer, all those years working in construction. Some of those years I lived in San Diego, but for many I lived in Tijuana and had to cross this border every day to go work in the US. I'd wake up in the morning and go. All of this was in that horse. So I placed it at San Ysidro. And people said, *why is this not finished? Why does it have two heads*? Because it was asking questions about how Mexican you are. Or how *Mexican-American* you are.'

Marcos paused for a moment, rubbing his hands together.

'That piece was one of my most simple and direct pieces. It was about this dichotomy: these two countries who just cannot separate themselves.'

From the Pacific coast of Oregon the land rose steadily as Marcos, David and Jose followed the 42nd parallel eastwards. It was the summer of 2014. They travelled through the mountains of the Western Cascades, passed beyond California to follow Highway 140 as it cut back and forth across the state line between Oregon and Nevada. Then came the high, arid plains of Idaho.

'A landscape smelling of sage,' Marcos described it in his journal. 'Millions of sage plants. Miles and miles of a unique landscape and an intense smell.' At night they would park the van by the roadside, set up their cots in the open air, listen to the 'song of the coyote' and look up into what Marcos described as 'the most star-filled skies I have ever seen'.[11]

Marcos was the driver and David the navigator. They called their journey, and the artwork it was creating, *DeLIMITations*.

'It was great for me to be seeing, all the time with my eyes open, looking at the road, looking at the land,' Marcos told me. 'I was going through the whole trip, looking at the landscapes – which are American landscapes now, but could have been Mexican landscapes, you know?'

Whenever they reached the location to place another monument, Marcos would set up his folding workstation beside the van and begin assembling the steel components: drilling the parts together, attaching them to the wooden base. Finally, they would fix the obelisk to the ground using sixteen-inch tent spikes, and then David would take his photographs.

'And then, maybe, we get ready to run!' Marcos laughed.

They travelled on, passing through tiny, ghostly towns and settlements, and immense grassy plains – once the home of the great wild bison herds, now grazed by thousands of domesticated cattle.

'I felt nostalgia,' Marcos told me, 'The nostalgia of the past – that is my past but is not my *personal* past. The past of my nation.'

He gave a big laugh again and shook his head.

'There is no worse nostalgia than to remember something you never ever had,' he said. 'I was travelling with *that* nostalgia. These places were never mine. Once it was Mexico's property, Mexico's land. But then the real property owners were the Native Americans. First, the Spanish robbed them, and then the Americans robbed Mexico.'

Following the line between Idaho and Nevada, they came upon a reservation belonging to the Shoshone-Paiute Tribes. There was an annual powwow underway, a celebration, complete with songs, drumming, fireworks. They met with the tribal elders and spent the night camped under the moon, on the shores of Mountain View Lake, some 1,600 metres above sea level. The next morning, they went looking for a place to put Monument 08. The ideal spot was a plot of land just off the road, beside a house fringed by a screen of trees.

'There were two Native American guys there talking to each other, but not paying attention to us,' Marcos said. 'And we started explaining: *we're doing this project that is marking the old border.* Turned out these two guys were from different tribes. One was Shoshone. The other was Navajo. And they were going to the rodeo. So they were strapping things up onto the roof of their car, and one of them said, *You can put it on my land, that's okay with me. I own all the way over to that corner post. You can put it wherever you want. But I'm late for the rodeo, and I've really got to go.*'

As they continued to pack up their car, the two Native American men started talking among themselves. Marcos heard one say to the other, *remember when we used to have a lot of fights between our tribes about the border here?* – and then they each started reeling off a long list of places that had once marked their tribal edgelands.

'The guys were ignoring us now,' Marcos said, 'but they had brought their conversation round to borders – borders that were much older than *our* border. They were talking about how things were before the white man arrived in their lands. And we felt blessed that they had allowed us to place the marker in their yard. But also, it was fascinating to hear them talk about their own idea of borders – of nations and power and empire.'

The two Native American men drove away, and Marcos and David assembled Monument 08. They took it to the very corner of the yard to set it upright, positioned it exactly on 42° north – surrounded by a wide open plain and an even wider expanse of sky.

'We knew that here, we were involved more in an act of *recolonisation* rather than decolonisation,' David said to me. 'So it had to be a collaboration: where we enjoined the people who were in that space to help us, to give us their permission to leave our artefact behind.'

When they reached the end of the border's westward route along the 42nd parallel, they were presented with a problem. The Treaty of Adams–Onís had never defined fully one portion of the line – the section that runs north–south from the present-day town of Leadville, Colorado, to the 'Source of the Arkansas River'. The true border was contingent on mapping that source.

In June 1845, the American explorer John C. Fremont – known as the 'Pathfinder' – was sent to find it by the US Army Corps of Topographical Engineers. Instead, he abandoned his mission to press on into Mexico, where he met with American settlers on the other side of the border in the Sacramento Valley, and proceeded to agitate for war.

In February 1846, his crew of sixty armed surveyors reached the summit of Gavilan Peak – now known as Fremont Peak – overlooking Monterey Bay, California, and raised the American flag. This direct provocation brought out the Mexican army, and, after a four-day stand-off, Fremont and his expedition retreated towards Oregon. They followed the course of the Sacramento River northwards. On 5 April, they came upon a large camp belonging to the Native American Wintu Tribe.

There, as one of the surveyors, Thomas Breckenridge, wrote, 'commenced a scene of slaughter which is unequalled in the West'. Men, women and children were massacred. Estimates of the number killed ranged from 200 to over 700. There were no recorded casualties among Fremont's party.[12]

By the end of that month, Mexico and America were officially at war. Come the turn of the year, all of modern-day California was under the control of the United States. The border that Fremont had been sent to map was gone.

'It put us into this strange conversation with the people who wrote the Treaty,' David said. 'And it allowed us to push back against Fremont, who was this kind of opportunist.'

So David and Marcos went looking for the source of the Arkansas River themselves. By tracing the tributary forks upstream from the main course of the river, they came to the tiny town of Medicine Bow, Wyoming.

'We decided to run the borderline through the middle of it,' David said. 'Straight down Maple Street.'

They put Monument 16 in the front yard of the house of a woman called Laurie.

'And we had this very engaged talk with the people in Medicine Bow about what this meant: that they had a historic border running through their community, and part of their town might have been Mexico, and part might have been the US. It made them think about *place* in a different way.'

Today, Medicine Bow is positioned right in the centre of the United States. But once it could have been a border town.

'It brought the history alive,' David said. 'And while obviously it doesn't have any real bearing at this point in time, we're the people who *actually* said where the headwaters of the Arkansas River are; we completed the Adams–Onís boundary. We got to make that official. In our own way.'

On they went in their Sprinter van, through the Rocky Mountains, following the Arkansas River hundreds of miles southwards, placing more obelisks along the way – in the high mountain landscapes, in laybys off the side of Highway 21, under a bridge just outside Smeltertown, Colorado. Next, they were curving east, into the flat prairies of Kansas, now on the trail of the Red River – the Rio Roxo – passing into Oklahoma and then Texas.

'Here Mexico begins to appear with more force,' Marcos wrote at the time, in his journal, 'to seep everywhere and sweat, or is it perhaps suppurating? Like an old wound that refuses to close.'[13]

I asked him about this idea of the border as a wound. Was that how he saw it, how he *felt* it?

'The wound is there in the landscape. But there is no scar. It is as simple as that. If you are shot in the arm, but have no scar, no one will believe you. So what we were doing with this project was to try to locate the scar that was not there – to prove that it existed. We marked the scar.'

It was high summer in Texas – oven-like heat, humidity, mosquitos. They rushed down the final stretch, placing obelisks wherever they could on public land: a derelict backlot beside a Methodist Church in Texarkana, right on the border with Arkansas; under the wrought-iron Burr's Ferry Bridge alongside the Sabine River at the easternmost point of Texas; amid the industrial ruin of the once massive naval shipyards of Port Orange.

Then, exactly a month after they had erected Monument 01, they reached the end of the line. As the last light of day faded on 31 July, they drove along a narrow dirt road, passed a massive oil refinery and a rig construction yard, and continued out into a huge saltmarsh. There, where the road stopped and the land gave on to the sea, was a circular concrete platform that had once held an old coastal artillery battery. The perfect place for Monument 47.

'I said to David, *I want to shoot this last photograph*,' Marcos told me. 'Because I realised I'd been building all the monuments and placing them all. And David had been taking all the photographs. And I wanted to shoot just one. The most interesting photo was to shoot backwards: to see Port Arthur and see the refineries in the background. But I insisted we shoot in the same direction that we were travelling. We shoot out over the Gulf of Mexico.'

I asked Marcos and David if they knew if the obelisks were still there. If the border – the scar – was still marked.

'I think some people went and stole them,' Marcos said. 'And that's okay; we were kind of allowing that, for people to go and steal them. And some of them were adopted by the local communities. And probably some of the most remote ones are still there.'

David told me that he had gone back to find one on the banks of the Red River. 'And it had been totally riddled with bullets and tipped over. And I think about that as sort of a metaphor for our current discussions around the border. You know: toppled on its side and shot full of holes.'

For both of them, however, this was just a part of the artwork, the inevitable process of change and decay.

'What happened to them – it is interesting, but it is not completely important to me,' Marcos said. 'Or rather, whatever happened to them is *equally important*. This was a gesture. We marked the scar. But it is not necessarily something that will – or should – be there for ever.'

Like any scar, it will fade.

'So let's do it, mark it – it is a colossal installation. But then forget about it. For the health of society.'

It was January in the grounds of a farmhouse set above the fork of the Brandywine Creek, almost exactly thirty miles west of the southernmost point of the city of Philadelphia. Two men were working inside a small, circular wooden structure, thirteen feet in diameter, with walls that were five and a half feet high. The structure had a conical roof, built so as to be able to rotate, with a folding aperture, out of which pointed a large telescope. It was night-time, and the temperature had dropped below freezing. The skies were clear.

The two men were wrapped in furs and blankets. One of them lay flat on the floor – the only way he was able to look through the narrow eyepiece of the telescope, which was held pointing directly upwards by a device called a zenith sector. On one side of the sector a weight was suspended from a piece of a string – a plumb bob designed to ensure that the telescope was precisely vertical. The other man held a candle to the side of the telescope, casting light through a small hole to illuminate four very thin wires – three vertical, one horizontal – which were arranged in the viewer to create a perfect centre where the middle vertical wire met its horizontal counterpart.

The white dots of stars moved through the viewer. Because of the earth's rotation, they were seen to move in an arc. Each star passed twice across the horizontal wires, as it rose and fell on either side of the vertical wire. All through the night the men said the names of stars to each other, like a litany. *Delta Persei. Capella. Castor. Alpha Cygni.* And they called out numbers too – recording the timings as each star crossed and recrossed each wire. They did this again and again, night after night, continually adjusting the telescope's viewing angle to try to find the point where the rise and fall of the star's arc took the exact same time on each side of the vertical. When they had this, they had found 'mid-heaven', the meridian, the moment when a star was exactly on a north–south line relative to the surface of the earth.

All of this was just to set the zenith sector accurately. Next, they followed more stars, tracking their movements across the sky and filling their journal with calculations and notations: times of ascension and declination; working out angles between the earth and the celestial hemisphere and the light of distant suns. Finally, on 28 February, after nearly two months of observations, they were able to determine their exact latitude on the surface of the planet: 39 degrees 56 minutes 18.9 seconds north.

They had carried out this same process already, thirty miles east, in the back garden of a house deemed to mark the southern limit of Philadelphia. Their observatory was then dismantled and moved to this farm, the delicate telescope and zenith sector transported on top of a feather mattress pulled as gently as possible by a horse-drawn wagon. The observatory's new location at Brandywine Creek was just ten and half seconds of latitude south of the house they had left in the city. On the ground, that translated to 365.8 yards. It was a distance that could be easily offset in their final calculations.

Soon they were on the move again, following in the wake of five hired labourers who had cut a swathe – a *visto* – southwards from the observatory through the dense forests that covered this landscape. The two men were attempting to measure exactly fifteen miles, stretching out their chains from one point to the next. It took two and a half weeks to reach their approximate mark. Once they had it, the observatory was transported once more. The stargazing began all over again.

It was late April now. Torrential rain obscured the skies for a whole week. By May, the weather had cleared, and eleven straight nights were spent lying on the observatory floor, squinting up through the telescope's lens. Another month of calculations and adjustments followed. Then, on 12 June, they had it: 39 degrees 43 minutes 18.2 seconds north latitude.

'The Point 15 miles South of the Southernmost Point of the City of Philadelphia,' they concluded in their journal, 'is situated in Mill Creek Hundred, in the County of Newcastle, in a Plantation belonging to Mr Alexander Bryan.' A thick oak post was hammered into the ground on this exact spot, painted white, and the word 'West' was carved into its western face.

This was the line of latitude that would form the border between the states of Pennsylvania and Maryland. Every previous attempt to locate it accurately had failed. Now, from the 'Post mark'd West' – the nexus point – more lines would begin to run out across the landscape. South, to carve in half a peninsula surrounded by the waters of Chesapeake Bay, the Potomac River and the Atlantic Ocean. East, along the partial curve of a twelve-mile radius circle – centred on the belfry of the courthouse of the town of New Castle – to meet and follow the course of the Delaware River upstream. And west. West into a landscape almost entirely unmapped. West – as decreed by royal charter eighty years earlier – by 'five degrees in longitude': before anyone had any idea what those five degrees might amount to, or how far they would stretch into the new continent.

The lines to the south and east were drawn first, marked with wooden mile posts – later to be replaced by great carved blocks of Portland Stone, shipped across the Atlantic from England. It took another year of celestial observations and measuring and surveying before the two men were back at the 'Post mark'd West', and were turning their own eyes westwards, to the final stretch of the border.

These two men were Charles Mason and Jeremiah Dixon. It was April 1765, and they were ready to run their gaze, their chains, their telescope and their astronomical instruments into the unknown distance. To unfurl their line and see where it would take them.[14]

Two and a half centuries before Marcos and David made their road trip to delineate the 1821 border, Mason and Dixon were marking the first precisely measured boundary line in North America. More than that, it was the first time, in history, that a perfect line of latitude was carved into the surface of the earth. Arrowing west into the continental wilderness, it was a line that would define – and at the same time divide – the nation still to come.

Charles Mason was born in Gloucestershire in 1728, the son of a baker and a miller. In his early twenties he drifted into the orbit of the Reverend Mr James Bradley – at that time the holder of the prestigious position of Astronomer Royal. Impressed by Mason's abilities in mathematics, Bradley took him on as his apprentice, and brought him to work at the Royal Observatory in Greenwich.[15]

Jeremiah Dixon was five years Mason's junior, and came from a large, colliery-owning Quaker family in County Durham. He grew up in the town of Bishop Auckland, trained as a surveyor, and, inspired by the astronomer Thomas Wright – who had built a large stone observatory above the nearby village of Westerton – took a keen amateur interest in the study of the stars. Dixon also became friends with another resident of Bishop Auckland, John Bird, the pre-eminent maker of scientific instruments for the Royal Observatory.

Mason and Dixon first met in 1760. A commission from the Royal Society paired them as companions for an expedition to the Indonesian island of Sumatra, where, on 6 June the following year, they were to make 'observations on the transit of the planet Venus over the Sun's disk'. These observations were to be just one part of a unique global experiment. Astronomers from many nations were co-ordinating their efforts to time this 'transit' – watching it from discrete locations all around the world – and sharing their results in an attempt to calculate precisely the distance to the sun and, by extension, the size, weight and shape of the earth.[16]

They set sail on 9 January 1761. Forty-eight hours out of Portsmouth, their ship, the *Seahorse*, was attacked by a French frigate. Eleven crewmen were killed, thirty-seven wounded, and the damage to the hull, mast and rigging was so severe that they were left with no option but to limp back to port. By the time *Seahorse* was repaired, they were already too late to reach Sumatra. Instead, at the very end of April 1761, they landed at Cape Town. There, on the flat ground below the slopes of Table Mountain, they built their observatory out of wood and canvas, checked, calibrated and rechecked their instruments – and waited.

At dawn on 6 June, Mason wrote, 'the Sun ascended in a thick haze, and immediately entered a dark cloud.' Twenty-three minutes later, they had their first sighting of Venus: a tiny indentation on the outer rim of the Sun, just visible through wisps of cloud. 'When I saw the planet first,' Mason said, 'its periphery and that of the Sun's were in a great tremor.'[17]

Both men were staring into telescopes fitted with darkening filters designed by Dixon's old friend, John Bird. The indentation became a fluid, flickering inkblot on the great blank circle. These were the crucial moments: recording the time that Venus first touched the Sun, and then the instant that it left the inner circumference and began to float free. For the next few hours they followed its progress. Cloud came, and for a while they lost it completely. As it approached the far side, however, the skies cleared. Timing was once again critical. They had to note as precisely as possible when Venus appeared to kiss the Sun's inner edge, and then when it was finally gone, the 'black drop': the planet's dark silhouette expelled entirely from the bright white surface.

Mason and Dixon's observation of the transit – an event that happened just twice a century, and for just a few hours – was the only successful attempt made in the southern hemisphere that day. Their account proved critical for informing the measurements required to calculate the distance to the Sun; and, at the same time, it sent their names circulating around the global scientific community, establishing them among the leading agents of a new, linear world. Technological innovation meant that lines could be seen and measured everywhere: lines running from the earth to the sky and back again; lines of distance; angles between lines; lines defined in degrees, hours, minutes, seconds. With their instruments and their astronomical knowledge, they could portion up the entire planet. In an era of burgeoning rationality and modernisation, this was a skill in great demand: a path to the future.

At the same time as Mason and Dixon were working on the Cape, Thomas Penn, then the owner of Pennsylvania, was making enquiries among the 'scientifik curious' of London for 'some very able Surveyors that were skilful in making Celestial Observations'. Penn and his counterpart Frederick Calvert, the owner of Maryland, were both desperate for a way to end the disputes – and violence – that had, for generations, plagued the blurred, uncertain boundary between their colonies.[18]

The problem could be traced back to two kings. When Charles I granted Maryland to the Calvert family in 1632, he decreed that it was to have a northern boundary which 'lieth under the Fortieth Degree of Northern Latitude'. Pennsylvania, granted by Charles II to the Penn family half a century later, was to be bounded to the south 'by a circle drawn at twelve miles distance from New Castle' and then 'by a straight line Westwards' along the 'Fortieth Degree', for 'five degrees in Longitude' from the Delaware River. Clear enough, perhaps: the main Maryland–Pennsylvania borderline was to run along the fortieth degree of latitude. Except neither king actually knew where this line was, nor how to identify it. And, with the creation of Pennsylvania, it now had to meet precisely with a circle drawn around the town of New Castle. These two royal charters had mixed, perhaps irreconcilably, the language of scientific exactitude with a complete ignorance of geographical reality.[19]

Almost as soon as his colony was established, William Penn, Thomas's father, was writing to Charles Calvert, Frederick's father, about the 'business of the bounds' and the need for them to be 'observing their just limits'.[20] Maps were drawn, but the two families could never agree on the results. All the while, land was being granted to colonists throughout the disputed region. Laws were different on either side of the line, as too was religious observance. Confusion reigned over where taxes were to be paid and to whom. Arguments between rival landowners spilled over into armed conflict and even murder.

It took until 1732 for a joint boundary commission to be formed to survey the border. Almost instantly, the commissioners were locked in intractable argument over the terms of the original charters, and no work was carried out. By 1750, the old commissioners had been replaced and the survey was finally beginning – under the new instruction, as ordered by George III's Board of Trade and Plantations, that the boundary should no longer follow the fortieth degree of latitude but should, instead, run west on a line set exactly fifteen miles south of the southernmost point of the Pennsylvanian capital of Philadelphia. Not least because, as it turned out, the fortieth degree of latitude actually ran *north* of the city.[21]

Over the next decade, successive survey teams tried, and failed, to make all this complex geometry fit. Time and again, lines ran off at the wrong angles or missed their targets. Writing in June 1762, the surveyor for Pennsylvania asked his employers, in defeated frustration, 'to be released from Trying to Do what I now Conceive to be Impossible.'[22]

A year later, Penn and Calvert were first introduced to Mason and Dixon, the latter pair not long returned from their Royal Society expedition. In August 1763, Penn wrote to inform his colonial secretary that an agreement had been reached and the two men would soon be on their way across the Atlantic, bringing with them 'their fine [Zenith] Sector, two Transit instruments, and two reflecting telescopes'.[23] Calvert wrote to his officials in Maryland asking God for a happy resolution to the issue and praying that this latest boundary survey would be the last. The recalcitrant border, he ventured, was set to be tamed finally by enlightenment innovation: the wayward line 'threaded by the Mathematicians'.[24]

A Saturday morning in June 1766. Charles Mason walked away from his surveyors' camp to climb the 800-metre-high Savage Mountain. Behind him were 165 miles of visto – an eight-foot-wide line that was being hacked into the landscape. A line that passed straight through forests, up and down hillsides and mountains, broke here and there to cross streams and ford the Potomac and Susquehenna rivers, and reached all the way back to the fields of Alexander Bryan's farm and the 'Post mark'd West'.

'From the solitary tops of these mountains,' he wrote, 'the eye gazes round with pleasure; filling the mind with adoration to that pervading spirit that made them.'

They had not yet travelled the line's full five degrees of longitude from the Delaware River. But they had collided with another border – of sorts. Savage Mountain was part of the crest of the Allegheny Mountains. As Mason observed, he was standing, exactly, on 'the Boundary between the Natives and strangers'.[25]

It was a border that had been created, once again, by a king. Three years earlier, George III had issued a proclamation forbidding any settlement west of the Alleghenies. These mountains were as far as they were permitted to go. Mason and Dixon's line had hit the terminus of colonial America.

This royal proclamation had hoped to placate those Native American tribes who fought alongside the British against the French in the Seven Years' War: to make clear the divisions in the land. As the Commissioners for Trade and Plantations said, it was time to halt the expansion and 'let the savages enjoy their deserts in quiet'.[26]

Except these lands were no deserts. Mason had seen them with his own eyes. Rather, they appeared to offer the promise of an almost super-sized abundance. In his journal he broke off from his lists of calculations to record, with astonishment, a giant hickory leaf seventeen inches long and twelve inches wide, a hailstone more than an inch and a half in diameter, a summer thunderstorm of such terrifying force that 'it seemed to threaten an immediate dissolution to all beneath it'. Nothing was small here. Mason described 'haws of a very large size, hops, wild cherry trees', 'very good tracts of land and the hills very rich', and 'dark vales of Pine through which I believe the sun's rays never penetrated'.[27]

He was far from the first to stand on this spot and wonder at what lay ahead. Many others had come before him, looked out from here towards the continent beyond. Some had already crossed, carved out their own space in the landscape, as was God's will. And what is the word of a king, they said, when set against the word of God?

This partition line had been porous from the start. Territory beyond it had been promised to private investors. Hundreds of thousands of acres had been sold. George Washington, a veteran of the Seven Years' War and the future first president of the United States, admitted in private letters that he 'can never look upon that proclamation in any other light (but this I say between ourselves) than as a temporary expedient to quiet the minds of the Indians'. The partition was already fracturing, he said. It was inevitable that, sooner or later, it 'must fall'.[28]

Tensions were high between the Native Americans and the colonists. Relations deteriorated continually into violence. For those natives who had attempted to integrate with communities east of the Alleghenies, there was open hostility driven by a conviction, held among many settlers, that the indigenous people had no place in *their* New World.

Mason knew what could happen, how far some colonists would go. In December 1763, the month after he arrived in America, an armed gang of Scots-Irish Presbyterians, calling themselves the 'Paxton Boys', attacked a village belonging to the Conestoga Tribe, about eighty miles west of Philadelphia. They killed six people, scalping and mutilating the bodies. The rest of the villagers were out working, and when news of the murders spread, they were brought to a newly built jail in the nearby town of Lancaster, to be sheltered there for their own protection.

Two weeks later, however, the Paxton Boys came to the town in even greater numbers, fifty or more of them. They broke into the jail and massacred every single remaining Conestoga – men, women and children. The following day, reports circulated that the gang were marching on Philadelphia, on a mission to kill any Native American or Quaker sympathiser they found there.[29] The city militia was readied, yet in the streets there was clear and vocal division. A mob supporting the Paxton Boys converged on the governor's residence to celebrate the killings. The gang ultimately dispersed before it reached the city, but the incident had given Mason an immediate insight into the fevered atmosphere of America – the extremity of the hatred and bigotry that was swirling around the landscape, driving some into fanatical, murderous fervour.[30]

Mason knew that he was drawing a border through a landscape already riven with divisions. Lines between colonists and colonists; lines between 'natives and strangers'; lines of racial purity; lines between civilisation and so-called savagery; lines between the god-fearing and the godless, prelapsarian ignorance and scientific mastery.

He turned away from the west, looked back to the east. For the next three months he and Dixon would retrace their route along the visto, inspecting the condition and accuracy of their line. It had been plotted by following five stars: *Vega*, *Deneb*, *Sadr*, *Delta Cygni* and *Capella*. To ensure they were always on the exact same degree of latitude, they had stopped every ten miles to take measurements in their mobile observatory. Now, at various points on the return journey, they were able to look both ways from a hilltop and see the line 'as the arch of a lesser circle very beautiful, and agreeable to the Laws of a Sphere'.[31] This was exactly as it should have been. A true line of latitude must always appear, when viewed over a distance on the earth, to bend with a small, almost imperceptible curve.

They followed this curve back to the 'Post mark'd West'. And then beyond it, even further east, to the Delaware River. The Boundary Commissioners had announced their desire to keep their line going, to run it out to its full extent, passing beyond George III's proclamation line. First, however, they had to make representations to the Six Nations Indian Confederation, into whose lands the survey must enter. While they awaited these negotiations, Mason and Dixon set out to establish the degree of longitude of the Delaware's western bank, and therefore exactly how much further west their borderline had to go. Their answer was 86.7 miles.[32]

Their final expedition did not get underway until June of the following year. The survey crew had swelled to some sixty-five men – half of them axemen required to cut the visto – and they were trailed by a flock of fifty-five sheep. As a condition for allowing the line to proceed, the chiefs of the Six Nations had provided an accompanying escort of fourteen Mohawks and Onondaga guides, along with an interpreter, Hugh Crawford, a war veteran and explorer who first crossed the Alleghenies as a young man and had lived among the Native Americans for decades.

Throughout the summer, they pressed on west, reached and then crossed their previous endpoint at Savage Mountain. On the other side, Mason wrote, is 'a Garden desolate . . . a wild waste'. At 199 miles 63 chains and 68 links west, they set up their telescope and zenith sector in a glade on the far side of the river and spent six nights observing the stars and verifying their position. A group of thirteen Delaware warriors emerged from the trees – one, Mason said, was 'the tallest man I ever saw' – and the natives stayed with them for several days, silently watching the surveyors as they, in turn, watched the skies. The calculations showed that they were 300 feet too far north of the true parallel, and so they adjusted, bringing their line back south, back on course.

Their journal became like a rhythmic poem of progress. 'Entered a glade . . . crossed a run . . . left the Glade . . . Continued the Line, Continued the Line, Continued the Line.' At the beginning of September, at 211 miles, they met the Laurel Mountains, 'a Wild of Wildes', a landscape of forests and limestone. Three miles further on, they made the crest of the mountain ridge, from where 'there is the most delightful pleasing View of the Western Plains the Eye can behold'. And somewhere, off into that far distance, 'the end of our Line may be seen'.[33]

At 219 miles, their line hit the east bank of the Cheat River. The Mohawk guides in the party objected to crossing, said that this was the limit: *here, and no further*. Crawford held a council with the guides and, after a long debate, they relented and agreed that the survey could continue. Two weeks later, they met the wide valley of another river, the great snaking course of the Monongahela. Once again, the telescope and sector were unpacked, and ten nights of stargazing followed. Mason and Dixon found that they were five chains south of the true line, so another correction had to be made. Yet, as they prepared to cross the river west, twenty-six of their own party refused to come. They feared for their lives in the lands ahead, had been unnerved by the comings and goings of natives in the trees around their camp.

Just fifteen men went on with them. Beyond the Monongahela, Mason recorded catching 'a lizard near a foot in length' and entering a landscape abundant in surface coal, which, it seemed, was 'found very plenty here'. It was into October now. At 231 miles 20 chains west, Mason reported that they 'crossed a War Path'. They continued that day for another mile and half, before the chief of their guides informed them that they had now gone beyond their limit. This was the final 'extent' allowed by the Six Nations, and he would 'not proceed one step further Westward'.[34]

Mason and Dixon's line had met the Great Indian Warrior Path. A north–south-running, continental highway, it was a line already drawn into the surface of this land by hundreds, perhaps even thousands, of years of passage. To take their visto across it, they were told, would be to erect a dam across a river. The two lines may touch, but not intersect. The surveyors could see their parallel continuing ahead of them, its invisible presence racing far away into the west. They were still some thirty miles short of five degrees longitude from the Delaware River. But this time, no compromise could be reached to allow them to continue.

They retreated back to the eastern edge of the Warrior Path, set up their astronomical instruments one last time. While they were in camp, they received a visit from the brother of the chief of the Delaware tribe, a man called 'Prince Prisqueetom'. His face, Mason wrote, was 'deeply furrowed with time' – he was eighty-six years old – but he spoke 'very good English'. He told them how, when he was younger, he and his brother thought they would 'go and see the great King over the waters; and make a perpetual Peace with him'. But he was afraid that, one way or another, he would never return home.

As they rested there, on the border of the Path, the old man told them of the beauty of the land ahead: 'Rich-weed and Pea vine, so thick you can scarcely get through it', 'verdant plains' and 'meadows by nature of miles square'. The next morning he was gone again, back to the west.[35]

Eight nights of observations showed Mason and Dixon that they had to adjust the endpoint of their line by 223 feet to the north. There, on 18 October, on the top of a high ridge, at 233 miles, 17 chains and 48 links from the 'Post mark'd West', they set up a new post. A 'W' was carved on its western side; earth and stone heaped around it to make a conical mound, five feet high. This was the absolute limit. There was still work to be done, though: the visto to be cut through the trees all the way up to this spot, the temporary wooden mile posts to be replaced with solid stone boundary markers, cairns to be erected on the summits of every mountain peak along the length of the boundary. But the line was finally capped.

Another year passed. Mason and Dixon double-checked their measurements, drew up maps of the whole extent of the Pennsylvania–Maryland border, and presented a full report to the Boundary Commissioners. It was not until the morning of 11 September 1768 that Mason came, at last, to a harbourside in the city of New York. At 11.30 a.m. he boarded the *Halifax Packet*, bound for Falmouth in Cornwall. As the ship pulled away from the shore, he wrote the very last line of his journal.

'Thus ends my restless progress in America.'[36]

Restless.

There is, perhaps, no better word to describe the borders of the United States of America. George Washington's prediction was correct. The proclamation line did fall. Colonists did stream west of the Alleghenies.

When the Revolutionary War with Britain broke out in 1775, it was a fight over bordering, a refusal to be contained by the imposition of boundaries. The Declaration of Independence that followed in 1776 was, among many other things, a manifesto *against limits*. Mason and Dixon's visto, completed just eight years earlier, had already cut an arrow into the heart of the continent, pointing out the direction of travel: west, west and always west. In its final stretch it had passed beyond the limits of Maryland and was no longer really bounding anything. It was just unspooling on and on, like a fishing line pulled forwards by fathomless possibility.

In 1783, the Treaty of Paris brought the war with Britain to an end. It also catapulted the western border of the United States from the Alleghenies to the Mississippi River, essentially doubling the size of the new nation with one pen stroke.[37] The Mississippi is, itself, a notoriously unreliable boundary. A 2,000-mile long river that cuts almost all of North America in two, from north to south, it constantly shifts and alters its course: its seemingly endless, coiled-spring meanders shape and reshape the land from one season to the next; its banks break to spread its waters for miles across its alluvial flood plain.

'One who knows the Mississippi,' wrote Mark Twain, knows that you, 'cannot tame that lawless stream, cannot curb it or confine it, cannot say to it, *Go here*, or *Go there*, and make it obey; cannot save a shore which it has sentenced; cannot bar its path with an obstruction which it will not tear down, dance over, and laugh at.'[38]

Twain could, just as easily, have been describing America.

This river border would last only twenty years. In 1803, the United States bought the region then known as Louisiana from the French – 800,000 square miles of territory that stretched from New Orleans to the northern ridgeline of the Rocky Mountains. A vast tract of land that doubled the size of the country once more, sent its western edge-point so far over the horizon that it seemed hardly worth considering an end at all.

There were some dissenting voices in the new republic, those who argued that the purchase was unconstitutional, that unchecked expansion threatened the stability of their emergent nation. But such opinions were in the minority. In response, John Randolph, who held the State of Virginia's seat on the House of Representatives, said that there 'was no particular boundary beyond which the United States could not extend'.[39] America, Randolph intimated, offered the world something new: a country always on the move, expressing its freedom through constant growth. A nation without limit.

Which meant that whatever borders the United States had at any one time were always temporal, contingent. As soon as they were conceived they were being instantaneously hurdled. When the 1819 Treaty of Adams–Onís set out its detailed description of the borderline with New Spain – and then, in 1821, the Republic of Mexico – settlers were already passing beyond it. They carried the frontier with them, pushing ever outwards, engaged in a constant conflict with the Native Americans whose lands they claimed – removing or exterminating tribes in the name of God, civilisation and progress. In turn, war with Mexico was seemingly inevitable: the moment that the former colonists, turned republicans, would announce themselves as an empire. By the mid-nineteenth century, it had become a key facet of government policy that the United States had a God-given right to claim all the lands from the east coast to the west coast of North America. They even had a name for it: 'Manifest Destiny'.

This phrase was first coined by the journalist John L. O'Sullivan in the summer of 1845. Agitating for the annexation of Texas, he railed against anti-expansionists and accused them of 'thwarting our policy and hampering our power, limiting our greatness and checking the fulfilment of our manifest destiny to overspread the continent allotted by Providence for the free development of our yearly multiplying millions'. For O'Sullivan, it was not just the land of the United States, but even its whole future, that was 'boundless'.[40]

It is hard to overstate just how deeply this notion of 'boundlessness' came to be rooted in the American psyche. At the end of the nineteenth century, a thirty-two-year-old historian from Wisconsin, Frederick Jackson Turner, summarised the concept in a paper that would later be described as 'the single most influential piece of writing in the history of American history'.[41] Turner presented what he called his 'frontier thesis'. As he put it, 'the existence of an area of free land, its continuous recession, and the advance of American settlement westward, explain American development'.[42] It was through this process of incessant movement, he wrote, that American identity itself was formed.

The border had begun as the Atlantic coast, Turner said. 'It was the frontier of Europe in a very real sense.' But, 'moving westward, the frontier became more and more American. As successive terminal moraines result from successive glaciations, so each frontier leaves its traces behind it, and when it becomes a settled region it still partakes of the frontier characteristics. Thus the advance of the frontier has meant a steady movement away from the influence of Europe, a steady growth of independence on American lines.' And so the more you move, and the more you expand, the more *American* you become. Democracy itself, he argued, 'came out of the American forest, and it gained strength each time it touched a new frontier'.[43] Which meant that a constantly moving border was a fundamental good. More than that, it was what made America *great.*

For Turner, the frontier was something almost mystical – and certainly unique – in the course of political history: a previously undiscovered engine for powering national success. It was, he wrote, 'a magic fountain of youth in which America continually bathed and was rejuvenated'; a 'field of opportunity'; 'the line of most rapid and effective Americanisation'; 'the outer edge of the wave'; a place to display 'dominion over inanimate nature'; a 'form of society rather than an area'; and a 'gate of escape from the bondage of the past'. It was also, all the time, 'the meeting point between savagery and civilisation'. And within this tension, he said, the frontier created the 'striking characteristics' of the 'American intellect' – 'coarseness and strength combined with acuteness and inquisitiveness; the practical, inventive turn of mind . . . that restless, nervous energy; that dominant individualism . . . that buoyancy and exuberance which comes with freedom'.[44]

Turner's thesis was, in many respects, a triumphant celebration of what he conceived as the struggle of the American people to build a new society. The borderline was hard-won at every step, but still it kept pushing west, changing everything as it went, bending and surging and leaping forwards, leaving a 'better' world in its wake. It offered a potent, accessible – and decidedly non-elitist – national myth: which of course ignored those who were overstepped, excluded or even annihilated in the process. Yet in his conclusion, Turner, albeit unknowingly, offered up a warning, a worrying vision of how this frontier past might inform the American future.

'Movement,' he wrote, has been America's 'dominant fact, and unless this training has no effect upon a people, the American energy will continually demand a wider field for its exercise.'[45] But the land cannot go on for ever. It must, inevitably, run out. And when it does, where does all that energy go? Where is the 'wider field' to be found? What happens if you finally delineate a nation that has been forged by the power of a moving border?

Ironically, Turner published his thesis just three years after the Superintendent of the US Census had reported in 1890 that 'at present . . . there can hardly be said to be a frontier line. In the discussion of its extent, its westward movement, etc, it cannot, therefore, any longer have a place in the census reports.'[46] In official terms, the frontier, that ever-shifting line that *was* American, had vanished.

Fifty years earlier, none other than Herman Melville had warned of the consequences when this mobile border had nowhere left to go. The land would be 'overrun at last . . . and then, the recoil must come'.[47]

Almost exactly a century after Turner's thesis, another American author was proposing his own theory on the origins and development of the United States. He too looked to lines – and frontiers and borders – for an answer. And, in particular, he returned to that first line, that arc of latitude cut into the continent by Charles Mason and Jeremiah Dixon. He even set out to explore this margin himself. He was said to have been seen walking the boundary between Pennsylvania and Maryland, pacing through forests, crossing highways, heading west.[48]

This may just have been rumour, of course. He is, after all, a famous recluse, a mystery man of American letters, variously described as 'the poet laureate of the deep state' and 'the postmodern Virgil'.[49] The author was Thomas Pynchon, and in 1997 he published *Mason & Dixon*, a 774-page, Henry Fielding-esque account of the two English astronomer-surveyors and their attempt to inscribe their boundary into the landscape. Except, in Pynchon's hands, what their story offered was a vehicle for an extended exploration and critique of the whole American project. The result was a kind of 'anti-Turner' – an alternative 'frontier thesis', a dark mirror which considered the drawing of lines and the constant expansion of borders not as a fundamental good, but rather as its exact opposite.

In the novel, Pynchon mocks the 'Geometrickally impossible territory' handed out by the two British kings, 'as if in playful refusal to admit that America, in any way, may be serious'. And so Mason and Dixon are really just surveying a line of make-believe. As the book's main narrator, the Reverend Wicks Cherrycoke puts it, 'there exists no "Maryland" beyond an Abstraction, a Frame of right lines drawn to enclose and square off the great Bay in its unimagin'd Fecundity, its shoreline tending to Infinite Length, ultimately unmappable, – no more, to be fair, than there exists any "Pennsylvania" but a chronicle of Frauds, committed serially against the Indians dwelling there, check'd only by the Ambitions of other Colonies to north and east'.[50]

As they cut their visto further and further into the continental interior, Dixon worries that the line has taken on a life of its own. It is, he says a 'tree-slaughtering Animal, with no purpose but to continue creating forever a perfect Corridor over the Land. Its teeth of Steel, – its Jaws, Axmen, – its Life's Blood, Disbursement. And what of its intentions beyond killing ev'rything due west of it? do you know? I don't either.'[51]

He wonders what the Native Americans must think, as they watch this 'invisible Thing that comes crawling straight over their Lands devouring all in its Path'. He suggests to Mason that all their constant cutting through the landscape has sent a clear message: 'as you see what we may do to Trees, and how little we care, – imagine how little we care for Indians, and what we are prepar'd to do to you. That Influence you have felt, along our line, that Current strong as a River's, – we command it.'[52]

Near the end of the novel, both Mason and Dixon come to conclude, mournfully, that the boundary they have drawn is nothing less than 'a conduit for evil'. It is just as one of their survey party, Captain Zhang, a Chinese expert in feng shui had warned them it would be. 'To mark a right line on the earth' is to invite 'Bad Energy', Zhang told them. And just as night follows day, so 'Bad History' follows 'Bad Energy'.

'Nothing,' he said, 'will produce Bad History more directly nor brutally, than drawing a Line, in particular a Right Line, the very Shape of Contempt, through the midst of a people – to create thus a Distinction betwixt 'em, – 'tis the first stroke. – All else will follow as if predestin'd, unto War and Devastation.'[53]

The proliferation of lines across the continent is, for Pynchon, the tragedy of America. He agrees with Turner that you can find the unique American character in shifting boundaries. But the problem, he suggests, is that this character – whatever its merits – is rooted in a pernicious binarism, an addiction to adversarial division. This mania for boundary lines and frontiers and borders offered the promise of separation and freedom from the bondage of the Old World – but only if you were white and Christian and Anglo-Saxon. And, once the continent was finally 'overspread', it was inevitable that these same lines would come to divide Americans from each other.[54]

In Zhang's 'Bad History', Pynchon is foreshadowing the ultimate divisive conflict still to come. Because Mason and Dixon's line was more than just a boundary between two states. It was also the dividing line between two separate Americas: the one that advocated slavery and the one that opposed it. What was 'predestined' to follow the line was the 'devastation' of *civil* war.

Pennsylvania would become the southern frontier of the abolitionist, industrial North; Maryland, the northern frontier of the slave-owning, agrarian South. Mason and Dixon's line, drawn in the name of reason and order, had, at the same time, been powered and funded by both the forced removal of Native Americans from the land and the forced labour of enslaved Africans in the colonial plantations. This was the true 'current, strong as a river's' that coursed along their visto: violent subjugation and binary division as America's foundational narrative.

Tensions mounted throughout the first half of the nineteenth century. By the summer of 1858, a series of national debates were being held on the future of slavery. Arguing in favour of abolition, against the slave-owning Illinois senator Stephen A. Douglas, was the man looking to take his seat on the Senate – Abraham Lincoln. Lincoln cast America as the latest battleground for a timeless, near-existential opposition. 'It is the eternal struggle between these two principles – right and wrong – throughout the world,' he said – with

Mason and Dixon's boundary as the hinge between them. On either side of the line were 'the two principles that have stood face to face from the beginning of time'. Douglas, on the other hand, argued that freeing the slaves and then letting them cross whatever borders they liked would ultimately make the prairie 'as black as night'.[55] Venus's inkblot on the white surface of the sun, expanding unstoppably into a total eclipse.

These stark differences could not be resolved through political rhetoric. Where reason failed, only force could follow. Three years later, the Civil War broke out. And another four years after that, Lincoln was assassinated at Ford's Theatre in Washington, D.C. For one half of America this was an unprecedented tragedy. For the other, the gunman, John Wilkes-Booth, was 'the great American Brutus', 'a lover of liberty' who had killed 'the enemy of his country'.[56]

Such deep-rooted divisions don't disappear, even when one side prevails. When the enslaved fugitive Harriet Tubman escaped across Mason and Dixon's line from Maryland into Pennsylvania in 1849, she spoke of how she looked down at her hands 'to see if I was the same person. There was such glory over everything; the sun came like gold through the trees, and over the fields, and I felt like I was in Heaven.' Understandably, in that moment, the boundary was the difference between, as she put it, 'liberty or death'.[57] Step north across the visto and you were in 'the promised land'. Such was the power of the line.

As Pynchon writes – imagining the surveyors' arc of latitude running down the main street of a village – 'laws continuing upon one side, – Slaves, Tobacco, Tax Liabilities, – may cease to exist upon the other'. Here, the line has the capacity to change your very existence: 'Slaves yesterday, free Men and Women today! You survey'd the Chains right off 'em with your own!'[58]

Tubman's joy did not – and could not – however, anticipate the struggles that would follow this 'emancipation'. The Fugitive Slave Law of 1850 that would empower slave owners to cross boundaries to recapture their 'property'. The chaotic Civil War that freed enslaved people in some states but kept them in bondage in others. The many lines – legal, political, social – that would follow over the next century and a half up to the present day, to act as barriers to integration and equality for all those once captive Africans who had become Americans.

Pynchon's point, in the end, is that all of these divisions remain, one way or another. They were there when he published his novel in 1997, and they are still here now, two decades on – perhaps the most pronounced they have been since the Civil War. Look for the origins of today's polarised America and you will find it in the very manner in which the continent was first taken, parcelled up and – as Pynchon's narrator, the Reverend Cherrycoke puts it – 'bickered' into 'Fragments'. The United States, built on the very idea of borders, founded on lines of inclusion and exclusion. The one place 'we should not have found them'.[59]

This, he concludes, is the failure of the original American dream: that there was once the possibility that the New World could have escaped the prejudices, injustices and hierarchies of the Old. But instead it took them, allowed them to evolve, and channelled them into the very flesh of the landscape: first through Mason and Dixon's line, and then through the innumerable lines that followed.

For a short time, America was the 'very Rubbish tip for subjunctive Hopes, for all that *may yet be true*, – Earthly Paradise, Fountain of Youth, Realms of Prester John, Christ's Kingdom'. This America was 'ever behind the sunset, safe till the next Territory to the west be seen and recorded, measur'd and tied in, back into the NetWork of Points already known, that slowly triangulates its Way into the Continent, changing all from subjunctive to declarative, reducing Possibilities to Simplicities that serve the ends of Governments, – winning away from the realms of the Scared, its Borderlands one by one, and assuming them unto the bare mortal world that is our home, and our Despair'.[60]

Turner's always advancing frontier erased American *possibility*. The great period of expansion, Pynchon argues, was equally a process of contraction. A narrowing of vision, a hardening of views, a cementing of inequality: a race to exhaust potential through an insatiable demand to run dividing lines out, across and around all the land that there was.

America today, he says, is 'haunted by the edge', by this lost border. And he pines for the fleeting moments when Mason and Dixon's boundary was still to run its full course. 'For as long as its Distance from the Post Mark'd West remains umeasur'd, nor is yet recorded as fact, may it remain, a-shimmer, among the few final Pages of its Life as Fiction.'[61]

In those last days of the survey, Pynchon still saw America as an expanse of hope. Before the visto touched it, and the inconvenient truth arrowed in. The truth that America *is the line* and the line *is America*. The outer edge of the wave. The conduit of bad history. The field of opportunity. The very shape of contempt. The eternal struggle between right and wrong. All swept up in that volatile current, strong as a river's.

To understand the United States today, that is still where you must go. To the line. To the border.

'We need to retell the story of the border,' David had said to me.

'If we don't recast it as something different, it will remain forever portrayed as a dangerous space. It has become part of our national mythology now. And so you have to tell a better story of the border to try to change that.'

I was driving south through Colorado's Rocky Mountains, on Highway 91, following the course of East Fork of the Arkansas River. It was late spring, a warm light was draped over the mountains, bringing out the rich green of their forested slopes and the rust-red of their bare rock, and the sun glinted in the remaining patches of snow.

(Actually, I wasn't driving. Or, more specifically, I was driving, but *virtually*. I should have been there, in the heart of Colorado, making my way through the mountains in a hire car picked up from Denver Airport. But the month before the trip, the United States closed its borders to all travellers from Europe. Countries all over the world

– including my own – went into lockdown. And so what follows is my recreation of the road trip that I was going to make, moving click for click down the highway using Google Earth . . . As I went, I listened back to the recording of my conversation with David and Marcos.)

Where the highway crossed the Fremont Pass, the valley opened up into the space left by an entire mountain that has been carved away for its molybdenum, an ore used to make the metal alloys in jet engine turbines. The road curved around again. The thin strip of the Arkansas tributary was on the left, the highway on the right. Just peaking up above a low hillock, I could see it. Surrounded by a clump of bright green bushes – Monument 20.

'We base so much understanding of place on an idea of borders being permanent,' David had said. 'There's this real notion of stasis that we project onto them, but historically that's not well supported. The idea that the borders of the United States are going to be like they are right now in say 100, 200 or 500 years? That's our desire speaking rather than anything that history would bear out.'

Another fifteen miles on, through the town of Leadville, the mountains receded from the highway and the land opened up into a wide, flat, grassy plain, which was threaded by the main branch of the Arkansas River. There, just before the road crossed the river, is a small parking area. At one end of it, framed by the riverbank and the plain and the distant mountains, was Monument 21. I zoomed in on its galvanised steel, still shining bright and untarnished. A couple were caught frozen, standing beside it to take a photograph.

'It is inherent,' Marcos had said to me. 'This idea of America for the Americans. This idea of "manifest destiny". That God talked to the president and said, "The destiny of this nation is to expand and conquer." I think this is just racist. The more they moved, the more they erased the rest of the people, just to put in place the ones who are similar to them. And this is inherent in the border today.'

Both Marcos and David had talked to me about the difference between the English word 'frontier', and the Spanish word '*frontera*'.

'*Frontier* to Americans is this vast plain of unlimited promise,' David said, 'where we realise our mythologies of freedom and independence and self-reliance, right? In Spanish, *frontera* is a limit, a demarcation. So right there we have this cognitive dissonance, embodied in these two different ideas.'

Marcos continued: 'The idea of the frontier in America is something that is at the edge *and then beyond*, that is waiting to be conquered. We don't have that in Mexico because we were a conquered country. For us, no, the *frontera* is just a line, it is a marker. You are not supposed to cross it, you know?'

He laughed then, deep and rich. 'We never thought that the limit could be expandable!'

Another twenty miles south, in the town of Buena Vista, I found Monument 22 behind a baseball field and a football pitch, overlooking the fast-flowing rapids of the Arkansas River. By this point, David was talking about what was happening at the current border with Mexico.

'We've commodified displacement at this point,' he said. 'We've reached the stage where there is an *exhaustion* of a perceived arena of *inexhaustible* resources. And so you get to the point where the migrant body becomes a resource: it's the last thing to exploit, that can be consumed for profit by a predatory industry that's capitalising on the fact that we've created this xenophobic image of the "other" arriving at our border'.

As David explained it, there is now new money to be made by the line, in processing those who, inexorably, are sucked into its orbit. Those dispossessed and undocumented are a resource that is unlikely to run out any time soon. David had told me a story about travelling to Tijuana in November 2018, at the same time as a 'caravan' of nearly 8,000 Central American migrants began to arrive in the city and converge on the San Ysidro Port of Entry to the United States. A makeshift tent city grew up in the open fields of a municipal sports centre a block away from the border. At the end of the month, on 25 November, thousands of migrants marched on San Ysidro to present themselves to the American authorities and request asylum.

What happened next was, perhaps, inevitable. A stand-off with Mexican police at the El Chaparral bridge leading to San Ysidro escalated as some migrants tried to push through, while others attempted to cross the last few hundred metres to the Port of Entry over the concrete banks of the Tijuana River. All of a sudden, the peaceful march became violent, and tear gas was being fired out into the massed crowds. Soon Mexican police were moving through the streets to round up any migrant they could find and load them into vans and trucks. David was right there, among the chaos in the streets of Tijuana, and it was at this moment that a young Honduran man ran up to him and asked urgently, 'How do I get across the border?'

All David could say to him was that it was not possible. 'Not here,' he had told the young man. 'The border is too strong.' And then he was gone again.[62]

'This was the moment,' David had said to me. The moment that he realised that 'it is never going to stop'.

'The fortification of our border is seen as a kind of definitive act to stem this problem,' he said. 'But it's not that. It's a futile act at the outset of what will be our new normal.'

How do I get across the border? There can be few moments today when someone, somewhere in the world, is not asking this exact same question. Our new normal.

At Smeltertown, Colorado, I looked for Monument 23 beneath the iron and concrete superstructure of a small bridge that takes Highway 291 over the Arkansas River. But it was nowhere to be seen.

The old 1821 line, as marked by David and Marcos, twisted east here, following the river out across the flat, empty plains than run off into Kansas. But I wasn't going that way. Instead, I continued south, for hundreds of miles: past Albuquerque and right through the middle of New Mexico, then west on Highway 10, clicking my way onwards into a parched landscape of desert and rock. Ahead of me was Arizona, Tucson and the Mexican border.

PART 3
CROSSING

6

HOSTILE TERRAIN

In October 2017, eight monoliths appeared in a patch of desert scrubland opposite the Mexican city of Tijuana. Four were made of reinforced concrete. Four were made of other materials: steel bars, metal tubes, brick facades and barbed wire. One slab was even coloured a striking navy blue – a cold, austere hue that suggested the sky on the very cusp of night. All rose up to a height of thirty feet.

These monoliths were commissioned by the US Customs and Border Protection Agency – eight prototypes for a border wall which, if ever fully completed, will run unbroken for 1,954 miles along the southern edge-line of America. According to their construction brief, they were to be 'aesthetically pleasing' and 'sympathetic to the local surroundings' (these two requirements for the US side only) and, more specifically, able to withstand at least half an hour of force from a 'sledgehammer, car jack, pickaxe, chisel, battery-operated impact tools, battery-operated cutting tools, oxy/acetylene torch or other similar hand-held tools'.[1]

The eight prototypes were not hidden from public view. Their designs and effectiveness were not assessed and tested in secret. Instead, they were erected alongside each other, spaced out a few metres apart in a single line, overlooking the fifteen-foot-high, rusting metal border fence that they were intended to supplement – or replace. They loomed over this fence, stared into the city, into the other country, beyond. There was no writing on any of these wall fragments, but there did not need to be. Their message was clear.

Two months after the eight border-wall prototypes were erected, a new, non-profit organisation called MAGA launched a campaign via an online petition to have them designated as a national monument. Under the Antiquities Act of 1906, either the president by proclamation, or Congress through legislation, can protect in perpetuity any significant natural, cultural or scientific feature on US Federal land. MAGA, an acronym for 'Make Art Great Again', argued that the eight prototypes had special 'cultural value' and were 'historical land art'.[2]

At the same time as the petition, MAGA was offering tours of the site as a 'major land art exhibition', which it called PROTOTYPES. Buses would leave from outside the Museum of Contemporary Art in San Diego and drive through the San Ysidro checkpoint into Mexico. Because access was restricted on the American side, the only way to see PROTOTYPES up close was from south of the border. The tour buses would continue through Tijuana to reach a dirt road in the neighbourhood of Escondido on the very eastern edge of the city. There, between the Megatruck stop and a scrapyard, a step ladder was set up alongside the current border fence to allow visitors to climb up and view the eight wall slabs in situ.

MAGA and its provocative campaign were created by the Swiss conceptual artist Christoph Büchel. When he first saw photographs of the prototypes, Büchel said he thought instantly of Stonehenge. 'Visually it is really striking,' he told *The New York Times.* As well as ancient parallels, he was also struck by the way the slabs offered a strange blend of Americana and science fiction – echoes of drive-in movie screens as parsed by the apocalypse, or the iconic monolith from the opening scenes of Stanley Kubrick's *2001: A Space Odyssey.* From the top of the step ladder, looking north, he said that 'you see everything, it's quite a strong conceptual impact', and so the prototypes have a unique, albeit unintentional 'sculptural value'.[3] The reason for preserving them, he said, was 'because they can signify and change meaning through time. They can remind people there was the idea to have this border wall once.'

MAGA and PROTOTYPES polarised the artistic community, particularly that of west coast America. In February 2018, hundreds of artists and curators signed an open letter condemning the tours to the wall, saying that they were 'concerned more with spectacle and irony than critically dismantling oppressive structures that undermine the lives of the most vulnerable'. They criticised *The New York Times* coverage of the project – which appeared under the headline 'Is Donald Trump, Wall-Builder-in-Chief, a Conceptual Artist?' – and argued that treating the eight slabs as 'land art' served only to 'aestheticize state violence and mock the lived experiences of those most affected by that violence'.[4]

Büchel had form for stoking controversy – he had converted a deconsecrated church into a mosque at the 2015 Venice Biennale, and once attempted to bury an entire jumbo jet in the Mojave Desert – and responded through a statement released by his gallery, Hauser & Wirth, that the prototypes should 'continue to stand as evidence of bigotry and fear in American culture, and serve as catalysts for transforming political discourse'. In his interview with *The New York Times*, Büchel had insisted that he was not the artist of this 'work' – rather its creators were the president, his administration and, by extension, the American nation itself.

'This is a collective sculpture,' he said. 'People elected this artist.'[5]

Jerry Saltz, the art critic for *New York* magazine, was inclined to agree. What he saw in Büchel's proposal was a 'glimmer of hope in the hopelessness'. It prompted him to imagine looking at them from the vantage point of some distant, more egalitarian future when 'these prototypes will be a perfect memorial to how close the United States came to giving in to the ghosts of racism, xenophobia, nativism, white nationalism, mediocrity, and a cosmic fear of the other'.[6]

In the end, Büchel and MAGA's petition received only 984 signatures: well short of their required goal of 1,600. In January 2019, it was revealed that all the proposed walls had failed basic 'penetrability' tests. The following month, the prototypes were demolished – the eight monoliths smashed down and broken up by the metal jaws and pneumatic drills of heavy machinery.

Büchel's concept of a 'National Monument' did not, however, disappear completely. Two years later, in April 2021, a Republican

Congressional Representative, Madison Cawthorn, put forward a draft bill which called for the establishment of a 'Southern Border Wall National Monument'. Dubbed the 'Donument Act' (a conflation of 'Donald Trump' and 'monument'), it proposed the designation of some 400 miles of border wall in California, Arizona, New Mexico and Texas – along with nearly 300,000 acres of surrounding borderlands – as a monument with 'permanent protection from alteration'.

'I will make every effort to protect and secure the southern border, and advance an America First agenda,' Cawthorn said in a statement announcing the bill. He continued that, if President Joe Biden 'refuses to finish the wall, you can be sure that American patriots will do everything in their power to protect it'.[7]

Just days before Cawthorn announced his bill, Arizona's Attorney General Mark Brnovich filed a lawsuit against the Biden administration, alleging that halting border-wall construction violated the National Environmental Policy Act and was 'having a devastating impact on the environment'. Not completing the wall, Brnovich said, had caused 'a dramatic increase of the number of people coming into this country crossing the border illegally'. As they moved north, he continued, migrants left 'trash' in their wake – clothes, backpacks, plastic bottles. 'That has an impact on wildlife, natural habitat,' he said, and 'it can also be fuel for wildfires.'[8] The Republican Senator for Tennessee Marsha Blackburn had expressed these same concerns in an interview given two weeks earlier. 'For all of those that are concerned about the environment,' she said, 'we have an environmental crisis. Because the migrants are running across the border, they're trampling through the ecosystem.'

Following this line of argument, *not* building the wall was hurting the landscape. The barrier was, in effect, a *suture*, binding the earth, closing a wound. What, Blackburn wondered, would happen without a wall when the rains came? 'We have roads that have been cut for putting in the wall . . . Those unfinished roads are going to wash.'[9]

While Cawthorn's bill had no chance of passing through a Congress controlled by a Democratic majority, it highlighted the precarious nature of a 'National Monument': that cultural significance is open to endless interpretation. If you take policies of isolationism, 'America First' and ostentatious security to their logical conclusion, then what more appropriate symbol of a nation could there be than a border wall? The identity of the United States and its people cut into the land, poured into concrete foundations, then unfurled over the crests of hills and mountains, snaking across desert plains and into the distance. Preserved for all time in a line of dark orange, eternally rusting steel.

'There was a backpack that we found that had a picture frame in it that said *Number One Dad* on it,' Jason De León told me. 'And someone had broken the glass and taken the photo out and left everything else behind. And I often think about the person that was carrying this framed photograph that says *Number One Dad* on it. I always wonder, who is the *Number One Dad*? Is it the dad who has to leave his kids and his country behind and go into the desert? Or is it the dad who stays, and watches their kids starve – but at least they are all together?'

For more than a decade, Jason has been collecting what people have dropped, discarded or lost as they attempt to cross the US–Mexico border through Arizona's Sonoran Desert. He has now amassed more than 8,000 objects, all catalogued, tagged, GPS-located and stored in archival boxes in a research laboratory at the University of California, Los Angeles, where he once studied archaeology as an undergraduate and now works as a professor of anthropology.

Jason had first travelled to the desert in January 2009. Around that time, he said, 'There was all this rhetoric about migrant *trash*. And that's one of the reasons I got interested in the first place, because people were posting pictures online and saying, *look at all this garbage that Mexicans are leaving out in the desert*. But that's all archaeology really is. The study of *trash*.'

He made contact with a local Arizona man, Bob Kee, a retired dental technician turned volunteer for the Tucson Samaritans. For years, Bob had been going out into the landscape, often several times a week, to leave food, water and medical aid for migrants. He took

Jason to a trail just beyond the small town of Arivaca, not much more than ten miles north of the border. After a couple of hours of hiking, they climbed up to a ridgeline that offered a view down onto an expanse of desert floor.

'And there was just all of this stuff,' Jason told me. 'Thousands of backpacks and those kinds of things. Water bottles everywhere. So from that first day that I went out, I thought that, okay, there is something here. But it was like a bar napkin sketch thing. Is this actually going to work? Who knows?'

If you were to go looking for the traces of *ancient* migrations, he told me, they were almost impossible to identify.

'The fingerprint is so shallow. It's notoriously difficult to study in the past, it really truly is.'

By the time that the materials being left behind by today's migrants were old enough to qualify as 'archaeology', they would already be gone. Cleared up and thrown away, or degraded, melted, turned to fragments and dust by the sun and the heat and extreme conditions of the Sonoran Desert. His idea was to create an archaeological record of the present, of *right now*. What was just trash to some was what Jason has described as, 'American immigration history in the making'.[10]

Jason was not, as he admitted readily to me, a conventional archaeologist. His original interest in the field stemmed from a trip, at the age of eight, to visit the pyramids of Teotihuacan in Mexico. And a love of the Indiana Jones films.

'For the longest time I just told people I'm going to be an archaeologist. Even though I didn't have any clue what that actually meant. So when I went to college, people said, *well, archaeology falls under anthropology*. I said, *okay, sounds good to me*. But it was this childhood fantasy. I didn't know what else to do with myself.'

Jason dropped out of university after just two months. He used his student loan cheque to buy a van and set off on a three-month tour of the US with his garage punk-reggae band Youth in Asia (say it quickly . . .).

'I thought that this was going to be my life,' Jason told me. Until the realisation hit him that it would also mean 'forever being broke and having no health insurance'.

He returned to academia, finished his undergraduate degree, then went on to complete a doctoral study, focusing on the trade of obsidian blade tools in Olmec Mesoamerica. Almost a decade had passed by this point, but still that sense of disillusionment hadn't quite left him.

'I felt like, *we're doing archaeology and the world's on fire. We're studying this thing that like six people care about.* And for me it became very difficult to work in Mexico and be thinking about issues of inequality in the deep past, thinking about stratification and social organisation from 3,000 years ago, when I'm watching inequality play out in real time.'

Jason was spending months working on excavations in Mexico for his dissertation. And all the time he was hearing from local people about how they were getting ready to cross, or had already tried to cross, the border into America.

'I met this one guy who was about my age, who had just come back from Arizona. And he tells me these stories about the border, about how he had almost died in the Sonoran Desert. And I'm thinking to myself, *well, I thought I knew a lot about the US–Mexico border because I travelled it so much.* I went to elementary school for three years in South Texas, so I was always around this border. But I came to realise that I didn't know anything about it. So those stories radically changed my thinking about what I should be doing with my life.'

Both of Jason's parents had served in the US Army and both were, in effect, immigrants to America. His mother was from the Philippines, while his father was from Mexico.

'On my dad's birth certificate it says that he was born in Texas,' he told me. 'Although it was very likely that he was born in Mexico and brought across when he was a baby. And then I had tons of other relatives who were undocumented. So I grew up around immigrant communities.'

As a boy, Jason said, he crossed constantly into Mexico.

'We spent so much time there. Going back and forth, grocery shopping and so on. It would be like, *we're going to go to Reynosa today.* Nowadays Reynosa is like *The Walking Dead*, it's so dangerous; you can't do it any more. But I sort of grew up thinking it was no big deal.'

The nature of the line and how you moved across it had flipped.

'And so all of those things I'd been thinking about up to that point – Mexico, borders, my family – they all circled around with the people I was meeting who had just crossed borders or who were getting ready to cross borders.'

By the end of his doctorate, he told me, he had no more interest in archaeology. Instead, he wanted to talk to *living* people.

'But at that point I hadn't really been thinking about bridging archaeology with migration. It wasn't until I took that trip to Arizona.'

At first, nobody among the local NGOs and humanitarian organisations had been willing to take him out into the desert. 'They all thought that what I wanted to do was ridiculous,' Jason said. That was until Bob agreed to be his guide.

'And once I got out there and I took stock of the scene, I realised that there was just so much work to do.'

Immediately after that first visit, Jason established what he called the Undocumented Migration Project.[11] Recruiting a team of students and graduate researchers, his aim was to combine aspects of archaeology, anthropology and forensic science to create a long-term study of unauthorised border crossing – and, in particular, to understand what he called the 'evolving material culture' associated with it. What this meant, in practice, was going out into the desert over and over again, following the routes of migrant trails and collecting whatever had been left behind.

To begin with, it was the personal objects that Jason was drawn to most. Pocket bibles with personal messages inside them. Love letters. Family photographs. He told me about a three-year-old's shoe that he had collected, which was covered in hand-drawn messages saying things like *I love you* and *Please don't leave.* A wallet with a joke driver's licence inside it. At some point the wallet's owner must have visited the UFO Museum in Roswell, New Mexico, and bought an 'illegal alien' driver's ID card.

'People are funny,' Jason said. 'They carry funny stuff with them. I think about that a lot.'

And then there was this one backpack, still with a shirt inside it; on the back of the shirt was an embroidered Statue of Liberty.

'For me that speaks to the fact that the Sonoran Desert really is, or has been, the Ellis Island for migrants for the past twenty years,' he said. 'We haven't thought about it in this kind of romantic way. And I hope we don't *ever* think about it in these terms. But there definitely is this parallel between these sorts of ports of mass entry.'

Over time, Jason's attention began to shift away from the very intimate, unique items towards the more everyday material – in particular, the water bottles.

'People are dying from lack of water, and every time I pick up one of those bottles I think about that. In a lot of ways the water bottles are one of the most moving and the most difficult kind of objects to handle because you know that they are this interface between life and death.'

Not long after he began the project, Jason noticed a significant shift in the nature of the bottles themselves. Before 2009, they had almost all been white. That year, however, all of sudden, he was finding black bottles everywhere.

'Boom, they just showed up overnight,' he told me. 'And I would say more than 70 per cent of all bottles are black now.'

This shift, it seems, is all about concealment: white bottles catch the light, reflect the sun, floodlights, torch beams.

'That's where the archaeology becomes really helpful,' he said. 'Because most people aren't weirdos who think about the water bottles.' Jason would ask migrants about their water bottles and 'they would look at me like I was insane. *Why do you want to know what colour the water bottle was that I was carrying?* Because they don't have a good sense of how things have changed. But the archaeology really gives you a sense of how people's own perspectives of what they're about to experience has evolved – along with the folks who are profiting from it.'

In towns all along the Mexican side of the border, whole economies have grown up around the manufacture and sale of the black water bottles, along with items like camouflage clothing and shoes with rectangles of carpet stuck to the soles – supposedly to help cover your tracks in the desert dust.

Back at the beginning of the project, Jason had found backpacks crammed with luggage: everything from cocktail dresses to hair driers. 'Things that they thought they were going to need on what they thought was going to be a really short journey. Two hours walking and they wanted to look their best when they got to the United States.'

Now, he said, ten years on, nobody was bringing anything other than the essentials. No books, no bibles, no family photographs. It was all food, first-aid equipment and water, backpacks. Camouflage shirts and trousers.

'But you only really pick up these changes if you are paying close attention to the objects that most people overlook.'

There were, however, other things that Jason and his team were finding. Bones. Often just tiny pieces – a sliver of a tooth, a splinter of sun-bleached skeleton. Sometimes a whole rib or an arm. Fragments of those people who never made it out of the desert.

Over the past twenty years, more than 7,000 people have been recorded as dying as they crossed the US–Mexico border. Nearly half these deaths have occurred in the Tucson sector alone, between New Mexico and the Yuma County line in Arizona: in that same strip of landscape first visited by Jason at the beginning of 2009. Here, the Sonoran Desert is characterised by saguaro and barrel cactus, thorn scrub, clinging grasses and parched, rocky gulleys and mountains. Summer temperatures regularly exceed 40°C, and in recent years have even topped 50°C. The region's hottest year on record, 2020, was also its deadliest. The remains of 227 migrants were found out among its borderlands.[12]

For two decades now, an aid organisation called Humane Borders has worked with Arizona's Pima County Medical Examiner's Office to monitor, record and recognise these deaths and, as part of this process, to create what they call a 'Migrant Death Map'. Overlain on a chart of southern Arizona is a rash of red dots: a scatter pattern that shows dense clusters along the line of the border with Mexico, but that spreads out far and wide across the landscape, with some lone dots even reaching as far north as the city of Phoenix.[13]

Each red dot is a person: a man or a woman or a child who died in their attempt to reach America. In the online version of the map, if you click on any one dot, you are given the barest hint of a story. A name – if, that is, they have actually been identified (for over a thousand dots, the name is still unknown). The day they were found and the condition of their bodies (in many cases this reads only 'skeletal remains'). The cause of death (if it was still possible to determine at the time of discovery). Unsurprisingly, exposure, heat stroke and hyperthermia are the most common. Their age (which ranges from babies just months old to, in one case, a man who was ninety-nine).

The Death Map presents a grim cartography of hope turned to human tragedy. A sort of real-time, spatial realisation of both the inexorable pull, and innate threat, of the border. For some families, anxious to know what has happened to their loved ones, the discovery of bodily remains – along with a specific location and cause – offers some meagre comfort. For many, however, there are no answers. Their sons or daughters or fathers or mothers or aunts or uncles or cousins have just disappeared. Entered the portal to the north – *el norte* – and never emerged out the other side. Everyone recognises that these official records are just a fraction of the real number of deaths in the desert. As a US government report acknowledged as far back as 2006, 'the total number of bodies that has not been found is ultimately unknown'. And, by implication, *never* would or could be known.

Increasingly, as Jason's project evolved, it was this uncertainty that came to occupy his mind. What actually happened to a body in the desert? Could it just disappear? Could it go from flesh to skeleton to fragments to . . . nothing? It was a prospect he found at once horrifying and yet, at the same time, vital.

'I was utterly shocked when I got into the literature and found that there was nothing,' he told me. No studies on the impact of the desert environment on human decomposition. No way of knowing if this landscape would preserve a person or erase them from existence.

'And even asking forensic scientists – they couldn't give me a good answer. They'd tell me, *well, we think some bodies mummify, some don't. We don't really know why that is. We're not sure if it's because of what they are wearing, or the time of year. Your guess is as good as ours.*'

Rather than guess, Jason decided to conduct his own research. He acquired juvenile and adult pigs from the University of Arizona's 'meat lab' and brought them out into the desert. For a number of reasons, including body size, fat distribution and anatomy, pigs are a common substitute for humans in forensic studies. To best recreate the circumstances of a person dying in situ in the landscape, Jason had to have the pigs killed on site. He then dressed them in various items of typical migrant clothing – jeans, underwear, T-shirts, shoes – and placed them in different contexts, from direct sunlight to partial and then complete shade.

I had heard Jason describe in an interview the incredulous response of the man who had delivered the animals to the desert site. 'I've seen a lot of weird stuff in this job,' the man had said to him, 'but I don't know what twisted shit you guys are on.' Jason had explained to him how no one really knew what happened to corpses in the desert, and so they were going to monitor the pigs with trail cameras, see how fast they decomposed and what type of wildlife scavengers would come. The man thought for a while and then said, 'You know, I had a cousin who crossed the border and disappeared. And we have no idea what happened to him.'[14]

'The footage is graphic,' Jason said to me. 'And it just gets worse and worse.'

In the first few days, not much happened – flies descended en masse, ants crawled all over the pigs' bodies, which had darkened and bloated in the sun. Then, whenever the carcasses reached what must have been the right state of putrefaction, the vultures came. Turkey vultures to be exact, big, black-feathered birds with bare, red, wrinkled heads. One or two would turn into half a dozen, then a dozen. In one video, Jason counted twenty-two vultures all feeding on the carcass at once, with another eight watching on, waiting their turn. The clothes were ripped apart, shoes torn off, to allow the birds to get at the rotting flesh. This process continued, day after day, for several weeks. In every experiment they conducted, the clothed bodies of the pigs would eventually be picked clean, reduced to skeletal remains scattered over a wide area. In most cases it was only possible to recover a proportion of the animal's bones – sometimes more than a third were missing.

In a grotesque irony, the fastest deterioration of a body came when they attempted to cover it up to 'protect' it from the sun and the scavengers. Jason had spoken to a number of migrants who had told him about this practice – how, if a member of your group died on the trail, you would give them a ceremonial burial beneath a makeshift cairn of desert rocks. As it turned out, these stones would then absorb the extreme heat of the sun, creating a mini-oven that would partially 'cook' the body, making it almost instantly attractive to scavengers. When they tried this with a pig, it went from fully fleshed to entirely skeletonised by vultures in just one day.

'The things we were watching on these cameras,' Jason said, 'it was gruesome. Now imagine a human in this scenario. The thought of what happens to people's bodies out there. It's a horrible thing to envision.'

Two weeks after conducting these first experiments with the pigs, Jason took a group of his students back to that original trail he had hiked with Bob Kee in 2009. It was now the summer of 2012, and, over the previous three years, he had continued to walk this route, witnessing how it had fallen steadily out of use. Very little new material was being dropped, and many of the objects that had once covered this landscape had deteriorated and disappeared in the intervening time. Jason's idea was to use the hike to demonstrate just how quickly the traces of migration could be erased.

The group made their way out of a dried-up ravine and climbed a steep slope of long, pale yellow grass towards a sparse clump of mesquite trees. On many occasions, Jason had sat in their shade, to rest or eat his lunch. It was there, just yards away from one of the trees, that they came across the body. A woman, collapsed face down, with a bottle of electrolyte fluids clutched beneath her arm. Jason would later describe this scene – in stark, vivid, unflinching detail – in his remarkable book, *The Land of Open Graves*, which emerged out of the Undocumented Migration Project.

'Her striking jet-black hair and the ponytail holder wrapped around her right wrist hint at the person she once was,' he wrote. 'I focus on her hair. It is smooth; the colour of smoky obsidian. It's possibly the darkest hair I've ever seen, and its texture gives the impression that she is still alive.'[15]

Jason called the police, and then he and his students waited with the body. They sat mostly in silence beneath the shade of one of the mesquite trees, in the hot breeze, until one of the group began to cry and was comforted by the others. Jason looked at the body and wondered about this woman's life.

'Was she a kind person? What did her laugh sound like? What compelled her to enter this desert?'[16]

After a while, someone remembered that they had picked up a discarded blanket earlier in the hike, and so they used it to cover the body. Four turkey vultures were circling in the sky above. It took five hours for the sheriff to arrive, and when he did, he came with a body bag, a stretcher and three Border Patrol agents. They had to turn the body over to get it into the bag, and Jason could not look away.

'I see what is left of her face,' he wrote. 'The mouth is a gnarled purple and black hole that obscures the rest of her features. I can't see her eyes because the mouth is too hard to look away from . . .

Whatever beauty and humanity that once existed in her face has been replaced by a stone-coloured ghoul stuck in mid-scream. It's a look you can never get away from.'[17]

The woman was taken to a storage freezer in the Pima County Medical Examiner's Office. She had no identification and had been carrying nothing other than that plastic bottle of fluids. But Jason became determined to find out who she was. He contacted an anthropologist friend who worked in the Examiner's Office, Robin Reineke, whose job it was to work with families whose relatives had died or gone missing while attempting to cross the desert. After several weeks Robin found a lead. A young migrant, who had encountered a group of local Samaritans the day before the body was found, had told them about walking with two people, an elderly man and a woman in her thirties, on the same trail that Jason and his group had hiked. Both his companions had fallen seriously ill while travelling with him, and he had had no choice but to leave them behind. The woman, he said, came from either Guatemala or Ecuador, and her name was Maricela.

Robin contacted the consulates of both countries, checked missing person reports, and was soon able to make a full identification. The body belonged to Carmita Maricela Zhagui Puyas, a thirty-one-year-old married mother of three who, in May 2012, left her husband and her children in Ecuador to attempt the journey to America.[18]

Jason told me that he could not shake the compulsion to make contact with Maricela's family. 'I felt like I needed to know who she was. And I hoped that on some level I could be helpful to them. I mean, I know that if someone I cared about died in the desert, I would want to know as much as possible about what had happened to them. So if someone had called me and said, *I'm the guy who came across this body. Would you like to know what happened?* – I think I would want that too.'

Eight months after Maricela's death, Jason arranged to meet with her brother-in-law. He lived in Queens in New York City, having made the journey from Ecuador to America a decade earlier, in 2001, when he was just seventeen years old. When Maricela told him over the phone that she was planning to migrate to New York, he pleaded with her not to. He knew, from his own experiences, just how fraught and dangerous the journey was. But she could not be dissuaded. She told him that she had no option; it was the only way to offer any kind of future for her children. At the beginning of June 2012, after she had reached northern Mexico and was preparing to walk across the Sonoran Desert, Maricela had sent a message to her sister-in-law via Facebook: 'I don't know how I'm going to get there but I am going for my family. God willing I will get there.'[19]

Before Maricela's body was returned to South America, her brother-in-law arranged for it to be transported to New York. He wanted her to complete her journey, even if it was in death. They held a wake for her in a local church in Queens, and then the next day her body was flown south again, travelling high over the borders of America, Mexico, Guatemala, Honduras, Nicaragua, Costa Rica, Panama and Colombia, back to Ecuador.

Jason told me that he and his team built a small, modest memorial to Maricela, on the trail beside where they found her, beneath the shade of one of the mesquite trees. They dug out a ditch and placed a round metal tub in the hole, encasing the bottom half of it in cement.

'A lot of cement. Because we wanted it to be permanent, Which meant we had to lug 150-pound bags of it across the desert.'

Inside the tub, they created a delicate mosaic of glass and ceramic tiles, patterned in blue, white and yellow. Behind these tiles were placed glass candle holders with faded images of saints on them. At the centre was a large silver crucifix, over which Jason had hung one of Maricela's necklaces, given to him by her family in Ecuador.

'We keep going back to check on it,' Jason told me. 'People have destroyed parts of it, and so we go back and rebuild parts of it. It is still there.'

It is a memorial to just one person, to a wife and a mother who, like thousands before her, was claimed by the border. But it also speaks to something larger. Why, for instance, was she there in the first place? She wanted to come to America, to find her way to New York. But why through the desert? Why cross via one of the harshest, most inhospitable landscapes anywhere along the borderline?

In 1993, in El Paso, Texas, the local Border Patrol began to put in place a new strategy that involved significantly increasing the visibility and presence of their agents along the length of the border fence in the city's downtown area. This process evolved into what became known officially as Operation Blockade. At one stage, the initiative saw some 400 border agents and their white-and-green patrol vehicles lined up along the banks of the Rio Grande for the entire twenty-mile stretch of the dividing line between El Paso and its Mexican counterpart Ciudad Juárez – a kind of visual, virtual, human wall. The result was that migrants, many of whom had previously just jumped the fences that bisected the two cities, began to gravitate away from the urban crossings and towards the edgelands. Or even further, out into the wilderness.

So pleased were the Border Patrol with the results in El Paso that, in 1994, this local initiative came to form the core of their new National Plan. They would, they said, 'improve control of the border by implementing a strategy of *prevention through deterrence*', bringing 'a decisive number of enforcement resources to bear in each major entry corridor', including hiring more than 1,000 new agents to work the line of the southwest border. The Border Patrol predicted that 'with traditional entry and smuggling routes disrupted, illegal traffic will be deterred, or forced over more hostile terrain, less suited for crossing and more suited for enforcement'.[20]

The concept was simple: funnel movement away from the population centres and use the landscape itself, the *hostile terrain*, as a barrier to entry. Scale up the approach in El Paso and apply it across the many hundreds of miles of the whole southwestern borderline. This National Plan not only admitted that the migrant 'influx' would adjust to the Border Patrol's changing tactics, and that 'violence will increase as effects of [the] strategy are felt', but it also included these same factors in its 'indicators of success'. Another document, produced by the US Government Accountability Office in 1997, went even further, suggesting that the 'deaths of aliens attempting entry' could be used for 'measuring the effectiveness of the strategy'.[21] Higher numbers of people dying would, in effect, show that the plan was working

In 2001, another Government Accountability Office report concluded that the plan's goal of 'shifting illegal traffic away from urban areas' had been achieved, but that this had come at a 'cost' to migrants. 'Rather than being deterred from attempting illegal entry,' it continued, 'many aliens have instead risked injury and death by trying to cross mountains, deserts and rivers.'[22] Not so much a deterrence, then, as a grand exercise in re-routing. Since the year 2000, over 6 million people have attempted to migrate through the Sonoran Desert alone. This strategy still remains in place today, two and a half decades after it was first conceived.

Jason was staggered when he first came across these documents, saw the policy and its consequences spelled out in black and white.

'With prevention through deterrence,' he said to me, 'the way that it's organised, is that it's this thing that can be weaponised and it can kill people. But you can also ignore it, because you don't see it every day. Bodies disappear. And then you can just say, *it's the natural environment that's doing it. It's the smugglers that are doing it.* People either blame the desert or they blame the smugglers – not wanting to recognise that all of these pieces are connected, and that all of our hands are dirty.'

In 2019, Jason and the Undocumented Migration Project began to think about how to bring this story to a wider audience. Their idea started with a blank wall. They would take this wall – and it could be any wall, anywhere, as long as it was around twenty feet wide – and draw a thick black line across it. This line would run sloping away from left to right, starting as a 'Z' shape, but with a very long tail which would continue diagonally downwards for two thirds of the length of the wall, before flattening out and running straight for the final third. What it would represent was the 400 miles of the Arizona–Mexico border, to scale, as it divides the Sonoran Desert. Above the wall, a massive grid would be formed out of squares of paper all marked with reference numbers – around 3,500 of them in total. These would be used as a guide to allow red pins to be pushed into the wall at exactly the right locations, with each sheet of paper then removed in the process. On the pins would be hung small rectangles of coloured card. Toe tags to be precise, each with the handwritten details of migrant bodies recovered in the Sonoran Desert since the year 2000: manila tags for identified bodies, and orange tags for the 1,000 people who were still unidentified.

Their aim was to make a wall-sized representation of the Migrant Death Map, which could be recreated anywhere, as long as there was space and volunteers prepared to install it themselves. This last factor was crucial, as Jason and his team saw participation as the most powerful part. The sheer amount of time involved in filling out the 3,500 toe tags with the name, age, sex, cause of death and condition of the body of each person, and then locating the exact place where they died on the space of the wall, could amount to a large, communal act of *witnessing*.

These maps first began appearing in locations across America in the autumn of 2020, to coincide with the run-up to the presidential election and highlight specifically the impact of 'prevention through deterrence' on the borderlands, going back twenty-six years to the time of the Clinton administration. It was this last aspect that gave the project its name: *Hostile Terrain 94* – a pointed reference to that 1994 Border Patrol National Strategy.[23]

By the end of 2022, Jason told me, the *Hostile Terrain* maps were on course to be installed in some 140 venues across six continents, including cities ranging from Los Angeles, Mexico City, San Pedro Sula and Manila, to London, Dublin, Madrid, Athens, Tangier and Melbourne, alongside locations with specific, intimate connections to migration, including Nogales in Mexico and the island of

Lampedusa in Italy. Beyond that, Jason told me, his plan was to turn the map into a permanent monument, to be built right on the line of the Mexico–Arizona border.

'It will be a giant metal wall,' he said. 'About twenty feet long and ten feet high. All of the 3,500 toe tags that are handwritten will be reproduced individually and cast in metal. And they'll be on chains, so the whole thing will chime. And then you can go and touch them and read every single tag.

'There *are* monuments along the US–Mexico border,' he continued – all those old boundary markers and, of course, large sections of the new border wall – 'but there is no monument to this human tragedy. And I think it's important we remember that *this was how stupid we were*. We need to remember the things that we have done – and continue to do – to people.'

'It's one of the most basic things you learn in any conservation or ecology class,' Laiken Jordahl told me. 'You have to preserve landscapes at scale. If you try to just protect them as these little islands, you are not going to protect the wildlife. If you want genetic diversity, if you want robust wildlife populations, you have to look at it at scale. And the border wall just slices a cold blade right through that.'

Laiken was talking to me from his home in Tucson, Arizona, where he works for the Centre for Biological Diversity, an organisation which specialises in using the US legal system to hold federal agencies and the government to account for any policies that threaten the environment – in particular violation of the Wildlife and Endangered Species Acts. As Laiken put it to me, 'We sue the government to make sure that they actually follow their own laws.'

The Centre can trace its origins back to 1989, when three men – Kieran Suckling, Peter Galvin and Todd Schulke – first met while working on a contract job for the US Forest Service. Their task was to look for rare Mexican spotted owls in the forests of southern New Mexico. After weeks of searching, sleeping during the day and hiking throughout the night, they came across an owl nest in an area that had been slated for clearance by an industrial logging company. They assumed that the Forest Service's legal commitment to protecting sensitive species would lead to the cancellation of the timber sale. Yet, when felling and extraction continued despite the discovery, they decided to take the story to the media, alleging that the Forest Service was breaching its own rules and destroying an endangered habitat in pursuit of a profit (a charge which the agency still disputes).[24] Either way, the logging stopped and the nest was left untouched. Unsurprisingly, their contracts with the Forest Service were not renewed. They left willingly. Later that year, along with a fourth man, John Silver, they hatched the idea for the Centre for Biological Diversity. An activist group that runs on lawsuits.

Laiken's own career path offered striking parallels. He grew up in Flagstaff, Arizona, within a – literal – stone's throw of the Grand Canyon.

'From an early age I found a lot of freedom from being in wild places on my own,' he told me. 'And then Flagstaff itself, we consider it kind of a border town with the Navajo nation. It's really like a tri-national place. My high school was one third indigenous, one third Latinx, so it felt like a really integrated community.'

After studying international development and habitat management at the University of Arizona in Tucson, he progressed into environmental policy work. First, he moved to Washington, D.C., interning for Arizona's Democratic Congressman Raúl Grijalva and writing brief papers on natural resources policies; then he moved on to work for the US National Park Service, as a 'wilderness fellow'.

'Which means nothing,' Laiken told me. 'Basically, the job was authoring these giant reports about the biggest threats that were facing the different national parks. And part of that is trying to capture the beauty of these places, how spectacular their different resources are. It's kind of interpretative writing but through a bureaucratic lens. The government trying to get *poetic*.'

His first posting came in the summer of 2015, at Grand Teton National Park in the mountains of Wyoming. He spent several months living and working there – studying the landscapes, writing his assessment – and then he moved on. From Grand Teton he went to Capitol Reef, the 'red rock' desert country of south-central Utah. Next came the prairies and ponderosa of Wupatki in northern Arizona, followed by the limestone canyons of Big Bend in the Chihuahuan Desert in far southwestern Texas. It was, Laiken said, the 'definition of a dream job'. When he had started at the Park Service, he told me, it was in the middle of President Obama's second term.

'And it felt like we were doing really great work looking at climate, looking at justice issues. It felt like there was some space within this giant bureaucracy to start looking deeper into the things that I was really passionate about.'

After finishing each posting, he would have a few months off before his next assignment began, and would go travelling to places like Mexico, Guatemala or Ecuador. He was, he told me, a passionate surfer and skateboarder.

'It's something I always do when I travel. It's the best way to make friends. There's just something so pure and natural doing it that way, just like the unbridled joy of surfing or skating.'

Laiken looked exactly as you'd imagine a surfing environmentalist to look: baseball cap, loose T-shirt, artful stubble, tanned skin. He was in his late twenties and spoke eloquently and earnestly – at once animated yet seemingly weighed down by experience, in a way that you would expect from someone much older.

In one of these trips, he told me, he 'skated all over Palestine'. Partly this was about reconciling with his own heritage. Laiken 'grew up pretty Jewish, bar mitzvah, all of that'. His grandparents, he said, were strong, vocal supporters of the Israeli state. His father, on the other hand, was 'a pretty outspoken advocate for Palestinian justice, which causes a lot of conflict'.

Going to the West Bank had shaped a lot of his thinking. 'It just gave me this keen awareness that wherever there are these borders, these different rules and resources, that's where you are going to find the most concentrated injustice.'

In December 2016, the Park Service posted him to Organ Pipe Cactus National Monument in southern Arizona. As Laiken describes Organ Pipe in his report (writing in that style of the 'government poetic'), 'erosive volcanic mountains cut through the centre of this expanse, giving way to sweeping alluvial bajadas, arroyos and sandy washes . . . This is an environment of extremes, where the elements are imposing and nature alone dictates the terms of survival.'[25] The park covers some 500 square miles in the heart of the Sonoran Desert. It also, crucially, has a thirty-mile-long southern boundary that runs right up against the US–Mexico border.

He had arrived there at a time of huge political upheaval. Donald Trump had just been elected president – partly on a ticket of building a 'huge, beautiful' border wall – but his inauguration was still to take place.

'And it was just so surreal to be working with this team of scientists and administrators who had devoted their lives to protecting this monument. A lot of them had been there for more than thirty years and knew that desert better than anyone – and then there was just this cloud. Nobody knew what was going to happen.'

For a while, the Park Service had been working with the Border Patrol to give agents courses on wilderness management, encouraging them to report wildlife sightings.

'You know you are kind of stuck with this giant law enforcement agency who can do whatever they want on the park. So you have to work with them and hope that you will encourage them not to destroy everything.'

I wondered aloud how receptive the agents had been to these courses.

Laiken gave a big laugh. 'Not in the least!' he said, shaking his head. 'Actually, you can't quite generalise. Because Border Patrol agents totally run the gamut, right? Half of them are people of colour, from immigrant families. Most of them are Trump voters. Lots of them are straight back from military deployment, these hothead, trigger-happy kids who see the entire world as a threat. And some of them are just really chill old dudes who spend more time in the desert than anybody, who love the desert.'

The truth is that the Park Service and the Border Patrol have competing, often entirely contradictory missions. Essentially, one is there to protect the landscape, the other is there to protect *entry into* the landscape.

'And as soon as Trump came in,' Laiken said, 'it was like, *well, I guess those meetings about wilderness conservation with the Border Patrol are over*.'

By the end of March 2017, he had completed his report. Over the course of more than a hundred pages, he detailed how the same issue kept cropping up at every stage of his assessment. The most immediate and significant threat to the integrity, character and future of Organ Pipe, he concluded, *came from the border itself*.[26]

'Wilderness land in the US – it's the most restrictive degree of land designation that is possible. You can't drive a car, you can't use a chainsaw, or light a fire or do anything that is considered interfering with the natural processes or the ecosystem. At Organ Pipe, you walked through the desert and there were just thousands of off-road vehicle tracks. The land was torn to shreds. And I mean it takes centuries for this soil base to even rebuild itself. It's called cryptobiotic soil, which means the soil itself is alive.'

He found data from Border Patrol vehicle logs that showed that, in one year alone, agents had driven over 17,000 miles off-road through the park. Organ Pipe is also home to the Sonoran pronghorn, an animal so threatened that its population had crashed down to just twenty at the start of the new millennium. 'And scientists found that they were being disturbed on average every four hours by Border Patrol activity in their critical habitat, as they are trying to recover as a species.'

In one passage of the report he described the 'eerie atmosphere' prevalent in what was supposed to be a wilderness. How 'trails and washes are often strewn with ragged clothes, discarded food containers and gallon-sized black water bottles'. Laiken was intersecting, albeit in an entirely different capacity, with the same materials that had first brought Jason De León out into the Sonoran Desert.

Even in the remotest regions of the park, he continued, you would have this 'paranoid gut feeling of being watched, which may often be justified'.[27] Smuggler groups were active in the heights of the Organ Pipe mountains, using spotters to relay Border Patrol activity. The park was also covered with an extensive network of motion sensors, drones and long-distance tower cameras. Set off one of the sensors, and a hiker would likely find themselves chased down by agents in ATVs, or even 'buzzed' by a helicopter, and then asked to verify their citizenship.

'There are no easy solutions,' Laiken said to me. 'But it became really clear to me that our existing border policies were funnelling all these people into one of the most beautiful and sensitive and rare and fragile landscapes anywhere on the border. It was those policies that were causing all of this mess, and causing Border Patrol to rip this wilderness to shreds.'

Over the past twenty years, hundreds of thousands of migrants had attempted to cross the border through Organ Pipe alone. At least 230 people had died in the park in the process.[28]

'It's a national monument that has been turned into a graveyard for migrants,' Laiken said, 'intentionally. You are out in the field hiking and you come across baby shoes and toys and blankets, and you have no idea if these people were scattered or apprehended or disappeared. It is such a site of extreme violence. And that violence has been put in these desolate places to hide that from the public. There is a reason that all this is happening in these very inaccessible places.'

After delivering his report, he said that it soon became obvious to him that no one in the Park Service was willing to have this discussion. No one was prepared to question border policy even when the evidence seemed overwhelming that it was this same policy that was threatening Organ Pipe's protected status so fundamentally.

'Until we can address the root cause of *why* people are being pushed to walk through this desolate, deadly, beautiful, fragile landscape, we are not going to get any solutions here. I knew that I was ready to leave the big bureaucracy. I wanted to work for a cause where we could actually approach these massive issues without constraints.'

In September 2017, he left Organ Pipe, left the Park Service, and came to the Centre for Biological Diversity.

It all happened, Laiken told me, 'one specific, fateful Friday evening' in the summer of 2019.

'It's what the Supreme Court usually does if they are going to issue a controversial ruling,' he said. 'They'll slip it in late on a Friday night to avoid the media fervour.'

For a year and a half, the Trump administration had attempted to secure approval and funding from Congress for the construction of a border wall. Time and again, these requests were denied. Trump's response, in February 2019, was to declare a 'national emergency' at the southern border. Congress rejected this declaration. Trump, in turn, vetoed that rejection.

The administration's next move was to attempt to redirect money from the US Defence budget for wall construction. The Pentagon notified Congress that $2.5 billion (a figure that would later rise to $6 billion) would be allocated to the wall, saying that a barrier was deemed to be 'necessary in the national interest'.[29]

Inevitably, legal challenges mounted against this 'reprogramming' of military funds. The Centre for Biological Diversity was one of many in the process of suing the government over its plans. When the first case about the wall was heard in the Northern District Court of California in May 2019, Judge Haywood Gilliam wrote in his judgement that this was 'not about whether the challenged border barrier construction plan is wise or unwise.' Rather, he continued, 'this case presents strictly legal questions regarding whether the proposed plan for funding border barrier construction exceeds the Executive Branch's lawful authority under the Constitution and a number of statutes duly enacted by Congress'.[30] Judge Gilliam ruled that it was indeed unlawful, and no actions could therefore be taken towards building the wall.

Still the Trump administration persisted. In July 2019, they managed to bring the case before the Supreme Court on appeal. On the 26th of that month – Laiken's 'fateful' Friday evening – the court delivered their verdict. It was just a single paragraph, a 5-to-4 ruling that overturned the District Court's decision, finding that those parties engaged in challenging the administration did not have the legal right to do so. As a result, the military budget could be reallocated and construction of the barrier could begin – and could continue – up until the time that any 'legitimate' legal challenges could be brought before the court.[31]

'It completely shocked all of us,' Laiken told me. 'I was out having a drink with my friends and as soon as I got the notification I just knew it was over. I knew that walls would be built all across Arizona. I knew that Organ Pipe was going to be finished. There was nothing left standing in the way. It was so stunning. I just ended up going to another bar by myself and binge drinking. It was like this realisation: *holy shit, this means the wall is coming to Arizona. This means that my life for the next few years is going to be fighting this thing.*'

In just a matter of weeks, the ground was broken for the first stretch of wall. By late August, access roads were being cut, long lines of wilderness bulldozed flat, trenches and foundations dug out in preparation for installing the barrier's distinctive thirty-foot-tall steel frames. And it all began at Organ Pipe.

'If you have an area that the environmentalists and the politicians care most about,' Laiken said, 'that's the area they are going to go for. They hope that it will nullify your resistance. They go straight for the heart.'

Given the possible threat of future legal challenges, the administration was anxious to move as quickly as possible. The speed of construction was, he said, 'just dizzying'.

'Because usually they'd have to go through all of these Environmental Planning documents, and public approvals. I mean none of this could ever have happened if *any* of the environmental laws were in place.'

Instead, alongside the Supreme Court ruling, the Trump administration was using a single clause in a fifteen-year-old act – originally designed to introduce stricter standards for driver's licences – which allowed the Department of Homeland Security the authority to 'waive certain laws, regulations, and other legal requirements . . . to ensure the expeditious construction of barriers and roads in the vicinity of the international border'.[32] 'Certain laws' included bypassing some twenty-eight acts designed to regulate federal works and protect the environment.

Soon, metres of wall were turning into hundreds of metres. Hundreds of metres into miles. Laiken was travelling back and forth along the length of the Arizona border, monitoring multiple construction sites, looking to document as much as possible. 'I knew that this was going to consume me,' he said.

There was, it seemed to him, an indiscriminate push to start as many discrete sections of the wall as possible, regardless of any particular connection to sites of heavy migrant traffic.

'There have been a number of places that have really felt like a punch to the gut,' he said. One of those was Guadalupe Canyon in the Peloncillo Mountains, in the far southwestern corner of Arizona.

'The amount of dynamiting that they did there – they just ripped this beautiful pristine mountain range apart. *And there's nobody there.* No one crossing. No Border Patrol. There's never anyone. Even if the goal really is a wall that will stop people from crossing, it was just so obvious that it wasn't going to accomplish that there. It was just destruction for destruction's sake.'

All this was happening against the backdrop of the worst drought in Arizona for hundreds of years. The wall's metal fencing was being erected on top of concrete foundations, which required water for mixing and pouring – a lot of water as it turned out. The Department of Customs and Border Protection estimated that they would need 80,000 gallons a day, or around 1.85 million gallons per mile. Based on more than forty miles of wall planned to be built across the

Arizona border, that amounted to nearly 80 million gallons in total.[33] The most readily accessible source was to be found beneath the ground, in subterranean caverns known as aquifers. In the Sonoran Desert, many of these aquifers are thousands of years old – deposits of meltwater that accumulated after the end of the last Ice Age, and which have been depleting ever since.

'It's a non-renewable resource,' Laiken said. 'Even if we get the wettest ten years in history, it's unlikely that the aquifers will replenish. You can't just recharge them.'

Tapping into this groundwater is normally regulated tightly by a number of state and federal laws. The waiver authority allowed them to be bypassed. Large conical water tanks became a fixture at construction sites. When Laiken had written his report on Organ Pipe he had identified two major, supplementary threats to the park, after the primary issue of border security: groundwater depletion and climate change.

'And so watching millions of gallons of water being pumped out of the ground to build the wall was just agonising.'

He began to wonder if, in some perverse way, this was deliberate. 'From a border security perspective, if you make the environment more hostile and deadly and lifeless, it's only going to further your goals of making it harder to cross, and then more people are likely to die. So sometimes it feels like they are willingly trying to make this place *hotter* and *drier*. There's just no incentive from their end to protect anything.'

Nevertheless, all the evidence from the past few decades suggests that migrants will not be deterred, whatever the conditions in the desert. And it's not just people who are fixated on crossing the border.

'Already we are seeing this phenomenon where species are moving north in order to find cooler weather habitats,' Laiken said. 'We've got a lot of wildlife in Mexico that will soon be tracking their habitats north, trying to survive. And they'll be met with this barrier. They'll watch their habitat disappear as it creeps north and they'll be left on the hotter, drier side of the wall, and they'll become extinct. That's something we're already seeing. It's accelerating every year.'

There was, he said, no equivalent to 'these kind of landscape-scale habitat fragmentations like the wall. There's no similar project that has ever split a landscape on this scale. And of course the whole ecosystem is just going to continue to degrade. How many more threads can we pull out of this patchwork before it all just unravels?'

Organ Pipe was, in effect, being turned into a walled-off National Monument. It created the impression that a fragile, protected landscape, a whole ecosystem, can just stop abruptly, as if it falls off a metaphorical cliff the moment that it meets the borderline with Mexico. The truth, as Laiken put it, is that 'it gets way more beautiful on the other side'. He described to me how the land opens out into the black, rocky expanse of a giant exploded volcano, how the biggest field of sand dunes in North America sweeps northeastwards from the Colorado River delta.

'From a conservation perspective borders *are* natural. There are so many naturally occurring collisions of ecosystems, lines where communities overlap and intersect.'

The irony, Laiken said, is that, in ecology, it is usually at these borderlines that you find the most beauty and biodiversity.

'And I think that's very applicable to humans as well. I think the border, in so many ways, *is* one of the most beautiful versions of America. These amazing communities all across the borderlands with these incredibly rich histories. These places of cultural exchange and opportunity. This is the culture that I think we need to be uplifting, preserving, identifying as a source of national pride.'

Laiken liked to imagine an alternative future for the border, one where the wall was dismantled and Organ Pipe was just one part of an ecological corridor that ran all the way south through Mexico to the Sea of Cortez. It was not, he said, an approach without precedent. In 1932, the Canadian National Park of Waterton was joined with the Glacier National Park in Montana. The result was the world's first 'International Peace Park': 1,700 square miles of transnational, protected landscape that largely ignores the existence a borderline between two countries in its midst.

'People can actually backpack across the border there, over these rugged mountains in the Rockies. Land managers work in unison to protect this connected landscape – which just happens to exist on both sides of an imposed line.'

Laiken's dream was to one day be able to hike through an 'Organ Pipe International Park' that stretched for a hundred miles down to the ocean – 'to slowly walk through the Sonoran Desert as it turns into the sea'.

In January 2021, just as quickly as it had begun, construction on the southern border wall stopped. The order came from the new president, Joe Biden, on his very first day in office. Three months later, on 30 April, it was confirmed that all further work was cancelled.[34] Forty-seven miles of new wall had been built in Arizona since August 2019.[35] But it was not contiguous wall. It was a series of sections and segments: lines of wall which, even when stretching for several miles, remained fundamentally incomplete. They had become, in a sense, instant ruins. Lonely lines of steel starting up, for no apparent reason, in the middle of a desert plain, or on the crest of a half-dynamited mountain. Construction sites were left abandoned, with piles of barriers stacked at the dead ends of excavated dirt roads leading to nowhere.

One of the very last sections to be built was in another area of protected land, on the slopes of the Huachuca Mountains at the very southern tip of the Arizona Trail in the Coronado National Memorial Park. Work carried on right up to the day of President Biden's inauguration. Sections of the mountains had been dynamited to flatten a path through the rock and, by the time the order came to down tools, a little under 400 metres of wall had been erected. One end stopped exactly alongside a historic boundary marker and a bench that had been installed many years before for hikers to take in the view.

Before the wall came, Laiken told me, you could sit on this bench and look south into Mexico and Sonora, 'and you wouldn't be able to see a single sign of human development. Just serene, beautiful, wild nature all the way to the Sierra Madre. Now there's this bench and there's the wall. And on one side of the bench the wall starts and runs for a quarter mile and then stops. And then on the other side, there's nothing.'

Indeed, so surreal is this intervention in the landscape, that Laiken could see value in just leaving it standing. 'Part of me thinks that this section of the wall should be preserved as a sort of reminder, a monument. It's not large enough to affect wildlife on a significant scale. And it's so obviously obscene and serves no purpose. It's like it proves the point itself, without any commentary.'

One person's monument to futility is, however, another's to unfinished business. Sit on that bench in the Huachuca Mountains, and the wall may appear as a presence – or an *absence*.

'It's been a wild time for the land,' Laiken said, 'but this issue, it isn't going to go away. I'm certain that the next Republican presidential nominee will be campaigning just as hard as Trump did to finish the wall. And let's imagine that they do finish the wall. Then what will they say?'

Would that be it? A full stop? An end to the 'problem' of the border?

'You look at places like Yuma or San Diego,' he said. 'They have two or three *layers* of wall now. So maybe it's just this perennial, perpetual, never-ending project?'

Why just draw it once, when you could draw it twice, then a third time? One thousand, nine hundred and fifty-four miles of border memorialised in triplicate.

There are far, far older monuments in this landscape.

In the northeastern corner of Organ Pipe, there is a steep, turreted ridge, a series of peaks formed of dark volcanic basalt. For the O'odham people, a Native American tribe who have lived in the Sonoran Desert for thousands of years now, this rock formation is a sacred site. According to their traditions, the whole earth began with the desert, and 'spread until it reached the edge of the sky dome, then it spun around until the edges were joined. From this union sprang a being.'[36] This being was the god I'itoi, and he first appeared at the very place where the rocky ridge is now, to teach the O'odham people their *him'dag*, their way of life. Central to this way of life is the idea that the land is not to be owned, but to be cared for – that every animal, plant, stick and stone is, in its own way, sacred.

Some call the ridge that stands there today I'itoi Mo'o or Montezuma's Head, others know it simply as 'Grandmother'. In one story, it is said that an old woman was returning home across the plain with her basket but grew tired and had to sit down to rest. 'Whereupon she was told by the others that there was no time for that as it would soon be dark and she would be turned to stone if caught there.'[37] The old woman, however, insisted that she could go no further. As the sun set the warning came true – the light dipped below the horizon, and she was transformed into solid rock. Her body became one peak of the ridge, her basket the other. (It is an ancient tale, but for those crossing this landscape today, it offers unexpectedly poignant resonances.)

For almost all their history, the O'odham lived undisturbed in the Sonoran Desert. They became experts in dryland agriculture, living on maize and beans and, when in season, the fruit and seeds of the organ pipe and saguaro cactus. Rainfall, its long absences and its sudden arrival, was central to their culture. You had to learn how to live in a perpetually precarious balance with the landscape.

'Like the people before them, these women gauged the movement of the summer sun and the amount of work that needed to be done,' writes the O'odham poet Ofelia Zepeda, recalling watching her mother and grandmother when she was still a child. 'The women planned their day around the heat and the coolness of the summer day. They knew the climate and felt confident in it. They knew the weather and its movements.'[38]

Much of their time was spent watching the sky, laughing at 'thunderstorms that threatened but were too weak to do any good', scorning the clouds that built up and then broke apart – the clouds 'that just lied to us'. And then, when the rains finally did come, they 'sat quietly watching the rivulets form on the dirt walls and small waterfalls pour from the edges of ramadas'. The rain, Zepeda writes, 'breaks the tension for the desert. Relief. Cycles continue.'[39]

The first outside influence came in the sixteenth century, when Spanish explorers made their way into O'odham lands. A process was set in motion then – of an open landscape being crossed and claimed and owned and divided. O'odham territory ranged all the way from northern Arizona to the shores of the Sea of Cortez. The tribe would traverse this great sweep of landscape back and forth, walking the 'salt trail' to collect salt, seashells and obsidian from the salt beds of Sonora. By the seventeenth century, their desert had become a part of New Spain. By the nineteenth century, it was part of Mexico. Then came the war between the Mexicans and Americans. In the aftermath, for the first time, O'odham was split in two by an international boundary.[40]

Over the next century and a half, the people were increasingly hemmed in and isolated. Their lands were taken by cattle ranchers and farmers in Mexico or by the US Air Force to use as a bombing range. Then Organ Pipe National Monument was itself designated on top of O'odham territory: the government 'protecting' the land by removing it from the care of the native people whose whole culture was based around protecting the land. For much of this time, however, the border was barely a presence: a thin line of cross-fencing. Families would travel back and forth between villages in America and Mexico. Pilgrimages would cross to ceremonial grounds south of the border, to perform the 'rebirthing' ritual called the *vikita* (the name for the white pigment at the base of an eagle feather). As one O'odham elder, Ophelia Rivas, put it, this ritual 'has been going on since the beginning of the world'.[41]

In the last twenty years, however, the line of division has hardened and solidified. The basic fence was replaced with vehicle barriers: long, low cross-hatchings of steel. Border Patrol checkpoints were set up all across the O'odham reservation. Gates allowing passage from one side of the land to the other – one country to another –

were closed. Those that remained opened were heavily policed. Surveillance watchtowers were built. And then came the wall. It cut through ancient grave sites, passed just yards away from the sacred Quitobaquito Springs. For perhaps as many as 15,000 years, these springs had been a site of travel, trade and intersection, a vital watering hole and stopping point on the salt trail.[42] Now, they collide with a barrier, a steel fence as imposing as it is incongruous. The O'odham had never seen a landscape intervention like this in all of their history. Their language, for one thing, has no word for 'wall'.[43]

In the Sonoran Desert, monuments have piled up upon monuments, overlapping, intersecting: the volcanic silhouette of the 'Grandmother'; ancient paths walked for millennia; sacred, life-giving springs and cacti; National Parks; a Southern Border Wall National Monument; a smuggler's trail, strewn with backpacks and water bottles; fallen rock cairns marking the disappeared bodies of unfortunate migrants; Maricela's shrine beneath the mesquite tree.

In one of her poems, Ofelia Zepeda writes of coming upon a memorial while out walking in the desert. From the way she describes it, it is easy to imagine that it could be Maricela's. There is a holy candle 'long melted' and a photograph 'of a young woman/with dangling earrings'. She notices that there is a stand of ocotillo – a succulent of the Sonoran Desert – growing beside the memorial. In spring, she thinks, this stand will 'burst/red, orange blossoms'. Then:

> Branches will bend forward.
> Birds, insects will visit
> All around her are the Tucson mountains
> Brown, mottled volcanic stones stand guard.[44]

These ancient mountains are also, Zepeda recognises, now on the flight path for Tucson International Airport. Day after day, she says, planes fly low over the memorial site, as if 'acknowledging the woman with the dangling earrings'. Monuments upon monuments. Lines crossing lines.

7
BORDER BURNING

Dusk settles over a forest on a mountainside. Lights glimmer a mile or so down below. A semi-circle of brightness: a tiny coastal city. Beyond the city, a wide expanse of sea fades into the horizon. Among the trees, preparations are underway. Men and adolescent boys – there are almost no women, no infants – take off their shoes and sandals and wrap the soles of their feet and the palms of their hands in duct tape.

Their beds are blankets on the ground, laid out beneath sheets of tarpaulin strung between tree branches and tied off with strips of fabric from torn T-shirts. They have to be ready to move at any time. Police hunt for them in the forests, raid their camps, and set fire to any shelters and belongings that they find.

Each camp – for there are many strung all over the mountains that curve around this coastal city – has a *chairman*, a leader. He (it is always a 'he') runs the operation, apportioning tasks like finding food, carrying water, hunting for plastic for new shelters, cooking. And making ladders – fashioning them from strips of wood bound together with whatever material can be scavenged, topping them with makeshift hooks formed out of bent carpenters' nails.

It has all been building up to this moment. Weeks or months in the forests for some. Years for others. This night the group will leave the camp – in their hundreds, maybe even a thousand or more. Each prays that they will not return, that this time they will make it. It is why they are here, why they have come – some travelling thousands of miles northwards to reach this point.

Now they move as silently as possible down through the forest, towards the lights. Their ladders are already waiting for them, stashed in bushes at the foot of the mountain, just metres from the edge of the city.

On the chairman's order the first wave breaks cover. Ahead of them are four huge fences. The first is a double fence, three metres tall and topped with rolls of razor wire. Directly below it, on the other side, is a two-metre-deep ditch. Next is a second fence, twice the height of the first, fitted with an overhanging flexible lip. Behind it are two more six-metre-tall fences, the spaces between them filled with 'nets' of barbed wire.

They throw their ladders at the first fence, hooking them into the dense clusters of razor wire. Once they have made it to the top, the second wave runs out and begins the climb. Then the third and final wave comes. There are hundreds of bodies on the fence now. And it is only once all three waves have made the summit of the first fence that the ladders are pulled free and the process begins all over again – with the next fence, and the one after that, and the one after that.

It is easier to climb the chain link in bare feet. The wraps of duct tape offer some protection from the razor and barbed wire, but not much. Most climbers are soon bleeding from their legs, hands and arms. By the time they reach the last fence – many do not reach it at all – massed ranks of military police with batons and riot shields are waiting for them. The fences are under constant video surveillance, including thermal imaging cameras. From the moment that the first wave emerges from the trees – perhaps even before – the authorities on the other side of the fence know they are coming.

This final stage is a numbers game, a brutal, physical lottery. That is why so many make the climb all at once. As they leap to the ground they hope that there will be too many of them for the police to contain. That there will be a chance – a slim chance – that they can break free. For those who do, the chairman's orders are very clear: *run*. Run towards a squat, low-rise complex of buildings, straight down a two-lane highway or across the lush fairways of a golf course. It is there, and only there, that they can claim asylum. Reach the gates of these buildings – which house the migrant detention centre – and they have made it. Temporarily at least. They have completed what they call 'the crossing'. Climbed a fence in Africa and come down on the other side, in another continent. In Europe.[1]

'Melilla, this place, is like a microcosm. They have their own rules, their own law of gravity. Things happen differently there.'

Carlos Spottorno was describing the city by the sea. *Melilla.* A Spanish enclave, just twelve square kilometres in size, set into a peninsula of land in northeastern Morocco less than seventy kilometres from the Algerian border. Bound by the Mediterranean on one side and a thirteen-kilometre-long half-moon of parallel barbed-wire fencing on the other, it is actually one of two enclaves; the other, Ceuta, is over 200 kilometres to the west, at the southern landing point of the Straits of Gibraltar.

These fingerprints of Spain in Africa have a long history, going back to the fifteenth century and the Christian *Reconquista*, the campaign to push the Muslim empire off the Iberian Peninsula and establish footholds all along the North African coast. It was in 1497, in the immediate aftermath of this centuries-long conflict, that the harbour of Melilla was first taken: one of the early land grabs of a Spanish crown already set on far greater expansion. By the terms of the Treaty of Tordesillas, signed four years earlier, the kingdoms of Spain and Portugal had agreed to divvy up the entire non-Christian world between them. There was to be a Spanish hemisphere, incorporating the Pacific and the Americas west of the line of longitude of the Azores, and a Portuguese hemisphere, incorporating the Atlantic, Africa and Asia south of the line of latitude of the Canary Islands.

While these grand divisions of a still largely unmapped earth were ignored by every other European power, they nonetheless established the ground rules for settler colonialism. The imperious bid by one continent to conquer, own – and ultimately *border* – the rest of the world.

Five centuries later, and Melilla and Ceuta remain today as Spanish territory. They are also now the only land border between Africa and Europe. Taken together, they offer just twenty-one kilometres where two vast – and vastly unequal – continents touch.

'So, Melilla,' Carlos said, pausing for a second and rolling his hands in the air as he looked for the right words, 'it has always been a *strange* place.'

Carlos is a Spanish documentary photographer, a former winner of both European and World Press Photography awards. Talking to me from his home in Madrid, he cut a rather dapper figure in shirt, suit jacket and glasses, with thick, wavy dark hair and a full beard contoured with faint stripes of grey around the chin. On the wall behind him was a blackboard with the words 'Ask Me Anything' written both forwards and backwards – a visual joke, I assumed, on the mirroring tendencies of video links. It was late December 2020. Large parts of Europe were about to go – or had already gone – into lockdown again as a result of the resurgent COVID-19 pandemic.

'All of this situation is bringing up all the borders to an everyday life level,' Carlos said. 'Everybody is now experiencing what it means to live in a position where you can't move. You're not allowed to move. We are now experiencing in the western world, maybe for the first time, what other people experience very often in their life. There are fault lines and cracks all around.'

Six years earlier, Carlos and fellow journalist Guillermo Abril were given an assignment by the Spanish newspaper *El País* that ended up taking them all along and across the external borders of the European Union, from the Moroccan coast to the Arctic Circle.[2]

'At the time things were happening in Melilla, it was everyday news in Spain,' Carlos said. 'And after the Arab Spring there was this noticeable increase in rafts going from Libya and Tunisia to Sicily. Also, the Syrian War had started, and Syrians were just starting to come to Europe from Turkey. So there were these three spots where borders were under pressure. Melilla, as the Spanish border in Africa; Sicily; and Turkey, Bulgaria and Greece.

'The editor told us to go and make a story about these three places. The basic idea was to, as they said, *put your feet on the line*. Don't see it from afar. The principle is that you need to put your feet on the line and see what happens, what the people have to tell you. The people who are trying to enter, the people who are trying to stop them from entering. Get the feel for what is going on.'

In January 2014, Carlos and Guillermo travelled to Melilla. In his notes from the time, Guillermo described it as a 'walled city', the whole place 'small and suffocating' with the feel of being in a prison.[3] Just three months before their trip, 366 migrants sailing north from Libya had drowned when their boat capsized off the coast of the tiny Italian island of Lampedusa. This was the beginning of what would become the greatest mass movement of people through Europe since the end of the Second World War.

Melilla itself had long been a magnet for migrants, the vast majority coming from 'sub-Saharan' Africa: Senegalese, Malians, Sudanese, Guineans, Nigerians, Congolese, Ivorians. Yet, at the beginning of the 1990s, there had been no fence here at all. It was only when Spain was integrated into the Schengen Area in 1995, and Melilla and its counterpart Ceuta suddenly became the European Union's outer border, that the barriers came up. Construction in Melilla began in 1996: a single stretch of small chain-link fence topped with a roll of barbed wire.[4]

A decade later – after five migrants were shot dead by Spain's Guardia Civil as they attempted to enter the city – the fencing grew another layer, and then another layer after that, rising to its current height of six metres. It was redesigned as a barbed, three-dimensional trap: all braided cables and razor wire, spotlights and watch-posts and movement sensors.[5] The physical realisation of the most unequal border on the planet. This is a line that marks an eightfold difference in GDP per capita. Put in crude terms, what this means is that, on average, each person on the European side of the fence is eight times richer than each person on the African side.[6] It is this extreme imbalance which helps to create what Carlos called Melilla's 'own law of gravity'. A tiny body, but, for some on the outside, it possesses a near-fathomless gravity well.

Failure, however, is the norm. Most migrants retreat or are repelled in their attempts to cross. Even if they do make it beyond the fences and into Melilla, they may be subjected to what are known as 'push-backs', *devoluciones calientes* – 'hot returns'. The police will round them up, unlock gates in the fencing and lead them through to the Moroccan side again. Expel them straight back across the border.[7]

There, if they are lucky, they may have the opportunity to slip away, to return to their shelters in their mountain camps. If they are unlucky, they are passed to the Moroccan military, who may transport them hundreds of miles away, to cities like Fez, Marrakesh and Rabat. Worse, many are taken out into the remote, desert landscape on the border between Morocco and Algeria and simply set loose without food or water. Often injured, ill, starved or beaten, they have little option but to begin their journey again, try to find their way back, somehow, to Melilla and the border.[8]

The truth is that many have nowhere else to go. They call themselves *harragas*. It is a Moroccan word, intended as a slur against migrants – meaning literally someone 'who burns', a reference to the police raids which torch their camps and incinerate all their belongings. Over time, however, the migrants have appropriated this term. They say that they are proud to be a *harraga*, a 'burner'. They have, in any case, already destroyed any documentation – passports, ID cards, records – that might allow the authorities to establish their country of origin. They have made themselves stateless, renounced their nationality, sacrificed their identity on the altar of hope. As the anthropologist Stefania Pandolfo discovered in her work among North African migrants, this dream – the inexorable pull of migration – is so strong that it is expressed in terms of obsession, drug use, even love.

'They describe the state of mind of the *harg* in a language of addiction,' she explains. '*l-harg keyjri f-l-'aruq bhal ddim, ana mbli:* "burning flows in my veins like blood, I am addicted".'[9]

They say that they have lost all 'desire, longing, for anything other than the burning itself'. They are already outside themselves. They have projected their existence beyond the border. 'My body is here, my Being is over there.'[10] And the only way to recover their essence, their soul, is to make the crossing and reclaim it. Until then, they live in limbo, as ghosts, as shadow people. They have burned their pasts, so that only their futures remain. Down in that city by the sea. Over that fence.

Those on the inside, however, are determined that Melilla must not be a place of opportunity, a site of transit. While the 'beings' of countless migrants may haunt the city's streets, the authorities are more dedicated than ever to ensuring that their bodies do not cross. Here, at Europe's extreme southern limit, the lines have been inscribed in the strongest and starkest terms. Yet, in the process, other things have become more blurred, more uncertain. Not least the law.

On 13 February 2020, the Grand Chamber of the European Court of Human Rights delivered a judgment in the first-ever case brought to challenge the legality of 'pushbacks'. The two applicants – 'N.D.' from Mali and 'N.T.' from the Ivory Coast – had scaled the Melilla fences in August 2014, only to be seized as they dropped down onto Spanish soil. Like many migrants before and after them, they were immediately handcuffed by the Guardia Civil and taken by exit gates back to the Moroccan side. First transferred to the police station in the city of Nador just a few kilometres south of Melilla, they were later taken 300 kilometres southwest to Fez and then abandoned.

In their complaint, they said that they had been 'subjected to a collective expulsion without an individual assessment of their circumstances and in the absence of any legal procedure or assistance' – an action prohibited by the European Convention on Human Rights.[11] The moment they hit the ground in Melilla, they had the right to claim asylum and remain in the territory while their individual cases were assessed. In October 2017, the Court judged that a violation had taken place, but the Spanish government appealed, and the case moved on to the Grand Chamber.

The delivery of the Court's final decision in 2020 – almost six years after the two men had crossed the fence – overturned this earlier ruling. There was no violation, they said, because the crossing of the fences represented 'culpable conduct' by the two migrants. In attempting entry through an 'unauthorised location' they had placed themselves in an 'unlawful situation'. And so the Spanish authorities could not be held responsible for offering no legal remedy for them to challenge their instant expulsion.

The Court justified their ruling on the grounds that Spain already provided 'several possible means of seeking admission to the national territory' for asylum seekers:[12] namely via the main port of entry to Melilla at the Beni Enzar border gate and through the consulate in the nearby city of Nador. The reality, however, is that sub-Saharan Africans can access neither. Moroccan police units have been assembled specifically to hunt them down. Often these are the same units that raid and destroy their forest camps – tasked with arresting and interrogating any black person found walking the streets of Nador.

Reaching Beni Enzar, in turn, requires passing through three separate Moroccan police checkpoints strung out over 300 metres of highway leading up to the borderline. If you are 'sub-Saharan', this particular 'possible means' is an impossible journey. Your skin colour has added another layer to the many barriers that have already been assembled to prevent your entry.[13]

From this judgement, human rights have become frayed at Europe's edgelines, subject to specific exceptions and sub-clauses. Cross the physical barriers and they will still meet a legal forcefield, as impassable as it is invisible.

For the European Union – and in particular for its border and coast guard agency, Frontex – the aim is to make Morocco the end point, not the jumping-off point. Migrants may travel this far, but no further.

In July 2019, the Spanish government authorised an outlay of €30 million to Morocco to fund the prevention of illegal immigration into Europe. This was on top of a €26 million public tender to purchase equipment, including hundreds of vehicles, drones, scanners, radars and technical surveillance equipment for border control. Earlier that same year, a fund of €140 million had been pledged by the European Union to Morocco to help it contain and cut off migration routes. Khalid Zerouali, the director of Migration and Border Surveillance in the Moroccan Interior Ministry, described this package as 'a good start'.[14]

The stemming and release of migrants has, for Morocco, become a useful tool for exerting political pressure. In February 2017, the country's agriculture minister Aziz Akhannouch issued a statement that any restrictions placed on their farming and fishing exports to Europe could see an increase in the 'migration flows' that his country had 'managed and maintained' with 'sustained effort'.

'How do you expect us to do the work of blocking African and even Moroccan emigration,' he said, 'if Europe doesn't want to work with us?'[15]

When Moroccan police and border guards relent in their pursuit of migrants, crossings spike almost instantly. The same day that Akhannouch made his statement, eighteen African migrants made it over the fences into Melilla. Less than a week earlier, over the course of just seventy-two hours, 853 people had managed to breach the barriers at Ceuta – almost half the number that had made it across in the whole of 2016.[16]

This constant tension, this constant uncertainty, bleeds into the very fabric of a place like Melilla.

'It's not surprising,' Carlos said to me, 'but this is where the extreme-right parties are growing the fastest. And this is what happens in those borders, those dark spots on earth where things are so unnatural that all the extremes grow quickly.'

In Spain's 2019 general election, a new, far-right political movement called VOX rose up to become the third largest party in parliament.

Their campaign rhetoric talked of a modern-day *Reconquista* – a crusade to liberate the nation from its various enemies, most specifically migrants, feminists, separatists and globalists. Their slogan has a very familiar ring to it. *Hacer España Grande Otra Vez*. Make Spain Great Again. Also familiar is their pledge, first made in 2018 by deputy party leader Javier Ortega Smith, to build an 'unbreakable concrete wall' around Melilla and Ceuta. VOX leader Sebastian Abascal later suggested, in yet another echo from across the Atlantic, that Morocco 'perhaps should pay' for the construction of this new barrier.[17]

Inevitably, for a party that speaks the language of division, a wall – and an 'unbreakable' one at that – offers a potent symbol of strength and security. VOX have continually used Spain's strained African border as evidence of the weakness of the political establishment. In the 2019 general election, they won over a third of the vote in Ceuta – enough to secure the enclave's sole seat in parliament – while both Ceuta and Melilla have elected VOX party representatives on to their autonomous government assemblies.[18]

These communities live on the raw, exposed margin of mass population movement. Many of them work, one way or another, in the *industry* of bordering – in the police force, the military or the Guardia Civil. Abascal praises them regularly as patriots, as defenders of the 'true' Spanish family – as 'the ones that protect the doors of our house'.[19]

Carlos and Guillermo spent time shadowing the Guardia Civil during their visit in 2014. I asked Carlos if he had a sense of how the border guards felt about their work. Was it pride in defending a nation, as Abascal projected on to them, or a fatalism or numbness in the face of such constant human struggle?

'What I remember well,' he told me, 'is that they felt in no man's land. Where politicians and public opinion would say to them, *be strong on the borders and don't let anyone in*. And at the same time, they were being accused of exercising violence, or being too violent, or doing all these "hot returns", which you are not allowed to do.

'So they felt abandoned. They felt very bad about this. They told us, *they are calling us from Madrid every day, saying, don't let anyone in.* Or even from Brussels, not just from Madrid. They had instructions from European institutions that the borders need to be protected. Yet whenever they did anything that went a little bit too far, that might be the end of their career.

'They were living under all this pressure. Wake up at 5 a.m. every day with an alarm: *There are 500 people jumping the fence, get your gear and get ready for battle!* So, for them, waking up at 5 a.m. ready for battle, that was something that happened many times a week. That was their life.'

Also, every day, some 35,000 people passed, legally, through the border checkpoints at Beni Enzar and El Barrio Chino. A visa exemption allows Moroccans living in the surrounding area to enter Melilla freely, although they are prohibited from staying the night. Any goods transported back and forth are free of any customs tax or duty – but only if they are *carried*, and therefore classed as 'personal luggage'. Vast, snaking queues, thousands of bodies long, form every morning from around 6 a.m., almost entirely made up of women, most often widows, divorcees and single mothers, young and old, who are the main providers for their families. Day after day, they walk or wait, bent double under the strain of carrying huge bundles trussed up in plastic and tarpaulin, often weighing up to eighty kilogrammes or more. They are known as *porteadores*, the so-called 'mule women'. Making multiple journeys from dawn till dusk, they carry goods into and out of Melilla, all for a daily wage of just €10.[20]

Their packages are always classed as basic needs items – food and clothing – but in reality they could be anything, not least high-value electronic goods like mobile phones. Customs officials let them pass without scrutiny. Some 45,000 people (more than half the population of Melilla itself) make their living as *porteadores*. The total number supported indirectly by this trade numbers over 400,000. It is, in essence, a form of sanctioned smuggling – *comercio atypico* as they term it in Spanish – and it accounts for the transfer of up to €600 million worth of goods each year.[21] As a result, the border itself has become a bizarre form of liminal factory, a mechanism for production and profit, powered by nothing more or less than the existence of a line of separation and a desperate, low-wage workforce prepared to cross it interminably.

Carlos remembered going to the checkpoint one morning, watching the gates open and the people clamouring to get in. The crowds were, Guillermo wrote in his notes, 'lined up like cattle', many 'crying out', some even collapsing. The throng of border crossers and *porteadores* was even larger than normal. They watched as a woman was pulled out of the line by the police. Carlos photographed the moment: the officials inspecting her documents while she looked away from them, into space. 'She wore the suffering of the whole world on her face,' Guillermo wrote. One of the policemen came over to them. 'We think she is Syrian,' he said.[22]

By this time, around 200 Syrians had already made their way into Melilla. The very first wave of arrivals from the civil war. Most of them were living in a tented village in a Muslim cemetery, down below the green expanse of the Melilla golf club.

Later, Carlos and Guillermo crossed into Morocco, telling the border officials they were teachers. They spent a few hours walking around the souk in Beni Enzar, pretending to shop, wary of being observed by the local secret service – and then they slipped away, walked beyond the city, trekking for half an hour up into the hills. It wasn't long before they reached the periphery of one of the migrant camps.

Shapes appeared in the eucalyptus trees above them, sentries, always on the lookout for police raids. They were welcomed, brought into the heart of a camp made up of one or two thousand people, most from Mali, Senegal and Ghana. Carlos photographed the activity: long lines of men carrying plastic water bottles filled up from a nearby mountain spring; a group playing football; others huddled around cooking pots simmering on open fires. Many showed their cuts and wounds: 'souvenirs', as Guillermo put it, of previous failed attempts to cross the fences.[23] They all spoke of fleeing war, poverty and famine.

'I was surprised by just how bad the conditions were,' Carlos said. 'Nothing *visually* was surprising to me. It was things I had seen before on the news. But again, when you put your feet on the line, you realise things that you can't feel watching on a screen. What it means to sleep rough, in the woods, in the rain, for months. You are there, and you feel like, *if I had to spend one night here, that would be a nightmare for me*. And these people have been here for six months, or a year, or more.'

One of Carlos's photographs stands out. A figure in silhouette, in front of a dozen or so threadbare, makeshift tents, framed either side by eucalyptus trees. He is looking out from the heights of the mountainside, over a wide vista that takes in the Moroccan town of Beni Enzar and, beyond it, the curved harbour of Melilla. The sea is a grey-blue expanse, the horizon disappearing into a heavy heat haze. It is a perfect portrait of border 'burning': of giving up everything you have ever known for the single cause of *crossing*. The figure looks ahead at their life to come. 'Nothing will stop us,' the migrants in the camp had said to them.

They returned to Melilla later that afternoon, got back to their hotel by the early evening. They sat talking over a drink in the bar – as Guillermo put it in his notes, at the exact same time that the migrants would be beginning to make their way down to the fence.[24] They talked of how, across Europe, and particularly in the north, so many people just did not know what was going on in Melilla.

'One of our goals was this,' Carlos told me. 'There were people – in Germany, say – who had no idea that this place even *exists*. And we wanted to try to change that. Because whatever is happening here – *it is going to get to their place, to your place*. Maybe weeks from now. Or months. Or years. And this is exactly what has happened.'

*

Carlos was, in a very different way, a product of border crossing. He was born in Budapest, in 1971. His father was a diplomat and his mother a fine arts graduate.

'There was no Spanish embassy in Budapest because it was still the time of the Iron Curtain. So my father went there with another two diplomats. They were very young at the time: twenty-eight years old. It was one of their first commissions and their assignment was to open an embassy. So there they were, living in a hotel for two or three years, looking for a building to turn into an embassy.'

After his birth, his parents met with a priest in Budapest to arrange a baptism. The priest would not use the Spanish name 'Carlos' and suggested a Hungarian equivalent. His parents refused and so they eventually agreed on a compromise: baptising him in Latin as 'Carolus'. Because Spain had not yet established official relations with Hungary his birth certificate had to be lodged in the nearest appropriate country – which was Austria. Somewhere in an archive in Vienna is the first official document recognising the existence of a *Carolus* Spottorno.

'But this is what happens,' Carlos said, 'when countries do not recognise each other.'

Throughout their time in Budapest, his parents were under surveillance from the Hungarian secret service and, by extension, the KGB. 'They found microphones in their own living room and everywhere. They had been in Cuba before and that was the same. So these are the kind of things that shape your mind. My mother still does not like to speak of many things over the phone. She thinks everyone is recording everything.'

When Carlos was three years old his family moved from Budapest to Rome. Three years later, they moved to Madrid. During that time his parents' marriage broke down. Carlos was just six years old when they divorced. When he was eight, his father was posted to the Moroccan capital Rabat – and Carlos and his mother went with him. It was an attempt by his parents to reconcile.

'Which was probably the worst place on earth to try that.' Carlos laughed. 'There was nothing glamorous. If it had been Paris maybe . . . But Morocco? No.' He shook his head, smiling. 'It was not the fault of Morocco, though. It was their own issues.'

After a year, his mother left Rabat and returned to Spain, to live in the mountains above the Andalusian city of Malaga.

'My mother at this time had become a hippie,' Carlos said. 'My father was a diplomat and my mother was a hippie . . . she decided to live in the countryside with no electricity or water for three years. And I went with her.'

At the same time, his father insisted that his son attend a prestigious school in Malaga. Carlos talked of how he would maybe take a shower once a week, how he never brushed his teeth, how the whole community up in the mountains would use their car batteries to get electricity into their houses. And then he would travel an hour and a half by bus every day, down through the hills, to go to the school in the city.

Carlos went on to study fine arts, just like his mother. He attended the Rome Academy, and lived with his father, who by this time had been posted back to Italy. He began his career as an art director in an advertising agency, but ultimately found the work rather empty. He had developed his own skills as a photographer and wanted to use the medium to tell stories about politics, the economy, social inequality. Given his unconventional upbringing, there was, perhaps, something inevitable about his transition into documentary journalism.

'I was exposed to conversations about international affairs, about politics, since I was a child, since I was very young,' Carlos said. 'And there was this kind of training with my father. He told me, *Whatever you see today in the news, in a week's time there is going to be a reaction. Pay attention! Everything is linked.*'

In early March 2014, a month and a half after their journey to Melilla, Carlos and Guillermo found themselves out in the middle of the Mediterranean Sea. They had managed to negotiate passage on board the 120-metre-long *Grecale*, an Italian naval frigate built for submarine warfare, now reassigned to Operation *Mare Nostrum* – Latin for 'Our Sea' – an open-ended search-and-rescue mission set up by the Italian Ministry of Defence in response to the Lampedusa tragedy the previous year. The vessel was one of thirty that had been charged with patrolling the waters between Africa and Europe, offering aid and assistance to any migrant boats that they found attempting to cross.

Over the course of the previous month, Carlos and Guillermo had been moving steadily east to west along Europe's external borderlines. At the beginning of February, they had flown to Istanbul and caught a bus that took them back into the European Union via a Greek checkpoint. From there they had continued to 'put their feet on the line', moving along the margin between Greece and Turkey.

For eighty miles the Greek–Turkish frontier follows the course of the Evros River northwards from the Thracian Sea. In the region of Orestiada, however, it cuts a corner, crossing straight over a tract of agricultural land for six miles. In 2012, a three-metre-high iron fence was constructed here and covered top to bottom – on the Turkish side – with concertinas of barbed wire. 'As far as we know,' a Greek border policeman told them, 'no one has ever crossed it.'[25]

This fence was bolstered along its whole length by the skeletal frames of 20-metre-tall watchtowers and a 500-metre-wide military exclusion zone: enter without permission and you risked being arrested and jailed. This, Carlos discovered for himself when he ventured inside the zone to photograph the border and was intercepted by the Greek military. They interrogated him and threatened him with prison, but in the end they were satisfied with deleting all the images from his camera – or at least the camera held around his neck. They did not search his bag and discover a second camera, the one which he had actually used to shoot across the borderline. Its memory card held a series of images of the landscape: those looming watchtowers, old landmine warning signs and a view, foregrounded by the regimented line of the fence, that gazed out of the European Union and into the Turkish town of Edirne.

Near one end of the fence was a detention centre for migrants – those who had been caught crossing from Turkey after making their way around the sides of the barrier and fording the Evros River. It was a compound hemmed in by double lines of fencing topped with more barbed wire. 'It is not a prison,' an official told Carlos and Guillermo when they came to visit. The centre held people from Afghanistan, Eritrea, Algeria, and a new group of Syrians who had made the crossing just days before. Everything was forbidden, however – taking photographs, talking to the migrants – and so they soon moved on, following the borderline further northwest, up to the point where it intersected with Bulgaria.

After crossing into Bulgaria, they arranged access to a local border patrol station, located in an old, Soviet-era military office near the town of Elhovo. They were told by the base commander that, for years, immigration into Bulgaria had been virtually non-existent. Yet in the previous six months, some 11,000 people had crossed from Turkey. The vast majority of them were Syrians. Now Bulgaria was receiving millions of euros from the European Union to pay for the constant surveillance of their 170-mile-long border with Turkey. Carlos photographed staff watching feeds from CCTV cameras, including thermal imaging. 'Immediately, it reminded us of Melilla,' Guillermo wrote.[26]

Just a month before, Bulgaria had begun constructing a twenty-one-mile-long section of fencing and razor wire to run through the plains and hills around the Lesovo checkpoint in the country's south-eastern corner. Just two and a half decades after the dismantling of the last physical remnants of the Iron Curtain in this landscape – hundreds of miles of fencing and minefields – a new barrier was emerging. (More sections would be built over the coming years until, by the summer of 2017, nearly the entire length of the border with Turkey would be sealed off, just as it had been during the Cold War.)[27] Carlos photographed the ground being broken for this first stretch of the border fence. Supplying the mesh, razor wire and surveillance technology were the same companies that had installed the barrier system in Melilla.[28]

They left Bulgaria soon after, heading west. At the beginning of March, they travelled to Lampedusa. Their request to accompany the local Coast Guard on patrol was, however, frustrated by storms out at sea. Instead, they visited a macabre site in one corner of the island – the 'graveyard of migrant ships'. It was, Carlos told me, an area several football pitches in size, full of great piles of rotting and rusting boats that had been pulled out of the water in the aftermath of rescue missions. The old vessels were 'stacked like the toys of a brutal god', Guillermo wrote.[29] A local activist, Giacomo Sferlazzo, had created an exhibit of objects found among the wreckage. Carlos photographed this detritus of broken lives: a water-damaged Nigerian passport; a tube of Colgate toothpaste and three toothbrushes; the warped cover of a bible with all its interior pages missing; a baby's bottle.

From Lampedusa they flew to Sicily, then travelled to Cara di Mineo: at that time the largest reception centre for migrants in the whole of Europe. It occupied the streets and houses of what was once an American military base. There were nearly 4,000 migrants living on site, double the actual capacity – with about ten to every house. The centre was, Guillermo wrote, 'a surreal landscape', an 'apocalyptic place'.[30] It was during this visit that they finally received the message they had been waiting for. Permission had been granted for them to come on board the *Grecale*; a helicopter was being scrambled to take them out into the Mediterranean. The navy offered no guarantees, however, as to when they might be able to return to land.

Almost immediately after arriving on the ship, they were met by its captain.

'We know you are journalists and we know what you want,' he said to them. 'But tell me, *what do you really want?*'

'We were quite clear,' Carlos said. 'We said, *we want to see a rescue operation. We want to see it and to be as close as possible.*'

The captain told them that they had come to the right place. But the seas were rough. There would be no crossings until the waters calmed.

Carlos and Guillermo were among the very first journalists to be allowed onto one of these rescue ships. It was, Carlos told me, a matter of opportune timing.

'The whole political and military system in Italy had suddenly decided it was a good moment to show what they were doing,' he said. 'They were fed up paying for this *Mare Nostrum* operation on their own. *Where is Europe?* they were saying. *Why is nobody helping us? Where are the German ships? Where are the French ships? There's nobody here except you and us, Spanish and Italians, taking care of this big burden. So, yes, we are going to show the news what is happening.*'

Over the previous decade and a half, an estimated 20,000 migrants had already drowned in the Mediterranean. That number was only set to rise: perhaps no matter what action was taken by the countries on Europe's southern sea border.

'When you keep the borders,' Carlos said, 'you have bad press always. Because borders are a dirty affair. So whoever is taking care of them is getting bad press. And you need political support.'

After three days on board, the weather started to clear, the winds died down, and the seas began to settle. On the evening of the fourth day, Guillermo wrote of how the horizon turned a 'bloody red' and the waters around the ship were smooth as glass. They were around eighty miles off the coast of Libya. For any boats waiting to make a crossing, conditions could not have been better.

Early the next morning, they were awoken in their bunks by the sound of helicopter rotors. They rushed to the command centre.

'We have contact,' the captain told them. 'Very probably migrants.' A call for help had been received from a satellite phone. The ship's helicopter radioed back with a description of a blue wooden boat. They had counted ten children, ten women, maybe a total of 150 to 170 people on board. It was, they confirmed, an 'SAR' – a search-and-rescue event.

The captain ordered the launch of the *Grecale*'s rescue boats, all of them filled with life jackets. Carlos and Guillermo asked for permission to go in one of the boats. The captain thought for a few minutes. '*Avanti*,' he told them finally in Italian. Go.[31]

'I had never seen anything like this before,' Carlos told me. 'I had been in refugee camps. But this was different. These people were under immediate stress and trauma. They had not been wounded, no one had died, the weather was good. It was as smooth as it gets. But still . . .'

As they approached the migrant boat, Guillermo wrote of the faces looking out at them, the mixture of terror and relief in their eyes. They were being transported into the rescue boats twenty at a time. 'Stay calm,' the chief engineer had told them. 'You are in Italy.'[32]

The rescuers soon discovered that the boat also had a hold, which was full of even more passengers. The vessel was little more than a wooden shell, just fifteen metres long. And it was carrying 219 people. The majority were Pakistani and Syrian, but there were also Moroccans, Nigerians – and even four Nepalese.

'I completely concentrated on shooting,' Carlos said. 'On getting the pictures, getting the material, the footage. This was one of the most intense moments of my life. I was thinking, *this is the key moment that will explain everything and you cannot fail.* Batteries need to work. The camera needs to work. You are seeing European history happening and you will not get a second chance.'

By the time that he had returned to the deck of the *Grecale*, however, he was overwhelmed.

'At some point I stopped,' he said. 'I took a rest for some minutes. I don't know what I looked like, but I remember the captain coming close to me and saying, *hey, guy, are you okay? You look like you are shocked.* And I said, *no, no. I'm okay, I'm just working.* But in fact I *was* shocked. And I was trying to digest what I was experiencing.

'I think I was lucky to be in a situation where things were not as bad as they could have been. That allowed me to concentrate on working under emotional conditions where I could concentrate on the quality of the images. If the situation was really bad, I'm not sure how I would have reacted to that. If I saw dead children, how would I react to that? Maybe very bad. I think I would be able to work, but I just don't know . . .'

Carlos paused for a few moments.

'I have a son,' he said. 'At that time he was six. Not much different to the boy we saw dead on the beach.'

That boy was Alan Kurdi: a three-year-old Syrian who drowned after their boat capsized as his family attempted to make a crossing from Turkey's Bodrum Peninsula to the Greek island of Kos. His body was photographed by a Turkish photojournalist, Nilüfer Demir, on 2 September 2015. Within hours, the image was circulating across the globe. It was a picture that was, at once, impossible to look at, and impossible to ignore. It made world leaders pick up their phones and call each other. It provoked a dramatic public and humanitarian response. But it was also a study of despair.[33]

'It strikes you,' Carlos said. 'Of course it does. You can't help thinking this could be mine. It is very easy to connect to that. It takes your biggest fears.'

Carlos and Guillermo were on the *Grecale* a year and half before Alan's death. They were witnessing events which, in 2014, were still relatively extreme – yet which would soon become commonplace. Among Carlos's pictures was one particularly compelling shot, an obverse of the horrifying image of Alan.

In the image, a young Syrian girl is captured at the exact moment that she is lifted up onto the deck from one of the rescue boats below. She is five or six years old, wearing a green anorak with its hood half up and a pink scarf tied loosely around her neck. Her whole body is dwarfed by the boxy form of her orange life jacket. One crewman in camouflage fatigues is passing her to another. Framing the scene is the gun-metal grey outrigging of the *Grecale*, a dull, overcast sky, and the opaque, faintly rippled surface of the sea. The girl's wavy black hair spills out from one side of her hood, one thick strand dropping in an 'S' shape from her forehead down to the tip of her nose. Her mouth is hidden by her scarf, but her eyes look

straight at the camera. Or, rather, straight *through* the camera. They are looking at you.

It is not so much that her gaze is inscrutable, as that it is open to endless interpretation. Are those eyes thankful or accusing? Plaintive or angry? Terrified or relieved? More than anything, perhaps, they are a place where you have no choice but to confront your own individual reaction to what you are seeing. That image of Alan's body on the shoreline could only be glanced at before the horror was overpowering. Here, however, the opposite is true. You cannot look away. The girl's eyes stare out: dark and penetrating and vibrantly, undeniably *alive*. It is going too far, perhaps, to say that this is an image of hope. But it is certainly one of *possibility*. A reminder that decisions can be made and unmade. That rescue was, once, an option.

Operation *Mare Nostrum* lasted for just over a year, from the beginning of October 2013 to the end of October 2014. In that time it saved more than 130,000 people from the sea.[34] But costs mounted, political will faltered, and, one by one, boats like the *Grecale* were repurposed. Some even said that the operation had created a 'pull factor', that it encouraged yet more migrants to make the dangerous crossing in even more unsuitable vessels. In October 2015, a year after *Mare Nostrum* ended, a boat carrying at least 950 migrants capsized between Libya and Lampedusa. Twenty-eight people were rescued, and only twenty-four bodies were recovered. The rest drowned, lost beneath the waves.[35]

In early March 2015, just hours before the finance ministers of the Eurozone were set to conclude the fractious negotiations surrounding the bailout of the collapsing economy of Greece, the country's Defence Minister Panos Kammenos gave a speech.

'If Europe abandons us in this crisis,' he said, 'we will flood it with migrants, and so much the worse for Berlin if jihadists from the Islamic State mix in amid that human tide of millions of economic refugees.'

Kammenos was the leader of the populist neo-right Independent Greeks party, which had formed a coalition government with the radical-left party, Syriza. He went on to say that, if Europe was to 'strike' Greece, then 'we will strike them. We will give to migrants from everywhere the documents they need to travel in the Schengen area, so that the human wave could go straight to Berlin.'[36]

For Carlos, this was one of the defining moments of the story they were trying to tell.

'There was this protocol of 2002 that says whenever a refugee enters a European country, they should stay in the country where they have entered. Of course, this protocol was signed before the big accumulation of refugees and migrants. When there are hundreds of thousands of people coming into Greece and Italy and Spain – the poorest countries in southern Europe – then it starts to create divisions between southern and northern Europe.'

This dialogue between those on the continent's edge and those in its interior was becoming increasingly combative. 'The south are saying, *we are protecting the border*,' Carlos said, '*but you don't even know where it is. You've never even heard of these places*. And if you ever hear us say, *there are troubles at the borders*, you say, *who cares? That's not our troubles*.

'And Kammenos decided this is going to stop, this is going to end. You are going to know the problem. No one who was not an extremist would have imagined doing such a thing: to *weaponise* people.'

Carlos and Guillermo's account of their journey the previous year – published by *El País* with the headline 'At the Gates of Europe'[37] – had won them a World Press Photo award. That summer, they persuaded the newspaper to allow them to continue the story. And so, in September 2015, they travelled to the small town of Röszke on the border between Hungary and Serbia.

Carlos arrived first, and telephoned Guillermo to describe a scene of utter chaos. 'I can see a curtain of smoke, riot police everywhere, it's a mess.'[38]

Hungary had just ordered the closure of its border with Serbia and was fast-tracking the construction of a four-metre-high, razor-wire fence along its 110-mile length. An estimated 160,000 migrants had already crossed. For Hungary's right-wing prime minister Viktor Orbán, the time had come to seal off the country.

'We have to make it clear that we cannot let everyone in,' he said, 'because if we allow everyone in, Europe is finished.'[39]

Orbán's government passed a law which made illegal entry into Hungary a crime. Large numbers of migrants had been corralled into an open field near the Röszke border checkpoint. When a group attempted to break through the fence, a pitched battle began. The Hungarian police used tear gas, water cannons and armoured vehicles to repel the migrants. Twenty-nine were arrested, while many more were injured.[40] Thousands had already arrived at this point, and hundreds of thousands more were on their way: making the long walk north from Greece, on through Macedonia, Kosovo and Serbia. With the way ahead blocked, the flow of people bent westwards, around the side of Hungary and into Croatia.

Carlos and Guillermo followed this new route to a large, make-shift migrant camp that had grown up around a railway station in the Croatian town of Tovarnik. The station had become an ad hoc, improvised border – a bottleneck formed of barriers and police who were regulating the movement of people onwards. The Croatian prime minister Zoran Milanović had just announced that he was prepared to allow the refugees free passage over his country's territory.

'We are ready to accept and direct those people,' he said, 'to where they apparently wish to go . . . Germany, Scandinavia.'[41]

Periodically, trains would arrive at the station, and there would be a scramble to get on board – family groups often breaking up in the process. The migrants did not know where the trains were going, just that they would take them onwards.

'I do not approve the policy of Budapest,' Milanović continued. 'I consider it harmful and dangerous. Not that the walls that are being erected will stop anyone, but they are sending a horrible message. A fence in Europe in the twenty-first century is not an answer, but a threat.'[42]

Soon, buses were arriving to supplement the trains. The deputy mayor of Tovarnik told Carlos and Guillermo that they had managed to move some 25,000 people in just four days.[43] On the refugees went, headed for the next border, the next hurdle, curving around the closed frontier of Hungary to reach the southern edge-line of Slovenia. There, the humanitarian effort had intensified: volunteers, many of them students who had travelled from central or northern Europe, were giving out clothes and food and offering medical aid. It seemed at that moment to Guillermo like an 'explosion of solidarity'.[44] These were the days just after the death of Alan Kurdi. Public and political attitudes had shifted dramatically. At least for a while.

Two months later, Carlos was in Paris, having dinner with a friend. All of a sudden a waiter called out loudly across the whole restaurant to ask for everyone's attention. There had been a shooting nearby. 'Don't panic,' he said, 'but you need to go.'

'I had to decide whether I should go to my hotel,' Carlos told me, 'which was in the direction of the shooting. Or walk away from the shooting but go nowhere. I decided to go to the hotel. For about ten minutes I was walking in the street, all the time thinking where am I going to hide? If I hear shooting, what will I do?'

It was the night of 13 November 2015. A series of co-ordinated terrorist attacks were taking place in the French capital that would kill a total of 130 people – including ninety audience members shot by gunmen at a rock concert at the Bataclan theatre. Islamic State later claimed responsibility, saying that the murders were in retaliation for French airstrikes on Syria and Iraq. Most of the attackers were born in France or Belgium, although some of them had previously joined the fighting with Islamic State in Syria, and were thought to have hidden themselves among the massive flow of refugees, slipping back into Europe unnoticed.

I wondered what Carlos was thinking in those moments. He had only recently returned from documenting the migrant crisis. And there he was, caught up in the immediate vicinity of the Paris terror attacks. Did it feel to him like everything was in chaos – as if some kind of continental breakdown was happening?

'That was exactly the case,' he replied. 'And it was not just my perception; I knew that people were going to link these two things. For extreme-right parties it was very easy to link these two things. So, in September, you have hundreds of thousands of people crossing the Balkans, women wearing the hijab, so obviously they are seen as Muslims. And then, two months later, you have this mass killing. In terms of propaganda, in terms of storytelling that criminalises refugees, it makes perfect sense. It is so easy to link. And link successfully, I'd say. I don't think these two things are unrelated to the Brexit vote. They are perfectly related.'

Still the refugees kept coming. A million or more had arrived in Europe by the end of 2015. It wasn't long before some countries were starting to refuse to take quotas of migrants that had been agreed earlier in the year. Attitudes were hardening again.

'Nationalism, mistrust between neighbours, xenophobia . . .' Guillermo wrote in his notes as the year came to an end.[45] He and Carlos had the feeling that something had 'started to crack' in the very fabric of Europe. From the great fault line of the exterior border more fissures had opened up, first between north and south, then along the borderlines between individual states across the European Union. All these cracks were connected, Carlos said. And if they could not be repaired, then 'the whole structure will collapse'.

In January 2016, Carlos and Guillermo's journey along Europe's borderlines finally came to an end. It was almost two years since they had made the trip to Africa's Mediterranean coast: to Melilla, the city by the sea. Now, some 2,500 miles away from the European Union's southern terminus, they had reached its northern counterpart – beyond the Arctic Circle, in the tiny Finnish border town of Salla.

Much of this last part of their story had been about looking outwards, towards the great weight which presses up against Europe's northeastern edgeline: Russia. Over the previous few weeks they had gone to Lithuania, Poland and Latvia, witnessed thousands of soldiers from eleven different NATO countries as they performed training exercises that imagined a border invasion by a fictious enemy called 'Redland'. And they had travelled on into Ukraine, seen how a real battle – a civil war being fought between the country's east and west – was casting the shadow of a much larger conflict. Both Russia and NATO were providing training, logistics and equipment to their opposing Ukrainian allies. As a geographical bulwark between two global power blocs, Ukraine had become the site of a proxy European border war. In February 2022, that proxy war became a real war. A Russian invasion – described by Vladimir Putin as a 'special military operation' – that was driven by a desire to wipe Ukraine's borders off the map. According to Putin, the objective was to right a historical mistake, to rub out the lines drawn around a nation of 40 million people. A nation which, he claimed, was never real in the first place. A pandemic spent pouring over old maps in the Kremlin archives had seemingly fuelled his personal, perverse mania for violently reclaiming Russia's historical edgelands.

'It was striking to see how, for people in the Baltic countries, the presence of the Russians is an existential threat,' Carlos told me. 'It is something that makes them feel uncomfortable every day of their lives. Because they feel like they could easily at any moment be invaded by Russians who say they are reclaiming part of their natural historic territory – just like they did with Crimea.'

For Carlos this emphasised one of the underlying themes of their story. 'Which is that: *we Europeans don't know each other*. We in Spain, say, have no idea about the fears of the Lithuanians. We barely know where Lithuania is. But it is not just Spanish ignorance. I'm sure the Lithuanians have no idea about our fears, or the things we are worried about. Or what the Greeks are worried about.'

Finland was their last stop. Here, the border with Russia runs for over 800 miles – it is Europe's longest single stretch of external borderline. The Finnish authorities took them on a flight on a twin-prop Border Guard aeroplane, a routine patrol that set out from Helsinki to cross the frozen surface of the Baltic Sea.

'Look at the ice,' Carlos had said to Guillermo. He began taking photographs through the plane window at a great ice sheet riven with cracks. 'In the Baltic Sea we found the cracks of Europe,' Guillermo wrote.*[46] It was for them, at that time, a potent and portentous – albeit unsubtle – visual metaphor.

'We had come expecting a big story about the Finnish and Russian border,' Carlos said. They thought they would find a sense of rising tension all along a frontier that runs through a vast expanse of territory: that the great tremors they had seen in Ukraine would be vibrating down the line.

'But in fact Russia was not a problem for them. The big problem was that 30,000 refugees had just arrived in their country of 5 million people. It was a shock to them.'

Most had come in just two or three months at the end of 2015. It made Finland the country with the fourth largest number of asylum seekers in the whole of the European Union – and with the largest percentage increase in overall numbers. Carlos and Guillermo travelled 200 miles north to a migrant reception centre in the small city of Kuopio. There, they were astonished to meet people who had passed through the same villages that they had visited in the Balkans – often the very same week that they had been there.

'They had gone from the Balkans to Austria, to Germany, to Denmark, to Sweden: and then Sweden had sent some of them to Finland,' Carlos said. 'We even met people who had been at that same train station in Croatia.'

* Carlos and Guillermo combined their previous work from 'At the Gates of Europe' with these subsequent journeys to the eastern and northern fringes of Europe to create a field journal – described by them as 'halfway between a photobook and a graphic novel' – called *La Grieta* (The Crack), which was first published in Spanish in 2016 by Astiberri. I was using the French edition – *La Fissure* –to quote from Guillermo's field notes. The translations are my own. There is, as yet, no English-language edition.

During their visit they saw migrant children attending the local primary school, heard how they were taking ice-skating lessons and would play in the snow as they walked home to the reception centre. But there were also signs of strain. Carlos photographed anti-refugee graffiti in the streets. There were stories of far-right groups harassing migrants, of vandals attacking the reception centres.

From there they travelled even further north, joining a troop of Finnish army border guards at the country's northernmost military base of Ivalo, on the 68th parallel. The soldiers took them out on a patrol, into the snowbound forest where temperatures dropped to -30°C. Carlos's glasses snapped in half from the cold and Guillermo's biro stopped working. They reached a long stretch of border fencing. This was not to keep people out, however. Rather, it was built to keep Finland's reindeer population *in*.

And then their last stop, Salla – one of the most northerly border crossing points between Finland and Russia. A place that has always billed itself – quite happily – as being 'the middle of nowhere'.

'We were in this police station at the border,' Carlos told me. 'And we didn't expect much. We expected a couple of border guards: bored, watching screens or feeds from cameras in the woods. We expected to find nothing at all. And suddenly this car arrives. Right at the moment when we were there.'

There were seven people crammed inside an old Lada. They climbed out on the Finnish side of the border.

'We were just a few metres away from them. But because of European law we could not speak to them.'

So Carlos asked if he could take a picture. The border guards hesitated and then shrugged, agreed that there was no law against *that*. Carlos laughed at the memory. 'The European labyrinth! Some things are possible. Some things are not possible.'

They approached the group, used Google Translate on their phones to ask permission to take a picture. At the same time, out of earshot of the border guards, they asked them where they were from. It was two separate groups who had banded together for this last stretch of their journey. A couple from Cameroon and a family of five from Afghanistan. Carlos took their photograph: the seven of them standing in a line on the snow holding their suitcases, with the chevroned barriers of the border immediately behind them, backlit by the massed floodlights surrounding the checkpoint.

'The people who know most about border laws are the migrants,' Carlos said. 'They are completely aware of everything. They know what to do and what to say. And here, they had figured out this way of buying these shitty cars in Murmansk and then driving for six hours to the border where they then claim asylum.'

Similar carloads had been arriving for the last few months. Sometimes three or four a day. The police guards at Salla had shown them a vehicle-dumping ground – a car park full of Ladas and Volgas abandoned by their occupants the moment that the border was crossed. It instantly put Carlos and Guillermo in mind of the 'graveyard of migrant ships' on Lampedusa. Indeed, another 250 miles north of Salla, not far from the coast of the Arctic Sea, there was another similar echo, this time the most bizarre of all.

At the Storskog border checkpoint, beyond the boundary of the European Union, Russia meets Norway. There, a loophole in the border rules between the two countries meant that, while Russia did not allow people to cross to Norway on foot, and Norway did not let drivers in carrying people without documents, bicycles were permitted at both ends without any checks. In the summer of 2015, the first refugee arrived in Norway by bicycle. By the end of the year, some 5,000 asylum seekers, most of them Syrian, had made this same crossing. Massive piles of discarded bicycles grew on the Norwegian side of the border – large numbers of them were children's, because these were the cheapest to buy. The Norwegian government soon moved to close the loophole. Then, in 2019 – at the cost of £500,000 – they built a chain-link fence along just 200 metres of the Storskog crossing. Yet another barrier rising on the extreme edge of the continent. A symbol at once pointed and futile.[47]

'This is such a rooted reaction,' Carlos said to me. 'It is so deep in our bones. To keep you safe, you close borders, close the door, close your eyes. *Close.* How do you keep safe from harm? *Closing.* And staying in the box. I think this is really deep in our brain. Maybe it is impossible to try to eliminate the concept of the border because, as they say, *your skin is the first border.* It is true. We have borders and we live with borders and we have come to rely on them.'

All the same, Carlos continued, thinking of the many fences and walls and barriers that he had encountered on his journey, 'when you create a physical barrier, you are calling for the destruction of that barrier. Sooner or later, this will happen. These physical borders are unsustainable. And they provoke, as they have provoked for thousands of times in history, clashes between people trying to cross from one side to the other.'

PART 4
BREAKING

8
THE MELTING BORDER

'The amazing thing is that, even though it is a relatively small glacier compared to the size of the surrounding ones; even though we had studied it for months on maps, and we had the conviction that we knew how it looked, and how to move, and the distances and everything – this was all completely shattered by the actual physical experience of being there.'

Marco Ferrari was in his late thirties, with short, close-cropped hair, a neatly trimmed beard and round, wire-framed spectacles. He was a lively, animated talker. Although an architect by training, he never chose to practise, but instead co-founded, with designer Elisa Pasqual, a design and research agency in Milan, called Studio Folder.

He was telling me about his agency's project to track the movement of a glacier. But not just any glacier. The Grafferner ice sheet is found at 3,000 metres above sea level in the Ötztal Alps. It is wedged into a deep valley between two ridges of high mountain peaks, the tallest of which, Similaun, tops out at nearly 3,600 metres. This glacier is also a border. Running right through its centre is the international boundary line dividing Italy from Austria.

On maps, this short stretch of border is drawn as a shallow curve bending outwards from Similaun over the ice to the summit of West Marzell, about a kilometre and a half to the northeast. It was designed – as is the case throughout the whole Alpine region – to follow the watershed. In the simplest terms, if rain or meltwater from the mountains flows north, funnelling into the Danube and draining into the Black Sea, then the land belongs to Austria. If it flows south, joining up with the Adige River and cutting east to empty into the Adriatic Sea, then the territory is Italy's.

On the glacier itself, however, there are no markers of the boundary line: just an ever-shifting expanse of snow and ice. The weather, the atmospheric conditions, the changing seasons – all sculpt and resculpt the Grafferner watershed at will. Here, the ridgeline between north and south is never the same twice – year to year, week to week, day to day, even minute to minute. Marco's plan was to find a way to delineate this high-altitude border: to design a method to measure its constant, incremental shifts in real time. Viewed abstractly, from a distance, the Grafferner appeared to offer the perfect test environment.

'But,' Marco said, shaking his head, 'it was much, much bigger than we thought it would be. It was huge, really huge. Also everything was white; there was no reference points. It is fairly flat, but still not as flat as we thought, and you couldn't see the horizon anywhere, you were just surrounded by hills and mountains. They completely impeded your view.'

Marco and his team made their first visit in April 2014, landing on the glacier in a helicopter. 'There was still a lot of snow on top of it,' he said, 'so walking across it was very demanding, especially if you had to criss-cross it several times. It was exhausting. We spent something like seven, eight hours on it. And also it was cold, and you feel the altitude, so it was incredibly tiring. Exhilarating, but very tiring.'

Marco paused, thought for a second, then continued.

'So our first impression was that, even though we'd planned our movements very precisely, we still felt like we were unprepared somehow. The conditions were so much wilder than we thought. We felt completely overwhelmed by it.'

Almost exactly a century ago, another team came to the Grafferner. They were surveyors working for the Instituto Geografico Militaire

(IGM), a branch of the Italian military that serves as the country's national mapping agency. Their task was to explore, measure and, finally, demarcate a new border.

In one of the many carve-ups that followed in the wake of the First World War, the 1919 Treaty of Saint-Germaine-en-Laye had transferred two whole regions of the former Austrian Empire to Italy. The German-speaking Südtirol became 'Alto Adige', while the predominantly Italian-speaking area of Trentino was also absorbed within the body of the new, enlarged Italian nation. The previous route of the border had been set in 1866 – just five years after Italy had formed into a single, unified kingdom. This post-war frontier jumped much further north, in some cases by over a hundred kilometres, right into the central Alps.[1]

Its guiding principle was this concept of the watershed. In 1713, France and Savoy had agreed by the Treaty of Utrecht to split their two territories by *l'eau pendante des Alpes*: the 'draining water' of the Alps. It was the first time that Europe's great mountain range had ever officially been divided in this way – its highest ridgeline conceived as a 'natural' breaking point, the place where gravity itself would determine the difference between one nation and another. And it set the precedent for all the Alpine splits to come.[2]

Principle was one thing. Practice, however, was quite another. For four years, from 1919 to 1923, the IGM surveyors tried to work out, in real terms on the ground, exactly where this theoretical watershed was. It was a huge, complex task, with teams spending weeks or months at a time navigating across hundreds of kilometres of the high landscapes and compiling their findings in field journals and diaries. Page after page of notebooks were filled with photographs, maps, drawings, annotations, mathematical calculations and neat, handwritten descriptions of the terrain. The surveyors reached the Grafferner sometime after 1921, approaching it from the east, along a rocky ridge just poking up above the level of another glacier, the Schlaf.

'From this point,' the surveyors wrote, 'the ridge gets increasingly narrow and hard to follow, due to its composition of brittle rock and boulders, which seem to defy gravity. Even the Austrian side gets scary because of the steep gap of ice that the ridge reveals – ice which eventually covers the rocky ridge between 3,492 and 3,573 metres and on which the boundary runs. The boundary here is extremely difficult to follow on foot.'

The surveyors still pressed on, up to the peak of West Marzell, which they found to be rocky on the Austrian side but encased with ice on the Italian side. 'From the West Marzell, the border runs along the watershed which divides the Similaun saddle in two and then rises up to the Similaun peak along a barely perceptible ridge, also made of ice.'

There, on the Grafferner, the surveyors conceded that the watershed dematerialised almost entirely. 'Overall, this tract appears as a conventional border only to those who don't observe closely the complex drainage of the waters.'[3]

Included among 'those' was the new fascist government of Italy, which came to power in 1922. To Mussolini and his ministers, the watershed was simply a device, a means of using mathematics and cartography to quantify and legitimate the Alps as an *eternal* boundary, a colossal margin of rock that had always cradled, protected – and made separate and distinct – the people of the Italian peninsula. Drawing it and marking it wasn't about establishing something new, but rather restoring something old: the mountain border as a symbol of a vigorous Italian strength that could be traced all the way back to the days of the Roman Empire. In this sense, it was less a watershed line and more the high-tide mark of an out-rushing wave of state-sponsored nationalism.[4]

While the surveyors were carefully and painstakingly working their way across the mountains, to the south of the border a government project was underway to 'conquer the soil' of the annexed – or, in the fascist lexicon, 'redeemed' – land. Driving this policy forward was the ardent nationalist Ettore Tolomei. For decades Tolomei had been fixated on this region and the idea of the Alps as Italy's true, natural extremity. In 1904, he had even climbed the 3,000-metre-high

Glockenkarkopf mountain, which he believed marked the northernmost point of the Alpine watershed. Claiming this as a first-ever ascent (despite the Austrian Fritz Koegl having reached the peak nearly a decade earlier), he asserted the right to rename the mountain as the *Vetta d'Italia*: the 'Summit of Italy'.[5] His blunt, unsubtle implication: if this was Italy's summit, then everything south of it was Italy's too.

Tolomei founded a publication, the *Archivo per l'Alto Adige*, which purported to occupy the high ground of journalistic and scientific objectivity, yet set out, one way or another, to prove the historical and innate 'Italianness' of Südtirol. A major part of his work was researching and compiling a huge list of Italianised names of places throughout the region: towns, villages, rivers, hills, mountains. Some were lifted from historical roots or sources; some were translations from the German, or German words with an Italian ending added; while a great many were simply Tolomei's own inventions. *Archivo* gained a significant readership throughout Italy in the years leading up to the First World War, so much so that the lists of alternative names it published had already begun to creep into maps, textbooks, newspapers – even transport timetables.

It was perhaps inevitable, then, that the fascist government would turn to Tolomei to oversee the post-war transformation of Südtirol into Alto Adige. On 23 March 1923, by decree of the king, Victor Emmanuel III, *Archivo*'s catalogue of place names – 16,735 in total – was adopted officially by the Italian state, replacing all German ones. Four months later, Tolomei appeared on the stage of the Municipal Theatre in the city of Bozen, now renamed Bolzano, at the foot of the Alps, to announce his thirty-two *provvedimenti* – 'measures' – for the reclamation of the region. These ranged from mandating Italian as the official language and replacing all Austrian civil servants with Italian nationals, to prohibiting any use of the name Südtirol, disbanding all political parties or press associated with the German-speaking community, and closing all German-language schools. At this point the Italianisation of names even went so far as to require the changing of individual surnames to their Italian versions. So extreme was this ruling that, throughout the region, German names were erased from gravestones.[6]

These stories still live inside this one border today: 'draining water', redemption, fascism, *provvedimenti*, prohibition, renaming, erasure. As the 1920s surveyors picked their way across the mountains and glaciers, conceiving and developing a network of points to knit together into a frontier, they were at the same time twisting the very nature of the Alps in this landscape, rotating its axis by ninety degrees. No longer was it a range of peaks threaded by valleys and passes – which had, for millennia, seen continuous movement north and south, back and forth. Now it was a hard line denoting *difference*, *otherness*. The watershed, co-opted by nationalism, had swung the gates shut.

All this happened less than a hundred years ago. In historical terms, this is a young border. An adolescent. And, like many adolescents, it has grown restless. Little by little – but all along its length – it is shifting. It is on the move.

Every summer when he was a boy, Marco and his parents would pack up the family car and travel north, out of Italy and on through Europe to Czechoslovakia, France or the Netherlands.

'On these trips,' he said, 'one of the things that struck me was this queuing at the border. You knew you were leaving a place and entering another one through this very explicit mark. And it was always an experience that somehow fascinated me.'

When he first began his project, he had no idea that he would end up on an Alpine glacier. Studio Folder had been commissioned to make a work for the 2014 Venice Architecture Biennale as part of a strand called *Monditalia* – architecture collaborating with music, film, dance and theatre to consider the political and cultural realities of modern Italy. All Marco knew from the outset was that he wanted to do something about borders.

He thought back to those childhood road trips in the 1980s. And then he thought about the impact of the Schengen Agreement in

1995, which began the process of abolishing internal European border checks. In the decades that followed, some 400 million people were granted the right to travel passport-free through twenty-six states that covered an area in excess of 4 million square kilometres. Borders grew so faint as to, in most practical senses, all but disappear.

But what, Marco wondered, had happened to all the checkpoints, all that border architecture – the buildings that he and his family had once queued up at and passed through? He started collecting archive photographs of border crossings around Europe, and then compared them to images on Google Street View of the same places now.

'In almost all of them, either the buildings were completely dismantled – so there was no physical trace of the border – or they were kind of abandoned, and the road passed around them, or passed through them, and there wasn't any sign of a checkpoint.'

Yet, at the same time, the lines that those buildings had once marked, and had represented physically in the terrain itself, had not gone away. They were still there on the maps.

'The maps didn't change,' Marco said, 'but the reality had changed a lot. So we wanted to investigate these apparent contradictions: how the Schengen Agreement not only modified the actual flow of people and goods between the countries. But also how it changed the European imagination around our understanding of borders. Because somehow, we as a generation, I think we grew up with this idea that borders in Europe weren't a thing any more, so that we could actually freely move. But then it was quite evident – even in 2014 – that this kind of belief was being shaken. There was all this enforcement of new border policies around immigration, and it became so obvious to us that not everyone could freely move, but only very privileged citizens with the passports of very specific countries. So we wanted to investigate all of this.'

From there, Marco and his team decided that their task should be to understand exactly what a border was as an 'object': the concepts and ideas that lay behind the creation of a border, how it was defined in law to be given real, physical weight, and how it was realised as a *construction*, an actual physical presence in a landscape. It was this idea that led them to the IGM.

The national mapping agency's archives are held in a complex of buildings grouped together behind the high walls and barbed wire of an army barracks on the outskirts of Florence. They remain today – as they were when first founded in 1861 – a branch of the military. And their chief task is to maintain Italy's land border: to know what it is, where it is, and to preserve its existence – its visibility on the ground – in the form of markers and boundary stones. Today this work is carried out by a staff of just two people: Simone Bartolini and Maria Vittoria De Vita.

'The archive is an amazing place,' Marco told me, his eyes lighting up behind his glasses. 'There are all these diaries and original surveys of the borders. And they are indexed and orderly on shelves. But then there is this huge part of the archive which is just completely unorganised and they had no idea what it contained. We were free for days on end to open all the books, all the drawers with all these maps. It was crazy, the wealth of material was just insane. But also the quality of the material. Because the surveys are, at once, incredibly technical – with calculations of trigonometric surveys and geodetics – but then you get all these photographs and notes from surveyors who were living for months in the territories. They would describe everything – from observations of the landscape, to where they were finding cheese and bread to eat to sustain themselves.'

In Marco's search for the 'materiality' of the border, the archive offered a discrete origin point. In one room, contained within three standard-sized filing cabinets, he found the official record of Italy's land borders – made up, he said, largely of written reports and lists of co-ordinates. Underpinning that, of course, was the myriad other documentary and record material that filled the archives: the maps, atlases, photographs and field notes. But in that one room, all the history, all the work that had gone into creating and measuring and remeasuring the route of the line, was distilled into these three filing cabinets. *Three* filing cabinets holding *four* borders inside them.

'Because,' Marco said, 'every border is a different border from the other one. You really can't say there is one Italian border.' Along the Alpine ridge, moving from east to west over more than 1,900 kilometres, Italy touches, in turn, Slovenia, Austria, Switzerland and France.

'And there are four borders, because every border has a completely different history, a completely different arrangement, and a completely different set of documents. The actual documents themselves look completely different: they have a different visual language.'

The contents of the filing cabinets were the net results of a century or more of measuring and calculating, negotiating and diplomacy, and, ultimately, *seeing*.

'This was something we discussed at length with the surveyors,' Marco said. 'Like, the kind of specificity with which a border is determined. First of all, there are national agreements, which are very vague. They describe in words: *the border has to go from this point to this point to this point to this point*. Then what happens is the words are translated into very generic maps. But the *actual*, final maps of the border are made by the surveyors. So all of the decisions that define the lines in such detailed precision are very personal – and can only be made in the context of the place itself.'

Marco outlined this process to me with brio, revelling in a kind of border deconstruction. He explained that the line we identify with the border has to somehow emerge from the landscape. And the only way for it to emerge is for the surveyor to see it – using their eyes and their measuring instruments. These allow them to pair and connect natural features, edges and slopes that can be co-opted and rendered as mathematical co-ordinates, put into the service of the line. To help that process, the surveyors build structures to use as sight aids or triangulation points for calculations – an artificial augmentation of the natural landscape.

'You see, the line emerges as a series of constructions – physical constructions – so the materiality of the border is enforced,' Marco said. 'But then, of course, there is the other part, which is cultural. That, for the border to be traced, it has to be an experience for hundreds of people who are moving and travelling along and across this line for years in order to draw it. The line is also about the life of these people over years and years.'

But what about now, what about the lives of the current custodians of the border, Simone and Maria? Given that the original, formative surveying work was done long ago, has the border as 'object' become more of an 'artefact', a fragment of history? What role has a modern IGM to play in *seeing* a landscape that had already been seen, the line running across it interpreted and drawn a century ago?

Before he was let loose in the archives, Marco had met Simone and Maria at the IGM headquarters, in an office away from the military barracks in a grand Renaissance building alongside the Piazza della Santissima Annunziata, right in the heart of Florence. At the very end of their conversation, Marco said the surveyors brought out a series of aerial photographs of the borderline. And then they started pointing out the glaciers – viewed from above, they were like blank spaces in the landscape, thick brushstrokes of white that stretched down from, or criss-crossed, the rocky black seams of the ridge line.

'Now that I'm thinking back about it,' Marco said, 'it was like they knew people must think their work was outdated, that it wasn't necessary any more. So at the end of the interview, to justify themselves, they showed us these images. They said, *now look, in the past few years we've been taking care of this new issue. We are really busy redrawing borderlines all across the Alps*.'

The aerial photographs demonstrated that the landscape of the border was changing fundamentally – and in some cases very rapidly – because the glaciers were melting, shrinking, even disappearing completely. This new landscape needed new surveyors to *see it* afresh. As the ice was disappearing, so the watershed, the dividing principle, was shifting – and, of course, the border was shifting with it. The line was refusing to stay still.

Simone and Maria explained that modifications of the border did happen from time to time, caused by everything from infrastructure developments – building roads, say, or laying power lines – to private property disputes or even landslides.

'The golden rule,' Marco said, 'is that the area of the state has to stay the same. So if Italy gains territory for some reason, it also has to cede territory back to Austria. So the balance is always the same. And every time this is a very lengthy process of exchange and adjustment and meetings and diplomatic negotiations.'

But with the glaciers the alterations were incessant. The surveyors had established that the shrinking ice fields were creating border anomalies at more than one hundred locations all along the Alpine ridge.

'The scale of the change that was happening because of the glaciers moving was completely impossible to tackle with the current legal framework of how borders were managed and defined,' Marco said.

The IGM approached the Italian Minister of Foreign Affairs with an idea. Following the original watershed principle, they could simply let the border move, without the need for territorial exchanges and diplomatic agreements. Wherever the line is subject to natural processes, those processes could redraw the line – and the surveyors would just follow nature's lead, as they mapped and remapped the boundaries.

This solution was first proposed in 1994 (although, even as far back as the 1970s, the IGM surveyors had been noticing that the glaciers along the border were shrinking and changing shape). A decade later, in 2005, it was passed into law as a bilateral agreement to regulate the border between Italy and Austria. In 2009, it was also implemented for Italy and Switzerland.[7]

The legislation stipulated that the border between these three nations will always follow the watershed line, even if that line moves.

It was creating a new type of border, a border that was, as the Italian parliament put it, 'no longer permanently fixed, but that depends on the gradual changes caused by the erosion and reduction of the glaciers, up to the extreme instance of their disappearance'.[8] It was a *confine mobile*, a 'moving border'. And it was the first-ever recognition in law, in history, anywhere in the world, that a border was not immutable, that it could, in essence, shift of its own free will.

To begin with, while Marco and his team recognised that this was an interesting legal development, they also thought that it was just a quirk, a curiosity.

'But in the following weeks we kept thinking about it, we kept coming back to it,' he said. 'And it became the focus, the fulcrum of our project. We realised how many things we could explore with it – the relationships between ecology, accelerating climate change and geopolitical equilibria across Europe. The gap between "natural" and political lines. And these were the kind of connections we were looking for. They became the centre of it all.'

The first aerial photograph that the surveyors had shown Marco was of a small glacier in the Ötztal Alps, which was shrinking and moving further and faster than most.

'There were huge changes to this glacier's – and the border's – geometry,' Marco said. 'It was still moving, but the ice had not retreated so much that, say, a rocky ridge had appeared.'

The most recent IGM survey had shown that the border here had slipped by more than a hundred metres from its 1920s original, the watershed bowing out further and further into Italy to give Austria more land. The glacier in the aerial photograph, which carried the borderline on its surface, was the Grafferner.

A room in Venice, in an old rope factory. Part of the Arsenale, the Serenissima's complex of long-abandoned shipyards and armouries. The room is dark, but for the spotlights trained down on a long white table. At one end of the table is a relief model of a mountainous landscape, milled out of two white plaster blocks, with a satellite image projected down on top of it. At the other end is a huge stack of paper. Printed on every sheet is a 1:3,000 scale map showing the route of the 1920s Italian–Austrian border, focused in on the area where it crosses the Grafferner glacier. The table has a rectangular space marked out on it, and a caption invites you to take a map, lay it inside the space, and push a button. Once pushed, a mechanical arm, set in the centre of the table, swings into life. The arm is an elegant, black-metal pantograph, and it holds in its hand – a squat little cuboid that looks like the headshell of a record player – a red felt-tip pen.

One hundred and eighty kilometres to the northwest, at an altitude of 3,300 metres above sea level, five sensors are spaced out along 1,000 metres of a watershed line sculpted by the snow and ice of the Grafferner glacier. These sensors are solar-powered, designed to withstand the extreme Alpine conditions, and they are constantly transmitting their precise GPS co-ordinates back to the installation in the Arsenale. Every time the button is pressed, the arm takes the sensors' positions – at that exact moment – and uses them to plot and draw the actual line of the border across the Grafferner. With purposeful, mechanical ease, the pantograph draws a red line across the map. It starts north of the dotted line of the 1920 border, then soon cuts across it southwards, pushing far out beyond it in a long, looping 'D' shape. The pen rises and then drifts down to a box at the bottom of the map where it writes Confine *– 'Border' – along with the date and time. A moving border is being drawn on demand, in real time, over and over again.*

It was to install the five GPS sensors that Marco first travelled to the Grafferner in April 2014. His team, working with local mountain guide Robert Ciatti, had picked their way across the glacier in an attempt to find and delineate the real ridgeline, using the most recent measurements given to them by the IGM.

'I'd say at first we thought of the sensors as more theatrical than actually scientific,' Marco explained to me. 'We did it with the idea of tracing the line just to see what would happen. It was a test.'

Once in place, they kept broadcasting their positions throughout the spring and summer of 2014.

'It allowed us to understand that we could actually see the movement of the border. Although this movement is very small in just five months, you could still see it in the data itself.'

But at the end of September, one by one, the signals went dead. There had been heavy snow in the mountains, and all five sensors were buried completely. Then, over autumn and winter, they were swallowed up, absorbed by the ice, pulled down into the body of the glacier. The installation at the *Arsenale* kept going until the Biennale closed in November, still using the last data broadcast in September to plot the line of the border.

This was not the end of the project for Studio Folder, however. Marco wanted to refine the system, improve its accuracy, its precision. At the same time, he wanted to overhaul the design of the sensors themselves, make them more robust and more capable of withstanding the extreme conditions up on the mountain. New versions were built. They could pick up more data than before; along with GPS co-ordinates, they also recorded air temperature, air quality and the sunlight index. They were still solar-powered, but fabricated with modified insulation around their batteries to prevent them from falling below their operating temperatures, creating what Marco described as a 'miniature greenhouse effect' inside their casings. Tests were carried out at -30°C in the University of Milan's 'Cold Lab': in the same space that 800,000-year-old ice cores from Antarctica are kept and studied.

This work carried on for two years, as Studio Folder collaborated with glaciologists and geophysicists to devise a new way of measuring the glacier with the upgraded sensors. By April 2016, Marco was back on the Grafferner, unloading half a ton of equipment from cargo nets lifted in by helicopter. This time, rather than five sensors, there were twenty-six. And instead of stringing them out in a line, the plan was to arrange a grid, five by five, with a final sensor set on a nearby rock, providing baseline measurements for altitude and atmospheric pressure. This would allow the watershed to be measured not as a simple line, but as a three-dimensional model: a 'living' sculpture, captured and translated by its constantly fluctuating data.

Small teams set off across the glacier with hand-held GPS receivers to mark the grid over an area of one square kilometre. They fixed the sensors with mountaineering screws, which passed through aluminium tripod bases, down past the snow cover, to bite into the glacier ice itself. The work took eight hours, but eventually the sensors were all in place. LED lights on each unit lit up to show that they had connected to the local cellular network and were actively transmitting their data.

This time, the drawing machine was 300 kilometres away, in a former munitions factory in the German city of Karlsruhe – home of the ZKM, the Centre for Art and Media. Within days of the installation opening, and just two weeks after the sensors had been put on the glacier, they stopped broadcasting. The signals cut out. The mountain guide, Robert, contacted Marco to tell him that there had been a huge snowfall.

'The amazing thing about Robert was that he was going every week to check on the sensors. He would go to the top of Similaun with binoculars and report back. He told us it had really snowed a lot, like three metres of snow. He said the sensors were buried for sure.'

Yet a few weeks later, the data link flickered into life. The new sensors were designed to reactivate once the solar panels started producing electricity again. As the temperature rose, the snow melted away, and the units all re-emerged into the light. The grid was back online.

I wanted to know how many different maps of the border the machine had drawn. Or rather – given that the sensors and the installation were, in a way, a closed loop, an autonomous system – how many times the border had *drawn itself*.

'I could say thousands or I could say none,' Marco replied, laughing. 'Both answers would be accurate.'

In the first exhibition in Venice, they had printed 9,000 copies of the map – these were all gone within the first two months of its six-month run, and so they had to print thousands more. Visitors were allowed to keep their maps, take them away. Marco has heard stories of them turning up all over the world, in South Africa, Kenya, New Zealand.

'Every map was different because the time was always different, so there is no one map similar to another,' Marco said. 'At the moment it is drawn, that map in your hand is the most accurate, most recent map of the border. But then the moment in which another visitor would trace another one, the map before is superseded.'

At the same time, Marco knew that the borderline itself, as drawn by the pantograph and the red pen, was a deliberate contradiction. While the sensors could detect tiny shifts in location and atmospheric pressure, the scale of the maps was too large for these shifts to really register, because any movement in the borderline would be less than the width of the felt-tip.

'In the second system the design was as precise as possible,' Marco said. 'But at the same time, it was part of the idea behind the project to also be a sort of critique of measuring. Because of the thickness of the pen, any change isn't visible in the maps. But still every borderline is different because the pantograph that draws it is just a little bit shaky!'

This was something that Marco intended, by design. He wanted to say that even this system, which looks incredibly well thought out and precise, cannot really be precise, 'because the glacier moves constantly all the time, so there is no point in drawing a really precise map. This idea of imprecision, and the impossibility of prefect measurement, was something we really wanted to convey in the installation. Even if the installation, aesthetically, looks incredibly precise and machinic.'

Marco returned to the Grafferner for the last time at the very end of September 2016. He'd come with his team to remove all the sensors, to dismantle the grid. It was another long day. The snow cover had all but gone, exposing the true surface of the glacier, the blue glassy sheen of the ice. As he was walking he spotted a faint glimmer of red in the ground. Looking closer he could see it was the casing of a sensor – one of the original five that had disappeared two years earlier.

'It was completely encapsulated in the ice,' Marco said. 'Just a tiny part was coming out. So we had to dig to take it out. It wasn't destroyed, but it was all battered and scratched.'

The glacier had embraced it, taken it for a ride. And then let it go. A border marker ejected by the ice. The other four sensors are still missing. But as the Grafferner slips and shrinks, the day will come, perhaps very soon, when they too will re-emerge, somewhere on the mountaintop.

It was seven in the morning, early September, just a few hundred metres south of the Italian–Austrian border on the Hochjochferner glacier. It had snowed in the night, leaving a fine white dust covering the ice and rocks. Clouds, glinting with tiny crystals, were all around us. It was cold, maybe four, five degrees below zero. But the sun was up now, and I could see a smudged hint of blue sky off to the west.

I was roped to the mountain guide, Robert Ciatti. Robert is now in his sixties, a lithe, sinewy, almost elfin figure. He had thick, wavy grey hair and his skin was a deep, nut brown, save for a patch of mottled, sun-damaged pink on the end of his nose. He led the way and I followed, our crampons crunching through the snow, occasionally ringing out high, discordant notes as the metal hit patches of stone or solid ice.

The Hochjochferner is a much larger glacier than the Grafferner. It lies a few kilometres to the west along the Alpine ridgeline and is made up of three rivers of ice that descend northwards into the valley below. Except now those tributaries no longer meet to become one sheet. Ridges of rock have appeared between them, splitting the ice into three entirely separate pieces. The border crosses the westernmost branch. I passed over it into Austria without realising, walking on the glacial shrapnel of broken, left-behind rocks. Alongside me was the looming presence of the 3,300-metre-high Schwarze Wand mountain – the 'Black Wall'.

The Hochjochferner, Robert told me, has shrunk in size by more than two thirds over the last century and a half. He gestured down into the valley, waved his hand along the dark-brown funnel of exposed rock that ran far off into the northeastern distance.

'Once,' he said, 'the ice filled up all of it.'

At that moment, a long thread of white cloud was nestled on the valley floor. Like a taunt. Or a visitation. A ghost of the glacier now gone.

Ice cover in the Alps reached its greatest recorded extent around the mid-nineteenth century, at the end of what is known as the Little Ice Age. The trend since then has been accelerating disappearance. Half of the glacier landscape from 1850 has vanished. Two thirds of this reduction took place over the course of a century and a quarter. The remaining third has happened in just the last thirty years. Where we are, in the Ötztal Alps, the total glaciated area decreased by just over 30 per cent between 1983 and 2006: from some 130 square kilometres of ice down to a little over ninety.[9]

Robert, Marco had told me, 'speaks about the glacier like it is his home. He knows these places so well and he has seen them changing dramatically.' *For me*, Robert had once said to Marco, *the glacier is life*.[10]

It was fascinating to follow him as he moved across the ice. Our progress was steady and methodical. We were on the middle sheet of the Hochjochferner now, heading directly across it towards a tall, red-brown cliff face. The ice shone darkly through the snow in patches of solid black and blue. Every so often Robert stopped, prodded at the way ahead with his hiking sticks, checking the solidity of the ground. We met a river, just a metre or so wide, running fast and true downslope. The water snaked side to side, cutting into the ice and carving banks of smooth, impossibly perfect curves. At times, the sound that dominated was not the wind or our footsteps, but the rush of water. Even if I couldn't see it, I could hear it, hurtling through channels and tunnels below my feet.

In the last thirty years, over the whole of the South Tyrol, nineteen glaciers have melted away to nothing. The number of glacier 'parts' has increased – from just over 200, to just over 300.[11] But this is no sign of a resurgence. Rather, it shows the inevitability of ice-sheet fragmentation. Just like on the Hochjochferner, glaciers are splitting off into smaller and smaller pieces, becoming a fractured mosaic of sheets and plates, all dwindling and receding.

To reach the highest section of the Hochjochferner, we had to climb. The way up was by *via ferrata* – 'iron path' – a series of steel cables, rungs and ladders fixed tightly to the rock of the cliff. At nearly 3,000 metres, it was hard, breathless going. The cables were still coated with a film of clear ice, the rocks slick underfoot.

By the time we reached the top, the sun had broken through and the clouds had dissipated. Ahead was the largest remaining section of the glacier. It had caught and held the previous night's snowfall and appeared as a blank white sheet.

The reflected glare was fierce, even with sunglasses. It was just after nine o'clock now and I could feel the heat building. The snow was already softening, melting into tiny pools all over the glacier's rocky margins. As we set off across the surface again, I could see that it was not as pristine as I had first thought. In places, where the slope steepened, it broke apart into a series of long wrinkles.

'Crevasses,' Robert said, noticing where I was looking. Line after line of them. Narrow fractures, a few hundred metres long by, at most, just a metre or so wide – but they dropped down deep.

Not long after, Robert held up his hand for me to stop. He poked at a patch of snow with his sticks and it gave way a little, then disintegrated, dropping down into a small black hole. He tested the surface around it and then nodded to himself.

'It's okay,' he said. 'Just watch your feet.'

He stepped across and I followed. The hole was half a pace wide, but I made the mistake of looking down into it as I passed over. There was no bottom. It just descended into a profound, dizzying nothingness. A tiny breach, yet I heard the echo of my movement come back up as I walked away, calling after me.

We passed around a long spine of rock which rose to join the high ridgeline, and turned to move alongside it, beginning to walk directly upwards. We had left the Hochjochferner behind now, and were on the surface of another glacier, the Kreuzferner. There was a kilometre to go to reach the ridgeline, up a glaciated slope that rose in altitude by another 300 metres. The snow was deeper and softer, and it started to feel very warm out on the bright-white mountainside. But Robert kept up his steady pace, our crampons crunching in rhythm. We talked little, just concentrated on moving, snatching breaths from the thinning air.

Up above us, in the near distance, I could see a black outcrop, topped by a tall wooden post. Soon we were stepping off the glacier and onto rock. We made our way up towards the post, which juts up from a tiny plateau. Now, at last, we could rest. This was as high as we would go: 3,278 metres above sea level.

I bent down to remove my crampons and Robert brushed at the ground in front of me. He revealed a flat stone plaque, fixed by iron clamps. Carved on the plaque were the letters 'I' and 'Ö': Italia and Österreich. The 'I' sat within an arrow, two lines pointing up like a child's drawing of a roof. But this was not just a symbol. This was the exact location and route of the border: Marco's 'line as an object', fixed onto the landscape itself. I was sitting on the watershed. Behind me, the ridge reared up another few hundred metres to the summits of Hauslabjoch and Finial. Ahead of me, however, the break line took a sharp, angled turn to the south, just as the plaque showed.

I pulled out my phone to take a picture and saw that I had a text message. It was from my mobile network, received an hour earlier. *Welcome to Austria*. I had only been a few hundred metres across the line from Italy, but it appeared that my phone knew I had crossed the border. It was a little disconcerting.

We sat up there on the watershed line and ate sandwiches, and Robert told me that these plaques were constantly having to be replaced. Not because of the extreme conditions, but because of vandalism. The enduring legacy of a century ago – the plaques defaced, scored through, or shattered into pieces. The 'materiality' of the border attacked by those who still object to '*their* mountains' being split in two.

After a while we set off again, downwards now. We were still following the borderline. It ran south, and we were just a few paces to the west of it, on the Italian side. There are no glaciers left on these south-facing slopes, not even any large slabs or plates of ice. The warming world has taken them, and rock is in charge now. It was a shattered, chaotic landscape: the mountainside entirely covered in fragments, big and small, broken-off and broken-up.

We dropped down into a small gulley, a little U-shaped depression where the slope flattened out and there were high rock walls on either side. This was the place I had asked Robert to take me to.

As the Alpine glaciers have melted and disappeared over the past decades, they have also given up their secrets. It is more than just rocks and the watershed that have re-emerged. Fragments of the past have been released by the ice too. Robert pulled out a photograph, held it over a flat, empty patch of snow right in front of where we were standing. It was a picture of this exact spot thirty years ago. The image was surreal, macabre, even. Two hikers, in garish, Day-Glo clothing, were squatting down in the gulley. At their feet was a body. The body was a dull orange, the same colour as the surrounding rocks. Only its upper half was visible: its back and shoulders, arms and head. It looked somehow shrunken, withered. It was face down, but its arms were stretched ahead of it and off to one side, as if it was trying to haul itself out of the ice, drag itself back into the world.

A man leaves his village to hike up into the mountains. He has done this many times before. He knows this landscape well, intimately even. He has a lean figure, the strong leg muscles of someone who is used to walking and climbing. But his knees and his back give him trouble now; the joints are getting worn and tired. He is in his mid-forties. It is early spring. He climbs up towards the ridgeline, the watershed. And he never returns.

The mountains claim him. He lies in that little U-shaped gulley. Snow falls on his body. Then melts, leaving him submerged in a pool of water. His body spins round. The water freezes, snow falls again. Then more snow. Layer builds upon layer builds upon layer. He is buried deep now, but the air can still permeate down to him. It draws the moisture from his body, dehydrates him – but not completely. As the years pass, the temperature drops, the snow compacts into ice. The ice builds up, ten metres, twenty metres. It covers the ridgeline completely, leaving him buried down in the gulley floor, cradled by rock, embraced by a glacial plug.

Then, in the summer of 1990, a warm wind blows into the mountains from the south. The snow, the ice, begin to melt very rapidly. The snow is not replaced that winter, and the next summer, the wind comes again, this time travelling all the way north from the Sahara, carrying with it the fine-grained sand of the African desert. The sand stains the ice and snow yellow-brown, speeds up the melting process even more.

It is a September afternoon that same year, and two hikers, coming down from the summit of Finail, decide to take a short cut. When they reach the gulley, they find a giant puddle of water. And then they see the body. A head and shoulders propped up against a flat rock.

They press on to a mountain hut at the head of the Tisen Pass, below Mount Similaun, to report what they've found. Because the gulley lies very close to the Italian–Austrian border, the police in both countries are called. The owner of the mountain hut, Alois Pripamer, goes to the site with his son Markus. They find fragments of clothing, the frame of a backpack, the shaft of an ice axe. Alois thinks he knows who the man is – a music professor from Verona, Carlo Capsoni, who disappeared while hiking here in 1941.

The next day, the Austrian police arrive, try to remove the body with a pneumatic drill. The weather conditions deteriorate, and they have to abandon the attempt. It takes another three days to get him out. In that time, Alois has been back again, gathering up a large collection of objects strewn around the man and collecting them in a plastic rubbish bag. An expert in forensic medicine from Innsbruck University, Rainer Henn, is brought in to oversee the final extraction. The man is chipped out of the ice using picks and ski poles. More fragments of his belongings emerge in the process: scraps of leather and string, a clump of hay. There is a knife with a wooden handle and a stone blade. Henn does not think that this body belongs to Capsoni.[12]

The man is zipped into a body bag, taken by helicopter to the Austrian village of Vent, and then driven on to the police station in the town of Sölden, where he is placed in a wooden coffin. From there, he travels by hearse to the Institute for Forensic Medicine in Innsbruck. Five days after he was first discovered, an archaeologist, Konrad Spindler, comes to view the body in the mortuary. He sees the man, but it is the objects laid out alongside him that interest him most. Almost immediately, Spindler tells the room, 'This man is at least 4,000 years old.'[13]

The body is thawing, and as a result, it is starting to decompose. The only option is to try to recreate the conditions up on the mountain – to fashion an artificial glacier. The man is wrapped in a sterile operating gown, packed into layers of crushed ice made from sterilised water, and placed in a cold cell at a temperature of -6°C. It is as near to 100 per cent humidity as they can get.

Tissue samples are taken from his body for carbon dating. The results show that he is, in fact, 5,300 years old. The glacial ice has preserved him for all this time, turned him into a 'wet mummy' – a form of freeze-drying that still retains a degree of moisture. All his organs remain intact, but the body has withered, shrivelled, reduced in weight from fifty to thirteen kilogrammes.[14]

As the weeks pass after the discovery, a new question emerges. Where exactly was he found? Everyone knows the location of the gulley, of course. But no one is quite sure on which side of the border it falls. The IGM are called in, along with their Austrian counterparts, to resurvey the stretch of the borderline that runs south from the Hauslabjoch ridge towards the gulley. When it was first drawn in the 1920s, the slope was completely different, a glacial expanse that made the watershed almost impossible to determine. The gulley itself was concealed beneath some twenty metres of ice.

The surveyors navigate down through this new landscape with their measuring instruments, tracking the course of the watershed among the rocks and boulders. The gulley, they discover, is ninety metres to the west of the line. On the Italian side.[15]

The man will have to move again. He is now deemed to be the property of South Tyrol. He is, at least, allowed a few years' rest. A new facility is built for him in the city of Bolzano, with a custom-designed cold chamber. On 16 January 1998, his new home is ready. He leaves Innsbruck in a refrigerated van and passes over the border by the Brenner Pass – escorted along a closed motorway by the Italian secret service, trailed by helicopters and a convoy of television news vans.

I paced around the gulley for a while, tried to imagine what happened here. A man's body, lying at 3,000 metres, just at the exact period, around 3,300 BC, that global temperatures started to cool. A peculiar and very particular combination of circumstances allowed the ice to take him and keep him, hold him for millennia, and then let him go, to return as a figure out of time. It seemed to me, at once, so unlikely, and so easy. You could just sit down, rest your back against one of those gulley walls, and do the same. Except that won't work now. The ice isn't there to take you. And the rock just doesn't care.

It was time to move on. Robert led off to the east, where the borderline became a defined, marked path. We were on the high, narrow ridge that overlooks the Tisen Pass, the main hiking route south into Italy. It took us over shattered, uneven terrain, the way ahead often disintegrating into heaped masses of precariously stacked slabs. At last, the ridge dipped down steeply to meet a flat saddle of land. There, with the dark bulk of Similaun rising up behind, was the mountain hut.

We went inside for soup and a beer, then came back out onto the terrace to sit in the warm sunshine. Robert pointed down at the rocks below us. A few metres from the hut was a tripod holding up a bright red cannister. It was one of Marco's sensors, one of the twenty-six built for his second experiment, left there by the team as a sort of monument.

The Grafferner was only another couple of kilometres away, over Similaun's peak, on the mountain's southeastern flank. Facing us, on its northwestern slope, was the Niederjochferner glacier. Thirty years ago, Robert told me, the Niederjochferner reached all the way up to the door of the mountain hut. Now, from where we were sitting, you couldn't even see its edge any more. It had receded hundreds of metres into the distance, over on the other side of a rocky rise.

After a short rest, we began the descent into Italy. The Tisen Pass was a red, raw landscape, a barren boulder field, cut through by a fast-flowing, meltwater stream. Heat throbbed off the stones. High-pitched marmot calls pierced the air. Far below was my guest-house, on the slopes overlooking Lake Vernago. From up in the pass, the surface of the lake was a striking, almost unreal shade of teal. The sound of the stream filled the valley, growing from a rumble to a full-throated roar. It was the sound of the departing ice.

The next morning, I drove from Lake Vernago, down through the mountains, to Bolzano. The city lies on the flat floor of a high valley, looking east to the Dolomites and west to the Ötztal Alps. Three rivers meet here: the Talfer, the Eisack and the eastern branch of the Adige. It's a point of confluence for the southern watershed, and as I walked through the city centre to the South Tyrol Museum of

Archaeology, the rivers were in torrent – green-blue, swollen, strong currents piling great tree logs and branches in thick heaps up against the grassy riverbanks.

I was going to see the man from the gulley. *Homo tirolensis*. The 'glacier corpse' (his name on the official government form recording his discovery). Today, he has a new name: Ötzi. A compression of 'Ötztal' and 'yeti', it was first coined by a journalist from Vienna, Karl Wendl, just a week after the body emerged from the ice. The media tried out more than 500 monikers, but this was the one that stuck: Ötzi, the iceman.

The museum takes up three floors of an elegant Art Nouveau building, originally constructed on the eve of the First World War as a branch of the Austro-Hungarian Bank. Come the end of the war, however, and it was occupied by the Banca d'Italia. This is Ötzi's home.

I found him on the first floor, in a darkened alcove set behind a long, curved information panel. Only one person can view him at a time. He lies, face up, on a slab of opaque glass, in a small room with white-tiled walls, which looks not unlike the interior of a – rectangular – igloo. This room is surrounded by pipes filled with a mixture of water and antifreeze, which keep the interior temperature at an unwavering -6°C. The body waits in darkness until you stand on a steel plate, look through a small, forty-centimetre-square window framed with burnished metal, and press a button. Then, all of a sudden, he appears, bathed in a glacial blue light.

It was a moment at once theatrical and shocking. His right arm was stretched out towards the viewing window, his hand so near I felt I could reach out and clasp it. I could see the tiniest details on the skin, the lines of wrinkles on the knuckles, the fingerprints. The fingers were clenched, as if they were grasping something. But the hand was empty.

His left arm was slung wildly across his body, his shrivelled, stick-like bicep pushed up underneath his chin. His feet were crossed on top of each other. He was so small and frail now. Like a child's body. Shrunken by the ice. He was covered by a thin, frozen film, the result of a sprinkler system that douses him regularly with sterilised water, to prevent his body from losing its humidity. The water had formed tiny icicle droplets at his extremities – his fingertips, his elbows. Beneath this icy carapace, the skin was a burnt brown-orange. It was uncannily like the crisped exterior of an overcooked roast chicken.

I looked at his face. His lips were pared back, his nose half collapsed, his teeth in a rictus. He still has his eyes. They were brown once. They are dried out now, but remain in their sockets, staring up into nothingness. There was even a single eyelash on his right eye. He sees nothing, but he is under constant watch. Air pressure, temperature and humidity in his 'cold cell' are monitored at all times. He is laid out on precision scales, and any variation in his weight sets off an automatic alarm.

Spread out around the rest of the museum floor were his belongings: displayed in pillar-like glass cabinets filled with air enriched with 99 per cent nitrogen, to kill bacteria or insects. There was his axe with its blade of pure copper, his bearskin cap, his longbow, quiver and fourteen arrows. His hide leggings and his deerskin shoes, the U-shaped hazel wood frame of his backpack. His calf-leather belt with a pouch holding a scraper, a drill, a flint and a tinder fungus for lighting fires. The trappings of a life metaphorically and literally frozen in a moment.

It struck me that, taken together, this all amounts to a sort of secular, rigorously scientific, ritual burial. A man laid out in an elaborate, custom-made building, with all his precious things, the objects that defined his life, arranged around him. This is what normally typifies the discovery of well-preserved ancient human remains – embalmed mummies, turf bog burials. Evidence of some kind of ceremony to prepare a body and a spirit for the afterlife. The irony, however, is that what makes Ötzi unique is that his original 'burial' was natural, an accident of location, weather and climate change. His death was sudden, unforeseen. Or, at least, it was unforeseen by *him*. Because research has now revealed exactly how he came to be lying face down against the rocks of the gulley wall.

He was murdered.

For the first decade after his discovery, it was thought that he had died when overcome by a snowstorm, or as the result of a climbing accident. But, in 2001, an X-ray of his body discovered a flint arrowhead lodged just below his left shoulder, only a few millimetres from his lung. He had been shot in the back, perhaps from as far as a hundred metres away: otherwise, the arrow would have passed all the way through his body. Instead, it severed his subclavian artery and stuck fast. He would have bled to death in minutes.

A forensic profiler, Detective Inspector Alexander Horn of the Munich Police, was approached by the museum to help piece together Ötzi's last moments. Using a newly commissioned autopsy report, and even examining the still-preserved contents of his stomach and digestive tract, Horn built up a picture of the circumstances surrounding the killing. Ötzi had made camp, cooked and eaten a meal of ibex meat, einkorn wheat – possibly as a form of bread – and some fatty cheese or bacon. Half an hour later, as he rested by the fireside, the arrow hit him from behind. CT scans revealed skull fractures and significant trauma to the back of his head – either from a fall after he was shot, or a blow from his killer to finish him off.

For Horn, it was certain that robbery was not the motive. Ötzi's belongings were seemingly untouched, including the valuable copper axe. Rather, this was a deliberate, premeditated homicide. 'The aim of the offender was to kill him, and he decides to take a long-distance shot,' Horn said in an interview with *The New York Times*. 'Most homicides are personal and follow violence and an escalation of violence. *I want to follow him, find him and kill him.* All the emotions we have in homicide, these things have not died out in all these years.'[16]

And so Ötzi collapsed face down in the snow. His right hand, the one that stretched towards his cold cell's viewing window, *had* been holding something after all. It was grasping his stone knife in a last, vain attempt at self-defence. He would hold it for another 5,000 years, until it was prised from his fingers in 1991, when his body was cut from the ice. The knife now has its own separate display case. Yet the straining muscles remain in that hand. It is a reminder that, for Ötzi, there is no rest. The memory of sudden violence is preserved in the very fabric of his body.

Was it a coincidence, I wondered, that he died just metres away from a borderline? What was he doing up there in the mountains? Where was he going? And was it possible that he had crossed some ancient territorial margin? Could that have been the transgression that killed him?

I sought out one of the museum's archaeologists, Andreas Putzer. Andreas is a calm, measured presence. He talked deliberately and precisely, stopping every so often to adjust his glasses and run his hand through his long, silver-brown hair.

'Ötzi opened the ice to us,' he said, 'because the general opinion was that humans didn't use this environment in this period. But Ötzi told us a completely different story.'

A whole new field of research emerged as a result of Ötzi's discovery, a complete reassessment of life, trade, culture and movement around and across the prehistoric Alpine landscapes.

'We do have division of territory in this period,' Andreas continued. 'You have for example, in Ötzi's time, in the Copper Age, these cult places marked with stone menhirs, carved stones. These stones are always close to a settlement, and the settlements have a distance between them of two or three kilometres. We think that these cult places mark the territory of a clan.'

All the same, Andreas said, the picture is incredibly faint and fragmented. 'Where the borders were in prehistory is very hard to define – we need more sites.'

In recent years, other cult sites, dating from the Bronze Age – 2,000 years after Ötzi's time – have emerged. 'In the Tisen valley,' Andreas told me, 'where the iceman was found, there is a cult site at the beginning of the valley. In the next valley we have another. And in the next. So I think these places are markers for territory. If you came from the north, you'd see these places and they show you, *that is my territory, or the territory of my community*.'

Yet Andreas did not believe that the mountains were ever divided, not like they are now. 'We don't find these cult sites, these stone markers, high on the mountain. So we think that the closest mountain area is probably the territory of the village. And the thing is, now, we know that the cultural groups in the north and the south of the Alps were connected. The Copper Age is the first example of globalisation that we have – groups are in contact. We find stone axes, made in northwestern Italy, turning up in Austria, Germany and France. The people were in contact, and there was a lot of trade that we are now discovering through analysis of the raw materials in their tools and objects. The iceman probably got his copper axe *because* this area was a trade route across the Alps.'

Ötzi's life, Andreas said, was all about movement. 'We know that he grew up in a different area. We know that he used materials that came from far away. So he represents the connection with other cultures, but also the intention to move and to see other places.'

It is then another irony that a borderline has had such an impact on his modern afterlife. *Which side of the line is he on? Which nation 'owns' him? Where does he belong?*

Andreas nodded vigorously. 'From a historical point of view this Alpine crest was not a border. The people on both sides of the valley had properties on both sides. What we have today is a virtual border made by politicians after the First World War. From an economical point of view, a cultural point of view, it was never a border between Austria and Italy. From the Mesolithic period to the Iron Age, we have finds that show that the passes were used to *cross* the Alps. The Alpine crest, the watershed, this so-called natural border was never a border for humans.'

Andreas paused for a moment, rubbed at his temples. He told me he was born and brought up here, in Bolzano. That he didn't see himself as Italian, or Austrian, but as Tyrolean. Identity in this region, he said, has always been about connection, has always been shaped by outside influences.

'But now we have this political border that is mostly in our heads. Except increasingly it is not. For people here, in Ötztal, in South Tyrol, *there is now a border*. Because the interaction between the people across the mountains in the last hundred years is decreasing with this border.'

The landscape changes. The line changes the landscape – or at least how it is perceived. Gravity as a force for nationalism. The line has weight.

I went back to the cold cell for one last look through the window at Ötzi. It is a peculiar fate for a human. Every year, 300,000 people come to gawp at him. Many, like me, may never have seen a dead body before. And here's one, separated from you by just a few inches of glass and wall. A murder victim warped by ice and lit by spotlights. It is entirely conceivable that he can be preserved for ever, his decomposition arrested, just as it is now. His flesh frozen in limbo.

The level of care undertaken by the museum is remarkable. Every month, the same square centimetre of his skin is photographed. Images are compared with previous photographs using special software to check for even the most minute changes in luminosity, colour and deformation.

These images, it occurred to me, are just like the surveyors' aerial photographs of the mountains. Ötzi's body becomes the landscape of the Alps in microcosm. Tiny glaciers fill the ridges, valleys, depressions and expanses of his flesh and bones. They are monitored and maintained in prefect equilibrium, constantly replenished and reformed, never allowed to melt or diminish. Ötzi can survive indefinitely, in an artificial, climate-controlled box. Whereas for the mountain glaciers, those immense ice blocks that once preserved *him*, there is no climate control. The temperature rises, and they just continue to disappear, one after another.

*

A forest of pine and fir. Cattle plodded idly among the trees, the bells around their necks ringing a discordant chorus. One stood obdurate and unmoving on the track ahead. I picked my way around her while she stared at me dismissively. Soon the trees gave way to high pasture, open slopes of wild grass and bare rock.

I was hiking from Vernago to the summit of Schröfwand – the 'Rugged Wall'. It was over 1,000 metres above the lake shore, and the path was steep, direct and punishing. From the top I hoped to have a clear view of the south face of the Grafferner: the 'ablation zone' where the glacier melts away into the valley below. That was if I could see anything at all. Another few hundred metres up, the path disappeared into a dark grey canopy of cloud.

Sheep and goats were grazing on these steep upper slopes. More bells, the tinkling now incessant, almost eerie as the view closed in around me. These animals have moved across the Alps for millennia – maybe, some argue, going as far back as Ötzi's time. Farmers on the Italian side herding their flocks north every summer over the watershed to the high pastures of the Ötz valley in Austria. The sound of bells drifting back and forth across the borderline.

I was hot with the effort of the climb now, muscles straining. But inside the cloud, the temperature had plummeted. Sweat cooled instantly on my temples and chilled the skin. I couldn't see the summit, so focused on the steps in front of me, breathing hard. The grass had gone. It was just rock now. The path zigzagged sharply up through boulders and sheer cliffs, and I had no idea how far there was to go. And then the ridgeline leered at me suddenly, out of the gloom, a long black overhang of knife-like serrations.

Up on top of the ridge was a scene of obliteration. Broken rocks everywhere and the route onwards marked with wooden posts jammed awkwardly into crevices. It was like walking on a great sea of smashed crockery. The lower peak of Schröfwand is a protruding ledge, marked with a giant iron cross. At its base was a makeshift shelter, built of stacked stones and a wooden crossbeam. I was thick in the cloud now and could see nothing apart from my immediate surroundings.

Exhausted and dispirited, I sat down in the lip of the shelter and ate my lunch. The air crackled with tiny flakes of snow, brief and almost imperceptible, like speckles on an old black-and-white film. I was 2,800 metres up, inside a grey cocoon. I waited ten minutes, then twenty, but the cloud did not budge. I felt the cold seeping in, my legs stiffening. With nothing else to do, I set off again, scrambling up the last little stretch to Schröfwand's true pinnacle. And then it happened.

The clouds were thinning, parting. All of a sudden I could see back down into the valley towards Lake Vernago. To the north, threads of grey were breaking off from the mass. The black shadow of Similaun appeared, a figure behind the curtain, waiting its cue. I was moving quickly now, rocks tumbling and skittering in my wake, worried that the view would vanish as quickly as it had appeared. But the clouds continued to lift, sunlight flashed on white, and there it was: the face of the Grafferner. It was not much more than a kilometre away from where I was standing. But between us the earth plunged almost straight down into the valley of the Grava River.

I stood on the very edge of the precipice. Below me was a grey sea. Across the valley, the Grafferner was reduced by distance and perspective to almost laughable simplicity. It was an upside-down white triangle: point angled down the mountainside; base a perfect straight line running between two peaks, Similaun on one side, and Kleine Similaun on the other. From here, all the complexity of the watershed collapsed. Why not just call it a line? Why does it matter?

'There were many times where I was thinking this is completely pointless,' Marco had said to me. 'Why am I obsessing around this, this glacier, this tiny little stretch of border? But then I'd think, no, being precise and forensic really pays off in terms of how much you can understand from certain processes. Processes that might seem very peripheral and marginal.'

At the heart of Marco's project, he had said, was the desire to challenge the western political mindset. To unpick a belief system shaped by the ideal of a stable planet, where any change is slow, rational and predictable. But when notions of territory and national identity are woven into seemingly 'natural' boundaries, what happens when those boundaries are altered rapidly and uncontrollably?

'We were looking at the problem in almost a laboratory situation,' Marco had said. 'The glacier is completely absent of any other layers of politics. But it shows how, even when the border is completely identified with a natural feature, it is still a political construction. So the project tried to somehow dismantle this idea of a natural border, completely destroy it, make it look impossible. *Even here*, it says, *it is not possible to draw a border*.'

Marco believes we are lacking in arguments and ideas that let us think about territory in different ways. 'Because the framework that we grew up with, and that we teach, implies borders as the primary form of organisation of territory. And this is insane. We lack images of how things could be different. Of how we can imagine the movement of people in a different way. The purpose of our project was to create an alternative image, to give a visual image that is different, an understanding of territory that is different.'

Is our fixation with borders, I had asked him, ultimately down to a lack of imagination? Is territorial organisation a design problem, waiting to be solved?

'I think it is very interesting to consider representation,' he had said. 'The way in which we represent things, and the images that we build of the world – they are the ways in which we then act in the world. In order to change the way in which politics works, first of all we need to create different images. Because borders today do not work. They don't exist in nature. They are an inefficient, counter-intuitive, problematic way of managing lots of different provinces and states. We really have to get rid of them.'

The high clouds were splitting apart to reveal a bright blue inkblot sky. All of the Grafferner and the bare slopes below it were draped in sunshine. White snow against rust-red rock.

When Marco last travelled to the glacier in 2016, he was accompanied by a team of glaciologists. They used ground-penetrating radar to send signals down through the glacier to hit bedrock, building up a picture of a future landscape – the mountainscape as it will be when stripped of the ice. They were surprised by how deep it went. The Grafferner, they thought, has ten, maybe even twenty years left.

Viewed from the summit of Schröfwand, the glacier sits perfectly between the black mountains, its 'V' of snow like grains in an hourglass descending to a narrow neck. Below the neck, of course, the ice has gone, transformed into meltwater. Over the next decade or so, all that ice will run out of the top of the hourglass until there is no more ice left. And then it will not be just this tiny stretch of border that is changed, but borders all across the globe.

Think of the Grafferner as a kind of natural doomsday clock, counting down the inexorable progress of climate change. It will warm and shrink and disappear and many more glaciers will go with it – across the Alps, the Andes, the Himalayas, Greenland, Alaska, Antarctica.[17] As this one border melts, others will be lost beneath the rising seas. Flood plains submerged. River deltas inundated.

All that ice has to go somewhere. Pour enough water down a watershed, and you can redraw the world.

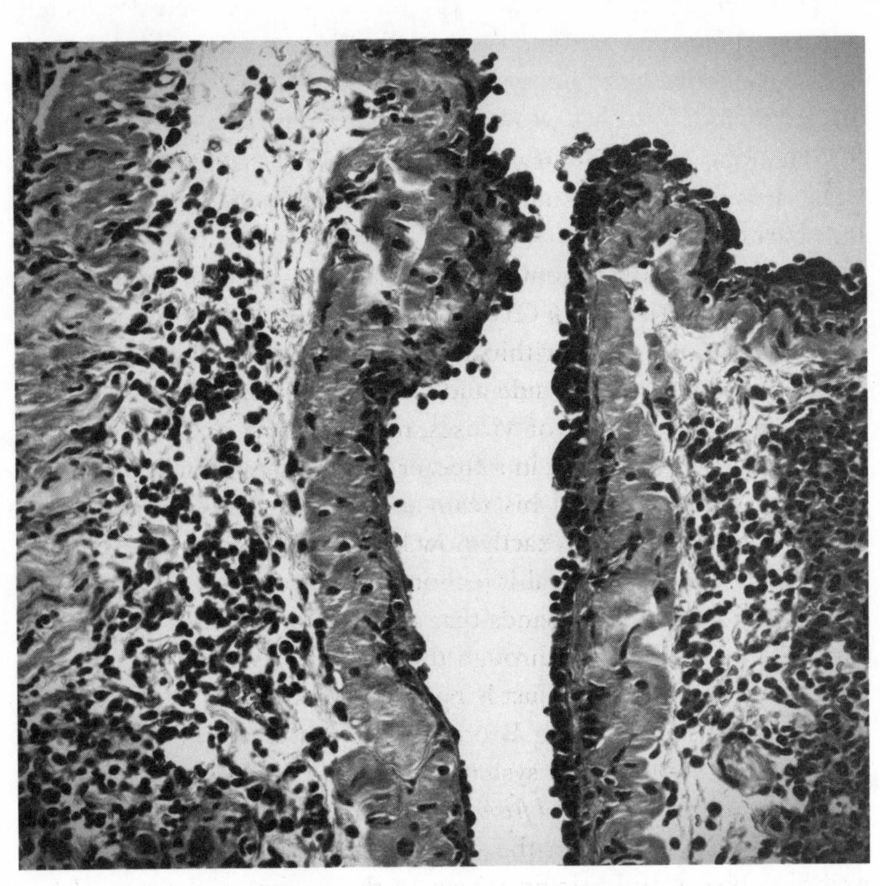

9

'THIS WALL OF FLESH'

'The first point of entry,' Benjamin told me, 'is the ability of the virus to get to its source of energy. That's when it starts: when that barrier is broken.'

Professor Benjamin tenOever is a virologist at the Icahn School of Medicine in New York City. He was talking to me from his laboratory, a series of rooms within Icahn's research buildings, bound by Madison Avenue on one side and Central Park on the other. There, he has created a 'library' of viruses, row after row of them, lined up inside tiny cryotubes kept in a freezer with an operating temperature of -80°C. Benjamin and his team use them to try to understand, down to a cellular level, exactly how host bodies, and more generally 'life' itself, respond to viral infection.

'It's a process that demands that a virus has evolved a way to grab onto a cell and then get through the first wall of defences,' he said. 'Because the cells are not just lying there defenceless. They are being surveyed constantly – Big Brother is definitely a real thing in the human body. Your entire system is continually trying to investigate any given cell: it is *stop and frisk* all the time. And you are also always perusing what is outside the cell – so that each cell is randomly grabbing pieces and bringing them to the surface and saying, *I have this in me, and I have this in me, and I have this in me*. And the immune system and Big Brother are looking at them and saying, *okay, I made that, I made that, I made that.* Until they finally get to a point where they say, *I have never seen that before.*

'And that's what starts it. That's when the call to arms and the call for reinforcements goes out. When the system sees that something *different* is there. That is the smallest scale of border breaking there is.'

It was the beginning of October when the ships arrived. Two or three at first, twelve of them in total, all rounding the hook of land that curls to a sharp point, like a crab's pincer, to form the sheltered harbour of the city of Messina on the island of Sicily. The ships were on their way home, travelling back to Genoa with goods and cargo picked up from ports as far eastwards as Crimea on the Black Sea. They nosed their way in among the many other vessels jostling in the busy harbourside. Within days of their arrival, the Genoese sailors, and anyone who had come into contact with them, began to fall ill.

The first sign was a swelling about the size of a lentil, an angry boil that appeared on the thigh or arm. Soon, the sailors started coughing up blood. They suffered three days of incessant vomiting. Then they died.

'And with them,' reported a local Sicilian, Michael Platiensis, 'died not only anyone who had talked with them, but also anyone who had acquired, or touched, or laid hands on their belongings.'[1]

As soon as the port authorities realised that the common link was the Genoese ships, the remaining sailors and their vessels were expelled from the harbour and sent back out to sea.[2] But the illness did not leave with them. It had taken hold in Messina and was moving at an incredible rate.

'Breath spread the infection among those speaking together,' Platiensis said, 'with one infecting the other, and it seemed as if the victim was struck all at once by the affliction and was, so to speak, shattered by it.'[3] As with the sailors, death 'was sure' within three days. Whole households were taken by it, all the way down to the family pets. 'Sex and age made no difference . . . everyone died alike.'

Some decided to give up Messina entirely. Many headed for the nearby city of Catania. But, as Platiensis recognised, 'the illness, already carried within them, was consuming their bodies'. A large number collapsed on the way, falling down by the roadside, on the seashore, or in the middle of woods or vineyards. Those who did reach Catania found lodgings only in time to 'breathe their last'. The Catanese insisted that their bodies be buried a distance outside the city in 'good deep graves'.[4] When more refugees from Messina approached Catania, they were turned away – and so they wandered, in small, listless groups, in desperate search of aid or shelter.

Just like before, it was already too late for Catania. The illness gripped the city, and only seemed to have increased in severity. The swellings now started off as big as 'hazelnuts', then grew even larger, turning into tumours the size of hen's eggs. Soon, Platiensis said, Catania was all but wiped out. At the same time, because of the travels of the stricken Messinese, the illness had reached every corner of Sicily. By January of the following year – just four months after the Genoese ships had first docked in Messina – it was all over Italy, and was racing, seemingly unstoppably, onwards: leaping the Alps, seeding itself in France, Spain, Hungary and Germany; striking north into Scandinavia; crossing the channel into England; and finally reaching Europe's northwestern extremity in Scotland.[5]

Giovanni Boccaccio witnessed first-hand the arrival of the disease in his home city of Florence. Just like Platiensis, he described the infection first presenting with swellings the size of an egg or an apple that would develop in the groin or armpits. But then the symptoms 'began to change, and many people discovered black or livid blotches on their arms, thighs and every other part of their bodies'. These marks, he continued, were a 'certain sign of impending death'.[6]

Nothing, it seemed, could halt the spread. 'The advice of doctors and the power of medicine appeared useless and unavailing,' Boccaccio wrote. And so, with science confounded and no known remedy available, he watched on as, one by one, the carefully constructed hierarchies and boundaries of society first frayed, then broke apart, and then disappeared entirely.

'All sorts of fears and fantasies,' he said, consumed the thoughts of those who remained free of infection, 'almost all of whom took one utterly cruel precaution, namely to avoid the sick and their belongings, fleeing far from them.' So extreme was this instinct for self-preservation, that he saw brothers abandoning brothers, uncles their nephews, sisters their sisters, and wives their husbands. 'Even worse, and almost unbelievable, is that fathers and mothers refused to tend to their children,' he said, 'treating them as if they belonged to someone else.'[7]

Day and night, thousands were dying in their homes and in the streets. Bodies were left untouched wherever they lay, blackened all over with gangrene from multiple organ failure. Respect for the authority of laws 'both divine and human, had declined just about to the vanishing point,' Boccaccio said. And so, he concluded, 'people felt free to behave however they liked'.

Some lost themselves in frenzied hedonism, resolved that the 'surest medicine for such an evil disease was to enjoy life's pleasures, and go about singing and having fun, satisfying their appetites by any means available, while laughing at everything'. Others 'formed themselves into companies and lived in isolation from everyone else' or 'abandoned their own homes, their relatives, their properties and possessions and headed for the countryside', as if believing that the illness 'would strike down only those found inside the walls of their city'.[8]

Boccaccio turned this into the basis for a story, a fantasy of escape. He wrote of how ten attractive twenty-somethings – seven women and three men – left Florence for an estate in the surrounding countryside. There, they hoped to ride out the storm and entertain each other with stories, 'having as much fun as possible' while the world outside drowned in disease and decay. 'We are the ones who have been abandoned,' cried the leader of the group, Pampinea. And so 'how can it be wrong,' she asked, 'for us or for anyone else to use whatever remedies we can in order to preserve our lives?'[9]

Ten friends told a story each day, for ten days of isolation, and a hundred tales formed the collection that Boccaccio called *The Decameron.* In these stories, they poked fun at the establishment and the elites, picking apart the hypocrisies of the society that had crumbled so quickly and so completely around them. In the process, they began tentatively to imagine something different, at once restoring the rituals of companionship and civility that had typified Florence before the illness struck, and, simultaneously, using their tales to explore new ways of thinking, of being and of behaving. They understood, even if only subconsciously, that if they and their city, and society in general, survived, they would be changed for ever.

This happened in the mid-fourteenth century. The Genoese ships had docked at Messina in October 1347. Over the next four years, between one third and one half of all Europeans – and a total of perhaps 200 million people worldwide – died.[10] In Boccaccio's Florence, nearly two thirds of the population died. Society was devastated on a scale that was unprecedented in human history. But it was not destroyed entirely – and soon it began to evolve and adapt in response to the terrifying threat of disease.

As Boccaccio recognised, along with many others, this 'plague', this 'Black Death' had 'begun some years before in the East, where it deprived countless beings of their lives before it headed to the West'.[11] Which meant that it *moved.* However, it was not borne on some great, cross-continental wind; rather, it was carried – it seemed – by people. It came with the Genoese into Sicily. It travelled with countless other sailors docking in ports all across the Mediterranean. It journeyed among trading caravans, taking the long overland routes of the Silk Road. It moved and it was always going to come. There were just too many links in the chains of trade, travel and commerce between east and west to stop it. In the aftermath of that first, terrible outbreak, the question was how to break those chains.

In 1377, the Adriatic port city of Ragusa – modern-day Dubrovnik – passed a law establishing what they called a *trentino*. Anyone attempting to enter the city from any place known to be stricken by illness or disease had to first remain in isolation for thirty days. At the beginning of the fifteenth century, the Republic of Venice adopted this same idea but extended the isolation period to forty days: *quaranta giorni*. A *trentino* became a *quarantino* – quarantine.[12]

Ships and their sailors had to remain at anchor long enough for symptoms to emerge. Those who had already fallen ill or were strongly suspected of carrying the plague were escorted by guard ships to a specially built hospital – a *lazaretto* – on an island in the Venice lagoon. There, yet more levels of isolation were imposed. Individuals had to occupy separate cells, each of which had its own garden plot and cooking facilities. Social contact in the *lazaretto* was forbidden. If inmates died, they were buried in lime, in graves that were at least twelve feet deep.

To even get this close to the city, however, ships had to pass through multiple rings of surveillance, control and containment. Armed boats patrolled the Adriatic to form an outer perimeter, constantly monitoring the seaways. Observation towers and sentry posts were constructed along almost the entire Italian coastline. They were positioned to be visible from one to another, to allow rapid communication by semaphore in daylight or beacons in darkness. They warned of illegal landings and signalled for assistance from armed infantry or fast-moving cavalry units, who hunted down anyone attempting to enter unchecked.[13]

Inland, lines of temporary, tented guard posts were established along territorial edges whenever the epidemic flared up. In many cases, these sanitary control measures were the first time that the external borders of republics, principalities and city states – until then vague, indistinct or even non-existent – were ever realised in any physical sense in the landscape. Lines on maps, often little observed, suddenly came to life. Borders were emerging, being created, as geographical demarcations between the polluted and the pure. Dirty and clean. Diseased and disease-free. Public health had become an issue of all-pervasive spatial control: all the way from the external rings of the patrol boats down to the quarantined sailors confined to their solitary cells in the *lazarettos*.[14]

As time passed, methods of surveillance grew ever more sophisticated. Cities across Italy established Magistracies which held legislative, judicial and executive powers over all public health issues. These were supplemented by extensive and frequent inter-state communications, as information was gathered and shared about disease anywhere in Europe, North Africa and the Middle East. Letters were sent back and forth every two weeks, sometimes every day if there was a crisis. Spies reported on the health conditions in cities to ensure that states were not concealing plague epidemics out of fear of the economic impact it would have on trade. By the seventeenth century this practice was institutionalised – conventions bound cities together in common public health practices and allowed them to place their own independent representatives within Magistracy offices in all major ports or harbours.[15]

Whenever news arrived of the spread of contagion, bans or suspensions were issued, forbidding people, ships, cargo or correspondence from any infected place from entering another state, apart from via specified quarantine stations. Attempts to ignore or breach these orders were punishable by death. The prevalence of illness in certain areas, however, came to create an assumption that some regions were, by their very nature, *always* insanitary. 'Experience has shown,' explained a booklet produced by the Venetian board of public health, 'that in the Ottoman Dominions, the Plague is never utterly extinct: Hence it is an immutable Law with the Magistrate of the Office of Health, to consider the whole Extent of the Ottoman Dominions and every State dependent on it, as always to be suspected to be in an infected Condition.'[16] For Ottomans, access to the Republic of Venice – and other states across Europe – was only ever possible after quarantine. To put it simply, to enter the West from the East, you had to be 'purified'.

At the beginning of the eighteenth century, Austria even attempted to create a system of biological controls along its entire 1,000-mile frontier with the Ottoman Empire. Detailed maps were drawn up to illustrate the steps to be taken in the event of an outbreak of contagion. Black dashes and dots ran across the landscape, bisecting everything from mountain passes to major roads, denoting where to set up 'plague cordons'.[17] Dark triangles represented locations for establishing quarantine stations and *lazarettos*. Also running through the maps, winding across rivers, roads and mountain ranges, was a thick yellow line. This was the line of infection.[18] Anyone north of it was to be considered healthy and in need of either protection or evacuation. Anyone south of it was automatically presumed to be a carrier, a threat, a pollutant.[19]

Despite the sophistication of these measures, serious incidences of the plague still continued in Europe and around the world for some five centuries, because, ultimately, no one understood what it was. The discovery of the root cause only came at the very end of the nineteenth century, through the work of the Swiss-French doctor Alexandre Yersin, who was treating a virulent outbreak of a fatal disease in the city of Hong Kong.

Examining the lymphatic tissue of a recently diseased patient under a microscope, Yersin identified the presence of a bacterium which he traced back to oriental rat fleas. This bacterium multiplied in the stomach of the flea and caused a blockage in its digestive tract, starving it and forcing it into a feeding frenzy. In biting anything it could land on – whether rats, other animals or people – it would regurgitate the bacterium into its victim. In humans, *Yersinia pestis* (as the bacterium became known, taking its name from Alexandre) would travel to the lymph nodes in the groin or armpits, depending on which was closest to the bite, where it was able to fight off the immune system while rapidly proliferating.[20] This internal struggle caused angry, egg-shaped swellings – the same ones that were so often mentioned by medieval writers. In the process, bacteria could also reach the lungs, turning the disease pneumonic, allowing transmission from person to person in tiny saliva droplets expelled by coughing. *Breath spread the infection* – just as Michael Platiensis had described in Sicily.

What Yersin had come to Hong Kong to treat *was* the plague. It had waned and all but disappeared by the mid-eighteenth century – only to return in China and India a hundred years later. Clustered inside its insect hosts, it had lived on, breaking out into humans whenever the opportunity arose, just as it did in Hong Kong. And it still remains today. Each year, over 2,000 cases are reported worldwide – most recently in Madagascar and Mongolia, but even including some small but regular outbreaks in the southwestern United States, in New Mexico and Arizona.[21]

Here, then, is another landscape to consider. A landscape that Yersin ventured into in order to make his discovery: hidden from the naked eye, tiny, microscopic. A landscape of cells and proteins and molecules. A landscape that has developed its own, incredibly sophisticated systems of surveillance and control. Not over centuries, but over billions of years. Because this is a landscape that is under constant attack and always has been. A landscape that never stops watching its perimeter for incursions or unauthorised entry – that is on the lookout, day and night, for pathogens attempting to overwhelm or evade its border defences. Pathogens like bacteria, prions, protozoa – and viruses.

'We have never been in a world without viruses,' Benjamin said. 'Ever.'

Benjamin had thick, short black hair and wore large-framed reading glasses. He was in his early forties, with a wide smile and lively eyes that betrayed a boyish enthusiasm.

He told me that he had always been fascinated by the origins of life. Growing up in Canada, in rural Ontario, his childhood was dominated by 'prayers and bibles and churches'. Evolution wasn't discussed, he said. Rather, it was assumed, as a matter of faith, that life had emerged as a 'six-day-creation kind of thing'. All the same,

Benjamin's father was a large-animal veterinarian. He used to ride along with him as he made house calls, which exposed him to medicine and the sciences from a very young age.

When he graduated from high school he entered into a pre-med programme at McGill University in Montreal, with the intention of training to become a physician. That was, however, until he enrolled in a microbiology course. Every day, his teacher would cover a different virus: its origins, characteristics and strategies for survival and self-replication.

'He just made it all come very alive,' Benjamin told me, 'to the point where I took on his passion, I suppose. I don't think I ever looked back. I was so hooked.'

The study of viruses allowed him to gaze into the past – several billion years into the past. It offered up tantalising theories as to what life was and where it came from, allowed him to unpick the biblical creation stories that had so dominated his childhood.

'Because of that,' he said, 'I feel like I do have a slightly different motivation and interest in this space. My fascination in evolution digs a little deeper than most people.'

As he explained it to me, 'our best guess, which is a pretty good one at this point, is that life started with RNA'.

Ribonucleic acid: single-stranded molecules made up of tiny building blocks called nucleotides. Where DNA has two strands and a regular structure of millions of nucleotides, RNA is irregular, capable of assuming near-infinite shapes, and is much smaller, comprising just thousands or even hundreds of nucleotides. As Benjamin put it to me, if you think of a cell as being like a computer, 'DNA is the hard drive, RNA is the software, and the actual application is the protein.'

In essence, DNA determines our operating capacity, encompassing all the 'software' – the RNA – that our cells are capable of running. RNA's job is to marshal and instruct the proteins to carry out specific tasks.

'If you take a snapshot of all the software that is running in a cell at any given time,' he said, 'that's the RNA. The DNA is not changing. You can look at the hardware of the computer, but that doesn't tell you anything about how the programme works.'

One of the interesting things about RNA, Benjamin continued, 'is that it can also function to some extent both as DNA *and* protein. Because it is between them, in the middle, it can do a bit of both. And because it can do a little bit of both, it is by far the prominent theory as to how you could ever start life.'

There are, he said, many fundamental problems around the question of how life could have begun. 'But if you can take the leap of faith that, given a billion years, a random collection of nucleic acids can make a piece of RNA, then you eventually get a piece of RNA that has the ability to copy itself. *And that would be the beginning of life.*'

Today, it is possible to model a version of this exact process in a laboratory.

'We can engineer a piece of RNA as small as 150 nucleotides,' he said. 'A tiny piece of RNA that can just replicate itself over and over and over again. So it doesn't seem so far-fetched that, given a billion years, evolution could actually achieve something like that.'

Once RNA can self-replicate, it can also make mistakes. In reproducing, variations appear. It can start to diverge in infinite directions and begin elaborating on itself – taking the first of the incalculably large number of steps that are required to get from a piece of RNA to a single cell.

'That is the cusp, right there,' he said, 'where the definition of life goes into the grey. Because an RNA that can self-replicate is also a virus. So one could, and many people have – including myself – argued that actually the very first "life-form" that existed on earth was, by definition, a virus. It was an RNA that could self-replicate. *Because that's what a virus is.*'

Benjamin continued to outline to me the layers of molecular complexity that built up as the very first 'proto-cell' manufactured itself into existence. That piece of self-replicating RNA would have been contained by a cellular 'body' that held and protected it within a defined, restricted space. Yet even from that earliest moment, that original flicker of existence, the surrounding environment would have been teeming with threats.

'That first life-form,' he said, that first *proto-cell*, 'would have had viruses impacting it. Just like we do today. Once life has started, it instantly has this problem of viruses.'

In effect, at the very moment that cellular life began, it was in a desperate battle for survival. The whole purpose of a virus is to prey on cells. Should it prove *too* strong, penetrating and overwhelming the cell, then life would be snuffed out before it had even got going. This, Benjamin suggested, had likely happened lots of times: the origins of life on earth as a series of false starts. There and gone again, over and over. At some point, however, a cell began to learn how to defend itself.

'Once the cell has a strategy to deal with this problem of viruses that is at least somewhat successful,' he said, 'that is going to propel evolution to move forward in both directions. The virus is trying constantly to knock down the host for resources, and the host is trying constantly to get rid of the virus so that it can propagate its own life. And because of this battle, viruses can never be *too* virulent, otherwise you get those dead ends again.

'There is this very intricate dance, if you will, through evolutionary time, where viruses – they're not thinking, they're not conscious – but they are always trying to find different ways and test different strategies to get back into those energy resources. And as those strategies evolve, so too does the host have to evolve ways to block access to those same resources.'

The result is a billions-of-years-long struggle, what Benjamin has previously called a 'perpetual arms race'.[22]

'If I'm a host and I create a new weapon to fight a virus, the virus will create a new weapon to deal with my weapon. And then I have to think of something new. As a result everything is always connected to the thing before it.'

Follow that process for long enough and you get to us, to humans. Multicellular organisms of incredible complexity, yet still engaged, always and all the time, in this never-ending, host–virus conflict. If a virus attempts to cross the cellular threshold into you or me – to breach our own, personal, biological borders – a number of things happen at once.

'The cell that first detects the virus,' Benjamin said, 'it's very altruistic. It says, *I'm going to go down for this, but in my going down I'm going to do two things: I'm going to send out a call for arms, and I'm going to send out a call for reinforcements.* The call for arms is to tell all the cells around it that *we have a problem, I'm detecting a virus, I think I'm going to die, but the rest of you – make sure you are going to be okay.*'

This 'call to arms' takes the form of protein molecules – interferons – being released into the extra-cellular space and signalling to all the other proteins in the vicinity to, as Benjamin put it, 'fortify everything they can'. Man the barricades, batten down the hatches, raise the drawbridge – whichever metaphor you like. This process is all about buying time, to keep the virus at bay until the cavalry arrives. Because a second messenger from the cell, a different type of protein called a cytokine, is on its way to bring back the 'reinforcements'.

'And so in come the heavy hitters of the immune system. A whole other army of specialised cells. They are designed to grab that virus, or grab cells that were killed by the virus, find pieces of it – not necessarily RNA pieces, but protein pieces of it – and use them to begin making antibodies.'

In direct response to the presence of a virus in our system, our bodies are able to begin manufacturing specific adaptive defences. We engage in that same 'dance' once again, working, at a cellular level, to build our walls, fabricate our borders, in an attempt to keep yet another pathogen at bay.

'And that is why we are here today and why vertebrates do so well,' Benjamin said, 'because we have that ability.'

I kept thinking back to that idea of a virus as the earliest form of life. It was a theory that seemed to me at once elegant, and somehow terrifying. It forces you to confront the truth – or at least *a* truth – of where and what we all come from. Benjamin had talked of how that first cell, which had started off as a piece of self-replicating RNA, later evolved to become 'wired' in DNA. At that point, he said, it had transformed into a more sophisticated system, because it was suddenly capable of generating its own energy.

'And many people define life as something that can generate its own energy source. Generate its own energy source *and evolve*. And so viruses can evolve but they *do not generate their own energy source*. And that's kind of like the line of contention right there.'

Viruses are 'obligate parasites'. They are 'alive' when they can tap into an energy source to make more of themselves, but as soon as they leave that source, that cell, they become inert until they can find another. It is this period of 'inertion', however, that challenges at an existential level what life actually is.

Take, for instance, the story of a tiny coastal village in northwestern Alaska called Brevig Mission. In November 1918, the people there began succumbing to a deadly illness. In just five days, seventy-two of the village's eighty adult inhabitants died. The cause was a virus: A(H1N1), the 'Spanish Flu'. Emerging at the very end of the First World War, this extraordinary outbreak of influenza went on to kill an estimated 50 million people across the globe. It was a testament both to its virulence and to its infectious properties that even some of the most remote communities on earth – like Brevig Mission – could not escape the spread.

The villagers were buried in a grave on a hillside, marked with so many white crosses that it looked, from a distance, like a line of haphazard fenceposts. Because of the Alaskan climate, the bodies were held frozen below the ground by the permafrost. In 1997, a seventy-two-year-old Swedish microbiologist called Johan Hultin travelled to Brevig Mission to excavate the grave site.[23]

He had already tried this once before, four decades earlier, in 1954: taking lung tissues from four bodies, transporting them back to his laboratory in the University of Iowa, and injecting them into chicken eggs in an attempt to get the virus to grow. But nothing had happened. It was only a chance reading of a journal article by a microbiologist working at America's Centre for Disease Control and Prevention, Jeffery Taubenberger, who was attempting to sequence the genome of the 1918 virus, that inspired Hultin to make a second attempt.

Working in collaboration with Taubenberger and his laboratory, Hultin once again made the long journey to Brevig Mission and dug down into the permafrost. Seven feet below the ground, he uncovered the body of an Inuit woman – he nicknamed her 'Lucy' – who had been in her mid-twenties when she died in 1918. Removing the lungs from her frozen body, he placed them in a special preserving fluid and shipped them to Taubenberger. Ten days later, it was confirmed that the tissue contained the genetic material of the virus.[24]

Over the next eight years, work continued to first understand the origins and evolution of the virus, and then, finally, to 'reconstruct' it. In 2005, in the Centre for Disease Control headquarters in Atlanta, a microbiologist called Terrence Tumpey inserted the virus – in the form of DNA molecules called plasmids – into human kidney cells. For weeks, just as Hultin had experienced, nothing happened. Then, at the end of July, Tumpey looked at his cell culture once again. It had suddenly exploded with dots. The virus was self-replicating.[25] After more than a century of lying in the cell tissue of a body buried deep in the earth on the very fringes of Alaska, it had found its way back to an energy source. It had, to all intents and purposes, come back to life.

This was, as Benjamin had said, 'the line of contention, right there'. As some microbiologists have put it, viruses exist 'at the edge of life'.[26] They haunt that ultimate borderline, stalk its margins, cross back and forth over the course of centuries, millennia even. And, in the process, they blur and break the very concept – which is at once so binary and so fundamental to our own human existence – of what it means to live and die.

The steamships dropped anchor a short distance from a dry, barren shoreline: the sand and mountains near the southern tip of Egypt's Sinai Peninsula, where the Red Sea meets the Gulf of Suez. On board were hundreds of Muslim passengers returning to Europe from their annual pilgrimage to Mecca. Also on board – or at least suspected of being on board, until circumstances proved otherwise – was a tiny, microscopic passenger known as *Vibrio cholerae*, a comma-shaped bacterium that causes a disease so virulent that it has the potential to kill within hours. Cholera.

Rowboats came and ferried them to a 'deserted beach'.[27] Waiting there were long rows of military field tents, split into four separate groups to keep the passengers of the different ships apart. Hundreds of soldiers guarded the site – which was, in any case, bordered by a vast, empty plain. This was the El Tor quarantine station, one of five set up along the Red Sea coast in the later part of the nineteenth century to run parallel to the shipping lane that led to the Suez Canal, the Mediterranean and Europe.

All pilgrim passengers following this route had to prove their health before they could move onwards. If there were no reported cholera cases onboard their ship when they arrived at El Tor, and none emerged after forty-eight hours spent in the camp, they could continue.[28] If they reached the quarantine station with any declared infection, however, that period was extended to a minimum of fifteen days: renewed in full at each instance of a new case. Some found themselves confined for months at a time, exposed to the extreme heat and cold of the desolate landscape. That was, of course, if cholera did not end their journey permanently.

Cholera had been confined to just one small part of the world for almost all of human history – the Ganges river delta in northern India. Then, in 1817, it broke free. British influence in the subcontinent had opened up travel and trade to previously isolated regions. The bacterium made the jump from infected people to water sources and back again, in a chain that came to link up all of India. By 1818, *The Times* reported that cholera 'still raged' through the state of Calcutta 'with great fury'. The cause was unknown, but the effects were shocking: 'its attacks are sudden, and very speedily fatal,' the report continued. 'It is not an uncommon circumstance for a person to die within six hours after his first seizure.'[29]

In this initial surge, the disease travelled as far east as China, Indonesia and the Philippines, and as far west as the Caspian Sea, taking it to the very cusp of Europe. After a few years it receded, seemed to disappear from everywhere apart from its point of origin. Then came a second outbreak in 1829. This time, it pushed much further around the world, working its way overland through Russia into northern Europe and by boat to Egypt and the Middle East. Soon it was in Germany, France and Britain, then leaping across the Atlantic to Canada, America and even Mexico.[30]

In particular, cholera targeted the poor – ripping through society's most disadvantaged communities while sparing the wealthy and the elite. Riots broke out everywhere from St Petersburg and Paris, to London, Glasgow and New York. Wild rumours circulated: cholera conspiracies claiming that the illness was really a means of mass population control. Hospitals, doctors, nurses and health officials were all targeted for violent attacks.[31]

The disease was settling into a pattern, breaking in waves across the globe, seemingly reaching further each time, before subsiding, over the course of several years, back to its source. Still the exact cause remained unclear. Links were beginning to be made to the bacterium's spread in water supplies, although many experts still proposed that infection could occur through 'miasma': by breathing the contaminated air of carriers.

One area of specific concern, however, was the journey to Mecca. In 1865, some 15,000 pilgrims died from a cholera outbreak. Many also brought the illness with them on their return journeys: 60,000 were killed in the port of Alexandria as a result, and the chain of infection soon jumped over the Mediterranean to ravage Marseille. Before the year was out, cholera was back in New York City.[32]

Dr Achille Proust, a professor of hygiene at the University of Paris – and father of novelist Marcel Proust – drew a direct line of causation all the way to Mecca. Europe, he wrote, could not 'remain like this, every year, at the mercy of the pilgrimage'.[33] Worshippers were travelling from further afield and in greater numbers than ever before.

Steamships and railways had effectively compressed the world, made long-haul travel an option for almost anyone, regardless of their social status: even for those described as that 'dangerous class' of 'pauper pilgrims'.[34] And, of course, globalised travel didn't just benefit *people*. For a pathogen bent on self-replication what could be better than the chance to reach out to more host bodies than ever before? Cholera had become the first pandemic of the industrial age.[35]

For the authorities of the time, these lines of transport and exchange were seen as the key vectors. Following the same measures devised to combat the plague in medieval times, they saw fighting cholera primarily as a technique of organising space. Their strategy was all about interrupting those conduits of disease, corralling and isolating the infected, setting up networks of surveillance, and 'identifying the places,' as Proust put it, 'which must be strengthened against the invasion of the epidemic, and which may be considered veritable strategic positions'.[36]

Like, for instance, the quarantine station of El Tor on the Red Sea coast. Although set up under the auspices of the Ottoman Empire and administered by Egypt, it was a spatial intervention staged as a result of direct political pressure coming from Europe. Clear distinctions were being drawn along biological lines between east and west. Metaphorical and *literal* lines.

In 1866, an International Sanitary Conference was held in Constantinople to develop plans to regulate the annual pilgrimage to Mecca. During the conference – which lasted seven months – the Ottoman Empire asked to be granted entry to Europe's 'sanitary domain'. The request was refused, on the grounds that the standards of health and hygiene across its territories fell consistently short of what was required. Just as in the days of the Black Death, the Ottoman lands were once again branded unclean: their borders marked as the great margin of disease.[37]

With El Tor and its counterparts managing the route into the Mediterranean from the south, and similar safeguards being put in place to the north to control the ports of entry on the Black Sea coast, Europe was defining itself as a 'civilised' space. A clean zone, with a responsibility to protect itself from external, 'uncivilised' contaminants.

As a result, the body of the traveller was becoming the ultimate object of both scrutiny and suspicion – and borders the places where that *scrutinising* could take place. Throughout the nineteenth century, health emerged as the key – and often the *only* – concern for the management of movement from state to state. Foreign bodies, as ever, offered the threat of the 'unknown'. But most pressingly, this threat was unknown *illness*. Before the widespread use of visas or passports, the crucial document for a traveller to hold was one which certified that they were 'disease free'. Borders were being enacted, more than anything else, as *cordons sanitaires*. Rather than just arbitrarily marking territory, they had a clear and urgent purpose: as sites of biological inspection. As lines for physically dividing pure on one side from polluted on the other.[38]

Yet there was something else at play here too. Because El Tor, as a first barrier to entering Europe, was still a considerable distance away from the continent itself. Here was the outsourcing of a sanitary threshold to a remote desert shoreline. European powers were stepping beyond their own territories, engaging in a kind of biological colonialism – managing the threat of disease from a distance, before it even approached their borders.[39]

This policy mixed a genuine desire to improve global standards of health, with self-interest, racial profiling and insidious notions of national 'purity'. But at its heart was the recognition of one crucial, irreversible thing – *individual borders weren't enough*. The world had linked up. The myriad connections were only going to grow and take root: thread veins reaching out to touch every single part of the earth. No matter who you were or where you lived, you had no real choice any more. You had become part of one giant, interconnected, planetary immune system.

Benjamin told me a story from his final year as an undergraduate at McGill. It was 1998. Five years earlier, there had been an outbreak of a mysterious illness in the United States at a place known as 'Four Corners' (so called because it is where the borderlines of Arizona, Utah, Colorado and New Mexico all meet). People were arriving at hospitals with acute breathing difficulties and dying soon after, effectively drowning in their own fluids. The symptoms and presentation matched with no recognised disease, and it took virologists weeks to trace the source.

'They eventually figured out it was coming from the dust of infected mice,' Benjamin said. 'Mice would urinate in dust, the dust would get kicked up, and then people would breathe it in.' And in the process, a previously unknown variant of what was called a 'hantavirus' entered their bodies. Hantaviruses can be found in rodents all over the planet, but there are many different strains.

'I thought it would be interesting to see what strains were circulating in Montreal,' he said, 'and see how different they were from the one in Four Corners.'

He started laying mouse traps all over the university campus – in offices, in chemistry labs, even in the morgue – and would get up at five o'clock each morning to see what he had caught.

'I'd become the McGill exterminator,' Benjamin said, laughing.

In the space of four months he'd collected over 200 mice, removed their lungs, and 'homogenised' the tissue – crudely speaking, squashed and blended it into liquid form – to turn it into RNA, allowing him to look for the virus. Except he never quite got that that far.

'I didn't know what I was doing,' he said. 'I was twenty-two years old. I thought I'd followed all the rules. I'd contacted the Canadian Institute of Health Research. But finally one of my emails must have hit someone who was like, *Oh my God, this kid can't do this*. And they shut me down so fast.'

He was laughing again, shaking his head at the same time.

'It's an odd thing, because to catch a mouse in your house doesn't require a permit, but if your goal is to catch a mouse in your house to see if it has a virus, suddenly you need to have Biosafety Level-3 training.'

As for the mice, 'they are all still sitting in a freezer, catalogued beautifully with where they were caught and what they looked like when they were caught'.

Not long before I spoke to Benjamin, I had been re-reading *The Plague*, the novel by Albert Camus set in a quarantined town in French Algeria around the time of the Second World War (the novel's opening line gives the date as '194–'). The conceit of the story is that it has been pieced together from the notebooks of a doctor working in the town. At the very beginning of the narrative, Dr Bernard Rieux recalls leaving his consulting rooms one morning to find a dead rat on the landing outside, which he 'pushed aside without paying attention to'. That same day, he returns home to his apartment in the evening and, as he looks for his keys, watches another rat stagger out into the corridor.

'The creature stopped, seemed to be trying to get its balance, stopped again, spun round and round with a faint cry and eventually fell, blood spurting from its half open lips. The doctor looked at it for a moment, then went upstairs.'[40]

Rats continue to die all over the town: first in their hundreds, then thousands, coming up from 'basements and cubby-holes, cellars and drains, in long swaying lines'. While finding all this strange and disconcerting, the townspeople do not recognise the danger until it is too late. By the time that the first person dies – the concierge of Rieux's apartment building – the disease is already endemic. The government soon takes the decision to seal off the whole town, to quarantine the population inside its walls, and leave them to their fate.

Camus intended the novel as an allegory for the insidious spread of fascism – the plague as an ideological creep that begins slowly, then spreads rapidly and uncontrollably, with deadly consequences. Reading the book towards the end of 2020 offered rather more direct, literal parallels. When Benjamin told me about the mice at McGill,

I couldn't help but picture him in the role of Dr Rieux – and rather than ignoring that first rat on the landing, I thought of him taking it straight to a laboratory, extracting its lungs, and trying to work out the cause.

In the novel, when the true horror of the situation dawns on the townspeople, they lament that they 'had never thought that our little town might be a place particularly chosen as one where rats die in the sun and concierges perish from peculiar illnesses'.[41]

But then perhaps no one ever does. Benjamin told me about a meeting he had, nearly every Monday morning, involving the heads of four or five of the laboratories in the Icahn School of Medicine, where they would discuss and share information on their respective areas of influenza research. It was during one of those meetings, in January 2020, when they first discussed 'the news that was brewing up about a weird respiratory virus out of China'. Sitting around the table were four expert virologists, two of them already US National Academy of Science Members for their work on flu. And out of those four, only one of them – the most junior member of the group – was actually worried.

'We thought it sounded like SARS,' Benjamin said.

Severe acute respiratory syndrome coronavirus – SARS – was a 'beta coronavirus' which had first emerged around 2002, infecting some 8,000 people worldwide, with a fatality rate of around 10 per cent. A decade later, a new beta coronavirus variant appeared known as MERS: Middle East respiratory syndrome-related coronavirus, which infected just 2,500 people, but had a fatality rate of over a third.

'And both of them are really self-limiting,' Benjamin said. 'So when the hot weather came, SARS just disappeared – off the face of the planet apparently. Or at least it went back to just bats. And MERS: the truth was that it was endemic in camels, and it hit a few people, but it didn't obviously take off and it didn't seem like a big problem. So the three of us senior virologists were all taking this stance – that even if it is a virus, and even if it is a beta coronavirus, it's not going to have the legs, it's not going to go very far, and everything is going to be okay.'

Benjamin gave an involuntary rub at his temples.

'But, when the disease showed up in Italy, none of us believed that to be true any more.'

That first Italian case was reported on 21 February, in a small town in Lombardy, just north of Milan.

'As soon as that happened, you'd be hard pressed to find a virologist anywhere that didn't believe that this was going to go around the world.'

Two weeks later, a tiny screw-top tube arrived at Benjamin's laboratory in New York. Inside it was a red liquid: a sample of homogenised tissue taken from the lungs of a deceased patient in Seattle, who had recently travelled into the United States from Europe. And inside that tissue was severe acute respiratory syndrome coronavirus 2 – SARS CoV-2 – the virus that causes coronavirus 2019, or COVID-19.

Benjamin's laboratory was unusual in that it specialised not in researching any one specific virus, but rather in understanding what a variety of viruses do to host bodies. It was focused on that cellular borderline – on what happens once it is breached, and how immune systems either cope with, or are compromised by, infection.

'In some respects, it was just another virus for us to apply to what we were already doing,' he said, 'so it was actually a really seamless thing to adjust to.'[42]

Within another week, the US Defence Department had offered his lab a multi-million-dollar grant to focus the team's efforts entirely on coronavirus research.

'It was crazy. I had to turn my lab upside down. There was this massive government contract, and people just wanted answers. I was one of maybe only a dozen labs in the world that had a Biosafety Level-3 facility that could house both ferrets and hamsters, which just happened to be two of the animals that could be naturally infected with coronavirus. And so a lot of it was just that I had the right resources and the capacity to do this.'

At the same time as his work intensified, Benjamin saw the city of New York shut down all around him. The hospital alongside the Icahn School of Medicine at Mount Sinai closed its doors to all non-employees and stopped all elective surgery.

'It became a wasteland, it was just so quiet. And then they started building rooms in the lobby. If there was space anywhere, they just turned it into new rooms so they could increase their ICU capacity.'

Across the street was Central Park. A huge tent was erected on the East Meadow and rapidly converted into a makeshift hospital building.

'It looked like a war zone,' he said. 'And then the streets were actually empty – there was nobody. Nobody driving around anywhere. All you could hear were ambulances.'

Benjamin and his team worked around the clock, arriving at the laboratory in the early hours of the morning, leaving late into the night.

'I would take a scooter back and forth from my house,' he told me, 'and you could ride down the middle of the street because there was just nobody around.'

Daisy Hoagland, a PhD student working in Benjamin's lab, was guiding me through the contours of an unfamiliar, abstract landscape. The image we were looking at was like a rocky coastline as seen from directly above: a semi-circular bay giving onto a series of small, craggy inlets, rising up to a shore with a cliff-like escarpment behind it. Except that the colours were off: the 'sea' was white, while the 'rocks' and 'land' appeared in shades of red, purple and dark, navy blue.[43]

'You see where it looks blurry?' she asked me. 'It shouldn't.'

She was indicating the place where the sea met the shore. The land there had become smudged and indistinct, as if partly obscured by lapping waves.

'That indicates bronchial apoptosis.'

Apoptosis – the death of a cell.

'Those dark blue dots,' Daisy explained, pointing out what looked like heaps of boulders clustered all around the bay, 'indicate, for the most part, nuclei. Each one of those is a cell. And there's hundreds of cells lining the bronchial epithelium.'

The landscape that we were studying was the lung tissue of a hamster infected with SARS CoV-2 – COVID-19 – viewed at 400x magnification. The bronchial epithelium is the thin membrane of cells which lines the millions of alveoli – the tiny air sacs – that manage blood-oxygen exchange in the lung. The white space in the image, the sea, was a single alveolus, surrounded by the coastline of the epithelium.

'What we are seeing,' Daisy said, 'is how coronavirus can kill cells and then cause a massive release of debris and more virus. And that's what's happening here. The cells are dying and releasing things.'

Biological flotsam and jetsam, cellular bodies, washing up on the shore or being carried out to sea.

She took me on a tour of more landscapes. Next was the epithelium of another hamster lung, but at 200x magnification. We were, in effect, higher up now. Looking down at not just one bay, but at a whole stretch of coastline: the mouth of a river emptying into an ocean, creating curved spits like sandbanks. Here the shore was a hive of activity, dense clusters of dark dots all jostling for position.

'Those are all neutrophils,' Daisy said. 'Lots and lots of them.'

Too many, as it turns out. Neutrophils are immune cells, a type of white blood cell, one of the most common and numerous of our body's border guards.

'It's showing that there's an imbalance of the immune response. And it's all about balance. If you're weighing the scale too far a certain way, then that can be extremely harmful. It's like this beautiful, orchestrated symphony of things that have to happen at the right times. But here, the immune response – it's the wrong one. It's just causing more disease.'

The troops had just kept on coming, trampling the landscape beneath their boots.

We moved on to another view, at 100x magnification now. A wetland, a patchwork of lakes and water, contained within thin strips of land. Surrounding some of the lakes were little strands of pink.

'Those bits of pink? You are seeing oedema,' Daisy said. 'Severe vascular oedema.' Blood spilling out of the vein and into the surrounding tissue, causing fluid build-up and swelling which, if unchecked, can lead to shortness of breath, complete respiratory failure – and death.

I found these images, in some senses, both shocking and surreal – or perhaps even *unreal*. This internal, cellular terrain was entirely alien to me, comprehensible only through metaphor and analogy. But all the same, what Daisy was showing me was the frontline of viral infection, exactly what was happening when the coronavirus crossed the borderline into a host body.

'It's crazy,' Daisy said to me, 'that there is a whole world that we don't see or completely understand. And that will never not fascinate me.'

As a teenager growing up in New Jersey, Daisy enrolled in a vocational high school for biotechnology, before going on to study microbiology at the University of Vermont. After graduation she flirted briefly with the idea of leaving science to work in international development. Ultimately, however, the pull of medical research was too strong for her to ignore (*Dear God, somebody give me a pipette*, she found herself saying after just two weeks working with a non-profit organisation in Berkley, California. *I just feel so unfulfilled not being at the bench.*) She joined Benjamin's lab in 2018, working initially on a viral engineering project focused on influenza. That was until the second week of March 2020, 'when everything just rapidly switched overnight'.

By that time, Daisy had already contracted coronavirus herself – along with her sister, her mother and her father, whom she had visited in New Jersey just before travel restrictions were imposed. It was an instant induction into the realities of a pandemic – even more so given that she was a virologist.

'It's very weird sometimes,' Daisy said. 'This virus, a virus that I study: you can picture it doing things to your cells. It's a strange feeling. You know too much.'

As soon as quarantine protocols allowed, she was back with the team at Mount Sinai. The lab's study of the virus had moved on rapidly, to the point where they were beginning to infect first ferrets, and then hamsters, in order to track exactly what coronavirus did within a host body. Hamsters offered the best model. They are the smallest rodent to share the same 'receptor' as humans: a protein on the surface of a cell, called ACE2, that the 'spike' protein of the virus first attaches to in order to force its way into the body.[44]

This work was carried out at the centre of Mount Sinai's own biosafety laboratory: a kind of nucleus of viral research where live 'handling' of the virus can take place. Daisy described the process of entry to me: how she had to pass through a series of anterooms like cell walls, before reaching the final space that leads on to the infectious area.

'So you put on an N95 facemask, a slash resistant gown, shoe covers, a head covering, a face shield, two pairs of gloves that have to be different colours so you can see if one's ripped'.

Inside, everything was under 'negative pressure'.

'Negative pressure is sucking all of the air,' she explained, 'so when you open the door there is no chance of viral particles that are aerosolised leaving, because the air is always being sucked up through filtered vents'.

She told me that the first time that she went in was terrifying.

'I started seeing stars and I had to leave. There was just so much pressure. Psychological pressure, and also the *negative* pressure – if you're not used to it, you can get lightheaded. And we were all working crazy hours: twelve-hour days, seven days a week. And a few months in, by June, there was this crushing pressure, because you are just a trainee, but you also know that you are a key piece that is working as hard as possible to figure out this puzzle. I was feeling that as a kind of existential pressure.'

Inside the laboratory, at the heart of those interlocking rooms, Daisy and her colleagues were putting COVID-19 to the test, trying to tease out what its strategies were. Looking to find a way to overcome them. Outside, in the streets of New York City, the experiment was live, uncontained and unfiltered. The virus was at large in countless human host bodies, announcing its presence over and over through the wailing of so many ambulance sirens.

'You are working on coronavirus every day,' she said, 'then you are doing your grocery shopping walking past this giant tent hospital in Central Park.'

Daisy shook her head and was silent for a few moments.

'It's insane,' she continued. 'Sometimes I think about it and think, *did I get the long-term effects of COVID? Am I hallucinating all of this right now?* Genuinely, it sometimes feels that way. I'm doing my PhD at the epicentre of a pandemic – and more than that, I'm doing it on RNA viruses when the pandemic that changes the world strikes. It just feels very surreal a lot of the time.'

Benjamin's team revealed that coronavirus did something very unusual, something that virologists had never seen before.

'Take influenza,' Benjamin said to me. 'When influenza first comes into a cell, it shuts down both the call to arms and the call for reinforcements. Because both are bad for it.'

At that first stage of infection, flu disrupts the immune system by preventing interferons warning other cells of the danger; stopping cytokines from getting messages out to the white blood cells.

'It has shut down communications', Benjamin said. 'So your infected cells try to release message one, and it is shut down. Then they try to release message two. *Shut down.*'

The body does not know that there is a breach, takes time to realise that one small part of it has gone dark, and the flu uses that time to replicate and multiply.

'But with coronavirus,' he said, 'once it breaks the border of that first cell, it only shuts down the call for arms, not the call for reinforcements.'

The release of interferons – the 'call to arms' – represents the immediate threat to the virus.

'It needs to make at least thousands of copies of itself at that first wall-breaking in order for this to be a successful infection that will pass on to the next person,' he said. And so all its efforts go into neutralising the immediate threat, while wilfully ignoring the inevitable arrival of the body's heavy artillery.

As Benjamin put it, 'The virus is saying, *I don't care. I'm going to leave the call for reinforcements on. That buys me five days to generate a couple thousand versions of myself, get out of Dodge, get to the next cell and make another thousand copies – and that's going to be my strategy.*'

This strategy, however, has the potential to cause catastrophic damage in the tissues of a host body.[45]

'Because you've left the faucet on for this call for reinforcements, the virus is bouncing from place to place in the lung and you're just constantly calling in for more and more reinforcements. And so your lungs fill with all these cells that are designed to bring on an inflammatory response – which is supposed to be localised, but by the time they get there, the virus is everywhere.'

Just as Daisy had shown me in the hamster tissue samples, the immune system's response goes into overdrive. The virus is killing cells and making copies of itself, while massed armies of neutrophils follow in its wake, compounding the damage. The air sacs fill up with the shrapnel and detritus of this cellular war: all those bodies washing up on the shoreline. Airways in turn become clogged and breathing becomes difficult – sometimes even impossible.

'This is a really messy virus,' Benjamin said. 'It leaves a lot of debris.'

So much so, that the debris can escape the site of original infection – most often the respiratory tract, the lungs – and end up in general circulation.

'If you look in other places,' he said, 'deep in the brain, the heart, the liver, the kidneys, the spleen, the pancreas, the intestines – everything shows this massive inflammation. So, that call for reinforcements: there are signatures of that everywhere.'

As we talked on, I couldn't help but think of the parallels between this microbiological world and the 'macro-political' world: the one that we inhabit. Benjamin was more than happy to indulge the analogy.

'If you viewed each organ as a country,' he said, 'what is happening is that the country of the respiratory tract has warned all the other countries that this is a serious problem. And so all the different organs put up their own borders in their own ways, and each one is unique too. The defences that the brain has to offer are very different to the defences that the lung has to offer.'

So far, so sensible – the body is prepared, it has fabricated barriers along all its many internal borderlines, creating a hostile environment for the virus. The problem, however, is that all this bolstering on the margins comes at a metabolic cost.

'So, as the lungs scream, *oh my God, it's coming*,' he explained, 'and the kidneys react to that message by saying, *okay, we are ready*, and they fortify their defences. But in so doing, their function as a kidney also gets compromised. As does the function of the brain, as does every other organ – because it takes a lot of energy to create those defences and that's energy that you can't use for your normal life.'

All the cracks begin to show under this strain – people arrive in ICUs with gastrointestinal symptoms or issues with their heart.

'These are not the result of the virus any more,' he said, 'but rather the result of all the body's organs expending energy that they don't have to expend.'

The system becomes fixated on the entry of foreign bodies, and it tears itself apart trying to keep them out. It is tempting to suggest that there is no virus more appropriate for our current age.

In the year 2099, a man begins to write a history of the world. It is the last history, the last book – the last anything – that will ever be written. Because this man is the *last* man alive on earth.

His name is Lionel Verney, and he has come to wander alone among the empty streets of Rome, picking his way through its abandoned palaces, churches and ruins. He has made the Palazzo Colona his home: 'Its grandeur – its treasure of paintings, its magnificent halls were objects soothing and even exhilarating.' He haunts the halls of the Vatican; embraces the vast columns of the Forum, leaning his 'burning cheek' against their 'cold durability'; he visits the great libraries of the city, selects whatever books catch his eye, and then finds some 'shady nook' on the banks of the Tiber to sit and read them.

His only companion is a shepherd's dog, whom he finds still herding sheep in the Campagna, keeping the flock together, 'fulfilling his duties' by repeating the 'lessons learned from man, now useless, though unforgotten'. In yet another empty house he finds a writer's study, where the pages of a half-finished manuscript lie scattered about. It is this discovery that inspires him to pen his own account of what has happened. He dedicates it 'to the illustrious dead': invoking their 'shadows' to 'arise, and read your fall!'

Seven years earlier, in 2092, a plague had arrived. It originated, it seemed, on the 'shores of the Nile', and soon spread into Constantinople – at that time besieged by the armies of Greece, who had been fighting a war with Turkey for nearly two centuries. After devastating the conflict-torn city, the plague was carried among the soldiers returning to Athens. There, people began to fall like 'ripe corn before the merciless sickle' of the disease, and the city's ancient temples were repurposed as morgues. In June of that year, reports came from the east that, one morning, 'the sun rose black'. The streets of Isfahan, Peking and Delhi were said to be strewn with 'pestilence-struck corpses'.

Lionel had received all this news while living among his small group of friends in England. 'We, in our cloudy isle,' he said, 'were far removed from danger, and the only circumstance that brought these disasters at all home to us was the daily arrival of vessels from the east, crowded with emigrants.' It still seemed distant to them then, a calamity several steps removed. They heard how 'nations, bordering on the already infected countries, began to enter upon serious plans for the better keeping out of the enemy'. But, for their government at home, 'there was no necessity for an earnest caution. England was still secure. France, Germany, Italy and Spain were interposed, walls yet without a breach, between us and the plague.'

Gradually, however, they saw the normal busy networks of trade and travel between Britain and the rest of the world begin to break down. Cargo ships did not arrive from foreign ports; passenger vessels went missing. Where once the 'busy multitudes assembled for pleasure and profit, now only the sound of wailing and misery is heard'. The reports from abroad grew ever more desperate. They heard how the 'vast cities of America, the fertile plains of Hindostan, the crowded abodes of the Chinese, are menaced with utter ruin'. The disease was closing in. 'We called to mind the plague of 1348, when it was calculated that a third of mankind had been destroyed. As yet western Europe was uninfected; would it always be so?'

The answer, inevitably, was *no*. By the end of August 2092, the disease had taken hold in France and Italy. Borders and walls could not stop it. In any case, as Lionel came to recognise, this talk of territories had been rendered absurd: 'The nations are no longer!' It spread, finally, into England, leaving nowhere on the planet untouched. 'All the world,' he said, 'has the plague!'

This nightmarish, apocalyptic vision of the future was written by Mary Shelley eight years after her gothic masterpiece *Frankenstein*. It was originally published in 1826 as *The Last Man*.[46] Shelley had worked on it in tandem with the spread of the first cholera pandemic around the world. Clearly, the emergence of a fatal disease, whose transmission confounded medical experts, was a potent source of inspiration. So too, however, were Shelley's personal circumstances.

Over the course of just a few years she had lost her husband Percy Shelley, her great friend Lord Byron and her own infant daughter. 'The Last Man!' she wrote in her journal in May 1824. 'Yes, I may well describe that solitary being's feelings, feeling as the last relic of a beloved race, my companions extinct before me.'[47] Her novel was the first major literary work to contemplate the extinction of humanity by a disease. Dismissed – even ridiculed – by critics on its initial release, it offers rather more potent, and alarming, resonances today.

Near the end of my conversation with Benjamin, I asked him again about what he had described as that 'arms race' between viruses and our immune system. Because it occurred to me that in the context of an arms race, there is always the possibility that a threshold can be crossed, a line of no return. With the invention of nuclear weapons, humans have established the prospect of mutually assured destruction. Was there a risk, I wondered, if you followed his metaphor, of something similar happening at a microbiological level? Could the game of cellular one-upmanship go too far?

'Let's say that you view the earth as one massive life-form,' he said to me, 'which you can, given the way that energy exchanges itself within different bodies at every level on the planet. And the one thing that viruses do – not because they think about it, but just because this is the nature of viruses – when any population gets too big, it is viruses that knock them down.'

This was something, he told me, that you could see across all sorts of different species and organisms, all the time. A large, growing population provides an environment for a virus to evolve, spread and thrive.

'Then that population drops, and the virus can't sustain itself, or the remaining population is resistant to that virus and it falls off the radar and that population can now grow again. Until the next thing comes along.'

Such is the pattern of existence.

'But then, as humans,' Benjamin said, 'we really messed with this. Because the development of antibiotics and vaccines *are* a nuclear weapon for infectious diseases. And one could argue that if a virus or a bacterium or a fungus emerges in the context of us using those weapons – which we are using – it could be truly devastating.'

He outlined a scenario where something like *Staphylococcus aureus* – the bacterium MRSA – evolves or mutates and becomes impermeable to the nuclear weapons we throw at it. 'And then what's going to happen is that we could lose literally half the population. But you'll find groups of people who, through some genetic mutation, are no longer susceptible to this one particular threat. And then the war starts again. And that's just how things have happened for millions of years.'

All the same, our memories remain very short. They do not like to linger on disease. At the very end of Camus's novel *The Plague*, the stricken town is saved. Cases of the illness drop off and then vanish. The quarantine gates are opened, crowds fill the streets, and cries of happiness rise above the town. Dr Rieux, however, is comparatively unmoved. 'This joy was always under threat,' he thinks. Because he knows that 'the plague bacillus never dies or vanishes entirely, that it can remain dormant for dozens of years . . . and that perhaps the day will come when, for the instruction or misfortune of mankind, the plague will rouse its rats and send them to die in some well-contented city'.[48]

Benjamin said, 'It's funny to me, you often hear people say, *Oh, this is a one-in-a-hundred-year pandemic, so once this one is done we've got another hundred years*. And the truth is that that's a gambler's fallacy. I don't think that is really how things work. And so a virus like SARS CoV-2 – you can see that these are becoming more commonplace. And I think that they will continue to do so, because we are breaking the rules.' It was inevitable, he suggested, that viruses will adapt, and quickly, to the challenges that medical science have presented. That the fallout will come from the 'nuclear weapons' – the antibiotics and vaccines – that we have deployed. Because this is a war that will never be over.

In a pandemic – the metaphorical front line of such a war – borders become at once crucial and immaterial. They are closed, hardened, sealed. Yet somehow they still remain porous. It just takes one person to slip through and bring the pathogen with them. And then those borders break apart and shrink. Follow them down the levels: from your country to your city, your town, your village, your house, your flat, your room.

Eventually, territory means nothing beyond the immediate landscape of the self. Our skin and blood and bone. Our cells and proteins and DNA and RNA. At that point, as Shelley wrote in *The Last Man*, 'our minds, late spread abroad through countless spheres and endless combinations of thought, now retrenched themselves behind this wall of flesh, eager to preserve its well-being only'.[49]

10

A GREEN LINE ACROSS A GREAT SHORE

In the mid-1930s, Edward Stebbing, a professor of forestry from the University of Edinburgh, travelled to West Africa in search of a borderline. This borderline was an elusive one. It was not marked on any map – or not in anything other than the vaguest terms. And it was changing constantly: from season to season, from year to year. It took no notice of national borders, was erratic and haphazard, and it ran for thousands of miles. What Stebbing was looking for was a line of transition. He wanted to find, as precisely as possible, the margin where the savannah became the desert.

'I had now been looking out for this disappearance of the savannah for some days,' wrote Stebbing, 'in other words, over several hundred miles. On several occasions I had thought I had found the real desert – treeless desert – only to be disappointed. I had known there would be no really marked boundary, nothing so distinct as between the so-called savannah forest and the high mixed deciduous forest, where fingers and tongues of one or the other are interpenetrating.' Instead, it was, he said, rather more complicated than that. 'The encroachment by the sand,' he continued, was often 'stealthy and almost invisible and unperceivable'.[1]

This border existed, literally, at a granular level. Drawn and redrawn by roots and soil and earth and the fluctuations of the underground water table. Stebbing's journeys took him from the shores of Lake Chad in the east to Gao in French Sudan – now Mali – in the west, a distance of nearly 1,000 miles. His route passed back and forth over the national borderline separating northern Nigeria from southern Niger, across shifting, uncertain landscapes. He wrote of travelling through 'interminable miles of the dry deciduous bush, backed eventually by low hills of sand overlying rock'; passing large herds of cattle, sheep and goats; of seeing scrub forest and grass on the low hills burning at night, 'the irregular lines of fire creeping up the hillsides: even here – within a few miles of the great desert!'.[2]

These arid reaches gave way to long stretches of forests and baobab trees, or explosions of greenery around the Komadugu Yobe River, a tributary flowing into Lake Chad. 'It is a curious sight to see this beautiful green high forest running as a narrow belt across the country, clothing each bank of the river,' Stebbing wrote, 'and to contrast it with the desert-like savannah forest stretching away on either side to the north and south, with the yellow sand of the outer borders of the desert showing here and there as low sand hills away to the north.'[3]

Whether in plain sight or somewhere over the horizon, the desert was always a looming presence for him: a spectre, a haunting. 'At Dogonduchi the desert reappears,' he wrote. 'The town is on the edge of a scarp, and one looked down on to long, flat-topped rounded-ended ridges . . . with, here and there, rounded or bluntly pointed outcrops of dark rock projecting up to fifty feet or so from the sandy plain.'[4]

Stebbing travelled in an army truck, always setting out at dawn, before the temperature rose sharply into days typified by 'heat and unquenchable thirst'. He would stop regularly, walking the land to look for the tell-tale traces of change. Soil layers that were 'gradually overlaid with sand in an ever-thickening carpet'. Scrub forest opening out – a sign that water supplies had become intermittent and the water level had dropped. Increasingly, he wrote, 'a set of conditions are produced under which the savannah forest is represented by more and more open patches of decadent thorn bush accompanied by masses of a tussock grass'. These grasses clung on, for a time. But they were the final stage in the deterioration of the soil. Soon, they too would disappear. By this point there was no stopping the redrawing of the line. 'The desert,' he wrote, 'has conquered.'[5]

The desert in question was the vast expanse of the Sahara – and the blurred borderland through which Stebbing was travelling was the Sahel. Taken from the Arabic word *sāhil*, meaning 'coast' or 'shore', the Sahel runs like a belt across the widest point of Africa, 7,000 kilometres of savannah, steppes and thorny shrublands that divide the ocean of sands to the north from the rainforests to the south. What concerned Stebbing was that this land appeared to be changing – both rapidly and seemingly uncontrollably.

'The desert is advancing!' he exclaimed. 'How, or how fast, I have yet to learn.' The more he travelled through the region, however, the more concerned he became. The people of the Sahel, he wrote, 'are living on the edge, not of a volcano, but of a desert whose power is incalculable and whose silent and almost invisible approach must be difficult to estimate. But the end is obvious: total annihilation of vegetation and the disappearance of man and beast from the overwhelmed locality.'[6]

Before taking up his post as a professor at Edinburgh, Stebbing had worked for over a decade as a forest entomologist and zoologist for the Indian Forest Service. He'd written a three-volume work, *The Forests of India*, detailing examples of early conservation practices going back to the nineteenth-century surgeons-turned-foresters of the East India Company medical service – early proponents of the idea that environmental degradation could affect the state of human health. In India, they had warned of the severe repercussions of unchecked deforestation.[7]

Stebbing's expedition to West Africa was, in many respects, a continuation of this work, and it resulted in one of the earliest modern accounts of what would become known as 'desertification' – how the impact of human activity on a landscape can impoverish its ecosystem, degrade and dry out its soil, and see its biomass deteriorate or even disappear completely. (The term itself was first coined in 1949 by the French botanist André Aubréville in his book *Climats, forêts et désertification de l'Afrique tropicale.* 'The desert always menaces,' he wrote of the Sahel. So much so, he said, that you could see 'real deserts that are being born today, under our eyes'.)[8]

For Stebbing, there was no doubt that 'proof of the steady advance of the Sahara exists'. But, he asked, was there any way to stop it? 'It should not be beyond the power of man to put up a barrier to this threat,' he said; to create a 'forest belt' to 'reproduce what previously existed' and to check the encroachment of the desert. What he envisaged was a great line of forest, a thousand miles long and seven miles wide, which 'must be on a scale sufficient to deal with the force opposed to man. Piecemeal efforts will certainly not meet this silent invasion.'[9]

Tabi Joda lives and works on the western fringe of Lake Chad on land that was once underwater. He grew up in this region too, in the far northwest of Cameroon, in the high forests that straddle the border with Nigeria.

'Those trees were the toys that we had,' he told me. 'They were the only things that we had to play with. We were learning how to jump from one tree to the other. Those were the kinds of things we would grow up learning – that and playing soccer. We used to prepare our own ball from latex from the trees. I had never seen a real ball.'

He held up a mass of light-brown fibrous material to show me. It looked like a cross between a clump of seaweed and giant, living rubber band. He pulled at it, making it stretch out and grow translucent, then let it snap back into shape.

'When you fold it all together,' he said, 'you can make a traditional ball – a football made out of the forest.'

Tabi was in his late thirties, had a small, impeccably trimmed goatee beard, and spoke excellent English inflected with a French accent. When he talked it was in long, lyrical paragraphs – a delivery not unlike that of a spoken-word poet, full of rhythm and building momentum and long emphatic pauses. Our conversation was at once disconcerting and uniquely pleasurable.

'When I was younger,' he said, 'there was still a lot of vegetation, a lot of forest. Before we just used to move twenty metres from my house and you could get these trees that we would harvest for latex – now you have to go kilometres, you have to go very far.'

He pulled absently at the rubber in his hands, stretching and snapping it again and again.

'This was not how it used to be,' he continued. 'There were trees here before. I used to see monkeys from my classroom – in the trees around my school, playing in the schoolyard. But I wasn't seeing them any more. *Where are those monkeys? Where are those baboons?* I used to hear the bush fowl, the wild chickens – they would wake me up in the morning. *Bu-bak, bu-bak, bu-bak* – they make a sound like that, early in the morning, at five o'clock. They are no more. What happened? Of course it is obvious. The trees are no longer there. The forest is gone.'

When Stebbing's report on the Sahel was published in the *Geographical Journal* in the summer of 1935 – with the attention-grabbing title of 'The Encroaching Sahara: The Threat to the West African Colonies' – it so alarmed the British and French governments that they founded a joint Boundary Forest Commission to explore the problem. Summarising their findings in 1938 – once again in the *Geographical Journal* – the commissioners largely dismissed Stebbing's 'gloomy view of the future', noting tartly that many 'observers with considerable experience in West Africa' were 'not in accord' with his conclusions. Rather, they said, the 'displacement of sand on some bare farmlands need not cause anxiety', and so the 'establishment of a vast shelter belt of trees is therefore unnecessary'. In their opinion, 'the natural forest formations appear to be stable except where they are being interfered with by man'.[10]

Except where they are being interfered with by man. It was this last point that was crucial. Stebbing and the commissioners were, in a sense, arguing over the semantics of an allusion – that potent image of the desert *moving*, its dunes surging outwards like the waves of a rising ocean. It was an idea at once arresting and terrifying. But it wasn't borne out by the evidence (Stebbing himself later admitted to regretting using the term 'encroaching').[11] What *was* changing, however – sometimes slowly, often imperceptibly – was the landscape along the Sahara's great southern shoreline. The Sahel wasn't being *overcome* by the desert: it was *becoming* a kind of desert. Both Stebbing and the Boundary Commissioners recognised elements of this change, but no one could really agree on the cause or what it meant. Was it climate? Farming? Overgrazing and overpopulation? Was it just part of the natural cycle of the region, where rainfall and water levels always fluctuated?

Decades passed. Colonial rule had steadily and comprehensively changed the management of the land over several generations. Regimented agricultural practices were introduced to separate crops from trees. The French administration introduced the mass growing of crops like groundnuts and cotton for export back to Europe. The demands for increased production and profit drove farmers to expand their fields and work more and more marginal lands, ploughing their soils, enriching them with fertilisers or dousing them with pesticides. This, in turn, reduced the grazing spaces available to the Sahel's nomadic herders. So too did the shift to a post-colonial world, as nations declared their independence and in the process etched their borders sharply across the desert and the savannah, blocking off herding routes that had been in use for centuries. Farmers and pastoralists increasingly fought over access to territory – and in the process soils and grasses were being either overworked or overgrazed. The old rhythms of the landscape had been dismantled and broken. And then the rain stopped falling.[12]

It began in the 1950s. Each year, the rains seemed to come less and less. The heavy clouds did not muster, or if they did, they rushed on by. There was nothing to stop the sun flaring down and the heat building. Trees had either been cut down for timber or reorganised in mass plantations, and so there was no shade for the fields and the crops. In places the topsoil began to dry up, crust and turn to dust.

By the late 1960s, the water level in Lake Chad was dropping. One of Africa's largest inland sources of freshwater, the lake is also a nexus point where the borders of Cameroon, Nigeria, Niger and Chad meet. Its basin takes in almost a tenth of the whole continent. The lake had always been subject to seasonal fluctuations, but this was different. By 1971, it was down to a third of its normal size. Its diminished waters offered the most immediate, visible symbol of the crisis to come. Crops began to fail; vegetation and grasses withered and disappeared. With nothing to graze on, livestock died – many countries experienced losses of a third to nearly a half of all their animals. The drought spread to touch the lives of nearly 30 million people across the whole length of the Sahel, from Senegal in the west to Ethiopia in the east. Famine and disease were consuming the land.

By the mid-1970s, the rains returned. Parts of the Sahel began to recover, people were back working the soil, crops were growing. But this was just a brief respite. Lake Chad – that bellwether of impending drought – had shrunk once again, even worse than before. By 1984, it was a quarter of what it had been two decades earlier. Once again, crops and vegetation had dried up all across the region. And once again, hundreds of thousands of people were displaced or worse. The death toll since the onset of the first drought at the end of the 1960s had reached over a million.[13]

The Sahel had become a great band of desiccation and dust. Not a bulwark against the vast desert to the north, but its mirror. Sometimes, when the wind blew, the air was so thick with clouds of degraded topsoil that it blotted out the sun.

There were many reasons, Tabi said, for the degradation of the land. In his own community, one of the most basic was wood.

'There was a very strong appetite for the sale of wood,' he said.

'It became an economic factor – the selling of firewood, the demand for rosewood and timber. And that led the people to cut down the forests.'

Tabi left his village to study at university. 'And each time I was going and coming back,' he said, 'I saw piles and piles of wood all along the roadsides. People in my family also contributed to that. Some of the money that was used in helping me go to university *came from that.* So, I was also part of the problem, right? I am not exempting myself. It had become an economy that was supporting lives, buying food for families and putting it on their tables, supporting their children.'

But, of course, it was a finite resource.

'Take for example a tree like a bush mango,' he said. 'It has a very big trunk. If you cut it for timber it will give you $200 from the timber – *and that $200 comes at once.* But if you harvest the bush mango, this tree gives you maybe $5 each year. And another tree is giving you $5, and another maybe $8. Then multiply that by ten trees, or twenty: it is already more than you are going to get in that one week from the timber. And when that tree is cut – *it is gone.* That's all. You've lost that tree for life.'

Tabi had watched it happen to tree after tree. He had seen it since he was a boy – the 'toys' he grew up with disappearing one by one, turned into those regimented log piles stacked up on every roadside. That border with the desert? His village had, in a sense, helped manufacture it on the ground, driven by economic pressures to strip the earth down to nothing.

'The land has lost so much of its value,' he told me. 'The land is bare.'

This was something, he said, that you could see from the largest scale – across countries, across the whole continent – down to the smallest.

'This is one thing that people hardly talk about,' Tabi said, 'but each time you fell a tree you end up destroying many other trees that are growing.'

Seeds are trampled and uprooted in the process. Saplings never get the chance to grow, deprived of protection from the sun and nutrients from the soil. This is, perhaps, an apt metaphor for life in the Sahel: that in a marginal land, it is all too easy to upset the equilibrium, to knock things off-kilter and set in motion a chain of unforeseen consequences. It is never just one tree.

'So many young people here are vulnerable,' Tabi said. 'Because the moment their income streams subside, the moment that they cannot get this income – especially the adolescents when they are getting towards being adults – what happens? They start thinking, *Oh, my cousin went to Germany by travelling across the Sahara and getting a boat into the Mediterranean, and then arriving in Lampedusa. And then he was given asylum and finally he was able to stay within Europe. So I'm going to do the same.*

'The world has become really, really borderless – yet there are still borders within this *borderlessness*. So many borders. And so at the end of the day you have climate refugees. You have irregular migrants, who are pushed out by these landscape degradations.'

Tabi was almost one of them. In 2004, he and a group of his friends had prepared to make this same trip. His goal was to reach Spain – to travel first into Nigeria from Cameroon, then on through Niger and Algeria to Morocco: a distance of over 1,600 miles, most of it across the Sahara. The night before he was supposed to leave, he stayed up late, thinking, questioning.

'I went to school because I wanted to be valuable to the community, right? And it was then, just in the nick of time, that I came to terms with who I was. It was at that point that it bore down on me that I had something more than just this thing I wanted to do, this *leaving*. That I could go back to my society and make an impact.

'And then something happened in the night, coincidentally. I had kept my shoes for the journey, but when I woke up in the morning, I could only see one shoe. I couldn't find the other. And so, in the course of searching for it, that added to the decision I had had in the night that I shouldn't go. That kind of sealed it.

That there was no point. I told my friends, *sorry, I will not leave with you on this journey*.'

Instead, Tabi turned back to the place where he had come from, that he had always known.

'Immediately – it didn't take more than one week – I just moved into the landscape. And I told myself, *I'm going to turn this dry land into a forest*.'

Imagine a line of trees. It begins on the western coast of a vast continent and runs inland from the ocean. This line is fifteen kilometres wide. It is not straight, but rather it arcs eastwards at first, for hundreds of kilometres. Then it bends sharply north and begins to draw – if viewed from above – what looks like one flattened, elongated 'S' tilted onto its side. This first 'S' flows into a second, by which time the line has been travelling for more than 3,000 kilometres. Now it begins to straighten, running onwards with only the faintest curve, for thousands of kilometres more, until it is in sight of a great sea. It kisses the coast before bending away southwards and then curving back again, in the shape of a fisherman's hook, to reach its terminus on the continent's eastern shore. Imagine nearly 8,000 kilometres of forest snaking, uninterrupted, through the land – from ocean to ocean. Imagine the largest living structure on the planet, three times the size of the Great Barrier Reef. And then imagine a name for it: 'The Great Green Wall'.[14]

This vision can be traced, in part, back to Thomas Sankara – dubbed 'Africa's Che Guevara' – the Marxist–Leninist revolutionary leader of Burkina Faso in the mid-1980s. Sankara's programme for the social, economic and ecological transformation of his own country had included a commitment to planting 10 million trees. It held within it the echo of Edward Stebbing's 'forest belt', but on a much grander scale – a green barrier against desertification to serve as a model for all the other countries throughout the Sahel. Solid blocks of trees that could one day join together to link the Atlantic coast to the shores of the Indian Ocean. 'You cannot carry out fundamental change without a certain degree of madness,' Sankara said in 1985, two years before his assassination in a military coup. 'We must dare to invent the future.'[15]

In 2005, Nigeria's president Olusegun Obsanjo resurrected this idea at a summit of the heads of state of the Sahel–Sahara region. It received strong support in particular from the Senegalese leader Abdoulaye Wade – who is credited with first describing it as a 'great green wall' – and in 2007 it was formally adopted by the governments of the African Union.[16]

The intention, at this initial stage, really was a literal wall. Trees would be planted in solid blocks, following a route determined by using average rainfall figures. A band of landscape was identified – approximately 15 kilometres wide – that received between just 100 and 400 millimetres of rain per annum, a dry corridor that snaked all the way along the Sahel. And the wall would follow this line, beginning in Senegal, travelling east through Mauritania, Mali, Burkina Faso, Niger, Nigeria, Chad, Sudan, Eritrea and Ethiopia, and ending in Djibouti.[17] In this form it had a potent and seductive visual appeal. A colossal, trans-boundary, ecological borderline. A symbol of pan-African fortitude and resilience facing off the great Saharan desert to the north. A line not *in* the sand, but *against* the sand.

'Today the word "wall" somehow has negative connotations,' Camilla Nordheim-Larsen, programme co-ordinator for the Great Green Wall at the United Nations Convention to Combat Desertification (UNCCD), said to me. 'But we try to explain it as a wall that doesn't divide people but unites them. And so this is the first wall that is a natural wonder, where man comes together with nature.'

Camilla was talking to me from Bonn, Germany, where the UNCCD have their headquarters. She wore black-framed glasses, had shoulder-length blonde hair, and spoke in the kind of perfectly structured English common to almost every Scandinavian I've ever met. After studying international development at the universities of

Oslo and then Toulouse, she joined the UN, working first on women's issues in Asia, before moving into the field of desertification in 2002.

'I'm an economist by background, so it wasn't self-evident that I would go on to work on this area,' she told me. 'But, really, I've come to think that land and land resources have not been given the focus that they should globally. Everyone in the world is talking about climate change; kids know about what the changing climate is doing to them, and that's really great and important. But to me there is not enough focus on the need for healthy soils. Because it's where we produce our food and build our houses and live, and the value of healthy soil should have much more international attention. I think this has the potential to lift millions out of poverty.'

In the Sahel, Camilla said, around four fifths of the population – estimated at around 135 million people – live off the land, either directly through agriculture or by working in related jobs.[18]

'And so healthy lands are actually linked to all these other global issues we are talking about today: to climate change, to food production, to jobs, to migration and to security. To me that is a really interesting angle as an economist.'

It is this sentiment that has come, gradually, to pivot the Great Green Wall away from its literal origins. To begin with, everything was geared towards mass plantations – great swathes of land bulldozed for regimented ranks of trees, ordered like some vast forest army. Countries were chasing ambitious targets around numbers of trees planted and acres of land to be 're-greened'.

But, as Dennis Garrity, Chair of the Global EverGreening Alliance and former Director General of the World Agroforestry Centre put it in a 2020 research report on African dryland restoration, 'most large-scale attempts at land restoration had disappointing results or were disastrously unsuccessful'.[19] Many saplings failed to grow to maturity and foundered in the harsh conditions, with little care or attention given to them after the initial planting. Studies suggested that the mortality rate for planted trees was often 80 per cent or higher. In some places fast-growing, non-native species were introduced, like pine or eucalyptus, which ended up exacerbating the very problems they were supposed to counteract – drawing water from the land, pushing out native species, and creating a form of unintentional, managed degradation.[20]

For Garrity, implementation was always 'top down, with little care or awareness of local realities', using practices that 'were rarely suited to people's needs' and too expensive to be either sustainable or scalable. Billions of dollars, he said, had already been wasted in such schemes, often supported by multilateral banks and development agencies.[21]

When the UNCCD came to review the progress of the Great Green Wall in 2020, they reported that just 4 per cent of the 2030 target of 100 million hectares of land had been restored. This, however, rose to 16 per cent when taking into account re-greening work on terrain that fell outside the specific route of the Great Green Wall or by including restoration that had not been carried out under its specific auspices.[22]

In Niger, for instance, in one of the poorest countries in the world, some 5 million hectares of land had been rehabilitated since the mid-1980s, the work of hundreds of thousands of smallholder farmers. Most remarkable of all, this had been achieved *without planting a single tree*. Instead, farmers had simply managed and nurtured the natural regrowth of native rootstocks or seeds lying dormant in the seemingly lifeless earth – reawakening what is sometimes called the 'seed memory' of the soil.

This was a quiet landscape revolution that went almost entirely unnoticed by the wider world, until a Dutch agroforestry specialist, Chris Reij, visited the region in 2004. Reij had worked in the Sahel for decades and had vivid memories of driving through southern Niger during the height of the drought in the 1980s, when there was so much sand and dust in the air that he had to have his car headlights on in the middle of the day.[23] Yet on his return two decades later, this same barren landscape was entirely unrecognisable, so extensive was the vegetation and tree cover.[24] Working with another researcher, Gray Tappan of the US Geological Survey, Reij analysed satellite imagery of the region, French government aerial photography from the 1970s, and even commissioned his own aerial survey.

The results were staggering. In comparing the modern and historical images they demonstrated that 'vast expanses of savannah devoid of vegetation in the early 1980s are now densely studded by trees, shrubs and crops'.[25] Because the land lay up against the northern border with Nigeria, it offered a direct comparison with a tract of country with the exact same soil and the same rainfall. On one side, the land was sparse and bare, while on the other, there was this long, solid block of greenery. Strip away lines on maps, and this stretch of the border between Niger and Nigeria was still visible from space. As Reij and Tappan put it, the farmers 'have literally "constructed" new agroforestry parklands on a massive scale'.[26] Rather than keeping trees and crops separate, as per the western model for mass agricultural production, they had brought them back together again, to work in concert *alongside* each other. One of the end results was almost 200 million regrown trees.[27]

It was success stories like this that began to transform the meaning and purpose of the Great Green Wall. The name remains, but now, as Camilla put it, 'it's metaphorical, it's a way to look at a mosaic of landscape interventions going across Africa, linking these thousands of communities together in a common purpose and a common goal'. The wall, if you like, has already fallen – as all walls must inevitably do. And emerging from its semantic ruins is this *mosaic*, a grassroots jigsaw that the Sahelian countries and their development partners must piece together if the project is ever going to achieve its goals.

'On the ground we know now what works,' Camilla said. 'The communities know what they need and what they want. But connecting that with the investment and really getting that to the size that we need, that is the challenge, I would say.'

For her, looking at it as an economist, you need to grow 'economic trees' alongside the real ones. 'You need to give the populations living on the land a reason to want to invest in their soils. Meaning that they have an incentive to take care of the land. Because it gives them income. For us the land restoration aspect is mainly linked to livelihood before anything else.'

In this new approach, perhaps appropriately, the words of the wall's spiritual father, Thomas Sankara, can be heard once again. 'The world that we are fighting for will never be built by technicians,' he said. 'It will be built by ordinary humans, who will transform themselves in the process of transforming the conditions of their lives.'[28]

At the same time as Nigeria's Olusegun Obsanjo and the other heads of the Sahelian states were first discussing the Great Green Wall in 2005, Tabi had returned to his maternal community in northwestern Cameroon.

'There was one very particular thing that struck me,' he said. 'I planted two trees at my school, when I was still a boy. One was an avocado tree, the other a moringa. And I remembered that they had grown very big, and soon they were harvesting avocado from the tree and it had big foliage. All of this was buried down in my mind.'

And so Tabi started a nursery, growing and nurturing trees on a small tract of land. 'And while I was doing that I was also learning more – how do we make these a productive thing for the community? How do we manage this?'

It didn't take long for him to see the results. 'I saw the landscape changing. And it kept changing. Fruit started bearing. You grow trees and trees take three to four years to become mature. What is it that the trees offer so you can do things differently? Well, you can start looking at how, along this line, you can grow these crops, or introduce beehives that help multiply the good variety of trees so that they are producing all year round. Then you can harvest fruits to sell in the market or use the leaves to make one product or another. You start stabilising the ecosystem, introducing agroforestry where people can actually plant and chop down crops alongside grazing animals. And that's what you need for restoration to be sustainable.'

It was at this stage that Tabi began to think bigger. 'I said to myself, we have one billion people in Africa. What if this becomes a signature of every individual on the continent? What about redirecting efforts and thoughts towards restoring Africa entirely. Putting one billion trees in place – then Africa blossoms, thrives.'

This notion inspired him to start – and name – his own agroforestry business: One Billion Trees for Africa. He began going out to other communities, first in Cameroon and then, over time, all across the Sahel region and beyond – to Chad, Niger, Nigeria, Burkina Faso, Togo, Mali and Ghana. Tabi's approach was to present them with a business model, explaining why they needed to foster the growth of new trees and why they should avoid cutting down the ones they already had.

'If you are telling people, don't cut down these trees, what are you giving them in return?' he said. 'Because you are not giving them money. And so you need to help them resist the pressures that are making them burn or cut down their trees, right? Because this tree is yours and this life is yours. And we get them to see tree cutting and tree burning as a whole burden, a threat to their life and a threat to their future. Instead of chasing big money that is not sustainable, you tell them they can chase long-term little income that *is* sustainable.'

Tied into his economic argument was an emotional one. Tabi was proposing a way to change, fundamentally, the fortunes of families so often torn apart by landscape degradation.

'You can tell people, *look, you can actually take care of your child. He or she can remain in this community and become part of the wealth of this community without going to Europe. Without trekking, risking their life across the Sahara and the Mediterranean Sea. Because millions have died in the sea there.* I say, *hey, my brother, my sister, my son, what do you think we can do? Okay, I'm going to share with you, this is what we did in Cameroon. We did it like this and it worked like this.*'

To date, Tabi has taken his agroforestry model to some thirty-three communities across eight countries, overseeing the growth of more than 2 million trees. After initial site visits to examine the land, he remains in contact with every one of his projects over WhatsApp and is constantly receiving messages updating him on progress or asking for further guidance and advice.

'I tell them to plant this tree when the rains are beginning – and don't put much soil under it. Or they tell me, *yesterday an unfortunate thing happened – a cow smashed our trees and destroyed them. What do we do?* So I have all the information from all the places. I can, on a daily basis, know very well what is happening in Burkina Faso or Niger or Chad. I hear from these communities because we are working with people. We are a community of communities.'

Through word of mouth, Tabi came to the attention of co-ordinators of the Great Green Wall, who asked him if he would become an ambassador for the project. Its vision and the aims of his own agroforestry work were perfectly aligned. All the same, when I asked him about the missteps and mistakes that had happened in the early development of the Green Wall, he shook his head and was silent for a long time.

'It's a big shame,' he said finally. 'A big shame. I would like the leaders of the world to hear me say it is a big shame. Why do I say it is a shame? I feel heart-broken, because I come from this region. This is where my parents, my grandparents, my siblings, my relatives live. So I am speaking from the point of view of *he who wears the shoes knows where it pinches.* Billions and billions have been invested in planting trees. I repeat again: *planting trees.* But planting trees is not enough. It is not enough. There is no point planting a tree when you can't grow this tree to fruition. And this is where our governments, the UN and the World Bank and so many donor agencies have failed. Let these words reach their ears: *they have failed.*'

Tabi was tugging again at the clump of fibrous rubber in his hands, stretching it out further and further so that it cracked loudly whenever he let it go.

'We hear people talking about the Great Green Wall, how it's *shaping the narrative in the Sahel.* But no one can shape a narrative about how your life looks better than *you.* We see the Sahel suffering a top-down, imposed, or superimposed narrative. When we should be generating narratives organically from the mouths and feelings of those people on the front line.'

He continued to shake his head. There was, he said, a disjointed nature to the project, a lack of co-ordination and tangible results: all those trees planted and not grown. I asked him if he was worried that it might not succeed.

'It worries me that it slows down the effort,' he replied. 'But in my heart, I still see the Great Green Wall as the best hope for Africa. I still see it as something that can really transform lives. Something that can bring a strong departure from the fractured, disarticulated communities, characterised by lack of food, by human suffering, by a lot of climate-driven resource violence. It can turn them into thriving systems and it can transform lives. And, of course, it can go far and wide in reducing all of these artificial borders.'

As Tabi put it, the Great Green Wall is a 'borderless' mosaic.

'So that tells the people that wildlife can actually flow within it, livelihoods can flow within it, people can flow within it, right? It is uniting Africans towards a cause that can actually transform Africa, that can go to the logical result of a more borderless Africa where we are more connected by the culture of development – not by the culture of political and administrative limitations and barriers.'

He threw the rubber up in the air and caught it. Once, twice, a third time.

'As Africans,' he said, 'we are living within lots of artificial borders, imposed borders. And I feel really not just Africa, but I think the entire world needs to redefine what we call borders. The whole world should see itself as an entire ecosystem.'

In 1921, England experienced what remains one of the most severe droughts in the country's history. The landscape turned from green to brown to pale yellow. The leaves on the trees were showing their autumn colours in the middle of July; crops burned, withered and failed; the earth hardened and cracked. Kent, on the southeast coast, suffered most of all. The seaside resort of Margate recorded just 236 millimetres of rain over the whole year – still the lowest annual precipitation in Britain since records began.[29] This made it an official desert: the definition for any region that receives less than 250 millimetres of rainfall a year.

Living in the town, as that parched summer turned into an equally hot, dry autumn, was the poet T. S. Eliot. He had come to recover from what the staffing records at the bank where he worked described as a 'nervous breakdown'. It was during this time, as he sat beneath the shade of the promenade looking out over Margate sands, that he wrote much of his most famous work, *The Waste Land.* In the final section of the poem, Eliot described his narrator moving through an 'arid plain', a place where there is 'no water but only rock'; where the 'dry sterile thunder without rain' has turned the streams to dust and left the 'dead mountain mouth of carious teeth that cannot spit'.

As scholars of Eliot have suggested, England's relentless, unchanging drought may just have been getting to him, and leaving its mark on the page. 'If there were water we should stop and drink,' he wrote; yet 'amongst the rock one cannot stop or think.' In fact, it was hard to do anything at all: 'here one can neither stand nor lie nor sit'.[30] Humans were not meant to live like this, he suggested, in the midst of such extreme heat. It was unnatural: it broke down the mind and the body and the spirit. *You cannot stand nor lie nor sit nor think.*

Eliot's sweltering convalescence in Margate came back to me when I spoke to Marten Scheffer, an ecologist and mathematical biologist at Wageningen University in the Netherlands. He was telling me about a time, several years earlier, when he had travelled to a conference in the city of Mérida, near the tip of the Yucatán peninsula in Mexico.

'I found it intolerably hot and humid,' he said, 'and I started to wonder, *this can't be good. I can't really think here.*'

He began to look for any studies exploring when humans functioned best – under what circumstances and what conditions.

'And I just didn't find very much,' he said. 'I kept being fascinated in the back of my mind. I thought maybe we could just take it from the angle that we do in ecology a lot, that you try to reconstruct the "niche" of an animal or a plant. You just look wherever it lives and where it doesn't live, right?'

As Marten put it, you find polar bears at the North Pole; you don't find reindeer in the desert. In the past he had used this technique in the study of tropical rainforests. Very often, he said, you can find what is known in ecology as a 'sharp border' between different environments. In the mountains, for instance, there is the sharp border of the treeline – a distinct, visible threshold above which trees no longer thrive.

'But also you get this sharp border between savannah and rainforest,' he said. For years he had focused on trying to identify the critical rainfall levels needed to shift from one state to the other. 'You can identify this climate envelope where you know you will get the forest, and then you can predict what will happen with climate change.'

It was while discussing this work with a visiting scientist from Nanjing University, Chi Xu, that Marten's idea began finally to take shape.

'We were sitting in my office, and one day we were thinking, well, maybe instead of for forests or trees, we can just do that for people. And we thought it was probably a silly and crazy idea, but why not see what happens?'

Marten was in his early sixties, had the distinctive pale, freckled skin of a northern European, with a trim beard and grey-white hair. Nature, he told me, had always been his passion. As a young boy he had lived in a house with his great-grandfather, a medical doctor who, for more than thirty years, had kept a series of journals full of observations on the natural world. Marten went on to study biology, had a brief flirtation with palaeontology ('I had to get all these dusty bones of mice from an island – I found it very boring'), and then settled on ecology.

'I went to the mathematical side, the theoretical side,' he told me. 'Trying to understand complex systems and tipping points in nature and how they work. And from that I started being more and more interested in tipping points in society. Basically I'm just restless, curiosity-driven.'

What Marten and Chi Xu went searching for was what they called the 'human climate niche'. Was there an ideal envelope for people? Was it possible to determine, by mining the vast existing datasets on demographics, land use and climate, the optimum conditions for humanity as a species to thrive?

The work took some three years – not because the results were difficult to isolate or identify; on the contrary, they were *so* clear and *so* striking that they felt the need to check and recheck their methodology and calculations.

'We did all the maps, we did all the computational work, and we got a clear concentration of humans in certain temperature regions. And we looked at that further and further and thought, well, maybe that's just a coincidence. Maybe where most people are is just because of some historical reason.'

And so they started looking backwards: to medieval times, to the classical world, all the way back to the mid-Holocene period.

'To our surprise we saw the same pattern,' Marten told me. 'And that was *really* a surprise. Because we thought, if people are limited to those temperatures, then they were limited to this optimum range, not too hot, not too cold.'

The data showed that, for the past 6,000 years at least, human populations have lived in the same, strikingly narrow slice of the total available climate space on earth – characterised by areas where the mean annual temperature is between 11°C and 15°C. And crucially, it is this temperature 'band' that is, by far, the most dominant, unifying factor. More so than rainfall, and certainly more so than soil fertility, which appears to have had only a limited impact on human distribution.[31]

'I could have imagined this for the Stone Age,' Marten said. 'But now we have moved everywhere we can. We've built houses, we have clothes and heating and air conditioning, and all kinds of techniques for agriculture. In that sense it is very surprising. I mean, it's not that there are *no* people living in very hot and very cold places; people live everywhere. But the bulk of the people still live in the same places that the bulk of the people have always lived. And so that suggests that there is some fundamental reason.'

As Marten put it, *all species* ultimately have their ideal environmental niche. And, despite technological advances, humans – as just another organism – are unlikely to be the exception.

They began to probe the question: why this particular temperature band? For one thing, they found that around half the global population relies on smallholder farming – on the hard, manual, outdoor labour of farmers that can be impacted severely by extreme temperatures. They looked at data showing strong correlations between heat and impaired physical, cognitive and psychological performance, with knock-on effects on mood, behaviour and mental health. And then, in another research paper examining the impact of climate on economic productivity, they noticed remarkable parallels to their own results.[32]

'These economists looked across 166 countries and asked, if they had a little bit of a hotter year, or a little bit of a colder year, what did that do to the economy? And piecing together all this information they came to the same optimum temperature for productivity that we found. There seems to be something to it. *We really do not do so well when it becomes too hot.*'

This, however, was one part of their research. Given that they appeared to have identified a tight, historically stable relationship between mean annual temperature and human distribution, what about the future? With the impacts of climate change, it was inevitable that this human niche would shift. What they wanted to explore was exactly where and how far. Using the latest projections of the Intergovernmental Panel on Climate Change (IPCC), they modelled the world that was waiting a half-century over the horizon.

'And it was just so striking how much that niche is moving in space,' Marten told me. 'It will move more in the next fifty years than it has moved over the past six thousand.'

They produced a series of maps to illustrate the exact nature of this geographical change. Showing 'suitability for living' in shades of blue – from light as the least suitable to dark as the most – you could see the inexorable drift of the 'climate niche' between now and 2070 as a sort of mass ink-blotting across large portions of the northern hemisphere and the very continental tips of the southern hemisphere. At the same time, the colour had leached away all over the equator and the tropics. The Sahara, the Sahel, the Arabian Peninsula, India, northern Australia, the top half of South America and the bottom half of North America became so pale as to be almost white.[33]

'To double-check we took another approach,' Marten said. 'We looked at the hottest places on earth where people live – a few spots in the Sahara and so on – and we looked at where those temperature conditions will be in the future. And you see that this will spread to areas where *many* people now live.'

Currently, less than 1 per cent of the earth's land surface experiences mean annual temperatures around or above 29°C. By following the IPCC figures for 'business as usual' – meaning with no mitigation of the present trajectory of climate change – they predicted that this would rise to almost one fifth of the globe.[34]

'And if you then just extrapolate,' he continued, 'and suppose the hypothetical situation that humans will in the future avoid living in places *where they have never lived*, and try to follow that niche, and avoid the extremely hot places, how many would have to move? And you get this staggering figure of 3.5 billion people.'

As Marten said, 'We have to be really careful in extrapolating that to migration because people don't want to move. They only move when they really have to move.'

If you take migration out of the equation, then, by 2070, potentially one third of humanity will be living in conditions currently found in only a handful of places on the planet, most of which are concentrated in the Sahara Desert. Of course, some have argued, in response, that this will never happen, that climate mitigation and technological advancement will slow down the warming process and allow humans to adapt.

'I think that's pretty much bullshit,' Marten said to me. 'Because we don't see anything in this mitigation. It's just not happening. But even if it goes well, we're still looking at quite a bit of temperature rise because of the slowness in the system. And now there are more people saying that we are in line with the worst-case scenario.'

As for adaptation, he was not optimistic.

'You can adapt to everything if you have the money. You can install good air conditioning, use good cheap energy. It's not a problem if you don't have to work in the field because you can send a robot out there and just stay inside. But all of that requires resources. And, unfortunately, the places that are going to get hottest are the poorest places on earth.'

Look at the wider ecological landscape and many species are already on the move – towards the poles, retreating from valleys to spaces higher up the mountains, always seeking more temperate landscapes. Year by year, kilometre by kilometre, researchers are noting these shifts. All sorts of organisms following their own climate niches.

'For instance, you see it happening with plants,' Marten said. 'Their reproductive success becomes better in the formerly colder places. And becomes worse and they die more often in the now hotter places. And that's what moves them. That's how it has always been on earth. And, of course, it's a natural thing to do. If the climate changes you move to a different place.'

As Marten explained, some countries have a large 'climate gradient'. In places like China or Chile for instance, there would be the opportunity to move internally to still find the human niche in another part of your national territory. But what if you can't move? What if there is something blocking your way?

'It becomes much more challenging internationally when you would like to cross a border, of course,' he said. 'Other species don't know the borders and they move; they just move. But this whole thing with the borders, you've got this locked-in situation – and it is going to create trouble for us. We've constructed the borders, and we're stuck.'

Marten's work had highlighted the 'niche' as a different kind of borderline. A borderline entirely beyond the control of any individual state or government, yet which, at the same time, has come to determine where almost every human being on the planet actually lives today. For millennia it has stayed in almost exactly the same place – prompting the shift from hunter-gathering to farming and ushering in the very beginnings of civilisation; watching over the growth of society, from the siting and construction of all the planet's major cities to the creation of bordered nation states, and the arrival and acceleration of the industrial age.

Operating within the stability of this niche, humanity has grown, thrived and exploded over the earth. The niche has *made us*. And now we, in turn, are moving the niche, exerting control over it through our innate uncontrollability. By our actions, we are sending it racing away across the globe. Leaving us, as a whole species, chasing our own shadow.[35]

'And we have to ask what will the reaction be?' Marten said.

If billions of people – even just hundreds of millions – are forced to move in the future because extreme temperatures make where they currently live uninhabitable, how will the world cope?

'The obvious response, and this is what you are already seeing, is that some will say, *well, we can't handle this influx – we need to close the borders, we need to make a wall and so forth*. And I wonder if that is sustainable in the long run. You can't really close off. And if you *can* close off, what you will see is a lot of misery on one side of the border that creates a tension that everyone will feel in the end. Globally, no one can avoid that tension.'

As Marten put it, we have to start thinking, now, about the fundamental question: what is safe for humanity if we want to keep thriving on this planet?[36] Ecologists already do this work for coral reefs and rainforests. What, he said, about doing it for societies?

'It is reversing in a way this question, to not say, what is dangerous? But asking, what is safe? You can say temperature is one. But inequality is another one. There are safe and unsafe limits to inequality. And the two are not independent, because if you are pressing on two places at once, it is more dangerous.'

Wrapped up in this, of course, is a global response to the shifting climate niche.

'We're going to have to confront situations where we have to think about redistributing people across the planet,' Marten said. 'You can either just try to lock borders or you can try to anticipate. And if you want to make a kind of graceful transition to a new situation, you have to at least start thinking about the questions you should ask. About international cooperation, integration and law. About labour possibilities, about food supply, about agriculture. About ecological carrying capacity of places, about cultural integrations, about how to weave societies together so that they don't fall off a cliff edge.'

But, Marten continued, those questions are not being asked.

'People prefer not to think or talk about them. Which is not a good idea. You see all this isolationism and pulling back. That's exactly the wrong direction, of course. It is something we really need to rethink: our borders. When you look at the future of humanity, it's an important thing. We can't just all lock ourselves up in our own countries.'

'What happens when a country disappears?'

This, Caroline Zickgraf said to me, is one of the biggest geopolitical questions associated with climate change. Not 'disappears' in the sense of one territory breaking up into a number of other territories, or the same geographical area suddenly being given a different name. No, what about when the *land itself* is gone?

'What defines a nation?' she asked. 'Is it borders or land? Does land define a nation, and so do other countries just absorb an entire displaced people? What happens when a government is still there, but its country isn't? Do you have governments in exile?'

Caroline was talking to me from Brussels, where she works as Deputy Director of the Hugo Observatory, the first scientific research centre to be created specifically to explore the links between environment, climate change, migration and politics. (As her Twitter bio puts it, 'I'll study anything that moves. Well, people mostly.')

She was telling me about the impacts of coastal erosion and rising sea levels on global communities. Caroline had previously worked as a researcher in Guet N'Dar, a fishing quarter in Senegal's second biggest city of Saint-Louis where 97 per cent of the population is dependent directly on fishing – both men and women, catching fish, selling fish, smoking fish, salting fish.[37]

'Anything that happens to the fish dramatically affects these people's ability to feed themselves,' she said.

The community of Guet N'Dar is one of the most densely populated in all of Africa, living on a very narrow finger of land called the Langue de Barbarie. The Senegal River is on one side and the Atlantic Ocean on the other.

'And due to erosion the land is carving away. You're already seeing houses being destroyed. And then there are changing currents, increasingly large waves and storm surges, more fisherman dying in more dangerous waters.'

At the same time, the fishing grounds are shifting. As one fisherman had said to her, 'The fish are migrating; so must we.'[38] Large numbers of the community are having to move northwards, a few miles across the border into Mauritania, spending sometimes up to ten months of the year outside their own country, because otherwise their livelihoods would be unsustainable. The fishermen then use this income to build new houses for their families, either on less crowded parts of the peninsula where the land is not so susceptible to erosion, or in the city of Saint-Louis itself.

'They are using international migration to finance really localised relocation away from sea-level rise.'

As Caroline described it, 'From a European perspective there is always this idea that everybody is coming to Europe. And that's why climate and migration matters. Which I find frustrating, because it's not what happens. There's a lot of hubris in that: the idea that everybody is just desperate to come to Europe. As if that was a choice that they would want. What I've seen in Senegal is that people do not want to go to Europe. They want to stay near to their homelands and, even in this dynamic, where these fishermen move internationally, it is so they can come back. It is so they can stay.'

The situation changes, however, if there is *nowhere to come back to*. Guet N'Dar may, in time, be inundated and destroyed by erosion. The community is trying to adapt, and, while its ultimate loss may cause hardship and movement, it is still just one small sliver of Senegal. But what about those places facing an immediate, all-encompassing threat?

'That's particularly a concern for countries in the South Pacific,' Caroline said. 'Small island developing states, low-lying atolls in the Indian Ocean, the Maldives. What happens when these places don't in a physical sense exist, and yet, in all other senses, *do exist*.'

Take, for instance, Tuvalu, a series of coral islands and atolls in the Pacific Ocean that is home to a population of around 12,000 people. For years now, Tuvalu has been viewed, from the outside, as a kind of laboratory for climate change – one of the first nations in history likely to be consumed by the rising seas, its people the original 'climate refugees'. Perhaps unsurprisingly, many Tuvaluans bristle at this portrayal, which tends to fetishise their plight as the inhabitants of a drowning world – a people fated to see their culture disappear beneath the waves.

'We wouldn't like to eventually get forced out of our place and be classed as environmental refugees,' as one Tuvaluan put it. 'That has a negative attachment to it. It's like considering ourselves like second-class citizens in the future. It devalues your feelings as a human being. It makes you feel small and negative about yourself. And it doesn't make you fully human.'

Or, in the words of another islander, 'We have been moving in history. Tuvaluans have been moving from place to place all the time. We have moved from island to island.'[39]

Those, like the Tuvaluans, who find themselves on this so-called front line of climate change *are* beginning to frame a response to the question: what happens to a disappearing country? For them, it is not about rescue and flight, but rather about migration being an innate part of their culture. And, indeed, an innate part of *all* human culture. One response to a vanishing land is to assert global citizenship. Culture is borderless, so why can't a nation be too?

'Climate change has made a laughing stock of our borders,' Caroline said to me. 'As if they are *real* borders. There's a big question mark about their sustainability. Not just as borders, but as a symbol of our geopolitical systems and states. In many ways, these systems are exactly why we are facing this existential crisis.'

The pressure is building, inexorably, on the fabric of the lines that we have drawn.

'If you talk about small island states,' she said, 'part of the reason that is a struggle is because *there is nowhere else to go*. But there's also a struggle where there is somewhere else to go, *but it's not yours*.'

Today, nearly 50 per cent of the world's population lives in coastal areas, while around 10 per cent – more than 600 million people – are settled in places that are less than ten metres above sea level.[40]

'And sea-level rise is going to push us in, or up, or whatever. And then, eventually, mass relocation becomes not a question of national governance, it becomes international. Which means, just like with a disappearing island, we need to shift our ideas of what nation states are and what borders mean.'

Disappearing islands and coastlines, the ghostly drift of the human niche, leaving great archipelagos of uninhabitability in its wake. Of course, it seems inevitable that borders will reach a point where they have to change. But change how?

'There's always an up and a down with borders,' Caroline said. 'They are never static; they are never fixed. There are moments when we feel like enforcing them more, putting on a big show of our borders.'

This, it seems, has only been exacerbated by fears over climate change. As if you could build a barrier to keep the heat and the sea and the uncertainty out. Which, of course, you can't. What you can do, however, is keep out the collateral damage. The people.

'Because what we know happens is that the scare stories don't motivate climate action; they put up walls,' Caroline said. 'You say, *we need to do something about climate change*. But what people hear is, *we need to do something about migration*.'

Out of this the concept of 'climate nationalism' has begun to emerge. Among some of the far-right, populist parties of Europe, there has been a shift away from a rhetoric that denies the impacts of climate change and a move towards an emphasis on the dangers that a warming planet presents to national interests.[41]

'People are used as pawns in this narrative of doom about climate change,' Caroline said. 'Which makes them more vulnerable. Because we've incited more walls, whether those walls are physical or otherwise. *Fortress Europe. Tighten. More restrictive policies*.'

Apocalyptic narratives talk of a 'human tide' or a 'human tsunami', of 'floods' of people. Of course, the natural response to a colossal wave is to repel it, to keep it out, to build up and increase borders in the face of a seemingly catastrophic threat. The Freedom Party of Austria (FPÖ) has said, 'Climate change must never become a recognised justification for asylum.' If it did, they warn, 'the dams will finally break, and Europe and Austria will also be flooded with millions of climate refugees'.[42] Dams, floods, tides, waves. Always this language of inundation. Other far-right leaders, like Matteo Salvini in Italy, invoke this fear at the same time as ridiculing it. 'What is the climate migrant?' he said. 'If he is cold in winter and hot in summer, does he migrate? Let's be serious. We already have so many. Is the climate migrant also one from Milan who does not like fog?'[43]

The prospect arises of borders not breaking, but rising up, higher and stronger – almost as if you could section off your entire slice of the earth, from the crust to the stratosphere. Pursue what parties like Italy's Lega call 'national climate adaptation', or which the FPÖ wraps up in their concept of Heimattreue – 'being true to your homeland'.[44]

As Caroline said, there's always an up and a down with borders. So perhaps it is inevitable that, for some, the lines have become so deeply ingrained that the logical endpoint is a kind of hermetic sealing, as if you could turn your whole country into one great, geodesic dome. Fabricate your edges as a solid, impermeable membrane; watch the waves break against them or rise higher and higher up their transparent sides. There are few futures I can think of more dystopian than that.

When I talked to Tabi about climate nationalism he gave a long, wry laugh, rocking backward and forward on his chair.

'Yes, okay, *let us destroy our air*,' he said, still chuckling. '*It is not your air. Let us frack because the earth here is ours, the water here is ours. It is none of your business. Or let us just deforest the Congo rainforest. Dry up the whole of the Sahel because it's none of your business, because it is our climate.*

'And tomorrow someone might say, *Africa is your space, so why not take care of your space? It's your bullshit space, we don't care. It's your climate, it's your problem*.'

Could the Great Green Wall be an antidote to this? A transnational, continent-sized, ecological border designed, specifically, as a magnet for communities and for collaboration. A wall to attract people, not repel them?

'If we can succeed,' Camilla said to me, 'we have a good model for what we can do elsewhere. I'd love to see Great Green Walls everywhere. In Latin America, Central America or across Central Asia. These kinds of co-ordinated efforts of corridor landscape restoration. Because you get the kind of scale you need to really achieve something.'

Perhaps, I had suggested to her, a Great Green Wall could run from the mouth of the Rio Grande to Tijuana, through the arid reaches dividing Mexico from the United States? Make a landscape of opposition one of production and cooperation?

'As a UN official,' she said, 'I don't have any position on these kinds of things.'

In 2019, another branch of the UN, the Food and Agriculture Organisation (FAO), announced a Great Green Wall for Cities initiative, to create half a million hectares of new 'urban forests' and restore 300,000 hectares of existing natural forests in and around cities in the Sahel and Central Asia. The artist's impression that accompanied the FAO press release showed an even larger green wall, running along its current route from West to East Africa, but then going much further: crossing into the Arabian Peninsula, Iran and Afghanistan; tracking the line of Himalayas in Pakistan and India; curving through China; ending finally on the Russian coast of the Sea of Japan. The drawing was a fiction, a figment. But, as Camilla said to me, that, in part, was the point.[45]

'What is most compelling about the Great Green Wall is the size, the scale, the brand,' she said. 'I've worked in this organisation for a long time, and in the past I've tried to convey to people what I'm doing, and they kind of glaze over, not understanding anything – but the Great Green Wall *they get*. Yes, it's a dream. But I think you need that kind of vision and dream to achieve massive things.'

Dream or not, what is certain is that, right now, the Great Green Wall maps exactly onto the fragile border of Marten's human climate niche. Temperature is rising faster in the Sahel than the global average, while, at the same time, the region's population is set to triple to 340 million in the next thirty years.[46] The wall was conceived originally as a barrier to *hold off* the Sahara. But perhaps you can turn it around now to see it as a means of *holding on* to the niche, as a mechanism for stopping the shadow of habitability from slipping away across the continents.

'I want to make Africa different,' Tabi said to me. 'Make my office this forest. This is where I will spend the rest of my life.'

Drawing a green line across a great shore.

This line's story will be told in the soil. 'I will show you fear in a handful of dust,' wrote Eliot, in another line from *The Waste Land.* Can the land hold on, can it resist, in the face of the heat or the drought to come? In the years that follow, will the shadow of the human niche still, each morning, 'stride' behind this Great Green Wall, then 'rise at evening' to meet it?[47] Or will it become untethered, float away? Humanity's ultimate border set loose on the winds.

ACKNOWLEDGMENTS

This is a book that could not have been written or published without the help, support and input of a large number of people.

Many very busy individuals gave up their time for interviews – either in person or virtually – and I'm indebted to them for their generosity and insight. Special thanks go out to Hans Ragnar Mathisen, Ivar Bjorklund, Baha Hilo, David Taylor, Marcos Ramirez, Jason de Leon, Laiken Jordahl, Carlos Spottorno, Marco Ferrari, Robert Ciatti, Andreas Putzer, Benjamin tenOever, Daisy Hoagland, Tabi Joda, Camilla Nordheim-Larsen, Marten Scheffer and Caroline Zickgraf. Our conversations were rich, fascinating, incredibly enjoyable and often lasted for several hours. Many took place during a global lockdown, and there was something so special about this ability to reach out to people in places ranging from Milan to Tijuana, New York to Cameroon, at a time when physical travel was impossible. Their contributions to the stories featured in this book are invaluable.

A huge thank you to the wonderful publishing team at Canongate – my editor Simon Thorogood, along with Francis Bickmore, Vicki Rutherford, Melissa Tombere, Jessica Neale, Anna Frame, Caitriona Horne, Jenny Fry, Alison Rae and everyone who has worked on *The Edge of the Plain*. Thanks also to Creative Scotland for their support towards the research and writing of this book.

I am, as ever, eternally indebted to my friend and agent Maggie Hattersley – whose last act before she retired was to sell this book (her work here was done!). Without her guidance, advice and support over the past twenty years, I'm not entirely sure I would be a writer at all. Thanks also to Jon Wood at RCW, who has been a huge help in ushering this book towards publication.

I'm also delighted to be published by the fantastic W. W. Norton in the United States. It has been an absolute pleasure working with my editor Helen Thomaides and her team, including Elizabeth Riley, Gina Savoy, and Michelle Waters on publicity and marketing, and Dassi Zeidel and Louise Mattarelliano on production. America's bordering story is a big part of this book and Norton is the perfect partner to bring it to readers in the US.

And a final thanks – of course – to Hazel, Brodie and Nate.

IMAGE CREDITS

All images the author's own aside from the following:

p. 60	PLAKLE, Creative Commons, by Wikimedia Commons
p. 162	DeLIMITations, Marcos Ramírez ERRE and David Taylor, 2014
p. 204	Yesica Uvina, Courtesy of U.S. Customs and Border Protection
pp. 240 and 262	Photos by Carlos Spottorno
p. 310	Reprinted from *Immunity*, Vol 54, Third edition. Daisy A. Hoagland, Rasmus Møller, Skyler Uhl, Kohei Oishi, Justin Frere, Ilona Golynker, Shu Horiuchi, Maryline Panis, Daniel Blanco-Melo, David Sachs, Knarik Arkun, Jean K. Lim, Benjamin R. tenOever. 'Leveraging the antiviral type I interferon system as a first line of defense against SARS-CoV-2 pathogenicity' (2021). With permission from Elsevier.
p. 346	© Jason Edwards, bio-images.com

NOTES

Introduction

1. A. Ghosh, *The Shadow Lines* (John Murray, 2011).

Prologue: The Edge of the Plain

1. S. N. Kramer, 'Sumerian historiography', *Israel Exploration Journal* 3, no. 4 (1953).
2. I. Finkel and S. Rey, *no man's land* (British Museum Press, 2018).
3. J. S. Cooper, 'Reconstructing history from ancient inscriptions: the Lagash–Umma border conflict', *Sources from the Ancient Near East*, vol. 2 (1983); Finkel and Rey, *no man's land*; Kramer, 'Sumerian historiography'.
4. The British Museum speculates that it was found by the Mosul-born archaeologist Hormuzd Rassam, the man who discovered the clay tablets containing our earliest work of literature, *The Epic of Gilgamesh.*
5. Finkel and Rey, *no man's land.*
6. Finkel and Rey, *no man's land.*
7. Finkel and Rey, *no man's land.*
8. Cooper, 'Reconstructing history from ancient inscriptions'.
9. I. J. Winter, 'After the battle is over: the "stele of the vultures" and the beginning of historical narrative in the art of the Ancient Near East', *Studies in the History of Art*, vol. 16, Symposium Papers IV: Pictorial Narrative in Antiquity and the Middle Ages, National Gallery of Art (1985); Cooper, 'Reconstructing history from ancient inscriptions'; Kramer, 'Sumerian historiography'.
10. Winter, 'After the battle is over'.

11. S. N. Kramer, *The Sumerians: Their History, Culture and Character* (The University of Chicago Press, 1963)
12. Kramer, *The Sumerians.*
13. Kramer, *The Sumerians.*
14. Kramer, *The Sumerians.*
15. Ole Grøn, 'Territorial infrastructure, markers and tension in Late Mesolithic hunter-gatherer societies: an ethnoarchaeological approach', *Muge 150th: The 150th Anniversary of the Discovery of Mesolithic Shell Middens*, vol. 2. (Cambridge Scholars Publishing, 2015).
16. C. Michael Barton, G. A. Clark and Allison E. Cohen, 'Art as information: explaining Upper Palaeolithic art in Western Europe', *World Archaeology* 26, no. 2 (1994).
17. Grøn, 'Territorial infrastructure, markers and tension in Late Mesolithic hunter-gatherer societies'.

1. Line of Bones

1. P. Koch, 'Sámi-state relations and its impact on reindeer herding across the Norwegian–Swedish border', *Nomadic and Indigenous Spaces: Productions and Cognitions* (Routledge, 2016).
2. E. Demant Hatt, *With the Lapps in the High Mountains: A Woman Among the Sámi, 1907–1908* (University of Wisconsin Press, 2013); B. Sjoholm, *Black Fox: A Life of Emilie Demant Hatt, Artist and Ethnographer* (University of Wisconsin Press, 2017); K. Kuutma, 'Collaborative ethnography before its time: Johan Turi and Emilie Demant Hatt', *Scandinavian Studies* 75, no. 2 (2003), pp. 165–80; K. Kuutma, 'Encounters to negotiate a Sámi ethnography: the process of collaborative representations', *Scandinavian Studies* 83, no. 4 (2011), pp. 491–518.
3. M. Tryland and S. J. Kutz, *Reindeer and Caribou; Health and Disease* (CRC Press, 2018).
4. R. Paine, *Coastal Lapp Society* (Tromsø Museum, 1957); *Ottars beretning* (Othere's tale in a new Norwegian translation by Arthur O. Sandved), Janet Bately (1984); See the 'Sami Culture' resource held on the website of the University of Texas, Austin: Sámi Culture; https://www.laits.utexas.edu/sami/dieda/hist/nor-sami.htm#ottar
5. K. Nickul, *The Lappish Nation: Citizens of Four Countries* (Curzon Press, 1997); I. Ruong, *The Lapps in Sweden* (AB Stockholm, 1967); N. Langston, 'Mining the boreal north', *Environment and Sustainability in a Globalizing World*, ed. A. J. Nightingale (Routledge, 2019); 'Christianity and the Emerging Nation States', Sami Culture, https://www.laits.utexas.edu/sami/diehtu/siida/christian/nationstate.htm.

6. J. Nordin, 'Embodied colonialism: the cultural meaning of silver in a Swedish colonial context in the 17th century', *Post-Medieval Archaeology* 46:1 (2012); J. Nordin, 'Metals of metabolism: the construction of industrial space and the commodification of early modern Sápmi', *Historical Archaeologies of Capitialism* (Springer, 2015); T. Aikas and A.-K.Salmi, *The Sound of Silence: Indigenous Perspectives on the Historical Archaeology of Colonialism* (Berghahn Books, 2019).
7. Nordin, 'Embodied colonialism'; Aikas and Salmi, *The Sound of Silence*; J. McCannon, *A History of the Arctic: Nature, Exploration and Exploitation* (Reaktion Books, 2013); Langston, 'Mining the boreal north'.
8. T. R. Berg, *Theatre of the World: The Maps that Made History* (Hodder & Stoughton, 2018).
9. Koch, 'Sámi-state relations and its impact on reindeer herding across the Norwegian–Swedish border'.
10. Quoted in Nickul, *The Lappish Nation.*
11. N. Kent, *The Sámi Peoples of the North: A Social and Cultural History* (Oxford University Press, 2019); Nickul, *The Lappish Nation*; M. and P. Aikio, 'A chapter in the history of the colonization of the Sámi lands: the forced migration of Norwegian reindeer Sámi to Finland in the 1800s', *Conflict in the Archaeology of Living Traditions* (Routledge, 2005).
12. Demant Hatt, *With the Lapps in the High Mountains*; Sjoholm, *Black Fox*; Kuutma, 'Collaborative ethnography before its time: Johan Turi and Emilie Demant Hatt'.
13. Demant Hatt, *With the Lapps in the High Mountains.*
14. Demant Hatt, *With the Lapps in the High Mountains.*
15. Demant Hatt, *With the Lapps in the High Mountains.*
16. Demant Hatt, *With the Lapps in the High Mountains.*
17. Demant Hatt, *With the Lapps in the High Mountains.*
18. Demant Hatt, *With the Lapps in the High Mountains*; Sjoholm, *Black Fox*; Kuutma, 'Collaborative ethnography before its time: Johan Turi and Emilie Demant Hatt'; M. Svonni, 'John Turi: first author of the Sámi', *Scandinavian Studies*, vol. 83, no. 4, winter (2011).
19. J. Turi, *Muitalus sámiid birra* ('An Account of the Sámi'), trans. T. A. DuBois (Nordic Studies Press, 2011).
20. Quoted by Sjoholm in introduction to *Black Fox.*
21. Quoted by Sjoholm in introduction to *Black Fox.*
22. Demant Hatt, *With the Lapps in the High Mountains.*
23. Demant Hatt, *With the Lapps in the High Mountains.*
24. Demant Hatt, *With the Lapps in the High Mountains.*
25. Demant Hatt, *With the Lapps in the High Mountains.*
26. Demant Hatt, *With the Lapps in the High Mountains.*

27. See also in J. Lundstrom, 'Names and places: the cartographic interventions of Hans Ragnar Mathisen' and M. T. Stephansen, 'A hand-drawn map as a decolonising document', *Afterall: A Journal of Art, Context and Enquiry*, vol. 44, winter (University of Chicago Press, 2017).
28. I. Bjorklund, *Sápmi – Becoming a Nation* (Tromsø University Museum, 2013).
29. Bjorklund, *Sápmi.*
30. Quoted in Bjorklund, *Sápmi.*
31. Lundstrom, 'Names and places'.
32. See Máret Ánne Sara's website: https://maretannesara.com/pile-o-sapmi/; A. S. Torp-Pedersen, 'You cannot beat a troll with its own tricks', *Contesting Histories: Art Practices Of/For Justice*, vol. 40, no. 3 (Kunstlicht, 2019).
33. See Maret Anne Sara's website for the artwork 'Pile O' Sapmi': http://www.pileosapmi.com; See A. S. Olsen, 'The Long Hard Cold Struggle', in *Kunstleritikk: The Nordic Journal of Contemporary Art*, 24 February 2017: https://kunstkritikk.no/the-long-hard-cold-struggle/; Office for Contemporary Art Norway, Máret Ánne Sara short film in 'Thinking at the Edge of the World. Perspectives from the North': https://www.facebook.com/oca.norway/videos/1015822229 7465294/; H. Hansen, 'Pile o' Sápmi and the connections between art and politics' (The Arctic Museum of Norway, 2019).
34. The Truth and Reconciliation Commission: https://uit.no/kommisjonen/mandat_en.
35. 'Minister says controversial copper mine needed for the green shift', *The Barents Observer*, 14 April 2019.
36. See Anders Sunna's website: http://anderssunna.com.

2. The Endless Margin

1. Herodotus, *The Histories*, 1, 82, trans. Tom Holland (Penguin, 2013).
2. Pausanias, *Description of Greece*, 2.3.85, trans. W. H. S. Jones and H. A. Omerod (Heinemann, 1918).
3. Plutarch, *Greek and Roman Parallel Stories* 306a–b, trans. F. C. Babbitt; T. Kelly, 'The traditional enmity between Sparta and Argos: the birth and development of a myth', *The American Historical Review*, 75(4) (1970).
4. Herodotus, *The Histories.*
5. D. G. Rocchi, 'Systems of borders in Ancient Greece', *Brill's Companion to Ancient Geography: The Inhabited World in Greek and Roman Tradition* (Brill, 2015).
6. *Homeric Hymn to Aphrodite*, quoted in J. McInerney, 'On the border: sacred land

and the margin of the community', *City, Countryside, and the Spatial Organization of Value in Classical Antiquity* (Brill, 2017).

7. McInerney, 'On the border'; Rocchi, 'Systems of borders in Ancient Greece'; G. Reger, 'On the border in Arizona and Greece: border studies and the boundaries of the Greek polis', *Historical Geography* 45 (2017), pp. 188–219.
8. S. G. Cole, 'Landscapes of Artemis', *The Classical World*, 93(5) (2000), pp. 471–81; McInerney, 'On the border'; Rocchi, 'Systems of borders in Ancient Greece'; Reger, 'On the border in Arizona and Greece'.
9. P. Petra, 'From polis to borders: demarcation of social and ritual space in the sanctuary of Poseidon at Kalaureia, Greece', *Temenos – Nordic Journal of Comparative Religion*, 44(2) (2008); Cole, 'Landscapes of Artemis'; McInerney, 'On the border'; Rocchi, 'Systems of borders in Ancient Greece'; Reger, 'On the border in Arizona and Greece'.
10. Reger, 'On the border in Arizona and Greece'; Cole, 'Landscapes of Artemis'.
11. McInerney, 'On the border'.
12. Euripides, *Bacchae*, trans. William Arrowsmith (Yale University Press, 1967).
13. McInerney, 'On the border'; Cole, 'Landscapes of Artemis'; Reger, 'On the border in Arizona and Greece'.
14. P. Vidal-Naquet, *The Black Hunter: Forms of Thought and Forms of Society in the Greek World* (Johns Hopkins University Press, 1987).
15. Vidal-Naquet, *The Black Hunter.*
16. C. Pélékides, *Histoire de l'éphébie attique des origines à 31 avant Jésus-christ* (De Boccard, 1962); Vidal-Naquet, *The Black Hunter.*
17. Vidal-Naquet, *The Black Hunter*; Reger, 'On the border in Arizona and Greece'.
18. Reger, 'On the border in Arizona and Greece'; Rocchi, 'Systems of borders in Ancient Greece'.
19. Rocchi, 'Systems of borders in Ancient Greece'.
20. Aristotle, *Politics*, 2.1265; quoted in Rocchi, 'Systems of borders in Ancient Greece'.
21. Aristotle, *Politics*, 7.10.133, trans. H. Rackham (Heinemann, 1932).
22. N. Bershadsky, 'Pushing the boundaries of myth: transformations of ancient border wars in archaic and classical Greece' (University of Chicago Press, 2013).
23. D. F. Elmer, 'Epikoinos: The ball game episkuros and Iliad 12.421–23', *Classical Philology* 103(4) (2008); L. O'Sullivan, 'Playing ball in Greek antiquity', *Greece & Rome*, 59(1) (2012), pp. 17–33.
24. Elmer, 'Epikoinos'.
25. Elmer, 'Epikoinos'.
26. Demosthenes, *Philippic*, 3.47–50; Vidal-Naquet, *The Black Hunter*, quoted in J. W. Humphrey, J. P. Oleson, and A. N. Sherwood, Greek and Roman

Technology: A Sourcebook: Annotated translations of Greek and Latin texts and documents (Routledge, 1998).

27. Dio Chrysostom, *Discourses*, 40 and 41, trans. H. L. Crosby (Harvard University Press, 1946).
28. Dioscorides, *Epigrams*, 7.229, trans. W. R. Paton (Heinemann, 1917).
29. Homer, *The Odyssey*, trans. Robert Fagles (Penguin, 1996).
30. G. Keyes (ed.), *The Letters of Rupert Brooke* (Faber and Faber, 1968), p. 676.
31. S. Sassoon, *Memoirs of an Infantry Officer* (Faber and Faber, 1974).
32. Private L. S. Price, quoted by M. Middlebrook in *First Day on the Somme* (Penguin, 2006); P. Fussell, *The Great War and Modern Memory* (OUP, 2000).
33. H. Williamson, *The Wet Flanders Plain* (Faber and Faber, 2009).
34. Fussell, *The Great War and Modern Memory*.
35. S. Sassoon, *Journals*: http://cudl.lib.cam.ac.uk/view/MS-ADD-09852-00001-00007/24.
36. E. Blunden, *The Mind's Eye* (Cape, 1934).
37. Major P. H. Pilditch, quoted in Fussell, *The Great War and Modern Memory*.
38. C. Carrington, *Soldier from the Wars Returning* (Hutchinson, 1965).
39. H. H. Cooper, quoted in Fussell, *The Great War and Modern Memory*.
40. T. E. Hulme, *Further Speculations*, ed. Sam Hynes (University of Minnesota Press, 1955).
41. D. Jones, *In Parenthesis* (Chilmark Press, 1962).
42. M. Brown, quoted in Fussell, *The Great War and Modern Memory*.
43. W. Owen, 'Exposure', *Poems by Wilfred Owen* (Chatto & Windus, 1920).
44. S. Casson, *Steady Drummer* (G. Bell & Sons, 1935).
45. E. Blunden, *Undertones of War* (Penguin, 1928).
46. R. Graves, 'The Kaiser's War', *Promise of Greatness* (John Day Company, 1968).
47. Quoted in Fussell, *The Great War and Modern Memory*.
48. I. Rosenberg, 'The Immortals': https://www.nationalarchives.gov.uk/rosenberg/war-poems.htm
49. Quoted in Fussell, *The Great War and Modern Memory*.
50. A. D. Gillespie, *Letters from Flanders* (Forgotten Books, 2018).
51. Gillespie, *Letters from Flanders*.
52. J. E. Winter and F. E. Winter, 'Some disputed sites and itineraries of Pausanias in the Northeast Peloponnesos', *Echos du monde classique: Classical views*, vol. 34, no. 2 (1990).
53. C. Watts, *Imperial War Museum*, quoted in Fussell, *The Great War and Modern Memory*.
54. Fussell, *The Great War and Modern Memory*.
55. D. Croxton, 'The peace of Westphalia of 1648 and the origins of sovereignty', *The International History Review*, vol. 21, no. 3 (Taylor & Francis, 1999).

56. J. O. Newman, 'Memory theatre: remembering the peace after three hundred years', *Performances of Peace: Utrecht 1713*, ed. Renger E. de Bruin et al. (Brill, 2015); M. Filho, 'Westphalia: a paradigm? A dialogue between law, art and philosophy of science', *German Law Journal* 8(10) (2007); R. Falk, 'Revisiting Westphalia, discovering post-Westphalia', *The Journal of Ethics*, vol. 6, no. 4 (Springer, 2002).
57. S. Patton, 'The peace of Westphalia and its affects on international relations, diplomacy and foreign policy', *The Histories*, vol. 10, issue 1, article 5 (2019); A. Hastings, *The Construction of Nationhood: Ethnicity, Religion and Nationalism* (CUP, 1997).
58. W. D. Smith, 'Friedrich Ratzel and the origins of Lebensraum', *German Studies Review*, vol. 3, no. 1 (German Studies Association, Johns Hopkins University Press, 1980); Hastings, *The Construction of Nationhood: Ethnicity, Religion and Nationalism.*
59. F. S. Fitzgerald, *Tender Is the Night* (Penguin, 1933).
60. Fitzgerald, *Tender Is the Night.*
61. Letter from Lutyens to Ware dated May 1917, quoted in T. Skelton and G. Gliddon, *Lutyens and the Great War* (Frances Lincoln, 2008).
62. S. Martin, *The Mythic Method: Classicism in British Art, 1920–1950* (Pallant House Gallery, 2016); R. Holland, *The Warm South: How the Mediterranean Shaped the British Imagination* (Yale University Press, 2018).
63. Fussell, *The Great War and Modern Memory.*
64. A. Burgess, *The Wanting Seed* (Norton, 1976).
65. Burgess, *The Wanting Seed.*
66. Fussell, *The Great War and Modern Memory.*

3. Limitless

1. Tacitus, *Agricola*, trans. H. Mattingly (Penguin, 2009).
2. Tacitus, *Agricola.*
3. Tacitus, *Agricola.*
4. Tacitus, *Agricola.*
5. Tacitus, *The Histories*, 1. 2, quoted by H. Mattingly, in Tacitus, *Agricola.*
6. W. Hanson and D. Breeze, 'The Antonine Wall: the current state of knowledge', *The Antonine Wall: Papers in Honour of Professor Lawrence Keppie* (Archaeopress, 2020).
7. Tacitus, *Agricola.*
8. T. Romankiewicz, K. Milek, C. Beckett, B. Russell and J. R. Synder, 'New perspectives on the structure of the Antonine Wall', *The Antonine Wall: Papers in Honour of Professor Lawrence Keppie.*

9. I. M. Ferris, 'Building an image: soldiers' labour and the Antonine Wall distance slabs', *The Antonine Wall: Papers in Honour of Professor Lawrence Keppie.*
10. R. Graves, 'The Virgil Cult', *The Virginia Quarterly Review* 38, no. 1 (1962), pp. 13–35.
11. Virgil, *Aeneid*, trans. R. Fagles (Penguin, 2006).
12. Virgil, *Aeneid.*
13. B. Knox, introduction, Virgil, *Aeneid.*
14. B. Knox, introduction, Virgil, *Aeneid.*
15. Virgil, *Aeneid.*
16. Graves, 'The Virgil Cult'.
17. R. S. O. Tomlin, 'Hadrian and Hadrian's Wall', *Britannia Romana: Roman Inscriptions and Roman Britain* (Oxbow Books, 2018), pp. 83–118.
18. Tacitus, *Agricola.*
19. D. Breeze, 'The end – and the future', *Bearsden: The Story of a Roman Fort* (Archaeopress, 2016), pp. 100–18; Hanson and Breeze, 'The Antonine Wall: the current state of knowledge', *The Antonine Wall: Papers in Honour of Professor Lawrence Keppie.*
20. A. Maldonado, 'The Early Medieval Antonine Wall', *Britannia* 46 (2015), pp. 225–45.
21. L. Keppie, 'The Hunterian Collection and its Museum', *Journal of the History of Collections*, vol. 26, no. 3 (2014), pp. 355–62; L. Keppie, 'Searching out Roman inscribed and sculptured stones on the Antonine Wall in 1723', *Britannia* 45 (2014), pp. 11–29.
22. R. S. O. Tomlin, 'Gods and men', *Britannia Romana: Roman Inscriptions and Roman Britain* (Oxbow Books, 2018), pp. 311–84; L. Allason-Jones, C. Driel-Murray and E. M. Greene, 'Roman women in Lowland Scotland', *The Antonine Wall: Papers in Honour of Professor Lawrence Keppie.*
23. D. Breeze, 'Life in the fort', *Bearsden*; Hanson and Breeze, 'The Antonine Wall: the current state of knowledge'.
24. R. Birley, *Vindolanda: Everyday Life on Rome's Northern Frontier* (Amberley, 2009).
25. C. P. Cavafy, *Complete Poems*, trans. B. Mendelsohn (Harper Press, 2013).
26. Josephus, *Jewish Wars*, trans. H. St. J. Thackery (Heinemann, 1928).
27. The Bible, Jeremiah 1:14.
28. The Bible, Joel 2:20.
29. The Bible, Ezekiel 38:15.
30. The Bible, Revelations, 20:7–8.
31. Josephus, *Jewish Antiquities*, trans. H. St. J. Thackery, Book I, 123, vol. 1 (London, 1930).
32. K. Czeglédy, 'The Syriac legend concerning Alexander the Great', *Acta Orientalia Academiae Scientiarum Hungaricae* 7, no. 2/3 (1957), pp. 231–49; F. Schmieder, 'Edges of the world – edges of time', *The Edges of the Medieval World*, eds G. Jaritz

and J. Kreem (Central European University Press, 2009); E. J. van Donzel, A. B. Schmidt and C. Ott, *Gog and Magog in Early Eastern Christian and Islamic Sources: Sallam's Quest for Alexander's Wall*, Brill's Inner Asian Library vol. 22 (Brill, 2010).

33. The Qur'an, 18:92–98.
34. Quoted in translation in van Donzel et al., *Gog and Magog in Early Eastern Christian and Islamic Sources*.
35. van Donzel et al., *Gog and Magog in Early Eastern Christian and Islamic Sources*.
36. van Donzel et al., *Gog and Magog in Early Eastern Christian and Islamic Sources*; A. Silverstein, 'Enclosed beyond Alexander's Barrier: on the comparative study of 'Abbāsid culture', *Journal of the American Oriental Society* 134, no. 2 (2014), pp. 287–306; V. I. Scherb, 'Assimilating giants: the appropriation of Gog and Magog in medieval and early modern England', *Journal of Medieval and Early Modern Studies* 32, no. 1 (2002), pp. 59–84; Czeglédy, 'The Syriac legend concerning Alexander the Great'.
37. van Donzel et al., *Gog and Magog in Early Eastern Christian and Islamic Sources*.
38. A. Gow, '*Gog* and *Magog* on *mappaemundi* and early printed world maps: orientalizing ethnography in the apocalyptic tradition', *Journal of Early Modern History*, vol. 2, issue 1 (Brill, 1998).
39. Schmieder, 'Edges of the world – edges of time'.
40. R. I. Meserve, 'The inhospitable land of the barbarian,' *Journal of Asian History* 16, no. 1 (1982), pp. 51–89.
41. Gow, '*Gog* and *Magog* on *mappaemundi* and early printed world maps: orientalizing ethnography in the apocalyptic tradition'.
42. van Donzel et al., *Gog and Magog in Early Eastern Christian and Islamic Sources*.
43. T. Zadeh, 'Of mummies, poets and water nymphs: tracing the codicological limits of Ibn Khurdādhbih's geography', *Abbasid Studies* IV, vol. 5 (Gibb Memorial Trust, 2013).
44. J. Griffiths, *The Great Firewall of China: How to Build and Control an Alternative Version of the Internet* (Zed Books, 2019); A. Collings, 'The Great Firewall: China and the internet', *Words of Fire: Independent Journalists Who Challenge Dictators, Drug Lords, and Other Enemies of a Free Press* (NYU Press, 2001), pp. 186–94.
45. Griffiths, *The Great Firewall of China*; Collings, 'The Great Firewall'.
46. 'Great Firewall father speaks out', *Global Times*, 18 February 2011, story archived at https://cryptome.org/0003/gwf-father.htm; Griffiths, *The Great Firewall of China*; J. Goldkorn, 'The Chinese internet: unshared destiny', eds J. Goldkorn, G. R. Barmé and L. Jaivin, *Shared Destiny* (ANU Press, 2015), pp. 106–23.
47. T. Zixue, 'The Great Firewall', *The Internet in China: Cultural, Political, and Social Dimensions (1980s–2000s)* (Routledge, 2006).
48. Zixue, 'The Great Firewall'.
49. Goldkorn, *Shared Destiny*.

50. Griffiths, *The Great Firewall of China.*
51. F. Schneider, *China's Digital Nationalism* (OUP, 2018), quoting Public Pledge of Self-Regulation and Professional Ethics for China Internet Industry. 26 March 2002, *Internet Society of China.* In original Chinese at https://www.isc.org.cn/hyzl/hyzl/listinfo-15599.html.
52. Zixue, 'The Great Firewall'.
53. Z. Rongwen, 'Scientifically understanding the natural laws of online communication, striving to boost the level of internet use and network governance', 16 September 2018, *Qiushi* – translation in R. Creemers, P. Triolo, and G. Webster, 'China's new top internet official lays out agenda for party control online', *New America,* 24 September 2018: https://www.newamerica.org/cybersecurity-initiative/digichina/blog/translation-chinas-new-top-internet-official-lays-out-agenda-for-party-control-online/.
54. Zixue, 'The Great Firewall'.
55. Quoted in Goldkorn, *Shared Destiny.*
56. Schneider, *China's Digital Nationalism*; Zixue, 'The Great Firewall'.
57. Rongwen, 'Scientifically understanding the natural laws of online communication, striving to boost the level of internet use and network governance'.
58. R. Meessen, B. Torossian and F. Bekkers, *A Horizon Scan of Trends and Developments in Hybrid Conflicts Set to Shape 2020 and Beyond* (Hague Centre for Strategic Studies, 2020); A. Riikonen, 'Decide, disrupt, destroy: information systems in great power competition with China', *Strategic Studies Quarterly* 13, no. 4 (2019); S. J. Brannen, C. S. Haig and K. Schmidt, *The Age of Mass Protests: Understanding an Escalating Global Trend* (Center for Strategic and International Studies, 2020).
59. Brannen, Haig and Schmidt, *The Age of Mass Protests.*
60. 'Google's ex-CEO Eric Schmidt says the internet will split in two by 2028', *Business Insider,* 21 September 2018: https://www.businessinsider.com/eric-schmidt-internet-will-split-in-two-2028-china-2018-9?r=US&IR=T.
61. 'Great British Firewall helps block 54m cyber attacks', *Financial Times,* 4 February 2018.

4. Walled Off

1. 'Jordan condemns Israel's plan to bring high-speed train to Western Wall', *The Times of Israel,* 18 February 2020.
2. Ateret Cohanim organisation: https://www.ateretcohanim.org/about/; and quoted in https://www.causematch.com/en/projects/ateret-2/.

3. 'Judge orders case reopened in long-running E. Jerusalem church property dispute', *Times of Israel*, 29 November 2019: https://www.timesofisrael.com/judge-orders-case-reopened-in-long-running-e-jerusalem-church-property-dispute/.
4. 'By the Jaffa Gate, final showdown looms in battle over Jerusalem's historic hotel', *The Observer*, 21 July 2019.
5. 'By the Jaffa Gate', *The Observer*.
6. D. Newman, 'Boundaries in flux: the 'Green Line' boundary between Israel and the West Bank – past, present and future', *Boundary and Territory Briefing*, vol. 1, no. 7 (University of Durham, 1995); M. Gieskes, 'The Green Line: potency, absurdity, and disruption of dichotomy in Francis Alÿs's intervention in Jerusalem', *The Imagined and Real Jerusalem in Art and Architecture*, eds J. Goudeau, M. Verhoeven and W. Weijers (Brill, 2014), pp. 33–58.
7. Digitisation on the UN website of the original British survey maps drawn on by Dayan and al-Tal were appended to the 1949 Armistice Agreement – even showing the Sellotape which was used to stick the two together. https://unispal.un.org/UNISPAL.NSF/5ba47a5c6cef541b802563e000493b8c/f03d55e48f77ab698525643b00608d34/$FILE/Arm_1949.jpg.
8. Memorandum by Sir Earle Richards of the Foreign Office, for the consideration of the Eastern Committee of the British War Cabinet, January 1919.
9. I. Black, *Enemies and Neighbours: Arabs and Jews in Palestine and Israel, 1917–2017* (Penguin, 2018).
10. S. Tamari, quoted in Black, *Enemies and Neighbours*.
11. L. Halperin, 'Petah Tikva, 1886: gender, anonymity, and the making of Zionist memory', *Jewish Social Studies* 23, no. 1 (2017).
12. Halperin, 'Petah Tikva, 1886'.
13. J. Poleskin, 'The Three Stalwarts of Petah Tikva', *Maccabaean* 33, no. 2 (1920).
14. D. Tidhar, 'Sender Hadad (Kriniker)', *Entsiklopediyah la-halutsei ha-Yishuv u-vonav: Demuyot u-temunot*, 19 vols (1947–71), in Halperin, 'Petah Tikva, 1886'.
15. United Nations Special Committee on Palestine, Report to the General Assembly, vol. 1, A/364, 3 September 1947.
16. Palestine Royal Commission Report, Presented by the Secretary of State for the Colonies to Parliament by Command of His Majesty (HM Stationery Office, July 1937).
17. United Nations Special Committee on Palestine, Report to the General Assembly.
18. United Nations Special Committee on Palestine, Report to the General Assembly.
19. J. Husseini, quoted in Black, *Enemies and Neighbours*.
20. S. Nusseibeh, *Once Upon a Country* (Farrar, Straus and Giroux, 2007).
21. A. Oz, *A Tale of Love and Darkness* (Vintage, 2004).

22. Nusseibeh, *Once Upon a Country.*
23. Oz, *A Tale of Love and Darkness.*
24. United Nations Security Council, S/1302/Rev.1, General Armistice Agreement, 3 April 1949.
25. Nusseibeh, *Once Upon a Country.*
26. Oz, *A Tale of Love and Darkness.*
27. Nusseibeh, *Once Upon a Country.*
28. E. Weizman, *Hollow Land: Israel's Architecture of Occupation* (Verso, 2007).
29. Nusseibeh, *Once Upon a Country.*
30. A. Hashimshoni, Y. Schweid and Z. Hashimshoni, Municipality of Jerusalem, *Masterplan for the City of Jerusalem, 1968* (1972), quoted in E. Weizman, *Hollow Land.*
31. Nusseibeh, *Once Upon a Country.*
32. Nusseibeh, *Once Upon a Country.*
33. N. Ibrahim, 'Olive groves in the West Bank have become a battleground', *Time*, 1 November 2019.
34. 'Forestry & green innovations', Jewish National Fund USA: https://www.jnf.org/menu-2/our-work/forestry-green-innovations.
35. R. Shehadeh, *Palestinian Walks: Notes on a Vanishing Landscape* (Profile, 2007).
36. F. Pearce, 'In Israel, questions are raised about a forest that rises from the desert', Yale School of the Environment, 30 September 2019: https://e360.yale.edu/features/in-israel-questions-are-raised-about-a-forest-that-rises-from-the-desert; J. Brownswell, 'Resistance is fertile: Palestine's eco-war', *Al-Jazeera*, 1 September 2011; I. Braverman, 'Uprooting identities: the regulation of olive trees in the Occupied West Bank', *PoLAR*, vol. 32, no. 2 (2009), pp. 237–63; Buffalo Legal Studies Research Paper (2009); Y. Galai, 'Narratives of redemption: the international meaning of afforestation in the Israeli Negev', *International Political Sociology*, vol. 11, issue 3 (September 2017).
37. Braverman, 'Uprooting identities'.
38. I. Pappe, *The Ethnic Cleansing of Palestine* (Oneworld, 2007).
39. Shehadeh, *Palestinian Walks.*
40. Interactive map produced by the research agency Forensic Architecture, based at Goldsmiths University of London: https://conquer-and-divide.btselem.org/map-en.html.
41. A history of al-Walaja produced by the NGO Zochrot (which means 'remembering' in Hebrew) to raise awareness of the Nakba: https://zochrot.org/en/village/49135.
42. Al-Walaja profile produced by the United Nations Relief and Works Agency (UNRWA) for Palestine refugees in the Near East: https://www.unrwa.org/resources/reports/al-walaja-miniprofile; UNRWA profile of al-Walaja prepared for the International Court of Justice: https://www.unrwa.org/userfiles/

image/articles/2013/The_International_Court_of_Justice_AlWalaja_mini_profile.pdf; UNRWA news report on al-Walaja: https://www.unrwa.org/newsroom/features/six-years-barrier-casts-shadow-over-west-bank-life.

43. UNRWA; G. Levy and A. Levac, 'Israel is turning an ancient Palestinian village into a national park for settlers', *Haaretz*, 25 October 2019.
44. Gieskes, 'The Green Line'.
45. Website of artist Francis Alÿs compiling his work on 'The Green Line': http://francisalys.com/the-green-line-yael-dayan/.
46. This story features in the display materials of the Walled Off Hotel's own museum.
47. Weizman, *Hollow Land*
48. E. Weizman, *The Least of All Possible Evils: A Short History of Humanitarian Violence* (Verso, 2011).
49. Quote from interview with E. Weizman, as recorded in *The Least of All Possible Evils*.
50. Quoted in Weizman, *Hollow Land*.
51. S. Haddad, 'Song of the Birds', *Palestine +100: Stories From a Century After Nakba*, B. Ghalayini (ed.) (Comma Press, 2019).
52. M. Kayyal, 'N', *Palestine +100*.
53. Z. Jabotinsky, 'The Iron Wall': https://www.jewishvirtuallibrary.org/quot-the-iron-wall-quot.
54. Y. Liebowitz, 'The Territories', *Judaism, Human Values and the Jewish State* (Harvard University Press, 1992).
55. Shehadeh, *Palestinian Walks*.
56. R. Shehadeh, *Language of War, Language of Peace* (Profile, 2015).
57. A. Oz, *Dear Zealots* (Chatto & Windus, 2017).

5. The Lost Border

1. From the project blog of the DeLIMITations artwork, M. Ramírez: https://delimitationsblog.tumblr.com (author's translation from Spanish).
2. Ramírez, 'DeLIMITtations'.
3. Ramírez, 'DeLIMITations'.
4. D. Taylor, *Working the Line* (Radius Books, 2010).
5. Treaty of Guadalupe Hidalgo in US National Archives Catalog: https://catalog.archives.gov/id/299809.
6. M. Dear, 'Monuments, manifest destiny, and Mexico, Part 2', *Prologue*, vol. 37, no. 2 (2005): https://www.archives.gov/publications/prologue/2005/summer/mexico-2.

7. Dear, 'Monuments, manifest destiny, and Mexico, Part 2'.
8. 'Photographic views of old monuments and characteristic scenes along the boundary line of United States and Mexico west of the Rio Grande', Library of Congress: https://loc.gov/item/2005689733; Report of the Boundary commission upon the survey and re-marking of the boundary between the United States and Mexico west of the Rio Grande, 1891–1896 . . . Part I. Report of the International commission. Part II. Report of the United States section, Library of Congress: https://www.loc.gov/item/02002130/.
9. Treaty of Adams–Onis, 1819: https://avalon.law.yale.edu/19th_century/sp1819.asp.
10. Treaty of Adams–Onis, 1819.
11. Ramírez, 'DeLIMITations'.
12. T. E. Breckenridge, *Thomas E. Breckenridge Memoirs*, 1894, University of Missouri at Columbia: Western Historical Manuscripts Collection.
13. Ramírez, 'DeLIMITations'.
14. M. Dixon, *The Manuscript Journal of Charles Mason and Jeremiah Dixon with Historical Prelude to their Survey*, 1763, available from the US Department of State and archived online: https://archive.org/details/JournalOfMasonAndDixon/page/n3/mode/2up.
15. H. W. Robinson, 'A note on Charles Mason's ancestry and his family', *Proceedings of the American Philosophical Society*, vol. 93, no. 2 (American Philosophical Society, 1949).
16. H. Woolf, 'British preparations for observing the transit of Venus of 1761', *The William and Mary Quarterly*, vol. 13, no. 4 (Omohundro Institute of Early American History and Culture, 1956).
17. T. MacKenzie, 'Mason and Dixon at the Cape', *Monthly Notes of the Astronomical Society of South Africa*, vol. 10 (1951).
18. E. Danson, *Drawing the Line: How Mason and Dixon Surveyed the Most Famous Border in America* (Wiley, 2017).
19. Dixon, *The Manuscript Journal of Charles Mason and Jeremiah Dixon with Historical Prelude to their Survey*; Danson, *Drawing the Line*.
20. Calvert Papers, Historical Society of Maryland, quoted in S. M. Walker, *Boundaries* (Candlewick Press, 2014).
21. Dixon, *The Manuscript Journal of Charles Mason and Jeremiah Dixon with Historical Prelude to their Survey*; Danson, *Drawing the Line*.
22. Letter from John Lukens to Charles Peters, 16 June 1762, Chew Family Papers, collection 2050, box 25, quoted in Walker, *Boundaries*.
23. Thomas Penn, quoted in T. D. Cope, 'Charles Mason and Jeremiah Dixon', *The*

Scientific Monthly, vol. 62, no. 6 (American Association for the Advancement of Science, 1946).

24. C. Calvert, quoted in Danson, *Drawing the Line*.
25. Dixon, *The Manuscript Journal of Charles Mason and Jeremiah Dixon with Historical Prelude to their Survey*.
26. Report of the Lords Commissioners for Trade and Plantations on the Petition of the Honourable Thomas Walpole, Benjamin Franklin, John Sargent, and Samuel Wharton, Esquires, and their Associates, 1772: https://www.gutenberg.org/cache/epub/26900/pg26900-images.html.
27. Dixon, *The Manuscript Journal of Charles Mason and Jeremiah Dixon with Historical Prelude to their Survey*.
28. Letter from George Washington to William Crawford, 17 September 1767: https://founders.archives.gov/documents/Washington/02-08-02-0020.
29. Danson, *Drawing the Line*; G. Grandin, *The End of the Myth* (Metropolitan, 2019).
30. Dixon, *The Manuscript Journal of Charles Mason and Jeremiah Dixon with Historical Prelude to their Survey*.
31. Dixon, *The Manuscript Journal of Charles Mason and Jeremiah Dixon with Historical Prelude to their Survey*.
32. Dixon, *The Manuscript Journal of Charles Mason and Jeremiah Dixon with Historical Prelude to their Survey*.
33. Dixon, *The Manuscript Journal of Charles Mason and Jeremiah Dixon with Historical Prelude to their Survey*.
34. Dixon, *The Manuscript Journal of Charles Mason and Jeremiah Dixon with Historical Prelude to their Survey*.
35. Dixon, *The Manuscript Journal of Charles Mason and Jeremiah Dixon with Historical Prelude to their Survey*.
36. Dixon, *The Manuscript Journal of Charles Mason and Jeremiah Dixon with Historical Prelude to their Survey*.
37. Grandin, *The End of the Myth*.
38. M. Twain, *Life on the Mississippi* (Dawson, 1883).
39. John Randolph, quoted in E. S. Brown, *The Constitutional History of the Louisiana Purchase, 1803–1812* (Wentworth Press, 2019); and quoted in Grandin, *The End of the Myth*.
40. J. L. O'Sullivan, 'Annexation', *United States Magazine and Democratic Review 17* (July–August 1845); quoted in J. Shapiro, *Shakespeare in a Divided America* (Faber, 2020).
41. J. M. Faragher (ed.), *Rereading Frederick Jackson Turner* (Henry Holt & Company, 1994).
42. F. J. Turner, 'The significance of the frontier in American history' (Annual Report of the American Historical Association, 1893): https://www.historians.

org/about-aha-and-membership/aha-history-and-archives/historical-archives/the-significance-of-the-frontier-in-american-history-(1893).

43. Turner, 'The significance of the frontier in American history'.
44. Turner, 'The significance of the frontier in American history'.
45. Turner, 'The significance of the frontier in American history'.
46. Turner acknowledges this at the start of his essay. Quoted from 'Distribution of population according to density: 1890', US Census Office, 11th Census, 1890, *Extra Census Bulletin 2* (20 April 1891).
47. H. Melville, *Mardi, and a Voyage Hither* (Harper & Brothers, 1849).
48. N. J. Sales, 'Meet your neighbour, Thomas Pynchon', *New York Magazine*, November 1996.
49. A. Nazaryn, 'A personal foray into the long-lost Pynchon tapes', *The New York Times*, 19 May 2017.
50. T. Pynchon, *Mason & Dixon* (Vintage, 1997).
51. Pynchon, *Mason & Dixon.*
52. Pynchon, *Mason & Dixon.*
53. Pynchon, *Mason & Dixon.*
54. Pynchon, *Mason & Dixon*; see also S. Olster, 'A "patch of england, at a three-thousand-mile off-set"? Representing America in "Mason & Dixon"', *Modern Fiction Studies*, vol. 50, no. 2 (Johns Hopkins University Press, 2004); A. N. Éigeartaigh, '"Toto, I have a feeling we're not in Kansas anymore": borders and borderlands in Thomas Pynchon's "Gravity's Rainbow" and "Mason and Dixon"', *Irish Journal of American Studies*, vol. 11/12 (Irish Association for American Studies, 2002); D. Cowart, 'The Luddite vision: Mason and Dixon', *American Literature*, vol. 71, no. 2 (Duke University Press, 1999); S. Cohen, '"Mason & Dixon" & the Ampersand', *Twentieth-Century Literature*, vol. 48, no. 3 (Duke University Press, Hofstra University, 2002).
55. Abraham Lincoln and Stephen A. Douglas debates: https://www.bartleby.com/251/; see also E. Osnos, 'Pulling our politics back from the brink', *The New Yorker*, 16 November 2020.
55. Quoted in Shapiro, *Shakespeare in a Divided America.*
57. Quoted by S. H. Bradford, *Scenes in the Life of Harriet Tubman*: https://docsouth.unc.edu/neh/bradford/bradford.html.
58. Pynchon, *Mason & Dixon.*
59. Pynchon, *Mason & Dixon.*
60. Pynchon, *Mason & Dixon.*
61. Pynchon, *Mason & Dixon.*
62. See more on this from David Taylor in 'Refuge and fortification', *Places Journal*: https://placesjournal.org/article/refuge-and-fortification-in-the-us-mexico-borderlands/.

6. Hostile Terrain

1. 'Eight ways to build a border wall', *The New York Times*, 8 November 2017.
2. Website of the PROTOTYPES artwork: https://www.borderwallprototypes.org.
3. M. Walker, 'Is Donald Trump, Wall-Builder in Chief, a conceptual artist?', *The New York Times*, 3 January 2018.
4. 'Artists, curators respond to Christoph Büchel's Border Wall Project', ARTnews (with link to full text of open letter): https://www.artnews.com/art-news/news/artists-curators-respond-christoph-buchels-border-wall-project-9775/.
5. Walker, 'Is Donald Trump, Wall-Builder in Chief, a conceptual artist?'.
6. J. Saltz, 'Trump's border wall prototypes: a kind of national monument to American nativism', *Vulture*, 17 January 2018.
7. 'Cawthorn drops the Donument Act': https://cawthorn.house.gov/media/press-releases/press-release-rep-cawthorn-drops-donument-act
8. 'AG lawsuit seeks environmental impact study on federal immigration policy', *Arizona Capitol Times*, 12 April 2021.
9. C. D'Angelo, 'There's plans to protect Trump's half-finished border wall as a monument', *HuffPost*, 14 April 2021.
10. J. De León, *The Land of Open Graves: Living and Dying on the Migrant Trail* (University of California, 2015).
11. Undocumented Migration Project: https://www.undocumentedmigrationproject.org/home.
12. Humane Borders: https://humaneborders.org/2020-was-deadliest-year-for-migrants-crossing-unlawfully-into-us-via-arizona/.
13. From webpage 'About Humane Borders': https://humaneborders.info.
14. 'Why no one understands immigration, and why we need to with Jason De León', *Factually!* podcast: https://podcasts.apple.com/us/podcast/why-no-one-understands-immigration-why-we-need-to-jason/id1463460577?i=1000469506298.
15. De León, *The Land of Open Graves.*
16. De León, *The Land of Open Graves.*
17. De León, *The Land of Open Graves.*
18. De León, *The Land of Open Graves.*
19. De León, *The Land of Open Graves.*
20. Border Patrol Strategic Plan 1994 and Beyond: https://www.hsdl.org/?view&did=721845.
21. Government Accountability Office, 'Report to the Committee on the Judiciary, US Senate and the Committee on the Judiciary, House of Representatives;

Illegal Immigration: Southwest Border Strategy Results Inconclusive; More Evaluation Needed', 1997: https://www.gao.gov/assets/ggd-98-21.pdf.

22. Government Accountability Office, 'INS's Southwest Border Strategy; Resource and Impact Issues remain after Seven Years', Report to Congressional Requesters, 2001: https://www.gao.gov/assets/gao-01-842.pdf.
23. Undocumented Migration Project, Hostile Terrain 94 art project: https://www.undocumentedmigrationproject.org/hostileterrain94.
24. 'Brazen environmental upstart brings legal muscle, nerve to climate debate', *The New York Times*, 30 March 2010.
25. L. Jordahl, 'Organ pipe cactus wilderness: wilderness character narrative and baseline monitoring assessment' (National Park Service, US Department of the Interior, March 2017).
26. Jordahl, 'Organ pipe cactus wilderness'.
27. Jordahl, 'Organ pipe cactus wilderness'.
28. R. Carranza, 'Trump is rebuilding Arizona's border fence – and taking groundwater from an iconic desert preserve to do so': https://eu.azcentral.com/story/news/politics/border-issues/2019/09/05/where-water-arizona-border-wall-coming-from/2157543001/.
29. H.R. 6157 (115th) Department of Defense and Labor, Health and Human Services, and Education Appropriations Act, 2019 and Continuing Appropriations Act, 2019: https://www.congress.gov/bill/115th-congress/house-bill/6157/text?r=8.
30. Judge Haywood S. Gilliam Jr, United States District Court Northern District of California, Sierra Club et al., plaintiffs v Donald J. Trump et al., defendants: https://assets.documentcloud.org/documents/6026005/California-Border-Wall-20190524.pdf.
31. 'Supreme Court lets Trump proceed on border wall', *The New York Times*, 26 July 2019.
32. 'Determination Pursuant to Section 102 of the Illegal Immigration Reform and Immigrant Responsibility Act of 1996, as Amended', Department of Homeland Security: https://www.federalregister.gov/documents/2018/10/10/2018-21930/determination-pursuant-to-section-102-of-the-illegal-immigration-reform-and-immigrant-responsibility.
33. Carranza, 'Trump is rebuilding Arizona's border fence – and taking groundwater from an iconic desert preserve to do so'.
34. 'Biden cancels border wall projects Trump paid for with diverted military funds', *The Washington Post*, 30 April 2021.
35. 'Trump's incomplete border wall is in pieces that could linger for decades', *The New York Times*, 16 March 2021
36. National Park Service National Register of Historic Places: https://npgallery.nps.gov/GetAsset/1073cb1a-5bb0-4114-a4ec-e396310a5654.

37. National Park Service National Register of Historic Places: https://npgallery.nps.gov/GetAsset/1073cb1a-5bb0-4114-a4ec-e396310a5654.
38. O. Zepeda, *Ocean Power: Poems from the Desert* (University of Arizona, 1995).
39. Zepeda, *Ocean Power.*
40. 'Border wall would cleave tribe, and its connection to ancestral land', *The New York Times*, 20 February 2017; Examining the Effect of the Border Wall on Private and Tribal Landowners, House Homeland Security Subcommittee: https://www.congress.gov/event/116th-congress/house-event/110571; E. M. Luna-Firebaugh, 'The border crossed us: border crossing issues of the indigenous peoples of the Americas', *Wicazo Sa Review*, vol. 17, no. 1 (University of Minnesota Press, 2002); G. L. Cadava, 'Borderlands of modernity and abandonment: the lines within Ambos Nogales and the Tohono O'odham Nation', *The Journal of American History*, vol. 98, no. 2 (Organization of American Historians, 2011); R. Hays, 'Cross-border indigenous nations: a history', *Race, Poverty and the Environment*, vol. 6/7 (Reimagine!, 1996).
41. M. Dicintio, 'Ofelia Rivas, the Tohono O'Odham, and the Wall', 19 January 2019: https://marcellodicintio.com/2019/01/19/ofelia-rivas-the-tohono-oodham-and-the-wall/.
42. F. Bell, K. M. Anderson and Y. Stewart, 'The Quitobaquito Cemetery and its History', US Department of the Interior, National Park Service, December 1980: http://npshistory.com/series/anthropology/wacc/quitobaquito/report.pdf.
43. 'There is no word for wall in our language', *El País*, 15 March 2017.
44. O. Zepeda, 'Ocotillo Memorial', *Where Clouds Are Formed* (University of Arizona, 2008).

7. Border Burning

1. I. Alexander-Nathani, *Burning at Europe's Borders* (OUP, 2021); I. Alexander-Nathani, 'Meet a boy who survived "The Crossing"', 5 July 2017: https://gpinvestigations.pri.org/meet-a-boy-who-survived-the-crossing-667e7234c397; E. Tyszler, 'From controlling mobilities to control over women's bodies: gendered effects of EU border externalization in Morocco', *CMS* 7, 25 (2019); M. Bausells, 'In limbo in Melilla', *The Guardian*, 10 May 2017; C. Spottorno and G. Abril, *La Grieta* (The Crack) (Astiberri, 2015).
2. C. Spottorno and G. Abril, 'A las puertos de Europa' (At the gates of Europe), *El País Semanal*: https://elpais.com/especiales/2014/europa-frontera-sur/el-relato.html.
3. Spottorno and Abril, *La Grieta.*

4. A. Ruiz Benedicto, M. Akkerman and P. Brunet, 'A walled world: towards a global apartheid', Transnational Institute, 18 November 2020: https://www.tni.org/files/publication-downloads/informe46_walledwolrd_centredelas_tni_stopwapenhandel_stopthewall_eng_def.pdf.
5. Ruiz Benedicto, Akkerman and Brunet, 'A walled world: towards a global apartheid'.
6. M. Graziano, *What Is a Border?* (Stanford University Press, 2018).
7. Spottorno and Abril, *La Grieta*; *The Black Book of Pushbacks*, 2 vols, Border Violence Monitoring Network, 18 December 2020: https://left.eu/issues/publications/black-book-of-pushbacks-volumes-i-ii/; 'Pushbacks in Melilla', Forensic Architecture, 15 June 2020: https://forensic-architecture.org/investigation/pushbacks-in-melilla-nd-and-nt-vs-spain.
8. 'Violence, vulnerability and migration: trapped at the Gates of Europe', Médecins Sans Frontières, 13 March 2013: https://www.msf.org/violence-vulnerability-and-migration-trapped-gates-europe.
9. S. Pandolfo, 'The burning: finitude and the politico-theological imagination of illegal migration', *Anthropological Theory* 7 (SAGE, 2007).
10. Pandolfo, 'The burning'.
11. Case of N.D. and N.T. v Spain, European Court of Human Rights Judgement, 13 February 2020: https://hudoc.echr.coe.int/spa#{%22itemid%22:[%22001-201353%22]}.
12. Case of N.D. and N.T. v Spain: https://hudoc.echr.coe.int/spa#{%22itemid%22:[%22001-201353%22]}.
13. 'Pushbacks in Melilla', Forensic Architecture; E. Tyszler, 'Humanitarianism and black female bodies: violence and intimacy at the Moroccan–Spanish border', *The Journal of North African Studies*, 26:5 (2021).
14. 'Spain will give Morocco €30 million to curb irregular immigration', *El País*, 19 July 2019; 'Spain and Morocco reach deal to curb irregular migration flows', *El País*, 21 February 2019.
15. 'Incursions at Spain's North African exclaves triple after Moroccan threats', *El País*, 27 February 2017.
16. 'Incursions at Spain's North African exclaves triple after Moroccan threats', *El País*.
17. Quoted in A. Santamarina, 'The spatial politics of far-right populism: VOX, anti-fascism and neighbourhood solidarity in Madrid City', *Critical Sociology* 47(6) (2021); and P. Pardo, 'Make Spain Great Again', Foreign Policy, 27 April 2019: https://foreignpolicy.com/2019/04/27/vox-spain-elections-trump-bannon/.
18. Santamarina, 'The spatial politics of far-right populism'; Pardo, 'Make Spain Great Again'.
19. Quoted in J. Boone, 'How is VOX making the Spanish flag wave again?', Tilburg University, June 2020: http://arno.uvt.nl/show.cgi?fid=151784.

20. S. Creta, 'Lives on hold: how coronavirus has affected the women porters of Melilla', *The Irish Times*, 6 July 2020; C. Malterre-Barthes and G. A. Bajalia, 'Crossing into Cueta', Migrant Journal 4, *Dark Matters* (2018); 'Morocco's "mule" women scratch a living on Spanish enclave border', Reuters, 25 August 2017.
21. Creta, 'Lives on hold'.
22. Spottorno and Abril, *La Grieta*.
23. Spottorno and Abril, *La Grieta*.
24. Spottorno and Abril, *La Grieta*.
25. Spottorno and Abril, *La Grieta*.
26. Spottorno and Abril, *La Grieta*.
27. R. Lyman, 'Bulgaria puts up a new wall but this one keeps people out', *The New York Times*, 5 April 2015; S. Nerov, 'Bulgaria's fence to stop migrants on Turkey border nears completion', Reuters, 17 July 2014.
28. Ruiz Benedicto, Akkerman and Brunet, 'A walled world: towards a global apartheid'.
29. Spottorno and Abril, *La Grieta*.
30. Spottorno and Abril, *La Grieta*.
31. Spottorno and Abril, *La Grieta*.
32. Spottorno and Abril, *La Grieta*.
33. P. Slovic, D. Vastfall, A. Erlandsson and R. Gregory, 'Iconic photographs and the ebb and flow of empathic response to humanitarian disasters', *PNAS* 114 (4), 24 January 2017.
34. A. Taylor, 'Italy ran an operation that saved thousands of migrants from drowning in the Mediterranean. Why did it stop?', *The Washington Post*, 20 April 2015.
35. R. Bauböck, 'Mare nostrum: the political ethics of migration in the Mediterranean', *CMS* 7, 4 (2019); 'Calls for action in Europe after migrant disaster in the Mediterranean', *The Washington Post*, 19 April 2015.
36. A. Tarquini, 'La minaccia di Kammenos alla Germania: 'Se Ue ci abbandona, vi sommergeremo di migranti mescolati a jihadisti"', *La Repubblica*, 9 March 2015; 'Greece's defence minister is threatening to "flood Europe with migrants"', *Business Insider*, 9 March 2015.
37. Spottorno and Abril, 'A las puertos de Europa'.
38. Spottorno and Abril, *La Grieta*.
39. 'Hungary closes Serbian border crossing as refugees make for Austria on foot', *The Guardian*, 4 September 2015.
40. 'Refugee crisis: Hungary uses teargas and water cannon at Serbia border', *The Guardian*, 16 September 2015.
41. 'Croatia to allow free passage of migrants, says prime minister', *AFP*, 17 September 2015.

42. 'Croatia to allow free passage of migrants, says prime minister', *AFP.*
43. Spottorno and Abril, *La Grieta.*
44. Spottorno and Abril, *La Grieta.*
45. Spottorno and Abril, *La Grieta.*
46. Spottorno and Abril, *La Grieta.*
47. 'Avoiding risky seas, migrants reach Europe with an arctic bike ride', *The New York Times*, 9 October 2015; 'Syrians fleeing war find new route to Europe – via the Arctic Circle', *The Guardian*, 29 August 2015.

8. The Melting Border

1. R. Steininger, *South Tyrol: A Minority Conflict of the Twentieth Century* (Transaction Publishers, 2003).
2. M. Ferrari, E. Pasqual and A. Bagnato, *A Moving Border: Alpine Cartographies of Climate Change* (Columbia University Press, 2018).
3. Quoted in Ferrari, Pasqual and Bagnato, *A Moving Border.*
4. R. Pergher, *Mussolini's Empire: Sovereignty and Settlement in Italy's Borderlands, 1922-43* (CUP, 2018).
5. Steininger, *South Tyrol.*
6. E. Lantschner, 'History of the South Tyrol conflict and its settlement', *Tolerance Through Law: Self Governance and Group Rights in South Tyrol* (Brill, 2018); Steininger, *South Tyrol.*
7. Ferrari, Pasqual and Bagnato, *A Moving Border.*
8. Ferrari, Pasqual and Bagnato, *A Moving Border.*
9. C. Knoll and H. Kerschner, 'A glacier inventory for South Tyrol, Italy, based on airborne laser-scanner data', *Annals of Glaciology*, 50(53) (2009), pp. 46–52.
10. Quoted in Ferrari, Pasqual and Bagnato, *A Moving Border.*
11. Knoll and Kerschner, 'A glacier inventory for South Tyrol, Italy, based on airborne laser-scanner data'.
12. A. Fleckinger, *Ötzi the Iceman* (South Tyrol Museum of Archaeology, 2018).
13. Quoted in Fleckinger, *Ötzi the Iceman.*
14. Fleckinger, *Ötzi the Iceman.*
15. Fleckinger, *Ötzi the Iceman.*
16. R. Nordland, 'Who killed the Iceman? Clues emerge in a very cold case', *The New York Times*, 26 March 2017.
17. M. Zemp, H. Frey, I. Gärtner-Roer, S. Nussbaumer, M. Hoelzle et al., 'Historically unprecedented global glacier decline in the early 21st century', *Journal of Glaciology*, 61 (228) (2015).

9. 'This Wall of Flesh'

1. M. de Piazza, quoted in R. Horrox, *The Black Death* (Manchester University Press, 1994).
2. Horrox, *The Black Death.*
3. Horrox, *The Black Death.*
4. Horrox, *The Black Death.*
5. J. A. Legan, 'The medical response to the Black Death', James Madison University, Senior Honors Projects, 2010–current. 103; S. K. Cohn Jr, *Epidemics: Hate and Compassion from the Plague of Athens to Aids* (OUP, 2018).
6. G. Boccaccio, *The Decameron*, trans. W. A. Rebhorn (Norton, 2013).
7. Boccaccio, *The Decameron.*
8. Boccaccio, *The Decameron.*
9. Boccaccio, *The Decameron.*
10. Legan, 'The medical response to the Black Death'.
11. Boccaccio, *The Decameron.*
12. A. Cliff and M. Smallman-Raynor, 'Containing the spread of epidemics', *Oxford Textbook of Infectious Disease Control: A Geographical Analysis from Medieval Quarantine to Global Eradication* (Oxford University Press, 2013); P. A. Mackowiak and P. S. Sehdev, 'The origin of quarantine', *Clinical Infectious Diseases*, vol. 35, issue 9, 1 November 2002.
13. Cliff and Smallman-Raynor, 'Containing the spread of epidemics'.
14. Cliff and Smallman-Raynor, 'Containing the spread of epidemics'.
15. Cliff and Smallman-Raynor, 'Containing the spread of epidemics'.
16. *Magistrato della sanità* (1752), quoted in Cliff and Smallman-Raynor, 'Containing the spread of epidemics'.
17. G. Rothenberg, 'The Austrian sanitary cordon and the control of the bubonic plague: 1710–1871', *Journal of the History of Medicine and Allied Sciences*, 28 (1973), pp. 15–23.
18. 'Mappa geographica qua preacautio contra pestem post factam locorum, iuxta Pacis Instrumenta, Evacuationem ac Demolitionem in Confinibus istis Cis-Danubialibus instituenda ostenditur' ('A Geographical map in which are shown the precautions that are to be taken against the plague within these Cis-Danubial regions after the evacuation and demolition of places in accordance with the peace treaties') Cliff and Smallman-Raynor, 'Containing the spread of epidemics'.
19. Cliff and Smallman-Raynor, 'Containing the spread of epidemics'.
20. M. Drancourt and D. Raoult, 'Molecular history of plague', *Clinical Microbiology and Infection: The Official Publication of the European Society of Clinical Microbiology*

and *Infectious Diseases*, vol. 22 (2016), p. 11: J-L. Ditchburn and R. Hodgkins, 'Yersinia pestis, a problem of the past and a re-emerging threat', *Biosafety and Health*, vol. 1, issue 2 (2019); C. E. Demeure, O. Dussurget, G. Mas Fiol et al., '*Yersinia pestis* and plague: an updated view on evolution, virulence determinants, immune subversion, vaccination, and diagnostics', *Genes Immun* 20 (2019), pp. 357–70.

21. US Centers for Disease Control and Prevention, overview of plague: https://www.cdc.gov/plague/index.html.
22. B. R. tenOever, 'The evolution of antiviral defense systems', *Cell Host & Microbe* 19, 10 February 2016.
23. D. Jordan, 'The deadliest flu: the complete story of the discovery and reconstruction of the 1918 pandemic virus', Centers for Disease Control and Prevention, 2018: https://www.cdc.gov/flu/pandemic-resources/reconstruction-1918-virus.html.
24. Jordan, 'The deadliest flu'.
25. Jordan, 'The deadliest flu'.
26. E. Rybicki, 'The classification of organisms at the edge of life or problems with virus systematics', *South African Journal of Science*, vol. 86, no. 4 (1990): https://journals.co.za/doi/10.10520/AJA00382353_6229.
27. M. M. H. Farahani, *A Shi'ite Pilgrimage to Mecca, 1885–1886* (University of Texas, 1990).
28. Farahani, *A Shi'ite Pilgrimage to Mecca, 1885–1886.*
29. *The Times*, 14 October 1818.
30. P. Zylberman, 'Civilizing the state: borders, weak states and international health in modern Europe', *Medicine at the Border*, A. Bashford (ed.) (Palgrave, 2006); Cohn Jr, *Epidemics: Hate and Compassion from the Plague of Athens to Aids.*
31. Cohn Jr, *Epidemics: Hate and Compassion from the Plague of Athens to Aids.*
32. C. Low, 'Empire and the Hajj: pilgrims, plagues, and pan-Islam under British surveillance, 1865–1908', *International Journal of Middle East Studies*, vol. 40, no. 2 (2008).
33. Dr Achille Proust, quoted in Low, 'Empire and the Hajj: pilgrims, plagues, and pan-Islam under British surveillance, 1865–1908'.
34. Low, 'Empire and the Hajj: pilgrims, plagues, and pan-Islam under British surveillance, 1865–1908'.
35. Zylberman, 'Civilizing the state: borders, weak states and international health in modern Europe'.
36. Dr Achille Proust, quoted in Zylberman, 'Civilizing the state: borders, weak states and international health in modern Europe'.
37. Zylberman, 'Civilizing the state: borders, weak states and international health in modern Europe'.

38. Zylberman, 'Civilizing the state: borders, weak states and international health in modern Europe'; A. Bashford, 'The age of universal contagion: history, disease and globalisation', *Medicine at the Border.*
39. Bashford, 'The age of universal contagion'; A. Bashford, *Imperial Hygiene: A Critical History of Colonialism, Nationalism and Public Health* (Palgrave Macmillan, 2003).
40. A. Camus, *The Plague* (Penguin, 1947).
41. Camus, *The Plague.*
42. The work that followed from the government grant was in this paper: B. R. tenOever et al., 'Imbalanced host response to SARS-CoV-2 drives development of COVID-19', *Cell*, vol. 181, issue 5 (2020).
43. D. Hoagland et al., 'Leveraging the antiviral type-I interferon system as a first line defense against SARS- CoV-2 pathogenicity', *Immunity*, vol. 54, issue 3 (2021).
44. Hoagland et al., 'Leveraging the antiviral type-I interferon system as a first line defense against SARS- CoV-2 pathogenicity'.
45. tenOever et al., 'Imbalanced Host Response to SARS-CoV-2 Drives Development of COVID-19'.
46. M. Shelley, *The Last Man* (OUP, 2008).
47. Quoted by M. Paley, introduction to *The Last Man.*
48. Camus, *The Plague.*
49. Shelley, *The Last Man.*

10. A Green Line across a Great Shore

1. E. P. Stebbing, 'The threat of the Sahara', *Journal of the Royal African Society*, vol. 36, no. 145 (1937).
2. E. P. Stebbing, 'The encroaching Sahara: the threat to the West African colonies', *The Geographical Journal*, vol. 85, no. 6 (1935).
3. Stebbing, 'The encroaching Sahara'.
4. Stebbing, 'The encroaching Sahara'.
5. Stebbing, 'The encroaching Sahara'.
6. Stebbing, 'The encroaching Sahara'.
7. J. M. Hodge, 'Colonial foresters versus agriculturalists: the debate over climate change and cocoa production in the Gold Coast', *Agricultural History*, vol. 83, no. 2 (2009); R. Grove, 'Conserving Eden: the (European) East India Companies and their environmental policies on St Helena, Mauritius and in Western India, 1660 to 1854', *Comparative Studies in Society and History*, vol. 35, no. 2 (1993).

8. A. Aubréville, *Climats, forêts et désertification de l'Afrique tropicale* (Société d'éditions géographiques, maritimes et coloniales, 1949); quoted in H. E. Dregne, 'Desertification of arid lands', *Physics of Desertification*, F. El-Baz and M. H. A. Hassan (eds) (1986).
9. Stebbing, 'The encroaching Sahara'.
10. B. Jones, 'Desiccation and the West African colonies', *The Geographical Journal*, vol. 91, no. 5 (1938).
11. Dregne, 'Desertification of arid lands'.
12. Dregne, 'Desertification of arid lands'; C. M. Somerville, *Drought and Aid in the Sahel* (Routledge, 2019); M. Rosenblum and D. Williamson, *Squandering Eden* (Bodley Head, 1987); P. G. Munro and G. van der Horst, 'Contesting African landscapes: a critical reappraisal of Sierra Leone's competing forest cover histories', *Environment and Planning D: Society and Space*, 34(4) (2016); S. Salgado, *Sahel: The End of the Road* (University of California, 2004).
13. Somerville, *Drought and Aid in the Sahel.*
14. M. Sacande and N. Berrahmouni, 'Africa's Great Green Wall: a transformative model for communities' sustainable development', *Nature & Faune*, vol. 32, no. 1 (2018); Great Green Wall initiative: https://www.greatgreenwall.org/about-great-green-wall; D. Goffner, H. Sinare and L. J. Gordon, 'The Great Green Wall for the Sahara and the Sahel Initiative as an opportunity to enhance resilience in Sahelian landscapes and livelihoods', *Reg Environ Change* 19, (2019), pp. 1417–28.
15. Quoted in A. Murrey, 'Thomas Sankara and a political economy of happiness', S. Oloruntoba and T. Falola (eds), *The Palgrave Handbook of African Political Economy* (Palgrave Macmillan, 2020); J. Carey, 'The best strategy for using trees to improve climate and ecosystems? Go natural', *Proceedings of the National Academy of Sciences*, 117 (9) (2020).
16. Goffner, Sinare and Gordon, 'The Great Green Wall for the Sahara and the Sahel Initiative as an opportunity to enhance resilience in Sahelian landscapes and livelihoods'.
17. Goffner, Sinare and Gordon, 'The Great Green Wall for the Sahara and the Sahel Initiative as an opportunity to enhance resilience in Sahelian landscapes and livelihoods'.
18. *The Great Green Wall Implementation Status and Way Ahead to 2030 (Advanced Version)*, United Nations Convention to Combat Desertification (UNCCD), 4 September 2020: https://catalogue.unccd.int/1551_GGW_Report_ENG_Final_040920.pdf.
19. N. Pasiecznik and C. Reij, *Restoring African Drylands* (European Tropical Forest Research Network, 2020): http://www.etfrn.org/publications/restoring+african+drylands.
20. R. Cernasky, 'New funds could help grow Africa's Great Green Wall. But can the massive forestry effort learn from past mistakes?', *Science*, 11 February 2021.

21. Quoted in Pasiecznik and Reij, *Restoring African Drylands.*
22. *The Great Green Wall Implementation Status and Way Ahead to 2030 (Advanced Version).*
23. Quoted in B. Bilger, 'The great oasis', *The New Yorker*, 11 December 2011.
24. C. Reij, G. Tappan and M. Smale, 'Agroenvironmental transformation in the Sahel: another kind of "green revolution"', IFPRI Discussion Paper 00914, November 2009: https://www.ifpri.org/publication/agroenvironmental-transformation-sahel; Goffner, Sinare and Gordon, 'The Great Green Wall for the Sahara and the Sahel Initiative as an opportunity to enhance resilience in Sahelian landscapes and livelihoods'.
25. Reij, Tappan and Smale, 'Agroenvironmental transformation in the Sahel'.
26. Reij, Tappan and Smale, 'Agroenvironmental transformation in the Sahel'.
27. Reij, Tappan and Smale, 'Agroenvironmental transformation in the Sahel'; Goffner, Sinare and Gordon, 'The Great Green Wall for the Sahara and the Sahel Initiative as an opportunity to enhance resilience in Sahelian landscapes and livelihoods'.
28. Quoted in Murrey, 'Thomas Sankara and a political economy of happiness'.
29. 'Southeast is suffering its worst drought for 90 years', *The Times*, 31 March 2012; P. Plester, 'Weatherwatch: the great year-long drought of 1921', *The Guardian*, 13 October 2011; S. T. Reno, *Early Anthropocene Literature in Britain, 1750–1884* (Springer, 2020).
30. T. S. Eliot, *The Waste Land* (Faber and Faber, 1925).
31. M. Scheffer, C. Xu, T. A. Kohler, T. M. Lenton and J.-C. Svenning, 'Future of the human climate niche', *Proceedings of the National Academy of Sciences*, 117 (21) (2020).
32. Scheffer et al., 'Future of the human climate niche'; M. Burke, S. M. Hsiang and E. Miguel, 'Global non-linear effect of temperature on economic production', *Nature* 527 (2015), pp. 235–9.
33. Scheffer et al., 'Future of the human climate niche'.
34. Scheffer et al., 'Future of the human climate niche'.
35. Scheffer et al., 'Future of the human climate niche'; J. Rockström, W. Steffen, K. Noone et al., 'A safe operating space for humanity', *Nature* 461 (2009), pp. 472–5; The website of the Stockholm Resilience Centre explains the concept of 'planetary boundaires'. https://www.stockholmresilience.org/research/planetary-boundaries.html.
36. Scheffer et al., 'Future of the human climate niche'; J. Rockström, W. Steffen, K. Noone et al., 'A safe operating space for humanity'.
37. C. Zickgraf, S. Vigil, F. De Longueville, P. Ozer and F. Gemenne, 'The impact of vulnerability and resilience to environmental changes on mobility patterns in West Africa' (KNOMAD, 2016).
38. Quoted in Select Committee on the European Union Home Affairs

Sub-Committee, 11 March 2020: https://committees.parliament.uk/oralevidence/234/html/.

39. Quoted in C. Farbotko and H. Lazrus, 'The first climate refugees? Contesting global narratives of climate change in Tuvalu' (University of Wollongong, 2012): https://ro.uow.edu.au/scipapers/4776.
40. Factsheet from the UN conference on oceans, held in New York on 5-9 June 2017. See https://www.un.org/sustainabledevelopment/wp-content/uploads/2017/05/Ocean-fact-sheet-package.pdf.
41. C. Zickgraf, 'Climate change and migration: myths and realities', *Green European Journal*, 20 January 2020.
42. 'How helpful is the term "climate refugee"?', *The Guardian*, 31 August 2020; G. Bettini, 'Climate barbarians at the gate? A critique of apocalyptic narratives on "climate refugees"', *Geoforum*, vol. 45 (2013).
43. Matteo Salvini originally quoted in Italian newspaper *Il Giornale*. See https://www.ilgiornale.it/news/politica/leuropa-spalanca-porte-libera-ai-migranti-climatici-1486186.html; A. Ruser and A. Machin, 'Nationalising the climate: is the European far right turning green?', *Green European Journal*, 27 September 2019.
44. Ruser and Machin, 'Nationalising the climate: is the European far right turning green?'.
45. 'A Great Green Wall for Cities', Food and Agriculture Organisation of the United Nations, 21 September 2019: https://www.fao.org/news/story/en/item/1234286/icode/.
46. 'Challenges', Great Green Wall: https://www.greatgreenwall.org/challenges.
47. Eliot, *The Waste Land*.

INDEX

INDEX

INDEX

INDEX

INDEX

INDEX

INDEX

INDEX